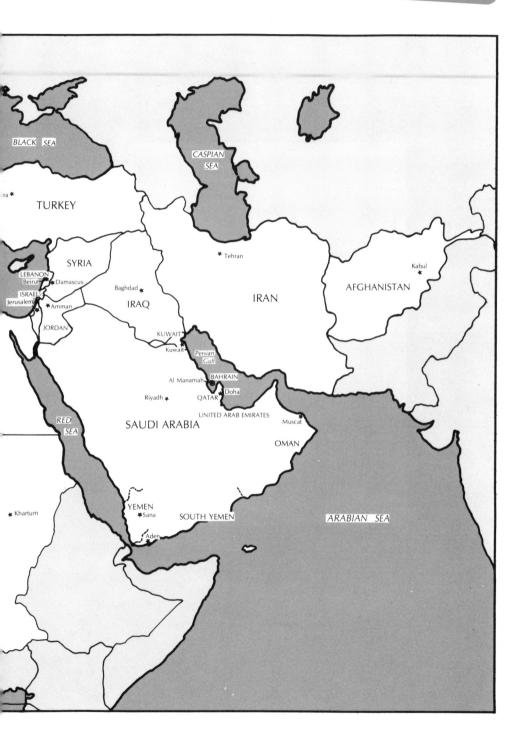

BLACK SEA

CASPIAN
SEA

TURKEY

ra ★

SYRIA

★ Tehran

Kabul
★

LEBANON
Beirut ★ ★ Damascus

Baghdad ★

AFGHANISTAN

ISRAEL
Jerusalem ★

★ Amman

IRAQ

IRAN

JORDAN

KUWAIT
Kuwait ★

Persian
Gulf

Al Manamah ★ ★ BAHRAIN

Riyadh ★

★ Doha
QATAR

RED
SEA

UNITED ARAB EMIRATES

SAUDI ARABIA

Muscat ★

OMAN

★ Khartum

YEMEN
★ Sana

SOUTH YEMEN

ARABIAN SEA

Aden ★

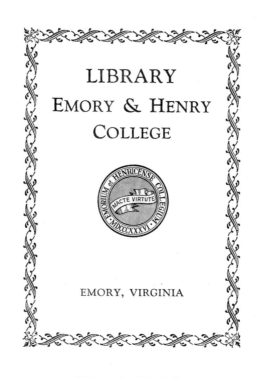

The Middle East Annual

The Middle East Annual

Issues and Events
Volume 3—1983

Edited by
David H. Partington

G. K. Hall & Co.
70 Lincoln Street, Boston, Mass.

Contents

Foreword

For most observers of Middle Eastern affairs the chronic instability of the region can no longer be attributed to the problems of postcolonial adjustment or to repeated Arab-Israeli conflicts. There is instead a vague awareness that all nations in the geographical arc from Morocco to Pakistan are afflicted with a deadly combination of severe internal problems and poorly functioning institutions. Moreover, this notion that the Middle East is in the throes of an internal crisis of unknown dimensions can no longer be left to specialists: such events as the 1973 Arab-Israeli war and the ensuing revolution in the price of oil and, more recently, the American military casualties in Lebanon, have made large numbers of Americans aware that political violence in this volatile area can have grave personal as well as international consequences.

A decade has now passed since the oil price increases of the early 1970s created a broad audience for the study of contemporary Middle Eastern issues. During this short period nothing has appeared in the United States that offers a convincing explanation for the recent course of events. One major reason for this unsatisfactory state of affairs may be that the facts, and even they are difficult to obtain, just simply do not fit the categories of thought employed in the United States to describe major political events.

Two examples of this confusion are well known. In Lebanon, a nation-state, politics are conducted not, it would seem, in terms of national issues but rather with reference to the interests of a bewildering array of confessional groups and personal factions. Even more disconcerting to Americans when compared with the rhythms of their own history is the political course followed by Iran since the revolution of 1979. That a developing country could elevate to power turbaned leaders whose training and whose world view bear little resemblance to what Americans regard as modern is a great mystery to the citizenry of the United States. Taken all together, these and many other expressions of the uniqueness of modern Middle Eastern history demonstrate again that patterns of change familiar to most Westerners do not apply to the history of the Middle East.

Historians have begun an attack on this major intellectual problem. To my mind they have developed enough evidence to show how societies whose past was molded by Islamic civilization are in the early stage of a radical transformation of their institutions; this disruptive event is taking place within a historical context entirely different from that of Europe.

At the risk of further oversimplification we can say that their work must take into account three paths. First, in marked contrast to Europe's development during the Renaissance and Reformation, Turkish ruling classes revived and strengthened the premodern institutions of Islamic civilization in the form of the sixteenth-century Ottoman, Safavid, and Moghul empires. When the West fell upon these states in the nineteenth and twentieth centuries, the societies they encountered were neither in advanced stages of decay nor in early phases of modernization. Thus the modern era of Middle Eastern history is revolutionary rather than evolutionary, and it begins within an institutional matrix that is not related to the experience of Europe. Second, Europe's conquest of the Turko-Muslim empires went hand in hand with the integration of the Middle East into an international economic order dominated by Western capitalism. Finally, European colonists and their Middle Eastern successors, the current political elite, established a third distinctive pattern when they introduced, from the outside and largely through the mechanisms of state bureaucracies, the revolutionary forces of modern technology and techniques.

These events have taken place so quickly and in such an unfamiliar manner that it is natural that theory should lag far behind events. But even the collection and recording of raw data is difficult. Only within the last quarter-century has the Middle East entered the modern era of statistics.

Why the *Middle East Annual* is so valuable for the advancement of American understanding of this strategic area's history is now clear; this effort truly fits the needs of those who seek an explanation for the modern travail of the Middle East. Because there is little previous experience that can assist analysis, scholars will have to proceed inductively to lay the foundation for a modern history of the Middle East. Furthermore, the press and the public will have to examine their attitudes toward the peoples of the region and make an effort to overcome any existing biases as they seek to arrive at a more sophisticated comprehension of the actions and motivations of those who are creating that history.

It follows that an accurate chronicle of events during a time of superheated change is indispensable. Important also are the scholarly efforts to relate the data for each year to previous history. Political information by itself rarely tells a story and nowhere is this truer than in the case of the modern Middle East. Endemic instability encourages sharp conflict both at the center and on the periphery of the region, leaving the way open for exploitation of these conflicts by the superpowers or by charismatic figures such as Muammar Qaddafi. The result of these clashes will not be just a shift of a border or two; it will have a great deal to do with the future shape of Middle Eastern political institutions and will also announce from time to time the score in the Great Game for predominance in this oil-rich crossroad between Europe, Asia, and Africa.

More demanding are the attempts to understand the responses of Middle Easterners to the recasting of their culture. Here the languages of protest and argument can only be interpreted by historians who are capable of both penetrating the propaganda barriers thrown up by civilizations and translating the symbolic messages of one culture into the language of another.

For 1983 the remarkable growth of Islamic fundamentalism touches all of these issues. It is at once a cry from a troubled Muslim heart, a utopian program totally out of touch with modern requirements, and an institutional means by which Islamic nations might shed outmoded institutions. It is also a measure of the influence in modern times of Islamic civilization, of the cultural distinctiveness of the Middle East, and of the severity of modern change. Should it be condemned as fanaticism? Will it facilitate change? Or will its popularity impede the modernization of the Middle East? It is too early to see the fate of this thoroughly Islamic reaction to change; but fundamentalists are nonetheless compelling Muslims to remember their past and non-Muslims to look to their unity at a time of great uncertainty. It is therefore a cultural event of major significance, and the *Middle East Annual* rightly draws attention to its importance.

With the publication of this third volume of the *Middle East Annual* the editors have provided scholars with an unrivaled opportunity to obtain the data and analysis necessary for an understanding of the complexities and turbulences of the contemporary Middle East. One hopes this still-fragile line of communication between two cultures will be strengthened and broadened through the publication of future volumes, so that Americans will come to appreciate the profound dimensions of the crisis of civilization through which the Middle East is now passing.

> Andrew C. Hess
> Professor of Diplomacy
> Fletcher School of Law and Diplomacy
> Tufts University
> Medford, Massachusetts

Introduction

David H. Partington

With this third volume of the *Middle East Annual: Issues and Events*, the editor and publisher continue their effort to provide a reference work for those who seek in-depth, dispassionate analyses of contemporary Middle Eastern problems. Intended for the general reader as well as the researcher and student, the *Annual* in its durable, library-quality format again presents five substantial essays by recognized authorities, a comprehensive chronicle of events, an extensive annotated bibliography of the year's monographic publications, and a bibliography of selected serials.

One of the dangers inherent in the study of an area's political events is the possibility of neglecting the social, intellectual, or spiritual dimensions of a development. The complex phenomenon often referred to as Islamic fundamentalism increasingly comes to the attention of Western observers. Indeed, a succession of violent, terroristic acts is popularly connected with the resurgence of Islam: the assassination of president Anwar Sadat of Egypt; the overthrow of the shah of Iran; and a string of car-bombings, the most devastating being the destruction of the U.S. Marines headquarters in Beirut on 23 October. In this issue of the *Annual*, professor John O. Voll provides an unusually perceptive account of the subject, relating the historical background of Islamic fundamentalism to its modern manifestations and analyzing its effects on the contemporary politics of the Middle East.

The international news of 1983 was dominated by the Middle East despite the fact that such events as the United States' invasion of Grenada, the shooting down of a Korean jetliner by the Soviets, and covert activity in Central America also captured world headlines. More specifically, the focus of this year's news interest was upon the consequences of the 1982 invasion of Lebanon by Israel. That invasion was the subject of unprecedented coverage by both conventional and electronic news media, whose effectiveness was so great that some basic American perceptions of Middle Eastern realities may have changed. The crucial question is the effect of the news coverage on the position of Israel in the mind of the American voter. Were the media agents of truth or of deception? Horribly graphic scenes of the devastation inflicted by the Israeli army on the Lebanese during the siege of Beirut raised strong doubts in the American conscience about the use of American weapons, provided for the defense of Israel, to advance the policies of Ariel Sharon. Because the media seemed in a position to change the direction of foreign policy, their impartiality was questioned. In this volume, media specialist Dr. Edmund Ghareeb, whose expertise includes the Arab media as well as the Western, provides our readers a study on the influence of news coverage on our perception of Middle Eastern events.

The Israeli invasion of Lebanon also had a powerful influence on the fortunes of the PLO. One of Israel's goals in the Lebanon war was to destroy the PLO. After Yasir Arafat was compelled to leave Beirut with his guerrillas during August 1982, many thought it was the end of the PLO in Lebanon. However, many PLO fighting men remained in eastern Lebanon, and in May of 1983 a rebellion against Arafat broke out within these PLO forces. The mutiny was led by officers who felt Arafat was abandoning the original PLO aim of military confrontation with Israel in favor of the path of negotiation leading to a settlement of the Palestine question.

Dr. Philip Mattar, a scholar whose speciality is the PLO, has prepared a highly informative, even-handed account of the PLO. Although much background is included, Dr. Mattar's essay concentrates its attention on events subsequent to August 1982.

During the course of 1983, United States policy in Lebanon failed utterly. Foreign military forces still occupy the country; the Lebanese army (trained and equipped by the United States) was defeated by the Druze militia; the Gemayel government failed to accommodate the interests of Shiites, Druze, and Sunnis for a greater share in government; and the U.S. Marines retreated from an impossible military mission. In the course of one year, the United States' diplomatic position went from one of influence to one where the president of Syria, Hafiz al-Assad, seems to have the upper hand.

One unknown factor in Assad's maneuvering has been the extent to which the Soviet Union (with which Syria is allied) would intervene in Middle Eastern affairs. For a number of reasons, the U.S.S.R.'s influence was at a low point at the beginning of 1983; yet by the end of the year, the ever-increasing embarrassment of the Reagan administration and the gradual rearming of Syria with advanced weaponry had signalled the rebirth of Soviet influence in the area. A noted analyst of Soviet foreign policy, professor Robert O. Freedman, has written for us an account of Soviet policies vis-à-vis its "client" Syria and their relation to events in Lebanon. Professor Freedman provides an extensive account of the failures and successes of earlier Soviet policies as well as detailed coverage of this year's events.

Another long-standing problem is that of Chad, where a conflict between two rival factions for the control of the government has from time to time assumed international dimensions, thanks largely to the interest of Col. Muammar Qaddafi of Libya in affecting the outcome of the dispute. During this year, Libya provided substantial military assistance to former president Goukouni Oueddei, who thereupon threatened to destroy the forces of president Hissen Habré. Oueddei's march to Ndjamena, the capital, was halted only after France, urged on by Washington, interposed a military force between Oueddei's troops and Ndjamena.

The United States' interest in Chad stems from a desire to counter any move by Qaddafi (despite the legitimate interest of Libya in northern Chad) and to maintain the stability of Sudan, whose government would be threatened were Qaddafi to control events in Chad. Professor Edouard Bustin's analysis of recent developments in Chad clarifies the internal and international complexities of this long-standing problem.

Here, then, is our selection of essays on the major events of the year. I wish to thank John O. Voll, Philip Mattar, Robert O. Freedman, Edouard Bustin, and Edmund Ghareeb for their contributions to our effort to provide authoritative discussions of current Middle Eastern problems. Mark Tyler Day deserves praise for compiling the extensive bibliography of monographic publications. Special thanks are due also to Ms. Karin Kiewra, associate editor, and to Mr. Ara Salibian, manuscript editor, both of G. K. Hall & Co., for painstaking work on all aspects of this volume.

Middle Eastern Chronicle:
The Events of 1983

David H. Partington

This chronicle is limited to political events, or happenings of political import, in that area of the world stretching from Morocco through India. It also includes pertinent events in the Western capitals. All citations in this chronicle are taken from the *New York Times*, and they are arranged in chronological order. Readers seeking a chronicle that is subdivided by topic and draws upon multiple sources are referred to the quarterly issues of the *Middle East Journal*. Another chronicle of unusual depth, and one that is especially useful for the events of Lebanon, can be found in the trilingual *Hālīyāt / Panorama de l'actualité / Panorama of Events*, which is issued quarterly by the Lebanese Center for Documentation and Research in Beirut.

1 January   Heavy shelling is exchanged between pro- and anti-Syrian factions in Tripoli, Lebanon.

2 January   Travelers in New Delhi confirm recent guerrilla attacks on Kabul's electrical system.

4 January   President Yitzhak Navon of Israel begins a two-week tour of the United States.

The Israeli army reports that Syria is preparing SAM-5 installations deep within Syria.

In Tripoli, Lebanon, clashes occur between pro- and anti-Syrian forces.

Iran ends three years of gasoline rationing.

5 January   President Yitzhak Navon of Israel, on a visit to the United States, informs the Reagan administration that deterioration in Israeli-Egyptian relations will make it difficult for Israel to support the Reagan peace plan.

The British Foreign Office cancels plans for Foreign Secretary Francis Pym to visit the Persian Gulf states; Saudi Arabia, Qatar, and the U.A.E. refused to welcome him, presumably in reaction to Prime Minister Thatcher's refusal to meet with a PLO member of a League of Arab States delegation.

A cease-fire is reached in Tripoli, Lebanon, after a week of civil strife among various factions, including the Syrians.

6 January   Heavy Israeli reinforcements move up to the cease-fire line in the Bekaa Valley.

7 January   In an ambush south of Beirut, twenty-one Israeli soldiers are wounded in a military bus.

The United States expresses official concern to the Soviet Union over the construction of SA-5 sites in Syria.

The deputy prime minister of Iraq, Tariq 'Aziz, says France is increasing its purchases of Iraqi oil and providing ever-increasing amounts of military aid to Iraq.

8 January   In Morocco, Prime Minister Bouabid announces that a new, centrist political party will be formed.

Lebanese prime minister Shafik al-Wazzan visits Damascus to seek a solution to the armed strife in Tripoli being waged by pro- and anti-Syrian groups.

The Sa'iqa group of the PLO claims responsibility for an attack on a bus in Tel Aviv.

9 January   Tariq 'Aziz, deputy prime minister of Iraq, and Mas'ud Rajavi, exiled leader of the Iranian Mujahedin-i Khalq, hold talks in Paris.

Civil disturbances occur between Arab residents and Jewish settlers in Nablus and Hebron.

10 January   Israeli military authorities close a Nablus high school (Arab) for one month following a protest by Arab youths.

Philip Habib, after conferring with President Reagan, departs for the Middle East.

11 January   Yasir Arafat, PLO chairman, flies to Moscow.

Artillery duels between Phalangists and Druze militiamen occur near Baabda, Lebanon.

Reports in New Delhi indicate that Afghan insurgents captured several Russians last week in the bazaar at Mazar-i Sharif.

12 January   Lebanon asks the Security Council to authorize the United Nations Interim Force in Lebanon to assist the Lebanese government in maintaining control throughout the country.

West German police arrest Ayatollah Khomeini's son-in-law for possessing 3.3 pounds of opium.

13 January	Israel and Lebanon reach an agreement on an agenda for future talks.
	Yasir Arafat concludes talks in Moscow; a joint statement calls for a voluntary confederation between Jordan and an independent Palestinian state.
	Greek officials assure Jewish leaders in Greece that the government's pro-Arab and anti-Israel outlook is not anti-Semitic in nature.
15 January	President Yitzhak Navon of Israel concludes his eleven-day visit to the United States.
16 January	The Israeli commission investigating the Beirut massacres finishes receiving testimony.
	Iraq claims its aircraft carry out successful raids on Iranian positions.
17 January	Ariel Sharon, defense minister of Israel, confers with President Mobutu Seko of Zaire on mutual security.
	U.S. officials believe that the U.S.S.R. has now shipped SA-5 missiles to Syria.
	Iraq bombs Iran's oil port on Kharg Island.
18 January	The Security Council extends for six months the mandate for UNIFIL, the United Nations Interim Force in Lebanon.
	Reports in New Delhi say a revolt occurred in Khost, Afghanistan, in which hundreds of Afghan soldiers defected to insurgent forces.
19 January	Iran announces a war budget of $4 billion for the next fiscal year.
	President Mobutu Seko reveals an agreement under which Israel will restructure the army of Zaire.
20 January	A statement is released revealing that Yasir Arafat, chairman of the PLO, recently met with three prominent Israelis: Uri Avnery, Major General Mattityahu Peled, and Yaccov Arnon.
	At a military tribunal in Tel Aviv, evidence is submitted in the defense of Major David Mopaz to the effect that the Israeli army chief of staff had ordered Arab demonstrators to be physically beaten.
	In the ongoing negotiations between Israel and Lebanon, four subcommittees are formed to take up these issues: (1) creation of a security zone in southern Lebanon, (2) Israeli-Lebanese relations, (3) withdrawal of foreign troops, and (4) guarantees of security for Lebanon.
22 January	Lebanon officially accepts the idea of using UN or multinational troops to man the early-warning posts demanded by Israel.

23 January	The Israeli government says the U.S. compromise plan to assure the withdrawal of foreign forces from Lebanon is unacceptable; Israel rejects the idea of a multinational force to man the electronic surveillance posts in southern Lebanon, insisting that only Israelis man them.
	Syria and Libya pledge support to Iran to overthrow the government of Saddam Hussein of Iraq.
	OPEC oil ministers, meeting in Geneva, tentatively agree to cut oil production this year to 17.5 million barrels a day; no agreement on a price structure is announced: the Persian Gulf states and the African producers disagree on a price differential.
24 January	OPEC oil ministers fail to secure an agreement on production quotas; Saudi Arabia, unable to settle the question of a price differential between Gulf oil and African oil, refuses to agree to production quotas.
	Philip Habib, U.S. special envoy to the Middle East, flies back to Washington as the State Department expresses extreme concern over the negotiations between Israel and Lebanon on the withdrawal of foreign troops.
25 January	President Hosni Mubarak of Egypt begins a state visit in Washington.
	The United States expresses concern over five nonviolent incidents involving U.S. Marines and Israeli troops in Beirut.
26 January	Israeli defense minister Sharon says the advance-warning stations Israel requires in southern Lebanon must be manned only by Israelis or others with knowledge of local conditions.
27 January	French president Mitterrand starts a three-day visit to Morocco.
	Egyptian president Hosni Mubarak, visiting Washington, expresses concern over the Lebanese negotiations.
	In Shtaura, Lebanon, a building used by al-Fatah's military intelligence branch is demolished by a car-bomb; between fifteen and thirty persons perish; responsibility for the bomb is claimed by the Front to Liberate Lebanon from Foreigners.
	Israeli defense minister Sharon calls on the U.S.S.R. to hold talks with Israel on mutual interests.
	President Hosni Mubarak of Egypt meets with American Jewish spokesmen in Washington.
29 January	Speaking before trade groups in New York State, Hosni Mubarak of Egypt calls upon the business community to invest in the private sector in Egypt.
30 January	Artillery battles between Christian and Druze militiamen spread to Beirut.

Secretary of State Shultz says that after a week of review the United States has no formula to speed the Israeli-Lebanese talks on troop withdrawal.

Yitzhak Navon, the president of Israel, announces he will not run for reelection; he wishes to be free to serve the Labor Party.

1 February Christian and Druze militias clash in Lebanon: seventeen dead and thirty-four wounded.

2 February Prime Minister Begin of Israel says he will not try to promote Jordan's participation in peace talks by ordering a freeze on Jewish settlement in the West Bank.

In a talk with representatives of the World Jewish Congress, President Reagan urges Israel not to establish new settlements in the West Bank.

In Beirut, a confrontation occurs between three Israeli tanks and one U.S. Marine when the Israelis attempt to patrol territory under Marine control.

3 February Secretary of Defense Weinberger requests the State Department to make a formal protest to Israel over the 2 February incident in which three Israeli tanks penetrated Marine-held territory.

The United States and Israel agree to erect a clear boundary in Beirut to separate their forces.

5 February The Research Center of the PLO in West Beirut is heavily damaged by a car-bomb; responsibility for the explosion is claimed by the Front for the Liberation of Lebanon from Foreigners. Eighteen persons are killed and 115 injured in the incident.

Christians Phalangists are reported to be terrorizing middle-class Palestinians living in Sidon, Lebanon; Israel says it will increase its patrols in the area to prevent these occurrences.

Greece informs the United States that plans to increase American military aid to Turkey will adversely affect the chances of reaching an agreement on U.S. naval bases in Greece.

The Food and Agriculture Organization reports famine in Chad.

7 February The Israeli commission investigating the Beirut massacres delivers its report to Prime Minister Begin.

The Israeli army announces that Druze and Christian militia groups reached an accord on cessation of hostilities.

President Reagan, in an address to television correspondents, accuses Israel of deliberate delay in withdrawing its troops from Lebanon.

Iran launches an invasion of Iraq at Fakeh in Misan Province.

8 February After four months of deliberations, the special judicial commission investigating the Beirut massacres makes its findings and recommendations public: top civilian and military leaders are indirectly responsible for the massacres, and certain high-level officers should resign; the prime minister should dismiss Defense Minister Ariel Sharon.

Iraq claims it has halted the latest Iranian offensive.

9 February　Secretary of Defense Weinberger rejects a proposed agreement with Israel on the sharing of military information gained in Lebanon.

Iraq reports it has repulsed a fourth Iranian offensive into Misan Province.

UN mediator Diego Cordovez reports some progress after seventeen days of discussions with Afghan, Pakistani, and Iranian officials.

10 February　The Israeli cabinet votes 16–1 to accept the recommendations of the judicial commission's inquiry into the Beirut massacres.

In Jerusalem, one person is killed and nine wounded when a grenade is thrown into a group of Israeli Peace Now demonstrators.

11 February　Ariel Sharon resigns from his position of defense minister of Israel; he is offered a position within the Begin cabinet, but without portfolio.

Moshe Arens, Israel's ambassador to the United States, is offered the post of defense minister of Israel.

The Israeli government delivers a formal protest to the Vatican over the activities of Archbishop Hilarion Capucci in supporting the PLO on Italian television; the archbishop had once been jailed by Israel for gunrunning.

Pierre Gemayel, leader of the Phalange party, denies that the Phalangists had any involvement with the Sabra and Shatilla massacres.

Iran celebrates the fourth anniversary of its revolution by holding anti-American rallies in Teheran.

12 February　The head of the Labor party in Israel, Shimon Peres, says he wants to confer with Prime Minister Begin on ways to preserve peace among rival political and social groups in Israel.

The brother of former president Anwar Sadat of Egypt is sentenced to one year in jail for corruption.

13 February　Ariel Sharon says he accepts the offer of Prime Minister Begin to remain in the cabinet as minister without portfolio.

Prime Minister Shafik al-Wazzan of Lebanon asks the United States to request Israel to stop the anti-Palestinian actions in southern Lebanon being waged by Christian militiamen.

14 February	Prime Minister Begin of Israel appoints Moshe Arens, the present Israeli ambassador to the United States, to the post of defense minister, replacing Ariel Sharon.
	Major Sa'd Haddad moves his militia forces into Sidon and sets up a garrison.
15 February	The Lebanese army assumes control of East Beirut from Christian militiamen.
	In testimony before the Senate Foreign Relations Committee, Secretary of State Shultz says the Arab states (principally Saudi Arabia) are withholding reconstruction aid from Lebanon until foreign forces vacate the country.
	Amnesty International criticizes Egypt for treatment of political prisoners.
	The president of Cyprus, Spyros Kyprianou, calls on the United States to pressure Turkey to remove its troops from northern Cyprus.
16 February	A confrontation occurs between an Israeli army patrol and the Lebanese army in East Beirut.
	President Reagan reveals in a press conference that AWAC planes were recently sent to Egypt to take part in training exercises; Egyptian president Mubarak is said to have requested help in monitoring Libyan aircraft.
	Iraq reports it has repulsed a new Iranian attack east of Amara.
17 February	U.S. officials explain that AWAC aircraft were sent to Egypt because of fear that Libya would attack Sudan.
	Egypt denies that joint military maneuvers with the United States, involving AWAC aircraft, are being held.
	The Israeli-backed militia of Major Sa'd Haddad expands its operations so as to control all of Lebanon south of the Awali River.
	An Israeli military tribunal finds that the former military commander of the occupied West Bank issued illegal orders to harass Arab residents of the area; four soldiers are found guilty and given prison sentences.
	At the Palestine National Council, which is meeting in Algiers, the leader of the radical wing of the PLO, Dr. George Habash, urges the delegates to totally reject the Reagan peace plan.
18 February	The U.S. Marines in Lebanon announce they will extend their patrol routes in East Beirut.
	The Pentagon informs Congress of its wish to sell 107 armored troop carriers to the Lebanese army.
	Libyan aircraft approach the carrier *Nimitz* and are chased away.

19 February	Moshe Arens, defense minister of Israel, criticizes U.S. officials for complaints about the slow pace of negotiations between Lebanon and Israel.
	Libya claims the United States is jamming its communications and carrying out acts of provocation.
	The Indian army is sent to Assam to halt violence between Muslims and Hindus.
	King Hussein of Jordan concludes a day of talks with President Petar Stambolić of Yugoslavia.
20 February	Dr. 'Isam Sartawi resigns from the Palestine National Council, which is meeting in Algiers. Dr. Sartawi, a leader of those Palestinians who advocate the recognition of Israel, has had Yasir Arafat's approval since 1976 to act as a contact person with Israel.
	Prime Minister Begin appoints Eliahu Lankin, present ambassador to South Africa, to be the Israeli ambassador to Great Britain; Lankin, a former commander in the Irgun Zvai Leumi terrorist group, faces opposition in Britain for his role in anti-British actions during the period of the Mandate.
	Secretary of State Shultz says that the Libyan threat against Sudan is over.
	The General Peoples' Conference in Libya approves expenditures for revolutionary movements in the Arab world.
	Persian Gulf oil exporters hold urgent talks in Riyadh after Nigeria cuts its price for oil to $30.
	The toll of deaths resulting from Hindu raids on Muslim villages in Assam on 18 February reaches six hundred.
21 February	Libya requests a Security Council meeting to consider the U.S. threat to its shores.
	U.S. officials claim the presence of AWAC planes in Egypt foiled Libya's plan to attack Sudan; Egyptian defense minister Abu Ghazalah claims the four U.S. AWACs were sent to Egypt only for training purposes.
	Usamah al-Baz, director of political affairs for President Mubarak of Egypt, warns Libya to stop destabilization tactics.
	Libya requests a Security Council meeting to consider the threat posed by the United States to its integrity.
	U.S. Marines in Lebanon assist in rescue operations during a blizzard.
	Turkey and the United States sign an agreement for the exchange of scientists and the pursuit of joint projects in health, energy, agriculture, and industry.
	Nikolai A. Tikhonov, prime minister of the U.S.S.R., begins a four-day visit to Greece.

22 February	President Mubarak of Egypt, visiting in Khartum, says Egyptian aircraft intercepted Libyan planes that had violated Egyptian airspace.

President Reagan offers to have the United States guarantee the security of Israel's northern border if Israeli troops are withdrawn from Lebanon; Israeli foreign minister Yitzhak Shamir rejects Reagan's offer, saying no security guarantee can take the place of a direct agreement between Israel and Lebanon.

Moshe Arens is unanimously approved by the Begin cabinet to succeed Ariel Sharon as defense minister of Israel.

Yasir Arafat is reelected chairman of the fourteen-member PLO Executive Committee by the Palestine National Council, which is meeting in Algiers.

The Palestine National Council, under pressure from radicals, adopts a stronger response to the Reagan peace plan, but does not reject it.

At the UN, Libya accuses the United States of provocation.

23 February Lebanese government sources express thanks for President Reagan's offer to guarantee the security of Israel's northern border.

President Reagan says the Palestinians need a "homeland," but does not advocate a nation state.

Moshe Arens is confirmed as defense minister of Israel by a vote of 65–51 (2 abstaining) in parliament.

In an interview in the *Los Angeles Times,* Moshe Arens suggests that a preemptive strike against the new Soviet-manned SAM-5 missiles in Syria is possible.

Persian Gulf members of OPEC agree upon a price cut for Saudi Light crude oil.

The Security Council, after two days of debate on Libya's complaint against the United States for provocation, fails to vote on the matter.

24 February Israeli foreign minister Yitzhak Shamir criticizes President Reagan for his support of a homeland for the Palestinians.

The foreign minister of Jordan, Marwan al-Kasim, states that Israel must withdraw from Lebanon and halt Jewish settlement in the West Bank before negotiations can begin on a comprehensive Middle East settlement.

In Turkey, prison sentences are given to the leader of the National Salvation party and twenty-three aides (the NSP is a Muslim fundamentalist party).

Estimates of Muslim deaths in the massacre in Assam by Hindus last week reach 3,500.

25 February	Eliahu Lankin, a member of the Irgun terrorist organization during the British Mandate of Palestine, declines the post of Israeli ambassador to Great Britain because of adverse British reaction to his appointment.
26 February	King Hassan II of Morocco and President Benjadid of Algeria hold direct talks on the Western Sahara issue.
27 February	Reports from Kabul say that bomb explosions have killed several people during the past week in Afghanistan.
28 February	The State Department asserts that the Reagan administration's proposed $2.48 billion aid program to Israel is sufficient; congressional critics claim it is not enough.
	Secretary of Defense Weinberger says the SAM-5 missiles in Syria, which are manned by Soviet technicians, are a serious threat to Middle Eastern security.
	Former Israeli defense minister Ariel Sharon files a libel suit against Time, Inc., and Time-Life International.
	Libyan troops, which were massed along the Egyptian and Sudanese borders, are pulled back.
	A delegation from Libya arrives in Chad to seek discussions on the Libya-Chad dispute; the president of Chad, Hissen Habré, expresses doubt that Libyan leader Qaddafi is prepared to cut off his support to dissidents in Chad.
	Hindus in Assam hold a twenty-four-hour general strike to force their demand that hundreds of thousands of Muslims be removed.
1 March	Israel rejects a U.S. compromise plan to resolve remaining differences between Israel and Lebanon on troop withdrawal; special envoy Philip Habib's proposals are accepted by Lebanon.
	The State Department expresses concern over the outbreaks of violence by Jewish settlers against Arab residents of the West Bank.
2 March	Iraq claims its navy has inflicted severe damage on Iranian oil facilities in the Nawruz field.
	Former president Carter begins an eight-day visit in Egypt.
3 March	Israeli police search the homes of Jewish settlers around Hebron for weapons, following several attacks on Arab residents.
	In Greece, large-scale protests are held against U.S. military bases.
5 March	UN officials report that 300,000 persons in Chad are in danger of starvation.
	Two Jordanians and an Iraqi are convicted in London of attempting to assassinate Shlomo Argov, Israel's ambassador to Great Britain, last June.

6 March	President Hosni Mubarak of Egypt reprimands the PLO for attempting to interfere in Egyptian affairs.
	Representatives of Sudan and the United States hold talks in Khartum.
	Israeli radio and television stations are forbidden to use the Hebrew word *ishim* (personalities) in connection with the PLO, because the Hebrew word has positive connotations.
7 March	Abu Musa, a senior commander of al-Fatah, attempts to seize control of two battalions of the elite Yarmuk Brigade in the Bekaa region of Lebanon.
	Israel orders a settlement of Rabbi Meir Kahane's followers to be evacuated from the West Bank.
	A conference of Third World leaders opens in New Delhi. In the opening address, Indira Gandhi calls for "early normalcy" in Afghanistan.
8 March	West Bank Jewish settlers are warned by Israel not to engage in violence against Arab residents.
	Former president Carter meets with PLO personnel in Egypt and with Prime Minister Begin in Jerusalem.
9 March	West Bank Arabs protest the visit of former president Carter to Israel.
	The Turkish ambassador to Yugoslavia is wounded in an assassination attempt; the Justice Commandos of the Armenian Genocide claims responsibility.
	Iraq proposes that the Third World conference arbitrate the war with Iran.
10 March	Iraq claims it sank six Iranian ships.
	India and Pakistan reach an accord on forming a joint commission to improve economic, industrial, and cultural relations.
11 March	Yitzhak Shamir, foreign minister of Israel, arrives in Washington with new ideas to solve the deadlocked negotiations on the withdrawal of foreign forces from Lebanon.
	Galip Balkar, Turkish ambassador to Bulgaria, dies from gunshot wounds inflicted by Armenian terrorists two days before.
12 March	Secretary of Defense Weinberger makes new proposals to Israel for an arrangement to share military intelligence; Israeli sources term them "insulting."
	Secretary of State Shultz confers with Lebanese foreign minister Elie Salem in Washington to seek a way to end the impasse in talks on Lebanon.
	OPEC, meeting in London, seeks an arrangement on reducing oil prices.
	The five-day Delhi conference of Third World countries ends:

the draft report's Middle East sections call for an international tribunal to try Israel for crimes against the Palestinian people.

13 March   Secretary of State Shultz confers in Washington with Israeli foreign minister Yitzhak Shamir on the negotiations being held on troop withdrawal from Lebanon.

Officials in Sudan report the discovery of seventy tons of arms and ammunition smuggled in by Libyan agents.

14 March   OPEC agrees to reduce the price of oil by 15 percent to $29 per barrel.

In talks with Yitzhak Shamir, President Reagan emphasizes the urgency of Israel's withdrawal from Lebanon.

Egypt and Israel resume trade negotiations that were broken off last June.

Two Israeli officials of the West Bank are put on trial for possession of illegal explosives.

Former president Carter says in Jordan that the West Bank settlements by Israel are illegal and an obstacle to peace.

15 March   Major General Moshe Levi is appointed chief of staff of the Israeli armed forces; he replaces Rafael Eytan, whom the Beirut massacre commission criticized.

U.S. policy in Morocco is criticized in Congress; the administration is urged to recommend diplomatic moves to King Hassan II to solve the Western Sahara issue.

The World Conference on Soviet Jewry opens in Jerusalem; five hundred Americans attend, including many political figures.

President Reagan sends a message to the World Conference on Soviet Jewry, pledging his support to efforts to increase Jewish emigration from the Soviet Union.

Former President Carter visits King Fahd of Saudi Arabia in Riyadh.

16 March   Yitzhak Shamir, foreign minister of Israel, returns to Israel from the United States, believing that some earlier differences have been resolved.

Five U.S. Marines and nine Italian soldiers are wounded in two separate incidents in Beirut; these are the first direct attacks on Americans and Italians since the peacekeeping forces arrived in September 1982.

17 March   In a letter released today, the commandant of the U.S. Marine Corps asserts that Israeli forces have persisted in harassing American troops in Beirut.

U.S. ambassador Samuel Lewis discusses the tension between Israeli and American troops in Beirut with Defense Minister Arens.

Chad asks the UN Security Council to assist in removing Libyan forces from the Aozou Strip, which Libya claims.

18 March
The Government Press Office in Israel rebuts U.S. Marine charges on three confrontations that occurred between Marines and the Israeli Defense Forces; the United States is accused of not honoring an agreement that delimited patrol zones in Beirut.

King Hussein of Jordan leads an Arab League delegation in a visit to Prime Minister Thatcher of Great Britain; the delegation includes Walid Khalidi, a member of the Palestine National Council.

19 March
King Hussein of Jordan confers with Philip Habib in London and states he will meet with Yasir Arafat next week.

Libya and the U.S.S.R. announce an agreement in principle for concluding a treaty of friendship and cooperation.

Negotiations between Greece and the United States over American naval bases resume after a week-long break.

Tzortziz Athanasiades is assassinated in Athens: his conservative newspaper was critical of the Socialist government of Prime Minister Andreas Papandreou.

20 March
The commander of American Marines in Lebanon accuses the Israeli troops there of indiscriminate gunfire and gross lack of discipline.

Special envoy Philip Habib confers with the foreign minister and the defense minister of Israel; no details of the talks are released.

The U.S.S.R. accuses the United States of training Afghan insurgents in the use of chemical weapons.

21 March
The Begin cabinet agrees to share military intelligence gained from the 1982 invasion of Lebanon with the United States and drops its insistence on a new accord governing such sharing.

22 March
The ten heads of government of the European Common Market countries issue a criticism of Israel's West Bank settlement policy and reaffirm their position that the PLO must be a part of peace negotiations.

The Israeli parliament elects Chaim Herzog to be the next president of Israel; Herzog, leader of the opposition Labor party, received a vote of 61–57, with 2 abstentions.

Special envoy Philip Habib confers with Amin Gemayel, president of Lebanon, on the withdrawal of foreign troops.

The Italian foreign ministry discloses that an Iraqi helicopter that crashed near Vicenzo on 21 March was to receive "maintenance"; industry sources reveal the helicopter was scheduled for installation of advanced electronic equipment.

24 March	The U.S. Marines unit in Beirut and the Israeli command agree on measures to avoid confrontations.
25 March	Philip Habib, U.S. special envoy in the Middle East, holds talks with Lebanese officials on the withdrawal of Israeli troops from Lebanon.
26 March	Amin Gemayel, president of Lebanon, says he cannot compromise Lebanon's sovereignty by allowing Israel to retain patrols in southern Lebanon.
	The foreign minister of Saudi Arabia arrives in Amman, Jordan, for talks on Middle East peace; Yasir Arafat is expected to join the discussions.
	An earthquake hits Iran; about one hundred persons perish.
	The Organization of African Unity urges its members to ratify a human rights charter.
27 March	Yasir Arafat cancels a meeting with King Hussein of Jordan; instead, he meets with King Fahd of Saudi Arabia to discuss responses to the American peace plan put forward by President Reagan.
	Iran claims it has repulsed an Iraqi thrust at Shahrani.
	Over 250 Arab schoolgirls in the West Bank become ill; poison is suspected.
28 March	The Ministry of Health in Israel finds no trace of poison at the Palestinian girls' schools at which some 250 students became ill.
	Iran asks the help of its Persian Gulf neighbors (except Iraq) for assistance in controlling an oil slick that was caused by Iraq's bombing of Kharg Island.
	Turkish journalist and publisher of *Cumhuriyet*, Nadir Nadi, pleads not guilty of incitement to violate existing laws.
	Pakistan announces the end of press censorship in effect since October 1979.
29 March	The Iranian Press Agency reports that women in Iran now have the right to divorce their husbands for moral or ideological reasons.
	Perez de Cuéllar, UN secretary general, expresses optimism that the U.S.S.R. favors UN efforts to mediate the conflict in Afghanistan.
	France reports it is ready to supply nuclear technology to Pakistan despite that country's unwillingness to conform to the standards of the International Atomic Energy Agency.
30 March	Israeli and Syrian forces exchange tank and mortar fire outside of Beirut.
	The Persian Gulf oil slick approaches Qatar.

31 March	President Reagan states he will not approve the shipment of seventy-five F-16 airplanes to Israel until it withdraws its army from Lebanon; these airplanes come under an agreement specifying their use for defensive purposes.
	Israel asks aid from the U.S. Centers for Disease Control to confirm the result obtained by Israeli scientists that the recent illness that afflicted hundreds of Arab girls in the West Bank was not caused by poison.
	The Turkish government charges thirty-three persons with conspiring to set up an Islamic state; a military court will try the case.
1 April	Yitzhak Shamir, foreign minister of Israel, decries President Reagan's decision not to approve the sale of seventy-five F-16 fighters to Israel.
2 April	Yasir Arafat confers with King Hussein of Jordan on the question of Jordanian participation in peace talks leading to the Palestinian "entity" referred to in President Reagan's peace proposals.
	U.S. Marines on patrol in Lebanon will henceforth carry loaded rifles.
3 April	Another 350 Arab schoolgirls in the West Bank become ill; mass hysteria is suggested as the cause.
4 April	Iraq offers a limited cease-fire to Iran to permit cleanup operations on a 7,500-square-mile oil spill in the Persian Gulf; Iran rejects the offer.
	In Istanbul, a military court postpones until 9 May delivering a verdict on the fate of Nadir Nadi, the prominent publisher of *Cumhuriyet*.
	Riots by Sikhs in the Punjab result in twenty killed and hundreds injured.
5 April	The Reagan administration urges Palestinian and Arab leaders to support King Hussein of Jordan in talks with the PLO.
	Yasir Arafat, after three days of talks with King Hussein, leaves Jordan with no sign that an accord has been reached on joining the American-sponsored peace talks with Israel.
	UN officials say the governments of Iran and Iraq have agreed in principle on means to clean up an oil spill from Iranian offshore wells.
6 April	The Security Council advises Chad and Libya to take their territorial dispute to the Organization of African Unity.
7 April	Efforts to reach an accord between Iran and Iraq to clean up the Persian Gulf oil spill are ended without success.
	The American Jewish Committee upholds UN Resolution 242 and suggests "territorial compromise through negotiations."

8 April	The United States informs King Hussein of Jordan that if he enters into peace negotiations, it will attempt to get Israel to abandon its settlement policy in the West Bank.

Yasir Arafat decides not to return to Amman for further talks with King Hussein.

10 April King Hussein of Jordan rejects the Reagan peace proposals, claiming that the PLO has reneged upon an agreed course of action that would have allowed Jordanian participation; the Jordanian cabinet adheres to the 1974 Rabat agreement which named the PLO as the only representative of the Palestinians.

Dr. 'Isam Sartawi, the leading moderate in the PLO, is assassinated in Portugal at the meeting of the Socialist International; the Abu Nidal faction of the Revolutionary Council of al-Fatah claims responsibility; Yasir Arafat accuses Israel of the deed.

Iran asserts it is now ready to cooperate with international efforts to contain the Persian Gulf oil spill.

11 April Teheran announces a new offensive against Iraq fifty miles west of Dizful; the action destroys hopes among Persian Gulf states for cooperation between Iran and Iraq in cleaning up the Gulf oil spill.

Iran begins shipping drinking water to Persian Gulf states whose desalinization facilities are threatened by the oil spill.

The UN engages in talks with the foreign ministers of Pakistan and Afghanistan in an effort to solve the Afghan conflict.

12 April President Reagan declares he will not abandon his peace initiative in the Middle East. Radical elements in the PLO, he avers, pressured Yasir Arafat not to go through with a plan for King Hussein to enter peace negotiations on behalf of the Palestinians.

The Begin government announces plans to expand sixty-eight existing West Bank settlements from thirty thousand to fifty thousand persons; Israeli officials deny that this plan is related to a possible forthcoming U.S. request that Israel freeze settlement activity.

The PLO calls for resumption of PLO-Jordanian talks.

To replace Dr. 'Isam Sartawi as its representative at the Socialist International meeting in Lisbon, the PLO appoints Ilan Halevi, a militant anti-Zionist Israeli Jewish leftist.

Both Iran and Iraq report heavy fighting in the Misan area.

13 April Israel's defense minister, Moshe Arens, says that the United States' decision not to sell seventy-five F-16s to Israel has provoked Israel to resolve to reduce its dependence on the U.S. arms industry.

A subcommittee of the House Foreign Affairs Committee has increased by $345 million the amount requested by the Reagan administration for 1984 grants and loans to Israel.

14 April	Egypt and Jordan resume normal trade relations.
	Iraq claims that almost ten thousand Iranians perished in the present Iranian offensive.

14 April   Egypt and Jordan resume normal trade relations.

Iraq claims that almost ten thousand Iranians perished in the present Iranian offensive.

16 April   The Islamic Museum in Jerusalem suffers a loss of rare items valued at $4 million in a robbery.

Iraqi president Saddam Hussein invites the Ayatollah Khomeini to an Islamic conference being held in Baghdad.

Iraq sinks an Iranian ship near the Nawruz oil field.

17 April   The Reagan administration decides to permit Israel to purchase American-made or -designed components for a jet fighter aircraft to be manufactured by Israel.

Iraq claims it sank four Iranian ships near Bandar Khomeini.

18 April   The U.S. Embassy in Beirut is badly damaged by a bomb blast; at least thirty-three persons are killed and eighty wounded. The Islamic Jihad organization claims responsibility for the attack. President Reagan says that terrorist actions will not deter the United States from its peace-making efforts.

Israel inaugurates a major new settlement in the West Bank south of Nablus; the Labor party and the Peace Now group mount major protests against the settlement.

19 April   The chief of staff of the Israeli army, Lieut. Gen. Rafael Eytan, retires; he had been found guilty of "dereliction of duty" in the episode of the Beirut massacre.

The United States and Morocco engage in joint military exercises.

The foreign minister of Iran, 'Ali Akbar Velayeti, denies Iranian involvement in the bombing of the U.S. embassy in Beirut.

Reports in New Delhi indicate a Soviet-led attack by the Afghan army is underway in the Herat area.

20 April   President Reagan asserts that the United States will not be deterred by the bombing of the U.S. embassy from its policy of seeking the withdrawal of foreign forces from Lebanon.

Brazil seizes four Libyan air transports carrying munitions and weapons to Nicaragua.

22 April   President Reagan announces he will send Secretary of State Shultz to the Middle East.

23 April   A member of the al-Sa'iqa guerrilla group is charged by Lebanon with the 16 March grenade attack on U.S. Marines in Beirut.

Long-range Iraqi missiles strike a residential section of Dizful and destroy two hundred houses and shops; the attack seems to be in retaliation for two bomb explosions in Baghdad on 21 April.

Soviet leader Andropov says in a *Der Spiegel* interview it is not his intention to stay in Afghanistan.

24 April The Turkish military government announces that political parties may be formed starting 16 May; former high-ranking members of banned parties will not be allowed to participate in political life.

25 April Secretary of State Shultz arrives in Cairo on a diplomatic trip aimed at reaching an agreement on the withdrawal of Israeli forces from Lebanon.

Prime Minister Papandreou of Greece warns the United States that negotiations on the future of American naval bases will stop unless there is an understanding on the duration of the agreement and a U.S. promise to preserve Greece's military position vis-à-vis Turkey.

26 April Secretary of State Shultz, in concluding talks with Egyptian president Mubarak, says the United States and Egypt have identical views on the need to withdraw all foreign forces from Lebanon and on the necessity for Beirut to exercise sovereignty over all of Lebanon.

The Persian Gulf states fail for the third time to agree on how to effect a truce between Iran and Iraq as a preliminary move for action to halt the oil spill from Iran's Nawruz field, thirty-four miles northwest of Kharg Island.

The Kabul government announces that all women and some male prisoners will be freed the next day to commemorate the fifth anniversary of the coup.

27 April Secretary of State Shultz opens talks with Israeli leaders in Jerusalem; Shultz receives assurances of cooperation in withdrawal negotiations.

28 April Secretary of State Shultz confers in Beirut with President Gemayel and other Lebanese leaders.

Israeli military officials report a major Soviet buildup of Syrian armed forces.

In Greece, mass protests are held against the presence of U.S. military bases.

29 April Prime Minister Begin of Israel and U.S. Secretary of State Shultz discuss a compromise position on the role of Major Sa'd Haddad and his militia in creating a security zone in southern Lebanon.

30 April Secretary of State Shultz says he is willing to interrupt his shuttle diplomacy between Jerusalem and Beirut to visit Damascus and discuss the withdrawal of Syrian troops from Lebanon.

The Greek and Turkish foreign ministers confer in Strasbourg on means to improve relations.

1 May	Iran and Iraq exchange prisoners—about thirty soldiers from each side—in Ankara, Turkey.
2 May	Yasir Arafat describes Secretary of State Shultz's negotiations in the Middle East as an attempt to promote imperialistic schemes.
	After meeting with Lebanese foreign minister Elie Salem, President Hafiz al-Assad of Syria describes the terms that Israel is demanding for withdrawal from Lebanon as unacceptable.
	Iran reports it has sunk an Iraqi gunboat that was attacking the Nawruz oil field.
3 May	Yasir Arafat and Hafiz al-Assad meet to resolve outstanding differences between the PLO and Syria.
	After conferring with Israeli officials, Secretary of State Shultz expresses the hope that an accord can be reached in a few days.
	American experts declare the bomb-damaged U.S. embassy building in Beirut to be unfit for further use.
	Administration officials reveal that the quantity and quality of American aid being sent to the Afghan insurgents is improving.
4 May	In Iran, the Tudeh party (Communist) is declared illegal and Russian diplomats are ordered to leave the country; this action follows recent televised confessions by party members who had passed military information to the U.S.S.R.
	Prime Minister Begin of Israel says he will call a cabinet meeting to decide on accepting the agreement worked out by Secretary Shultz.
5 May	Heavy rocket and artillery duels between Christian and Druze forces occur in the suburbs of Beirut.
	Major Sa'd Haddad, leader of a private, Israeli-backed militia in southern Lebanon, states he will refuse to accept any compromise on his demand to be overall commander of security forces in southern Lebanon.
	Chaim Herzog, a prominent member of the Labor party, is inaugurated Israel's sixth president.
6 May	The Israeli cabinet votes 17–2 to accept the draft agreement with Lebanon, dependent on Syrian and PLO evacuation of Lebanon; the text of the agreement will not be disclosed until Israel obtains clarification on certain points.
	Secretary of State Shultz announces in Jerusalem that President Reagan will lift the embargo on the sale of seventy-five F-16 aircraft to Israel.
	A total of 133 Jewish-American students at Harvard, Yale, and New York University law schools send a letter to Prime Minister Begin protesting the invasion of Lebanon and current policies concerning the West Bank.

7 May	Iran and Iraq begin a new effort to reach an accord on controlling the Persian Gulf oil slick.
8 May	Afghanistan orders the second secretary of the U.S. embassy in Kabul to leave the country.
9 May	The State Department expresses concern over the buildup of Syrian and PLO forces in Lebanon.
	The UN delegate of Israel, Yehuda Z. Blum, challenges the factual accuracy of a letter signed by 133 American law students; the letter protested the invasion of Lebanon and Israel's settlement policy in the West Bank.
	Two American companies are damaged by bomb blasts in Amman.
	The Soviet ambassador in Beirut orders thirty-nine women and forty-eight children—all dependents of Soviet diplomats—flown out of Beirut to the Soviet Union.
	In Turkey, a military court sentences the publisher of the newspaper *Cumhuriyet* to ten weeks in jail for publishing an article he wrote twenty-two years ago.
	One Afghan diplomat is ordered to leave the United States.
10 May	At a news conference in Paris, Secretary of State Schultz appeals to the Soviet Union to pressure Syria to pull its forces out of Lebanon.
	The House Foreign Affairs Committee votes 14–13 to cut off foreign aid to Turkey in 1987 if at that time Turkish forces still occupy Cyprus.
	It is reported in Islamabad, Pakistan, that Soviet and Afghan forces launched a major offensive ten days earlier against insurgents north of Kabul in the Shomali area.
11 May	Secretary of State Shultz concludes his seventeen-day diplomatic mission in the Middle East; on his return to Washington he expresses confidence Syria will remove its forces from Lebanon.
	Foreign Minister Yitzhak Shamir of Israel says in Parliament that Israel will pursue its own interests if Syria and the PLO do not withdraw from Lebanon.
	The International Committee of the Red Cross accuses both Iraq and Iran of violations of international law in their treatment of war prisoners.
12 May	Lebanese foreign minister Elie Salem arrives in Damascus to confer on the pullout of Syrian troops from Lebanon.
13 May	Yasir Arafat's faction within the PLO, al-Fatah, issues a statement denying there is a revolt in the ranks of the PLO in the Bekaa Valley.

Syria rejects Lebanon's efforts to persuade it to go along with the Shultz plan for joint security arrangements with Israel.

The General Assembly resolves, by a vote of 103–5, that Turkey remove its forces from Cyprus.

14 May The Lebanese cabinet approves the withdrawal agreement with Israel.

President Mubarak of Egypt urges the Arab world to support the Israeli-Lebanese accord on troop withdrawal from Lebanon.

Syria vows it will do everything possible to foil the Israeli-Lebanese agreement.

PLO officials announce that Yasir Arafat has returned to Lebanon.

15 May Hafiz al-Assad, president of Syria, meets political leaders from Lebanon who oppose the Israeli-Lebanese pact and assures them of his support.

Yasir Arafat calls on the PLO to wage war against Israel and the United States.

The foreign minister of Pakistan, Ya'qub Khan, arrives in Peking, China, on a two-day diplomatic mission.

Libya and Germany exchange prisoners at the Frankfort airport.

16 May In Turkey, the first political party to be formed since the military government took over, the Nationalist Democracy party, is registered with retired general Turgut Sunalp as its head.

17 May The United States and Israel sign a confidential agreement that recognizes Israel's right to retaliate against attacks directed from Lebanon.

Fierce fighting is reported in Chad in the Faya-Largeau area.

Thomas Sankara, the prime minister of Upper Volta, is arrested on suspicion of plotting against the president; Sankara is backed by Qaddafi of Libya.

18 May Syria rejects an appeal by President Reagan to withdraw its troops from Lebanon and refuses to receive Philip Habib, special envoy to the Middle East.

19 May The United States and Egypt amicably break off talks on an agreement for the use of military facilities at Ras Banas on the Red Sea.

Lebanese foreign minister Elie Salem commences a trip to European capitals to seek diplomatic support for the withdrawal of Syrian forces from Lebanon.

The Soviet ambassador in Afghanistan says the Kabul government will agree to a withdrawal of Soviet troops if there are international guarantees against intervention from abroad.

20 May	President Reagan lifts the ban on the sale of seventy-five F-16 fighters to Israel.
	Greece lodges a strong protest over alleged American and Turkish violations of its airspace over the Aegean Sea.
	The State Department accuses the U.S.S.R. of extremely heavy bombing raids on civilian targets in Afghanistan.
21 May	Iran charges Iraq with using French Exocet missiles to attack oil well installations in the Persian Gulf.
22 May	Yasir Arafat visits Palestinian positions in Tripoli, Lebanon.
	Violence between Druze and Christian factions breaks out in the Shuf Mountains; twenty-three are killed and one hundred kidnapped.
	Egypt announces it will construct military facilities at Ras Banas and that "limited use" of them will continue to be offered to the United States.
23 May	Greece and the United States resume talks on the future of American bases in Greece.
24 May	A Turkish military court sentences thirty-five Kurds to death for attempting to set up a separate Kurdish state.
	Diplomatic reports in New Delhi indicate a truce has been reached between an insurgent leader, Ahmad Shah Mas 'ud, and Soviet troops, affecting the Panjshir Valley of Afghanistan.
25 May	Syrian fighter planes fire two air-to-air missiles at Israeli airplanes over Lebanon; no damage is sustained.
	Iraq offers to sign an agreement with Iran that would ban attacks on civilian areas.
26 May	Turkish moves into Iraq against Kurdish insurgents are reported.
	Iran rejects a recent Iraqi proposal that both countries agree not to bomb or shell each other's civilian areas.
27 May	In a public statement, Secretary of State George Shultz informs Syria that its military buildup in Lebanon and along the Libano-Syrian border threatens the uneasy peace in the area; about one thousand new Syrian troops have moved recently into Lebanon, adding to the more than forty thousand troops already deployed in or near the country.
	Syrian foreign minister Mustafa Tlas claims the Syrian buildup is defensive in nature; Israeli defense minister Moshe Arens welcomes the statement by Tlas, and maintains that Israel will not be dragged into a war with Syria.
	Turkey sends troops into Iraqi territory in pursuit of "aggressors"—presumably Kurds.
28 May	Israel moves a large tank force toward the Bekaa Valley.

Peace Now, a pacifist group in Israel, begins a peace march south from the border with Lebanon.

The Ayatollah Khomeini criticizes President Reagan's recent statement on behalf of the Bahais in Iran.

29 May Rebellious junior officers in Yasir Arafat's al-Fatah group seize control of six PLO supply depots near Damascus.

Syrian and PLO officials begin discussions to prevent further dissent within Yasir Arafat's Fatah group.

President Amin Gemayel appeals for Lebanese unity at an Islamic rally in Beirut.

West German diplomats report that Iran seeks closer ties with Western nations.

30 May An Iraqi Kurdish spokesman reports that the recent incursion by the Turkish army into Iraq has trapped up to thirty thousand Kurdish civilians in remote areas.

31 May Reports reach New Delhi that insurgents in Afghanistan staged two major attacks last week against government positions in Kabul and in the Logar Valley.

Ruling authorities in Turkey close down the newly created Great Turkey party and confine fourteen politicians, including former prime minister Suleyman Demirel.

1 June Musa Awad, a leading civilian member of al-Fatah, announces that he and about twenty-four other leaders have joined in a rebellion against Yasir Arafat.

Syrian president Hafiz al-Assad predicts a new war with Israel and vows to undermine the U.S.–imposed agreement signed by Israel and Lebanon.

Prime Minister Begin of Israel, defending his policies in Parliament, says Israel has no plans to attack Syria.

2 June Philip Habib, special envoy to the Middle East, returns to Washington for a policy review.

The sponsors of a conference on Palestinian rights abandon plans to convene in Paris; the Mitterrand government objected that anti-Semitic incidents might occur and that terrorists would be attracted to such a meeting.

An official meeting between the United States and Israel to discuss the deportation of Nazis now living in America is canceled when the U.S. delegation refuses to meet in East Jerusalem, whose annexation by Israel has not been recognized by Washington.

Turkish military authorities take former prime minister Demirel and fifteen other former politicians into custody.

3 June Lebanese president Gemayel undertakes a new effort to gain support from Arab countries to persuade Syria to withdraw its troops; conversations with the Arab League and Saudi Arabia commence.

Dubai bans fish imports from other Persian Gulf countries because of contamination from the oil slick leaking from Iran's Nawruz oil field.

4 June   Heavy fighting breaks out between factions of the PLO in eastern Lebanon; Syria moves tanks into the Bekaa Valley.

Up to 150,000 persons demonstrate in Tel Aviv to demand the withdrawal of Israeli troops from Lebanon.

5 June   The Libyan chargé d'affaires in Beirut is wounded in an assassination attempt.

6 June   The foreign minister of Lebanon, Elie Salem, leaves for Washington to discuss ways to remove foreign troops from Lebanon.

A general strike in the Muslim areas of Lebanon marks the first anniversary of Israel's invasion of that country.

The Labor party in Israel calls for a state commission of inquiry into all aspects of the war in Lebanon.

Rebels within al-Fatah call for elections of new officers.

The Organization of African Unity, scheduled to convene in Addis Ababa, is unable to meet owing to continuing disputes over the seating of the Polisario delegation.

7 June   President Saddam Hussein of Iraq offers a limited cease-fire to Iran.

8 June   Israel's parliament votes 55–47 to reject a Labor party proposal to withdraw forces from Lebanon.

Iran rejects an offer from Iraq for a limited cease-fire during the month of Ramadan.

In Addis Ababa, the Polisario guerrilla front relinquishes its seat in the Organization of African Unity, thus clearing the way for those nations led by Morocco that had been boycotting the meeting to return and form a quorum.

Following an ambush of Soviet troops by insurgents, Soviet and Afghan forces subject villages near Paghman to day-long artillery attacks.

10 June   Ariel Sharon, former defense minister of Israel, asks for an inquiry into the Lebanon war in order to clear his name.

The prime minister of Greece, Andreas Papandreou, says that if present talks on the American bases in Greece break down (probably over the question of grant aid), then he will remove the bases within the next twelve or eighteen months.

11 June   The Organization of African Unity reaches a formula to end the dispute over the Western Sahara.

12 June	Morris Draper, U.S. special envoy to the Middle East, reveals in an interview that "serious discussions" have been held with the U.S.S.R. about the Lebanon situation.
13 June	Israeli and Syrian tank forces exchange heavy artillery fire in eastern Lebanon.
	Yasir Arafat visits the Bekaa Valley and meets with PLO field commanders.
	A high Saudi official visits Lebanon to attempt to mediate a withdrawal of PLO forces.
	The ruling generals in Turkey reserve the right to veto candidates put up by political parties.
14 June	The Lebanese parliament approves, 65–2, the agreement with Israel for the withdrawal of Israeli troops.
	Fighting breaks out between Druze militiamen and Christian Phalangists in the Shuf Mountains of Lebanon.
	Secretary of Defense Weinberger says he is willing to revive an Israeli–U.S. understanding to cooperate against the Soviet threat in the Middle East.
15 June	The Syrian government calls for guerrilla war against the Gemayel government of Lebanon.
	Riots in Srinagar, Kashmir, leave seven hundred wounded.
16 June	Iraq claims its air force inflicts heavy damage on Iranian troops on the northern front.
	The government of India halts all rail service in the Punjab after Sikh members of the Akali Dal party announce they will squat on railroad tracks to emphasize their demand for greater autonomy.
17 June	The September Martyrs regiment of al-Fatah joins the rebels against Yasir Arafat; it claims a major share of the recent attacks against Israeli occupation forces in Lebanon.
	Both Iran and Iraq report they have launched attacks in the Misan area of the war front.
18 June	The mutiny against Yasir Arafat's leadership of the PLO grows; new fighting breaks out between Palestinian units in eastern Lebanon, with a major clash near Shtaura.
	The pro-Arafat PLO news service, Wafa, begins functioning in Tripoli, Lebanon.
19 June	'Izz al-Din Sharif (a.k.a. Abu Ziyad), who is a senior aide to Yasir Arafat, is ambushed when he goes to confront a rebellion in PLO ranks near Damascus.
20 June	In Damascus, Yasir Arafat opens an official PLO debate on the mutiny against his leadership.

Secretary of State George Shultz confers with Wadi Haddad, a senior Lebanese representative, on the implications of a possible Israeli redeployment in Lebanon.

The official Lebanese report on the Beirut massacres is released; it exculpates the Christian Phalangist party and says the Israeli army bears responsibility for the event because it surrounded the refugee camps 11–18 September 1982.

21 June　　With Syrian support, Palestinian guerrillas opposed to Yasir Arafat seize control of eight positions from Arafat loyalists in eastern Lebanon.

Cairo expels twenty Palestinian students, all members of the Popular Front for the Liberation of Palestine, for security reasons.

Reports reach New Delhi that Afghan insurgents have opened intense attacks in the Kabul area.

The State Department recommends that the United States supply nuclear reactor parts to India.

22 June　　The State Department says Chadian dissidents, with backing from Libya, are poised to attack Faya-Largeau in northern Chad.

23 June　　Yasir Arafat accuses Syria of cutting off supplies to his guerrilla forces in eastern Lebanon.

The Lebanese government says the report released last week on the Beirut massacres was an "unauthorized first draft" that should not have been made public.

Military authorities in Turkey ban twenty-one founders of the new Social Democratic party from taking part in political activities.

Chad announces that 3,500 rebel troops with Libyan backing are besieging the town of Faya-Largeau; the rebels are loyal to former Chadian president Goukouni Oueddei.

24 June　　Yasir Arafat is expelled from Syria because of his "continual slanders against Syria."

In Iraq, Kurds repel an Iraqi army assault on their base at Shene, killing seventy Iraqi soldiers.

In Chad, the town of Faya-Largeau falls to the troops of former president Goukouni Oueddei.

UN–sponsored talks in Geneva on the withdrawal of Soviet troops from Afghanistan end with no progress made.

25 June　　Yasir Arafat flies to Prague to seek international support against dissidents in the PLO.

The government of Chad reports that rebels now control a third of the country.

26 June　　Libyan-backed rebel forces push southward from Faya-Largeau.

The French minister for cooperation and development makes an unannounced visit to Chad.

The Begin cabinet in Israel agrees to accept arbitration of a salary dispute between physicians and the state medical system after a thirteen-day hunger strike by the physicians.

27 June

The Lebanese government reports it has charged eight persons with the abduction and murder of American ambassador Francis E. Meloy.

President Reagan signs legislation for emergency and military aid to Lebanon.

The mufti of Jerusalem gives his opinion that the president of Syria, Hafiz al-Assad, may be killed because he has murdered many Muslims.

Over three thousand Israeli doctors call off their two-week-long hunger strike after the government agrees to arbitration of their demands for higher pay.

France agrees to lend Iraq five Super Etendard fighter-bombers.

France agrees to airlift thirty-five tons of military supplies to Chad to support the government of Hissen Habré.

28 June

Rebels within the PLO attack troops loyal to Yasir Arafat and seize part of the Beirut-Damascus highway.

29 June

Arafat loyalists, with supplies cut off by Syria, are driven out of Shtaura by PLO rebels.

30 June

Palestinian guerrillas in Lebanon agree on a cease-fire; a committee composed of various PLO factions is formed to oversee the truce.

France reports it has sent two hundred tons of military equipment to Hissen Habré's forces in Chad.

1 July

The PLO Executive Committee, meeting in Tunis, calls for a cease-fire between Palestinian groups in Lebanon and decides to send a mediation team to Syria.

Israeli foreign minister Yitzhak Shamir declares that his government is determined to see simultaneous Syrian and Israeli withdrawals from Lebanon.

Secretary of State George Shultz ends two days of talks in New Delhi with Indian leaders; he endorses the sale of American weapons to India.

2 July

PLO factions break a two-day truce; fighting erupts in eastern Lebanon.

A PLO mediation team flies from Tunis to Damascus.

Secretary of State Shultz arrives in Pakistan to pursue talks on Afghanistan.

3 July	Secretary of State Shultz visits the Khyber Pass in Pakistan and speaks to three or four thousand Afghan refugees.
	Colonel Qaddafi ends a three-day visit to Morocco; a communiqué says the two countries will establish fraternal relations.
	Zaire sends military assistance to the Chad government.
5 July	Israel announces its intention to pull back its troops in Lebanon and to redeploy them in better defensive positions.
6 July	Secretary of State Shultz confers with President Hafiz al-Assad in Damascus; after their meeting, Syria reaffirms its opposition to the Lebanese-Israeli agreement.
7 July	The prime minister of Lebanon, Shafik al-Wazzan, narrowly escapes a car-bomb attempt on his life in Beirut.
	In the West Bank, Israeli authorities dismiss the mayor and city council of Hebron after an Israeli student is killed.
9 July	Rebel forces in Chad claim the capture of Abéché, a strategically important town.
10 July	A Saudi emissary meets with President Hafiz al-Assad of Syria to discuss the revolt within PLO ranks.
	A special envoy from Fidel Castro confers with Yasir Arafat in Tunis on resolving the rebellion with the PLO.
	In Israel, the Begin cabinet approves the dismissal of the Arab mayor of Hebron, a major Arab city in the West Bank.
	Iraq claims its navy sank three Iranian ships in the Persian Gulf.
	The government of Chad admits the fall of Abéché to rebel forces and reports it has ordered a counterattack.
11 July	The government of Chad retakes the oasis of Umm Chalouba from rebel forces.
	Polisario guerrillas mount attacks on several Moroccan outposts in the Western Sahara.
	The World Wildlife Fund terms "catastrophic" the oil spill from the Iranian Nawruz field in the Persian Gulf.
12 July	The government of Chad recaptures the town of Abéché and pursues rebel forces toward Biltine.
13 July	Seven hundred troops from Zaire arrive in Ndjamena, Chad, to assist the government of Hissen Habré.
14 July	In Tel Aviv, police set up a special task force to deal with riots by Jewish religious militants.
	A Turkish diplomat is slain in Brussels by an Armenian assassin.

15 July	Units of the Lebanese army battle Shiite militiamen in West Beirut.
	Armenian terrorists explode a bomb at a Turkish Airlines counter in Orly Airport, France; five persons are killed; Prime Minister Pierre Mauroy pledges that all will be done to capture and punish the terrorists.
	The United States and Greece reach agreement on a new five-year pact for the operation of American bases in Greece.
16 July	Christian and Druze forces engage in heavy artillery battles southeast of Beirut.
	The Organization of African Unity, meeting in Addis Ababa, appeals for an end to foreign intervention in Chad; Libya is reported to welcome this statement.
	Ethiopian troops invade the Galgadud region of Somalia.
17 July	The government of Chad puts Libyan prisoners on public display.
	Somalia claims to have repulsed invading Ethiopian forces.
19 July	Amin Gemayel, president of Lebanon, meets with King Hussein of Jordan to coordinate policies on the crisis in Lebanon.
	Prime Minister Begin of Israel postpones a planned trip to Washington for personal reasons.
	The amir of Bahrain meets with President Reagan in Washington; discussions focus on efforts to remove Syrian troops from Lebanon.
	President Reagan decides to send Chad some $10 million in military aid.
20 July	The Begin cabinet approves plans to pull troops from the Beirut area and Shuf Mountains and to set up a new line of defense along the Awali River.
	Tariq 'Aziz, foreign minister of Iraq, claims that large supplies of weapons made in America are entering Iran.
	An Armenian, Varadjian Garbidjian, head of the French branch of the Armenian Secret Army for the Liberation of Armenia, is charged in France with responsibility for the bomb attack in Orly Airport on 15 July.
21 July	Yasir Arafat, as a concession to critics of his leadership, dismisses the two senior commanders whose appointments led to a mutiny against him among PLO units in eastern Lebanon.
	David S. Dodge, former acting president of the American University in Beirut, is freed from a captivity that began on 19 July 1982, with the help of Syrian authorities.

22 July	Philip Habib is replaced by Robert C. McFarlane, presently a deputy national security adviser, as chief Middle East negotiator.
	The Beirut airport is subjected to shelling while Druze and Christian forces intensify their artillery duels.
	The French embassy in Teheran is bombed; Armenian guerrillas claim responsibility for the attack.
23 July	Walid Jumblat, Druze leader in Lebanon, forms the National Salvation Front with leftist and Syrian-backed groups to oppose the Gemayel government.
	Egypt arrests twenty-five fundamentalists and charges them with plotting to overthrow the government.
	Iran starts a new offensive against Iraq, moving toward Ruwandiz.
24 July	In eastern Lebanon, new fighting occurs between forces loyal to Yasir Arafat and those backed by Syria.
	Iran claims major gains in its new offensive against Iraq.
	The Chadian government lays siege to Faya-Largeau, which was seized by rebels last month.
25 July	Defense Minister Moshe Arens and Foreign Minister Yitzhak Shamir of Israel arrive in Washington to discuss the Lebanese situation with administration officials.
	American military aid is airlifted to Chad; this is the first part of a $10 million effort approved by President Reagan.
26 July	Gunmen attack the Islamic College in Hebron in the West Bank; three persons are killed and thirty-three wounded.
	The Department of State warns Iran that any attempt to block the transit of oil shipments through the Persian Gulf will be countered by U.S. military force.
27 July	Four Arabs are wounded in the West Bank during protests over the recent attack on the Islamic College in Hebron.
	Armenian terrorists invade the residence of the Turkish ambassador in Lisbon and blow it up. The Armenian Revolutionary Army claims credit for the attack.
	Afghan insurgents cut off electric power to Kabul.
28 July	The Israeli army orders the Phalangist militia to close and vacate an office and barracks at Kafr Falus. The closure, which was ordered because the Phalangists were harassing Palestinians and Shiites in the area, incites thousands of Christians to demonstrate in protest near Sidon and Nabatiya.
	Secretary of State George Shultz applauds the Israeli pullback in Lebanon to the Awali River and hopes that Syria will likewise pull back.

Syrian troops pull out of positions in Tripoli, Lebanon, and rival militia groups battle for positions.

Pro-Arafat PLO troops, under heavy fire in eastern Lebanon from pro-Syrian insurgents, request aid from the Gemayel government to evacuate them via Tripoli.

29 July
Phalangist authorities call on their forces in southern Lebanon to accede to the plans by Israeli forces to close Phalangist bases.

30 July
Opposing Palestinian factions battle at Baalbak, Lebanon; Yasir Arafat accuses Syria of aiding those who contest his leadership.

Iran opens a new offensive against Iraq, the second within a week.

The loyalist forces in Chad recapture the town of Faya-Largeau, which had fallen to rebel forces on 24 June.

31 July
The United States accuses Libya of bombing the town of Faya-Largeau in Chad.

1 August
Sudan asks the United States and France to provide help to the government of Chad.

France announces it will send antiaircraft guns to Chad.

The aircraft carrier *Eisenhower* is placed on standby for operations near Libya.

2 August
The United States vetoes a resolution in the Security Council that is critical of Israeli settlement policies in the West Bank.

Special envoy Robert C. McFarlane meets President Gemayel of Lebanon.

Chad requests a Security Council meeting to hear a complaint about Libya's aggression in Chad.

American and Libyan jet fighters encounter each other over the Gulf of Sidra; no hostile action occurs.

3 August
Israel rejects Lebanon's request for a timetable for the withdrawal of troops.

Pentagon and State Department officials announce that two AWAC reconnaissance aircraft have been flown to Egypt. They also say that military advisers have been sent to Chad with Redeye antiaircraft missiles.

Debate begins in the Security Council on Chad's complaint that Libya has invaded its territory.

4 August
Libya claims it is neutral in the Chadian conflict and denies it has intervened.

Libyan aircraft bomb Faya-Largeau.

The United States announces it will increase aid to Chad from $10 to $25 million.

5 August	In Tripoli, Lebanon, a car-bomb kills twenty and injures fifty persons.
6 August	U.S. special envoy Robert McFarlane meets with Syrian foreign minister Khaddam in Damascus.
	Chad asks France for direct military aid.
	The United States confirms it has dispatched two AWAC planes with support teams to assist the government of Chad.
7 August	A car-bomb kills 33 and wounds 125 in Baalbek, Lebanon.
	France says it will not provide direct assistance to Chad in the form of combat planes or ground troops.
8 August	President Reagan notifies Congress of the deployment of two AWACs and eight F-15 fighter planes with support personnel to Chad to assist in opposing the Libyan-supported rebels.
9 August	Libya moves a force of tanks toward Faya-Largeau.
	France announces it is sending 180 paratroopers to Chad, adding to the 2,000 French troops already there; their mission is to train Chadians, not to engage in combat.
10 August	Druze militiamen and the Lebanese army fight artillery duels; the Druze shell the Beirut airport and seize three high-level government officials, demanding that the entire Gemayel cabinet resign.
	Rebels in Chad launch a major assault on Faya-Largeau, which the government is unable to resupply.
	France says it is sending 500, rather than 180, paratroopers to Chad.
	Armenian terrorists claim responsibility for a car-bomb explosion at the French embassy compound in Teheran.
11 August	Druze militiamen release three Lebanese officials they had captured; the officials are to present a list of ten demands to President Gemayel.
	President Reagan denounces Libyan military activities in Chad but says the United States will not become militarily involved.
	Faya-Largeau is reported to fall to attacking rebel forces of some five thousand troops, including two thousand Libyans.
12 August	Libyan planes attack Umm Chalouba in Chad.
13 August	Christian and Druze militias fight artillery battles in the mountains east of Beirut.
	Druze leader Walid Jumblat, whose militia has forced the closing of the Beirut airport, says he will keep the airport closed until the government of Amin Gemayel accedes to his demands for (1) resignation of the cabinet, (2) no Lebanese army heavy artil-

lery in Druze areas of Lebanon, and (3) a national reconciliation, to go into effect before the Lebanese army enters the Shuf.

The United Nations World Conference to Combat Racism ends with a call for sanctions against South Africa and Israel.

French paratroopers are deployed in the town of Abéché in Chad.

Somalia reports it has forced back an Ethiopian attack in the Ogaden area.

14 August

French paratroopers are deployed in Chad in the area of Salel to oppose the southward advance of Libyan-supported rebels.

On the thirtieth anniversary of Pakistan's independence, thousands riot, protesting the present government.

16 August

The State Department, in a classified memorandum, expresses concern for the safety of the 300,000 Palestinian refugees in Lebanon.

Hissen Habré, president of Chad, denounces the Libyan occupation of his country and says Qaddafi's aim is to annex one-half of Chad.

President Mitterrand expresses annoyance at American efforts to persuade France to adopt a hard line against Libya and to intervene actively in the civil war in Chad.

West and Central African leaders decide to call upon the Organization of African Unity to resolve the civil war in Chad.

17 August

The prime minister of Lebanon, Shafik al-Wazzan, refuses to conduct government business on this day as a personal protest against the welcome given to Moshe Arens, the defense minister of Israel, upon his visit to Beirut the previous day.

Rival Communist factions, the Parcham (flag) and the Khalq (masses) groups, battle each other near Herat, Afghanistan; about one hundred Afghan army and police personnel are killed.

18 August

The government of Chad claims that Russian advisers accompanied the rebel forces that seized Faya-Largeau.

19 August

Brig. Gen. Jean Poli, a marine paratrooper, is appointed to command French forces in Chad.

20 August

The Cairo airport is closed for two hours as Egyptian and American aircraft conduct exercises.

President Mobutu Sese Seko of Zaire visits President Habré of Chad as a gesture of support.

21 August

Special envoy McFarlane says the United States will not support the partitioning of Lebanon.

France sends ten combat airplanes to Chad in support of Hissen Habré's government.

22 August	President Samuel K. Doe of Liberia pays a state visit to Israel.
	The government of Chad asks for direct French assistance in the war against the rebels who control the northern third of the country.
23 August	Iran pays $419.5 million to the Export-Import Bank to settle claims deriving from the seizure of American hostages in 1979; the total amount paid by Iran to date out of its $1.42 billion escrow fund (set up on 1 January 1981) is $895.9 million.
	The United States removes its two AWACs and eight F-15 fighter escorts from Sudan; these had been sent to counter Libya's actions in Chad.
	Chad claims that five thousand armor-equipped Libyans are in Chad; the rebels are reported to have advanced fifty miles south of Faya-Largeau.
24 August	President Samuel K. Doe of Liberia, who is in Jerusalem on a state visit, accuses Colonel Qaddafi of Libya of planning to take over the continent of Africa.
	Iraq claims it has destroyed four Iranian naval vessels near Kharg Island.
	The French cabinet, having sent three thousand French troops to Chad, decides to seek a diplomatic resolution of the conflict.
25 August	The French consulate building in Berlin is bombed; the Secret Army for the Liberation of Armenia claims responsibility for the explosion, which killed one person and injured twenty-three.
	Yehuda Z. Blum, Israel's chief UN delegate, says his country plans to withhold a portion of its financial contribution to protest recent UN actions that defame and vilify Israel.
26 August	France and Zaire hold military exercises with Chadian government forces in eastern Chad.
27 August	Walid Jumblat, leader of the Lebanese Druze, confers with special envoy Robert C. McFarlane.
	President Reagan reaffirms his opposition to Israel's policy of settlement in occupied territories.
28 August	Marines in Lebanon shoot back at attackers; this is the first instance of Marines engaging in combat since their arrival in Lebanon.
	Prime Minister Begin of Israel informs his cabinet that he intends to resign.
	An Air France jet liner, hijacked over Europe, is held at the Teheran airport. The hijackers demand that France cease military aid to Chad, Iraq, and Lebanon. Iranian officials condemn the hijacking.

29 August	Two American Marines are killed and fourteen wounded during fierce fighting between the Lebanese army and Muslim militias.
	In Geneva, a UN conference on Palestinian rights opens, with delegates from 115 countries; the United States and Israel boycott the meeting.
	Thousands of Sikhs attack government offices in Punjab State.
30 August	Four French soldiers are killed in Beirut during continuing battles between the Lebanese army and Muslim militia groups.
	It is reported that Prime Minister Begin has agreed to delay the withdrawal of Israeli forces from the Shuf Mountains until the Lebanese army is able to maintain control there.
31 August	In a major operation, the Lebanese army seizes control of most of West Beirut from bands of Muslim gunmen.
	President Gemayel of Lebanon calls for a "national reconciliation dialogue." Walid Jumblat, Druze leader in Lebanon, characterizes this statement as treachery.
	Hijackers of an Air France jet surrender at the Teheran airport.
1 September	The United States orders two thousand additional Marines to the eastern Mediterranean.
	Yasir Arafat arrives in Geneva to address a UN conference on Palestinians.
	Iraq continues air attacks on the Iranian city of Marivan.
2 September	Yitzhak Shamir is elected head of the Herut party in Israel, succeeding Menachim Begin; Shamir is given promises of support by the major factions of the Likud bloc.
	In Chad, three thousand insurgents attack the oasis of Umm Chalouba.
	Turkish military authorities lift the ban on the publication of Tercümen, a leading conservative newspaper.
3 September	The United States asks Israel to delay its planned withdrawal from the Beirut region south to the Awali defense line.
	The departure of large quantities of Israeli armored equipment from Beirut signals the redeployment of Israeli forces to the Awali River area.
	Government forces in Chad defeat a major assault on Umm Chalouba and Kalait; the government claims that eight hundred rebel troops perished and six hundred were captured.
4 September	Israel completes the withdrawal of ten to fifteen thousand troops from the Beirut area, ending a fifteen-month occupation.
	Christians and Druze militias commence heavy artillery duels as Israeli forces leave the Beirut area.

5 September	Druze and Christian Phalangist militias battle for the second day in mountains near Beirut, apparently for control of Bhamdun.
	Chad says Libyan aircraft bomb Umm Chalouba.
	The UN asks Iran to stop recruiting children for its armies.
	Seven members of the banned Pakistan Peoples' party are arrested for advocating democracy in Punjab.
6 September	Druze forces capture the strategically important town of Bhamdun in Lebanon.
	Two more American Marines are killed by stray shells; President Reagan reaffirms that the Marines will stay in Beirut.
7 September	The Gemayel government in Lebanon asks the multinational forces to send troops into the Shuf Mountains to block an expected Syrian advance.
	Heavy artillery battles are fought near Beirut; two French soldiers are killed by stray shells, bringing to sixteen the total French losses. France sends flights of aircraft over Druze positions as a warning. Warships supporting the multinational forces move closer to the Lebanese coast.
	Officials of the Iraqi foreign ministry meet with State Department officials to discuss the Iran-Iraq war.
	Chad claims victory over rebels at Umm Chalouba.
	Greece and the United States agree on terms for a new defense and economic cooperation pact.
8 September	An American warship fires on Druze positions southeast of Beirut after gunmen fire on the Marines.
	The United States warns Syria it will protect the Marines in Beirut.
	Chad's president, Hissen Habré, complains that France is not directly assisting in the fight against the rebels; France, he suggests, seeks to partition Chad.
	Sixty-three persons are injured in antigovernment riots in Punjab Province.
9 September	Cease-fire talks are held in Beirut.
10 September	The governments that have contributed to peacekeeping forces in Beirut refuse a request from the Gemayel government that troops be sent into the Shuf area.
11 September	Druze forces in an offensive move seize two towns and batter the Lebanese army at strategic Suq al-Gharb; Druze leader Walid Jumblat rejects a truce offer and refuses to negotiate unless the Christian forces and the Lebanese army withdraw from the Shuf Mountains.

12 September	President Reagan authorizes the Marines in Lebanon to use "aggressive self-defense."
	A new force of American Marines numbering two thousand arrives off the coast of Lebanon.
	Reports from Afghanistan indicate that Muslim insurgents seized three towns in eastern Afghanistan.
13 September	The Syrian minister for foreign affairs warns the Reagan administration not to increase its involvement in Lebanon.
	The U.S. government authorizes the Marines in Lebanon to assist other members of the multinational force and the Lebanese army; this allows offshore naval and air power to be used.
	Druze militiamen, with Syrian support, attack the Lebanese army positions at Suq al-Gharb.
	President Gemayel of Lebanon assures the ambassadors of nations that contributed troops to the multinational force that Lebanon is prepared to hold talks on halting the civil conflict.
	Senator John Glenn of Ohio, who is seeking the Democratic party's nomination for president, says the United States should drop its pretense of evenhandedness in the Middle East and come out in full support of Israel.
14 September	Prince Bandar of Saudi Arabia and Robert McFarlane of the United States attempt to persuade authorities in Damascus to agree to a truce in Lebanon; Syria insists that the Lebanese army withdraw from the Shuf area.
	David Levy, the deputy prime minister of Israel, becomes the acting prime minister because of Begin's illness.
15 September	Prime Minister Begin of Israel submits his formal letter of resignation.
	Two American diplomats are told to leave Afghanistan because of spying.
16 September	The Lebanese army begins a large-scale attack against Druze militiamen and Palestinians in the Suq al-Gharb region; the Lebanese air force flies sorties against Druze positions.
17 September	U.S. warships lying off Beirut bombard Druze artillery emplacements in the Syrian-controlled region west of Beirut; Syria says it will retaliate if its positions are attacked.
	The Israeli interior minister estimates that up to seventy thousand refugees from northern Lebanon have moved into the Sidon area.
	President Saddam Hussein of Iraq cables the Islamic Conference's peace committee, saying his country desires peace and welcomes any effort to end the war with Iran.

18 September	Warfare widens in Lebanon; antigovernment forces shell the Lebanese air force base, and Libyan leader Qaddafi puts troops that are in Lebanon at the disposal of the Syrians and Druze. Yasir Arafat confirms that his fighters are supporting the Druze in the Shuf Mountains.
	Demonstrations, marked by violence, are held in Arab cities in Israel to commemorate the anniversary of the Beirut massacres.
	Afghan jet planes bomb a village in Pakistan close to the Afghan border.
19 September	U.S. warships shell antigovernment positions in an effort to assist Lebanese army units that are defending the town of Suq al-Gharb. This is the first instance of American force used in direct support of the Lebanese government.
	The French foreign minister, Claude Cheysson, criticizes the U.S. naval bombardment of antigovernment positions near Suq al-Gharb in Lebanon.
	The Ayatollah Khomeini declares Iran will cut oil supplies to any European country that aids Iraq in blocking Iranian oil shipments through the Gulf.
20 September	Two American warships, the cruiser *Virginia* and the destroyer *John Rodgers*, bombard antigovernment artillery positions southeast of Beirut.
	Reginald Bartholomew is designated U.S. ambassador to Lebanon.
	Yitzhak Shamir lines up sufficient support to form a parliamentary majority and create a new government in Israel.
21 September	American naval forces fire two salvos at antigovernment artillery positions that have been firing on Beirut.
	The United States blames the Soviet Union for sponsoring and supplying Syria's intervention in Lebanese affairs.
	The president of Israel, Chaim Herzog, asks Yitzhak Shamir to form a new government.
22 September	After a barrage of rockets fall on French and Italian positions in Beirut, eight French Super Etendard aircraft, launched from the carrier *Foch*, attack antigovernment artillery positions east of Beirut.
23 September	U.S. Marines come under fire at the Beirut airport; two American warships and a shore battery return the fire.
	The Senate Foreign Relations Committee votes approval of a resolution to allow the Marines to remain in Lebanon for eighteen months.
24 September	Shiite militiamen and the Lebanese army engage in tank and artillery duels in a Beirut suburb, Burj al-Brajneh.

Secretary of State Shultz says the Marines should stay in Lebanon as long as there is a need, regardless of Congress's efforts to impose the War Powers Act.

The Defense Department says 1,800 Marines are ashore in Lebanon.

Syria orders one thousand or more pro-Arafat PLO troops to leave their positions in the Bekaa Valley and move to northeastern Lebanon.

In Pakistan, over two hundred persons are arrested for protesting, as campaigning starts for local elections.

25 September Syria and Lebanon announce a cease-fire for all combatant groups in Lebanon: (1) neutral observers will be selected; (2) a committee is to be formed to expedite details of the cease-fire; (3) there is to be a meeting of national reconciliation among the major religious and political factions of Lebanon, to which Syria and Saudi Arabia are invited to send observers.

The U.S. battleship *New Jersey* arrives off the coast of Beirut.

President Hosni Mubarak of Egypt proposes to parliament that two of Sadat's emergency laws be repealed.

26 September Lebanese prime minister Shafik al-Wazzan offers to resign as a gesture to assist in the creation of a new and more representative government; President Gemayel asks him to continue in his post.

A cease-fire in Lebanon starts at 6:00 A.M.

27 September Foreign ministers of the four countries participating in peacekeeping efforts in Lebanon confer in New York and agree to keep their forces in Beirut to support the Lebanese government.

Palestinian and Lebanese prisoners in Israel ask the PLO to speed up negotiations for their release.

Amnesty International claims there is evidence Iran is torturing political prisoners.

28 September President Hafiz al-Assad of Syria informs the UN that he does not accept the use of UN observers to supervise a cease-fire in Lebanon.

The House of Representatives votes to invoke the War Powers Act and authorize the president to deploy the Marines in Lebanon for eighteen months.

Druze militiamen threaten retaliation if the Lebanese government reopens the Beirut airport.

Reports are confirmed that Jordan is preparing twenty M-48 tanks to be given to Lebanon; twenty tanks were sent in midsummer.

At the UN, Syrian foreign minister 'Abd al-Halim Khaddam denounces the four nations that have supplied the multinational peacekeeping force in Beirut.

29 September	The Beirut airport opens after being closed since 28 August.
	The U.S. Senate passes a bill applying the War Powers Act to Lebanon and allowing the Marines to stay for eighteen months; the House agrees to accept the Senate bill.
30 September	Yitzhak Shamir fails to bring Laborites into a cabinet of national unity; Labor demands withdrawal of Israeli troops from Lebanon, opposes Israeli settlements in the West Bank, and favors the Reagan peace plan.
	An Armenian guerrilla group claims responsibility for a bomb blast that destroyed the American, Soviet, and Algerian pavilions at a trade fair in Marseilles, France.
1 October	Lebanese Druze leader Walid Jumblat accuses Yasir Arafat of trying to destroy the Druze position in the Shuf area by stationing PLO forces there, thereby inviting future attacks by Israel.
	The Mubarak government in Egypt requests an extension of the state of emergency imposed after the Sadat assassination.
	Turkish officials release former Prime Minister Demirel and fifteen other politicians from a three-month exile.
	Secretary of Defense Weinberger visits an Afghan refugee camp in Pakistan.
2 October	Jordanian diplomats indicate that under certain conditions their government is prepared to hold new discussions with Yasir Arafat on a Middle Eastern settlement.
	President Amin Gemayel of Lebanon accuses Walid Jumblat, leader of the Lebanese Druze, of planning to partition Lebanon by setting up a Druze ministate, after Jumblat on 31 September created local administrative areas within territory under his military control.
3 October	Leaders of thirty-eight African states meet in Vittel, France, for the tenth annual French-African conference, seeking ways to end the civil war in Chad; Libya declines to attend.
4 October	In Tripoli, Lebanon, pro-Syrian Alawite and anti-Syrian Sunni forces battle through the night.
	Syrian and Israeli forces exchange artillery fire during the night in the Bekaa Valley.
	The French-African conference, meeting in Vittel, France, agrees unanimously that a solution to the war in Chad must preserve the unity and integrity of that country.
5 October	President Gemayel of Lebanon agrees to accept observers from nonaligned countries to supervise the truce that was agreed to on 26 September.
	Yitzhak Shamir, prime minister designate of Israel, informs Parliament he has formed a new government out of a coalition of

right-wing and religious parties, controlling 62 of 120 seats in Parliament.

6 October
Husayn Wahbi, leader of an Israeli-trained Shiite brigade in south Lebanon, is killed by a car-bomb.

In Washington, D.C., the mayors of four West Bank towns ask a federal court to revoke the tax exemptions of several Jewish organizations.

Spyros Kyprianou, president of Cyprus, leaves New York City without responding to a recent initiative by Rauf Denktash for talks on the federation of Cyprus.

Four thousand persons demonstrate in Lahore, Pakistan, against the military rule of Zia ul-Haq.

The Indian government, responding to acts of violence by Sikhs, takes direct control of Punjab State.

8 October
French police arrest seven Armenians in connection with the 15 July bombing at Orly Airport.

9 October
Yasir Arafat indicates readiness to reopen talks with King Hussein of Jordan on the Reagan peace plan.

Robert McFarlane, U.S. special envoy to the Middle East, meets in Damascus with Foreign Minister Khaddam.

French Etendard aircraft arrive in Iraq.

Iran threatens to block the Strait of Hormuz if Iraq uses its five Etendard aircraft against Iranian targets.

Libya prevents thirty-five French citizens from departing the country.

10 October
Yitzhak Shamir becomes prime minister of Israel by a vote of 60–53 in Parliament; his cabinet represents the former conservative religious and right-wing political parties of Menachim Begin's government.

Rival Palestinian factions engage in small-arms battles in Damascus.

Amnesty International accuses the government of Chad of allowing its troops to kill more than 160 civilians.

11 October
Druze leader Walid Jumblat refuses to agree to attend the Lebanese reconciliation committee's meeting at the presidential palace.

12 October
Heavy street fighting occurs in Tripoli, Lebanon, between Sunni Muslims and pro-Syrian Communists.

President Reagan signs legislation authorizing the Marines to remain in Lebanon for eighteen months.

Sa'd Haddad, leader of the Israeli-supported southern militia, temporarily gives up his command to Sharb al-Barakat because of ill health.

Soviet and Afghan government forces attack the town of Istalif in the Shomali Valley of Afghanistan; hundreds of villagers are killed, according to reports reaching New Delhi.

13 October   Representatives of the Lebanese government and most of the major warring factions meet to prepare for a council of national reconciliation.

The Reagan administration proposes a secret $225 million aid plan to assist Jordan in arming two army brigades to serve as a special strike force; Israeli representatives oppose the idea, which was first discussed in 1979.

Israel's finance minister, Yoram Aridor, resigns because of opposition to his plan to replace the shekel with the U.S. dollar.

14 October   Two Muslim groups, the Shiite Amal and Walid Jumblat's Progressive Socialist party, pull out of the truce panel overseeing the cease-fire in the Beirut area.

15 October   The cease-fire committee of Lebanon agrees to have observers from Greece and Italy monitor the truce; four hundred observers from each country are requested.

The Gulf Cooperation Council nations finish their first joint military exercises.

Jewish Orthodox extremists assault Mayor Teddy Kollek of Jerusalem.

18 October   The Lebanese government announces that the reconciliation conference between Christian and Muslim leaders will be held at the Beirut airport on 20 October; Walid Jumblat rejects the airport as the site of the conference.

President Reagan discusses Middle Eastern issues with his top aides: there is no intention to withdraw the Marines or to change their mission; secret financing and sale of four C-130s and other equipment to Jordan will proceed.

U.S. joint chiefs of staff review the rules of operations for the Marines in Beirut; so far seven Marines have died and fifty have been wounded.

19 October   The opening of the Lebanese national reconciliation conference is postponed because of objections by Walid Jumblat, and others, to the site of the planned meetings: the Beirut airport is deemed to be too closely controlled by the U.S. Marines.

President Reagan, speaking at a news conference, vows that the United States will not allow Syria to destroy the chances for stability in Lebanon.

Reports in Pakistan say 126 villagers were massacred last week in Afghanistan by Russian troops.

A new contingent of Marines has left for Beirut to relieve those now serving as part of the multinational force.

20 October	Iran starts a new drive into Iraq, attacking northeastern Iraq between Baneh and Marivan, ninety miles east of Kirkuk.
	The UN General Assembly defers action on an attempt sponsored by Iran and Libya to unseat the delegation from Israel.
21 October	U.S. officials reveal that a secret Jordanian rapid deployment force has been receiving U.S. military training for 2½ years.
	Switzerland agrees to host the Lebanese reconciliation conference.
	Indonesia announces it has warned Iran to stop spreading hostile propaganda.
22 October	Walid Jumblat ends his boycott of the committee that is planning the meeting of the national reconciliation conference.
23 October	The U.S. Marine headquarters at the Beirut airport is blown up by a truck-bomb; 147 are killed and 75 wounded. A similar attack on the French barracks two miles away occurs almost simultaneously.
	Israeli troops put down a riot of villagers in Sarafand, southern Lebanon.
	The government of Pakistan reveals it has arrested more than four thousand persons during the past month-and-a-half for political agitation.
24 October	French president François Mitterrand makes an unannounced visit to Beirut to see the French paratroop barracks.
	President Reagan says the mission of the Marines in Beirut is unchanged.
	Syrian units shell Arafat PLO forces northeast of Tripoli.
25 October	Jordan's ambassador to India is wounded in an assassination attempt.
26 October	Vice-president George Bush visits Beirut and declares U.S. policies will not change.
	President Mubarak of Egypt advises President Reagan not to retaliate for the bomb attack on the Marines' base in Beirut; he also urges the United States to insist on an Israeli withdrawal from Lebanon and to pursue the Reagan peace proposal of 1 September 1982.
27 October	Representatives of the four powers of the multinational forces in Beirut meet in Paris to discuss reprisals for the bombing of French and American installations on Sunday.
	Husayn Musawi, head of the Shiite Islamic Amal group, denies he had a direct or indirect part in the bombings of French and American installations in Beirut.

Opponents of Lebanese president Gemayel hold meetings in Damascus with President Hafiz al-Assad. Attending are Rashid Karami, Suleiman Franjieh, Nabih Berri, and Walid Jumblat.

30 October   Israeli defense minister Moshe Arens accuses Syria of responsibility in the bombing attack on Marine headquarters in Beirut.

In Iraq, the speaker of the national assembly says his country would accept a cease-fire in the Persian Gulf war.

Turkey's military authorities close down two daily papers, *Günaydın* and *Tan*, supposedly because they failed to carry a portrait of Atatürk on the sixtieth anniversary of the founding of the Turkish republic.

Turkey's Erzurum Province suffers a severe earthquake; over five hundred persons perish.

31 October   The Lebanese national reconciliation conference opens in Geneva; all factions are represented, and President Gemayel expresses thanks to Syria for help in arranging the conference.

The Security Councils call on Iran and Iraq to cease hostilities in the Persian Gulf.

Iraq claims it sank three Iranian naval vessels in the Persian Gulf.

The death toll from the earthquake in Erzurum Province of Turkey reaches 980.

1 November   At the Lebanese unity conference in Geneva, Syria's foreign minister, Khaddam, asks that the Israeli-Lebanese accord be terminated.

The Senate Appropriations Committee cuts out the provision for funding an eight-thousand-man Jordanian strike force in the 1984 military spending bill.

The count of victims of the earthquake in Erzurum Province, Turkey, reaches 1,233.

Insurgents in Afghanistan, according to reports reaching Pakistan, have shot down two Soviet transport aircraft.

2 November   Participants in the Geneva talks on Lebanese unity agree on a statement that defines Lebanon's national identity.

The prime minister's office in Israel says that the United States and Israel have agreed on ways to increase strategic cooperation.

The Israeli army shuts down Bethlehem University for two months following demonstrations that occurred after student council members who had put on an anti-Israel exhibit were arrested.

Donald Rumsfeld, a former secretary of defense, agrees to serve as President Reagan's Middle East envoy.

Turkish military authorities ban all public opinion polls until after the forthcoming elections.

3 November	The committee on national unity meeting in Geneva authorizes President Gemayel to open talks with other nations to seek a way to get Israeli troops out of Lebanon.
	In Tripoli, Lebanon, Palestinians backed by Syrian and Libyan forces begin to attack Yasir Arafat's PLO troops at the Baddawi and Nahr al-Bared camps; thirty-four people are killed and one hundred wounded in the artillery battles.
	Israeli military authorities bar two well-known Arabs from visiting Jerusalem to confer with the British minister of state, Richard Luce, who is visiting Israel.
	In the Iran-Iraq war, fighting flares up in the Penjwin area of Iraq.
4 November	A truck-bomb destroys Israel's military compound in Tyre, Lebanon, killing thirty-nine persons and wounding thirty-two; the Muslim Jihad claims credit for the attack, and Israeli authorities vow swift retaliation.
	American officials, reacting to terrorist attacks on French, Israeli, and American forces in Lebanon, indicate that the United States is determined to enter into closer strategic understandings with Israel.
	The Lebanese peace conference, meeting in Geneva, recesses for ten days to allow President Gemayel to confer elsewhere on how to facilitate the withdrawal of foreign troops from Lebanon.
5 November	Palestinian rebels surround the Nahr al-Bared refugee camp; this is one of Yasir Arafat's two remaining strongholds in Lebanon.
	The death toll in the previous day's bomb attack on an Israeli base in Tyre, Lebanon, reaches sixty.
	Israeli officials say they may reduce the sphere of Major Haddad's militia in southern Lebanon to areas where he is accepted by the local populace.
6 November	Rebel PLO forces, led by Syrian commandos, force Yasir Arafat and his troops out of Nahr al-Bared; Arafat falls back to the Baddawi camp and vows to fight on.
	The Gulf Cooperation Council convenes in Doha for a three-day meeting; economic and military cooperation are on the agenda.
7 November	Detachments of Yasir Arafat's PLO forces leave the Baddawi camp and move into Tripoli to set up rocket positions.
	Yasir Arafat seeks aid from the Gulf states; Khalid al-Hassan, a high official in al-Fatah, meets with leaders of the Gulf Cooperation Council, which agrees to send a delegation to Syria to urge President Assad to stop inter-PLO fighting.
	Thousands of Arabs in East Jerusalem and the West Bank hold rallies to show support for Arafat.
	American and Israeli officials declare their governments have no plans to attack Syria, which has called up reservists to counter

increases in American and Israeli forces.

Election returns in Turkey shows the Motherland party winning 212 of 400 seats in Parliament; the Populist party, in second place, wins 117; the Nationalist Democracy party (favored by the military) wins 71 seats.

8 November   Civic leaders in Tripoli, Lebanon, confer with Yasir Arafat to seek ways to keep the city from becoming a battlefield.

9 November   The representatives of major Lebanese factions meeting in Geneva agree on the principle of parity between Muslims and Christians in Parliament.

Arafat forces repel attacks by PLO rebels near Tripoli.

The military authorities in the West Bank close two Arab schools for a month after rock-throwing incidents.

The Gulf Cooperation Council ends a conference that was called to reach a cease-fire agreement in Lebanon; the discussions show that council members are weakening in their support for Yasir Arafat and are shifting to a policy of improving relations with Syria.

10 November   The House of Representatives votes 224–189 to allow Israel to use $550 million in military credits to finance the construction of a new fighter plane, the Lavie; approval comes over the objection of Secretary of Defense Weinberger.

Syrian batteries fire on U.S. reconnaissance planes over Lebanon.

Former Lebanese prime minister Rashid Karami, a Muslim, asks Yasir Arafat to leave Tripoli.

The search for bodies in the Marine compound in Beirut officially ends; 239 bodies have been recovered.

11 November   The first session of the conference of delegates from Lebanon adjourns in Geneva after a week of discussions; the principal question has been how to increase the share of Muslims in the government.

Syrian foreign minister 'Abd al-Halim Khaddam leaves Moscow after two days of talks with Foreign Minister Gromyko; the Soviets have stressed the need for unity in the PLO.

Turkey extends martial law provisions for four months.

12 November   Yasir Arafat states his conditions for leaving Tripoli: (1) guaranteed cease-fire; (2) observers from the Arab League to maintain the cease-fire; (3) the right to return to Tripoli any time in the future; (4) the withdrawal of rebel PLO forces.

The military government of Turkey enacts new press laws that would bring heavy fines and long imprisonment for editors and writers of articles that threaten national security and/or offend public morality.

13 November	President Hafiz al-Assad of Syria is hospitalized, reportedly with an inflamed appendix.
14 November	Fighting continues around Suq al-Gharb between the Lebanese army and Druze militiamen.
15 November	The Baddawi refugee camp, which is Yasir Arafat's last refuge in Lebanon, is attacked by anti-Arafat Palestinians with heavy Syrian support.
	Turkish Cypriot leader Rauf Denktash declares the Turkish area of Cyprus to be an independent republic; the United States condemns the move and says it will not recognize the new state.
	Islamic insurgents shoot down a Soviet-made MI-8 helicopter ten miles south of Kabul, Afghanistan, killing an Afghan general and eleven other persons.
16 November	Anti-Arafat Palestinian forces move into the Baddawi refugee camp.
	The Israeli air force strikes at military installations of the Islamic Amal militia in the Bekaa Valley.
	The president of Cyprus, Spyros Kyprianou, says his government is determined to reverse the declaration of independence made by the Turks of Cyprus, through peaceful means.
17 November	Fourteen Super Etendard jets from the French carrier *Clemenceau* attack bases of the Shiite militia group, the Islamic Amal, east of Baalbak in Lebanon; the Phalange radio reports there are hundreds of casualties.
19 November	The entire city of Tripoli, Lebanon, is subjected to artillery fire, mostly from rebel PLO forces, while portions of the Baddawi camp are still held by Arafat loyalists.
	President Gemayel of Lebanon flies to Saudi Arabia to meet King Fahd for discussions on withdrawing Syrian and Israeli troops from Lebanon.
	Syria says it is prepared to launch suicide attacks against U.S. warships; Maj. Gen. Mustafa Tlas says also that Syria's new ground-to-ground missiles can strike anywhere in Israel.
	President Habib Bourguiba of Tunisia legalizes two opposition parties.
20 November	Israeli aircraft attack pro-Syrian Palestinian bases east of Beirut near Bhamdun. These attacks are described by Israeli spokesmen as retaliatory in nature and in response to many attacks on Israeli soldiers.
	Special envoy Donald H. Rumsfeld visits Damascus and confers with Syrian foreign minister Khaddam.
21 November	Yasir Arafat and his forces are trapped in Tripoli by Palestinian rebel forces.

Iraq claims the destruction of seven Iranian ships between Kharg Island and Bandar Khomeini.

22 November Responding to Yasir Arafat's appeal that Arab leaders persuade Syria and Libya to stop support to the PLO rebels, the Saudi foreign minister starts talks in Damascus with the Syrian foreign minister.

A delegation from the Arab states' nonalignment movement visits Damascus for talks on the rebellion within the PLO.

Farouk Kaddoumi, foreign affairs spokesman for the PLO, travels to Moscow for talks on preserving the unity of leadership in the PLO.

Secretary of Defense Weinberger accuses the Iranians of exploding the truck-bomb at the Marine compound in Beirut on 23 October; according to Weinberger, this was done with Syrian authorization and direction.

Nicholas Veliotes, the new U.S. ambassador to Egypt, arrives in Cairo.

23 November Arafat sources report an agreement has been reached on a plan to leave Tripoli.

Syria rejects the Weinberger charge, saying that it is not responsible in any way for the truck-bomb attack on the American Marines in Beirut.

Soviet foreign minister Gromyko calls for PLO unity.

The UN General Assembly votes overwhelmingly for a resolution demanding the U.S.S.R. pull its forces out of Afghanistan.

24 November The Israeli-Palestinian exchange of prisoners takes place: 6 Israelis for 5,900 Palestinians and Lebanese; Israel closes the Ansar camp in southern Lebanon and returns the PLO archives taken from Beirut during the 1982 invasion.

Parliament convenes in Turkey for its first session in three years.

Turkey vetoes the publication of a final statement by the foreign ministers of the Council of Europe that condemned the declaration of independence by the Turks of Cyprus.

25 November The foreign ministers of Saudi Arabia and Syria announce in Damascus that rival PLO factions have agreed to a truce and to withdraw from the Tripoli area within two weeks.

The Lebanese government, having recently broken diplomatic relations with Iran over the issue of Iranian "revolutionary guards" stationed in the Bekaa Valley, orders all Iranian diplomats to leave the country.

The government of Chad says a meeting of reconciliation for the disputants in the civil war will take place in Ethiopia; no date has been set for the meeting.

26 November Rauf Denktash calls for a review of the UN's troops in Cyprus, claiming that countries contributing to the UN force take sides against the newly proclaimed Turkish Cypriot Republic.

27 November   Iran claims that "rebels" in Iraq have set off bombs in Baghdad, killing over one hundred persons. Iraq denies the report.

Israeli prime minister Yitzhak Shamir and Defense Minister Moshe Arens arrive in Washington for talks on the Middle Eastern situation.

Turkey announce plans to build a NATO-financed military air base in Thrace at Corlu.

28 November   The Higher Coordinating Committee, a delegation of Lebanese from Tripoli, travels to Syria to seek an agreement on the departure of rival PLO factions.

President Reagan approves an increase in military cooperation with Israel; the arms ban is lifted, and a working group is set up to find ways to assist Lebanon. Reagan also decides to reduce next year's military aid to Israel to $1.275 billion, but to consider it a nonrepayable loan.

29 November   The United States and Israel agree to establish a joint political-military group to examine ways to increase mutual cooperation. The agreement comes after two days of talks between President Reagan and Israeli prime minister Yitzhak Shamir in Washington. The United States makes military and economic concessions to Israel, but Israel appears to make no concessions to the United States.

West Bank Arabs cause civil disturbances to mark the thirty-sixth anniversary of a UN resolution calling for the partitioning of Palestine.

Heavy shelling occurs between Christian and Druze militiamen east of Beirut.

Members of the British Commonwealth meeting in New Delhi condemn the declaration of independence by the Turks of Cyprus and urge all nations not to assist the new republic.

30 November   Prime Minister Yitshak Shamir of Israel, speaking before the National Press Club in Washington, says the new U.S.–Israel accord on strategic cooperation can help restore independence to Lebanon.

Amin Gemayel, president of Lebanon, arrives in Washington; talks with President Reagan are to start the next day.

The government of Bangladesh asks the Soviet Union to reduce by one-half the number of employees at its embassy and to close down the Soviet cultural center.

1 December   While visiting Washington, Lebanese president Gemayel is advised to broaden the base of his government by bringing in opposition leaders.

Shaykh Halim Taqi al-Din, president of the Druze supreme religious council, is assassinated at his home by an unknown gunman.

King Hussein of Jordan announces he is ready to resume talks with Yasir Arafat on the future of the West Bank and Gaza.

2 December   Yasir Arafat, besieged in Tripoli, asks the UN for guarantees of safety for his forces when an evacuation from the port takes place.

Anti-Arafat Palestinians shell the port area of Tripoli.

Secretary of State Shultz reveals that Lebanon and the United States have agreed to establish economic and military committees to promote the unity of the country and the withdrawal of foreign forces.

Muslim West Beirut observes the funeral of the assassinated Druze religious leader, Shaykh Halim Taqi al-Din.

The legislature of the Turkish Federated State of Cyprus establishes a constituent assembly to draft a constitution for the Turkish Republic of Northern Cyprus; the vote is 26–14, with several members objecting to the tactics of Rauf Denktash.

3 December   The Security Council agrees to permit Yasir Arafat and his forces to be evacuated from Tripoli under protection of the UN flag.

Israeli jets, in their fourth air strike since 14 November, bomb Syrian bases near Sofar, twelve miles east of Beirut, in retaliation for a fatal attack on an Israeli soldier in southern Lebanon the day before.

4 December   The foreign minister of Syria, 'Abd al-Halim Khaddam, in notes to the UN and to various world leaders, asks for help to stop the aggressive American policy of escalating the military conflict in Lebanon.

American naval aircraft attack Syrian antiaircraft batteries east of Beirut; two planes are shot down.

Following U.S. air strikes against Syrian positions, the Marines are subjected to four hours of artillery attack by Syrian-backed militias; eight Marines are killed; American warships return the fire.

Druze spokesmen announce that their three-month siege of Dayr al-Qamar will be lifted.

President Reagan promises additional retaliatory strikes against Syrian positions if American Marines are attacked.

5 December   Druze leaders in Lebanon say that they did not intend to fire upon Marine positions on 4 December; they were aiming at Lebanese army forces positioned in close proximity to the Marines.

Syria warns the United States against new reconnaissance flights over its positions in Lebanon.

A car-bomb explosion in West Beirut kills fourteen and injures eighty-three.

Yitzhak Shamir, prime minister of Israel, says in answer to parliamentary critics that the U.S.–Israel accords reached recently in Washington contain no secret commitments.

6 December A time bomb destroys a bus in Jerusalem; four Israelis are killed and forty-six wounded. Both pro-Arafat and anti-Arafat factions of the PLO claim responsibility.

Syria shoots down two Israeli drone reconnaissance planes.

In Turkey, the group of five generals who have run the country since 12 September 1980, turn the authority of government over to parliament.

Sources in New Delhi say that Soviet forces in Afghanistan last week mounted an attack in the Shomali Valley, but gave up after suffering heavy losses of personnel.

7 December Final details of the plan for evacuating Yasir Arafat's troops from Tripoli are agreed upon between Arafat and the Palestinians who oppose him.

An Arafat spokesman says he did not authorize the previous day's bombing of a bus in Jerusalem.

Five West Bank Palestinian leaders condemn the bus bombing.

In Turkey, Turgut Özal, head of the Motherland party, is formally asked by the president, General Kenan Evren, to form a civilian government.

8 December Marines at the Beirut airport come under heavy attack from the Hayy al-Sollum area.

All four members of the multinational force in Lebanon say they will remain indefinitely and press for a broadly based government and for the withdrawal of foreign forces.

Prime Minister Yitzhak Shamir of Israel condemns the UN for agreeing to let Yasir Arafat and his troops be evacuated from Beirut on ships flying the UN flag.

In the United States, Israel's ambassador, Yehuda Z. Blum, asks that all plans to assist Yasir Arafat in his removal from Tripoli be rescinded.

Iraq claims the destruction of six enemy ships in the Persian Gulf.

9 December Yasir Arafat, reacting to a morning Israeli sea and air attack on the port of Tripoli, appeals to the UN for additional guarantees for security during the planned evacuation of his forces.

A Jewish group called Terror against Terror claims responsibility for placing hand grenades in two churches, a seminary, and a mosque in Jerusalem; the grenades were dismantled by security forces.

10 December Secretary of State Shultz, while visiting in Tunis, speaks out in defense of the recent U.S.–Israel agreement for strategic cooperation.

11 December The foreign ministers of Islamic states, who are meeting in Bangladesh, fail to reach an agreement on the conflict within the PLO, and delay acting on the Iraq-Iran war until a meeting of Islamic states next month in Morocco.

After a two-day lull, heavy fighting breaks out between the Lebanese army and Shiite militiamen south of Beirut.

The Israeli cabinet refuses to give a guarantee of safe passage to Yasir Arafat, who is scheduled to leave Tripoli, with four thousand of his followers, on Greek ships.

Ephraim Segal, an American-born Israeli settler in the occupied West Bank, is detained for killing an eleven-year-old Arab girl with his Uzi submachine gun after a rock-throwing incident.

Gen. Husayn Muhammad Ershad, head of the military government of Bangladesh, proclaims himself president.

12 December Car-bomb blasts at six locations in Kuwait damage the American embassy, the French embassy, and four other areas, leaving seven dead and sixty-two injured; Islamic Jihad is believed responsible.

President Gemayel of Lebanon travels to Great Britain for talks with Prime Minister Thatcher.

At the UN, Iran warns the United States that further involvement in Lebanon will bring new retaliations by Iran.

13 December American warships shell Syrian antiaircraft positions east of Beirut.

Israeli gunboats shell PLO positions around Tripoli.

In Turkey, a new civilian government headed by Turgut Özal takes office after approval by General Kenan Evren, the Turkish president.

14 December The U.S. battleship *New Jersey* shells targets in Lebanon after American reconnaissance planes are fired on from Syrian-controlled areas.

The American ambassador to Cyprus, Raymond Ewing, calls on Rauf Denktash.

15 December The U.S. battleship *New Jersey* uses its five-inch guns to support Marines under attack from Druze forces near Beirut.

Druze forces lift a hundred-day siege of Dayr al-Qamar, allowing Christian inhabitants and militiamen to be evacuated under an International Committee of the Red Cross.

Israeli gunboats shell Arafat forces at Tripoli.

Iraq bombs Iranian targets in Ilam and Dehloran in further retaliation for the bombings last Monday in Kuwait.

16 December	A new cease-fire goes into effect in Lebanon; representatives of the Lebanese army and various Muslim groups reach an agreement in Damascus; the Beirut airport reopens after having been closed for sixteen days.

Donald Rumsfeld, special envoy to the Middle East, meets Israeli leaders; Defense Minister Moshe Arens says Israel could prevent Arafat's evacuation from Tripoli.

Amin Gemayel, president of Lebanon, holds talks with Colonel Qaddafi in Libya.

Kuwaiti authorities report that the perpetrator of the truck-bombing at the U.S. embassy on 12 December was a pro-Iranian fundamentalist from Iraq.

17 December The evacuation of Yasir Arafat's PLO forces from Tripoli begins; one hundred wounded military and civilian personnel embark on a ship chartered by the International Red Cross.

18 December After two American aircraft are fired upon by Syrian ground batteries, U.S. warships retaliate by shelling Syrian positions. The Syrian government officially decries this act of aggression.

Kuwait charges nine Iraqis and three Lebanese with the recent bombings; all are Shiite Muslims.

Israeli ships shell PLO troops awaiting evacuation from Tripoli.

The foreign ministers of Lebanon, Saudi Arabia, and Syria fail to agree on a date for reopening the Lebanese reconciliation talks.

Donald Rumsfeld, U.S. special envoy in the Middle East, meets with President Hosni Mubarak of Egypt to explain the U.S.–Israel accord on strategic cooperation.

19 December Israeli gunboats shell the harbor of Tripoli; Arafat's evacuation is postponed for another day.

U.S. officials are angered by Israeli actions in Tripoli that caused the delay of plans to evacuate Arafat.

Five Greek transport ships and a French naval escort vessel sail out of Larnaca for Tripoli; the Greek captains ask new assurances they will not be attacked by Israeli gunboats.

Israeli planes attack Palestinian positions at 'Alayh and Bhamdun.

The Investigations Subcommittee of the House Armed Services Committee concludes that "very serious errors in judgment" on the part of U.S. Marine officers in Beirut led to the large death toll in the bombing on 23 October.

French paratroopers complete training the first Lebanese tank battalion; thirty French AMX-13 tanks provide the basis of a battalion, including 150 crew members and 140 machine gunners.

The General Assembly adopts a resolution condemning the U.S.–Israel accord for strategic cooperation; four other resolutions critical of the Israeli occupation of Arab territories are adopted.

Syria bans six religious societies: the Ba'th party national command claims they engage in illegal political activities.

In an address to the Turkish parliament, Prime Minister Turgut Özal extends the "hand of friendship" to Greece. Özal also pledges his government to improve relations with the United States and Arab countries.

20 December   Yasir Arafat and four thousand of his troops sail from Tripoli in five Greek ships.

21 December   Two car-bombs explode in Beirut, one at a French military command post in East Beirut, the other in western Beirut; nineteen perish. An unknown group, the Black Hand, claims responsibility.

Israel says it will continue to attack guerrilla bases in Lebanon; Israeli jets bomb a training camp for Shiite militiamen near Beirut.

Egyptian foreign minister Kemal Hassan 'Ali meets with President Reagan; the minister later says the departure of Arafat from Lebanon opens up hope for a new political approach to Middle Eastern problems.

Iranian agents set off bombs in Ankara and Istanbul directed against Iraqi officials.

The Polisario guerrilla group reports that Morocco is beginning a major drive in Western Sahara with some 25,000 troops on the march.

22 December   Yasir Arafat and Hosni Mubarak, president of Egypt, confer in Cairo; Arafat calls Egypt "the real supporter of the Palestinian people and the champion of the recovery of Palestine." One PLO group, the Democratic Front for the Liberation of Palestine, calls the meeting "irresponsible behavior"; the Reagan administration terms it "an encouraging development"; Israel calls it "a severe blow to the peace process."

Jordan ends a five-year trade boycott of Egypt.

Iraq claims it has sunk two Iranian ships.

23 December   The prime minister of Israel, Yitzhak Shamir, criticizes the United States for its approval of the Arafat-Mubarak meeting.

The president of Italy advocates the withdrawal of the Italian contingent from the international peacekeeping forces in Beirut.

24 December   A major break in Lebanon's eight-day-old cease-fire occurs when the Lebanese army and Shiite militiamen engage in battle near the Beirut airport.

The French contingent of the international peacekeeping forces turns its positions south of Beirut over to the Lebanese army, prompting attacks from the Shiite militias.

In Kuwait, seven more persons are arrested in connection with the 12 December bombings.

25 December   The Lebanese army reports successes in battles with Shiite and Druze militias in southern Beirut.

Syria invites Jesse Jackson, a contender for the Democratic nomination for president, to Syria "to discuss Middle Eastern issues." Jackson will also take up the problem of gaining the release of Lieut. Robert Goodman, a captured American pilot.

Iran orders three French diplomats to leave the country.

26 December   Yasir Arafat and a contingent of some one thousand followers arrive in Yemen.

The Lebanese army battles Shiite militiamen to the south of Beirut for the third day; fighting started when French units of the multinational force handed their areas over to the Lebanese army.

Butros Ghali, Egyptian minister of state for foreign affairs, says that if negotiations among Egypt, the PLO, and Jordan succeed, all Arabs will support them.

Prime Minister Yitzhak Shamir of Israel says the Reagan peace plan of 1982 is dead, even though Mubarak and Arafat become reconciled.

27 December   President Reagan determines that the U.S. military commanders should not be punished for lack of adequate measures in the 23 October truck-bombing of Marine headquarters in Beirut.

28 December   In Beirut, 249 members of the 2,200-man Italian contingent of the multinational force return home.

Israeli finance minister Yigal Cohen-Orgad is reported to be prepared to recommend a partial freeze on new settlements in the West Bank to reduce public spending; the Israeli Peace Now movement approves this, but various conservative groups oppose it.

29 December   The director general of the Egyptian foreign ministry travels to Israel for talks with Prime Minister Yitzhak Shamir; this visit is seen as a continuation of talks begun last month in Cairo as part of the Israeli-Egyptian dialogue.

A Jordanian embassy employee is assassinated in Madrid; this is the fourth attack on Jordanian diplomatic personnel in two months.

30 December   Yasir Arafat travels from Yemen to Tunisia to hold talks with PLO leaders to redefine policy.

The Israeli army closes all roads between northern Lebanon and the Israeli-occupied southern portion of the country.

Bombs explode in two mosques in Hebron in the West Bank.

France expels five Iranian students, claiming they were trained terrorists.

31 December   Lebanon protests to Israel the closing of passage points between Lebanon and the Israeli-controlled areas of the country.

Italy declares its intention to reduce its 2,200-man contingent in Beirut by one-half.

Jesse Jackson visits the captured American flier, Robert Goodman, in Damascus.

Islamic Fundamentalism: Historic Mission and Contemporary Mood

John O. Voll

Islamic fundamentalism is a major force in the contemporary world. It emerged during the 1970s as a visible and dynamic alternative to existing ideologies and world views, both traditional and Western oriented. It is controversial because it challenges not only the current social orders in Muslim societies but also the Western-oriented attempts to change those social orders. Even what the definition of the term *fundamentalist* should be, and whether or not it can legitimately be applied to the Islamic experience, arouses debate.

The suddenness with which Islamic fundamentalism captured the headlines of the world's news media can obscure its deep roots in Islamic history. What has come to be called Islamic fundamentalism is not new to the Islamic experience, however revolutionary its implications may be in the context of contemporary Muslim societies. Within the framework of historical continuity, fundamentalism takes many forms, which vary according to specific local conditions and the general context of the times.

The diversity of groups and individuals who have been called Islamic fundamentalists makes it difficult to arrive at a definition. What is often called fundamentalism represents more of a mood or a style than a special sect or clearly separate group. The spirit of basing faith, practice, and the social order on the fundamentals of Islam is part of the general Islamic world view. Muslims everywhere believe that God revealed His message for humanity through a series of prophets, culminating with the appearance of Muhammad in the seventh century. They believe that this message is most completely and accurately recorded in the Qur'an and that it was implemented through the leadership and practices of Muhammad and his community. All Muslims are confident that a community based on God's revelation can and must be built by Muslims on earth. The obligations of individual Muslims are those of regular prayer, the giving of alms, fasting, and making a pilgrimage to Mecca if possible. They are also expected to participate in the ongoing effort to maintain the community of believers on earth. All Muslims, whether fundamentalists or not, live within this framework and believe in these tenets.

At the same time, some individuals and groups are recognized as being especially dedicated to reshaping their society according to a strict interpretation of the fundamental sources of the Islamic tradition. Although it takes different forms in different places and eras, a special style of Muslim life and attitude aims at renewing and reshaping Muslim society in closer accord with the Qur'an and the traditions of the Prophet. This mood of sociomoral reconstruction is what is frequently called Islamic fundamentalism.

THE CONTEXT IN 1983

By 1983 both the Muslim and non-Muslim worlds had grown accustomed to the importance of movements and individuals called Islamic fundamentalists. Although such people were clearly active in 1983, the tremendous variety of the groups and their actions makes it difficult to survey their activities during the year.

These activities took place in all parts of the Islamic world and even beyond, in areas where Muslims represent only a small proportion of the population. In Indonesia, men were tried on charges of subversion because they had worked to establish activist Islamic communities that came into conflict with the forces of the state. One of these men was associated with an older group, the Dar al-Islam movement, prominent after World War II. Another was a younger man who appears to have been part of a newer generation of Muslim fundamentalists in Indonesia. (Execution of Islamic . . . 1983; Subversion trial . . . 1983).

In the far western part of the Islamic world, there were similar legal reflections of fundamentalist activity. In Tunisia, for example, thirty members of the fundamentalist Islamic Liberation party were sentenced in August 1983 to varying prison terms. Moreover, fundamentalist students were involved in disturbances on some university campuses. There was also a major attempt in Algeria to revise the legal code as it pertains to family matters in a more Islamic direction.

This militant dimension of Islamic fundamentalism, of course, attracts the most attention. No major region seems to have escaped fundamentalist activity. There have been reports, for example, that the Islamic Liberation party, whose members were tried in Tunisia, is based in West Germany and that its members are active in Europe as well as in the Middle East. Major political leaders in Malaysia have warned that a radical Muslim movement with outside support is operating within their country (Das 1983). In Egypt, the trials of fundamentalists continued for a time, as did the Syrian government's active campaign of suppression of such movements.

The prominence of reports like these can, however, obscure the more significant aspects of the resurgence of Islam. A heightened sense of Islamic identity and a growing conviction of the need for an authentically Islamic social order and personal life-style was manifested in activities other than militance during 1983. In India, for example, it was reported that the "last two years have . . . seen a rapid rise in conversions as Islamic organizations have launched a programme to convert both Hindus and Christians to Islam" (Arab money . . . 1983). Active publishing ventures in Western Europe and the United States reached the growing Muslim communities in those areas. Also in the United States, the American Islamic College was opened in Chicago.

Similarly, many governments continued to adopt policies that were more explicitly Islamic. President Zia ul-Haq in Pakistan expanded the application of specific Islamic legislation during the year, although his program of Islamization aroused opposition as well as support among the Muslims of his country (Gigot

1983; Tasker 1983). In the Sudan, the government of Ja'far Numayri began the strict application of Islamic law during 1983. Among other measures, Islamic punishments were introduced into criminal law and alcoholic beverages were prohibited. Even in non-Muslim countries, actions were taken that encouraged Muslim minorities. Thailand announced in April 1983 that it was establishing a government-sponsored Islamic foundation to assist Muslims in Thailand; to work out other ways of assisting them, Thai leaders held discussions with leaders in Libya, Saudi Arabia, and other Islamic countries (Formation . . . 1983; Delegation trip . . . 1983).

Thus, it is clear that though no major fundamentalist revolution occurred in an Islamic country in 1983, nevertheless there was much dynamism within the fundamentalist Islamic world. Because the activities were so diverse, it is difficult to use a general term like *fundamentalism* when discussing the contemporary Islamic experience, particularly if one expects the term to apply to a single group or movement. However, Islamic activity does not divide itself into neatly definable sectarian groupings, for, as has been noted, Islam is not just a religion, it is a way of life.

Islam has no sects or churches. Instead, the historical communities of Muslims hold differing views of what the Islamic community, or *ummah*, should be. Their different senses of the community are based on the Qur'an and the precedents set by God's Messenger, Muhammad, or the *sunnah* of the Prophet. This is the context in which contemporary Muslim activity should be seen.

Moreover, the activities of 1983 did not represent a new phenomenon within Islamic society. The concepts of renewal and reform, or in Islamic terms, *tajdid* and *islah*, are deeply rooted in the historical experiences of Islamic peoples. Thus, the fundamentalism of the current resurgence of Islam shows a major continuity with the past. At the same time, however, the fundamentalism of today also shows new features that reflect the special conditions of the contemporary era.

FUNDAMENTALISM IN HISTORICAL PERSPECTIVE

Throughout Islamic history, there have been individuals and groups who have called other Muslims to a stricter adherence to the Qur'an and the sunnah of the Prophet. At times, these people were so extreme in their positions that they exceeded what the Islamic community considered to be acceptable. On the whole, however, they served as a kind of conscience for the community.

In the long history of the Muslims, there has been a continual process of interaction between changing conditions and the Muslim vision of what God expects of humans. Muslims believe that the early community of believers around the Prophet Muhammad were witnesses to the revelation of God and were the first to accept that revelation. These early believers, then, became a special group in the history of Islam and their actions set significant patterns that shaped subsequent history. Although Muslim and non-Muslim scholars may disagree on interpretations and reasons for these actions, the importance of the early formative centuries is recognized by both groups. And both agree that in order to see the underlying continuities involved in contemporary Islamic fundamentalism, it is necessary to examine the early centuries.

Even in its earliest days the community of Muslims was not without its divisions. The Qur'an has special words for those who were hypocritical in their acceptance of the revelation and of Muhammad's mission. However, it was following the death of the Prophet in A.H. 11 (A.D. 632) that divisions within the community became more acute. Within a century, the Muslim community had expanded to the extent that Muslim rule extended from Spain to central Asia, but had also fought two major civil wars and was about to experience a third.

While there were many personal and group rivalries involved in these conflicts, they also involved differing visions of the ideal nature of the Islamic community itself. One major group emphasized the actual experience of the community and believed that those Companions of the Prophet who had succeeded him as leaders of the community were rightly guided. This majority came to accept the consensus of the community as an important source of guidance. This style of Islam is now called Sunni Islam. The alternate vision believed that continuing divine guidance comes to the community through special leaders or Imams who are the direct descendents of the Prophet and his cousin/son-in-law, 'Ali. The supporters of 'Ali, and then of his descendents, came to be known as the Partisans, or Shi'ah of 'Ali, and are the modern Shiites of contemporary news stories.

In this context of rapid change, the process of defining the social and ideological implications of the Islamic message gained critical importance. Muslim thinkers worked to define the legal, as well as the theological aspects of the revelation. The Qur'an, the definitive record of the revelation of God through Muhammad, was augmented by records of the memories of the actions and words of Muhammad and other early leaders of the community. These traditions, or *hadith*, became the second great source of guidance. For most Muslims, the body of reliable traditions became defined by a series of great collections that were compiled by the end of the third Islamic century. The most famous of these was made by Muhammad al-Bukhari (A.H. 194–256 [A.D. 810–870]). Special Shiite collections recorded the sayings and actions of the Imams.

Along with the collections of traditions, there was also a long process of defining the legal structures appropriate for Islamic society, resulting in the emergence of a number of major schools of legal interpretation. The most prominent of these were four Sunni schools (Hanafi, Maliki, Shafi'i, and Hanbali), although Shiite schools also emerged.

These developments were part of the gradual evolution of the social and political ordering of the society created by Muslims. Following the death of the Prophet Muhammad, a series of major political-social developments occurred that provided the critical context for the expression of the Islamic mission. At first, four successors to the Prophet (*khalifahs*, or "caliphs") led the Muslim community in its early expansion and created the basis for a large empire. The four caliphs had been close companions of the Prophet, and the era of their rule is called by Sunni Muslims the era of the Rashidun or rightly guided Caliphs. Divisions within the community led to the first civil war beginning in A.H. 35 (A.D. 656). The victors in this and another major civil conflict at the end of the seventh century were the Umayyads, the leading clan in pre-Islamic Mecca who had been late in converting to Islam. Under Umayyad leadership, the Islamic community became a major empire but there was much dissatisfaction. Believers loyal to the memory of 'Ali became organized as Shiite opposition groups, while pious Sunni scholars criticized the laxness of Umayyad adherence to the rules of the faith. By A.H. 132 (A.D. 750), a major revolution had brought an end to Umayyad rule, and a new dynasty of caliphs, the Abbasids, had come to power. Pious opposition to Umayyad rule had been important in the Abbasid victory but the new dynasty did not create a new political system—the Abbasid regime was also a caliph-imperial structure.

It was during Abbasid rule that the consolidation of the Islamic schools of law and the formalized collection of the traditions of the Prophet took place. The caliphate was no longer the primary focus of Islamic loyalty; instead, one could call for action in accordance with the Qur'an and sunnah of the Prophet. In this, "the precepts of the Qur'an and *sunna* superseded political or even religious loyalties" (Lapidus 1975, 382). A critical figure in this evolution was Ahmad ibn Hanbal (A.H. 164–241 [A.D. 780–855]), the founder of one of the four major Sunni schools of law. Hanbalism, merging "political activism, a popular religious movement, and the school of law as a scholarly and religious tradition of study," marked a new stage in the development of the Islamic community (Lapidus 1975, 383).

Since the earliest days of the Islamic community, there had been people calling for no compromise in adherence to the Islamic message. However, one needs a relatively comprehensive definition of the basic vision before this rigorism can be seen as a real movement of renewal or reform (Rahman 1970, 632). Early Islamic rigorism tended toward simple asceticism, rejecting the materialism of the Umayyads and becoming the basis of a separate community with its own body of rules and interpretations. When these rules were not accepted by the majority, the rigorism led to division within the community, as happened with the development of the Kharijites within the first two Islamic centuries (Laoust 1965, 36–48).

The emergence of Hanbalism in the third (ninth) century reflects the new conditions for reform and renewal. With the clear definition of an established canon of the Qur'an and the sunnah, the emergence of fundamentalism was possible. There was, in other words, an agreed upon set of fundamentals that could become the basis for judging conditions found in any society or community. These fundamentals could be used to define the reforms needed in a society and to judge the validity and authenticity of formulations and customs that had developed within Muslim societies following the days of the Prophet.

This fundamentalism is not restricted to followers of the Hanbali school of law but is a part of the broader Islamic sense of mission. In times of rapid change when the community is forced to adapt, new forms will be introduced that will reflect the diversity within Islamic history. But once a community has become established, it is natural that some want to preserve what has been gained. Throughout Islamic history, this preserving mood, or conservative style, was present among scholars, teachers, and leaders acting to maintain the main lines of existing conditions. Gradually, however, as society changed, the things being preserved by the conservatives also changed; in this sense, the conservative position was always a relatively realistic compromise with things as they were.

A second basic style was to adapt to change, adopting new ideas and integrating them into the broader Islamic framework. Part of the greatness of medieval Islamic society was its ability to create a dynamic synthesis of many different social and cultural traditions.

However, at times, adaptation to change or conservative compromise with the status quo aroused fear that the integrity and authenticity of the Islamic dimension of the community would be lost. In this case, there would emerge, after the third (ninth) century, calls for a purification of society and a return to the Islamic fundamentals as defined by a rigorous adherence to the Qur'an and the sunnah. It is important to recognize that this mode of Islamic experience is in sharp contrast to the conservative viewpoint. A fundamentalist is not a conservative.

Fundamentalism is a strong critique of existing conditions rather than an attempt to preserve them.

Throughout the past thousand years, there has been a dynamic interaction within the Muslim community among the conservative, adaptationist, and fundamentalist styles. They are not separate sects or identifiable movements. Their specific intellectual content or organizational structure varies according to the challenges being faced.

Although the fundamentalist response has taken many forms in the past millenium, commonly it is associated with one of three particular themes. The first is opposition to popular religious practices for which no justification can be found in the Qur'an and the sunnah. Some of these may reflect pre-Islamic religious customs or local practices. One such practice, for instance, was that of paying special respect to the tomb and memory of a local holy man. Over time, conservative teachers would come to accept such practices, but fundamentalists would oppose them. One of the important figures in the later definition of the Hanbali tradition, for example, was Ibn Taymiyyah (A.H. 661–728 [A.D. 1262–1327]), who vigorously opposed "popular" religious practices (Memon 1976). Similar positions were taken by the great eighteenth-century revivalist in the Arabian Peninsula, Muhammad ibn 'Abd al-Wahhab, and the nineteenth-century revolutionary in the Sudan, Muhammad Ahmad, the Sudanese Mahdi.

A second area of fundamentalist response was that of correcting the activities and attitudes of the Islamic scholars and leaders themselves. The religious establishments in various areas of the Islamic world could become conservative bastions in support of local social compromises. Too close an association with political leaders who were more concerned with the state than with the Islamic mission could be a target of fundamentalist criticism. Also, scholarly communities created a massive edifice of writings and schools of thought representing elaborations of the fundamentals of the Qur'an and the sunnah; some fundamentalists believed that maintaining this edifice had become an end in itself. As schools of legal thought and other groups became more formalized, many Muslim scholars came to believe in the importance of adherence to the decisions of the medieval thinkers. In contrast, from time to time, scholars would insist on the obligation to study the fundamentals of the faith and base judgments on informed analysis of original sources, rather than relying on later thinkers. This process of independent analysis is called *ijtihad* and the call to ijtihad was a common part of a fundamentalist's message. Some fundamentalists accused other scholars of unbelief or polytheism because they seemed willing to equate the works of medieval Muslim scholars with the Qur'an and the sunnah.

The third object of fundamentalist attack is the innovation inspired by non-Islamic cultures and ideas. Thus, in medieval Islam, a major and generally successful effort to integrate the Greek philosophical tradition into the broader Islamic civilization was mistrusted by fundamentalists, whose efforts reduced the impact of Greek thought.

It is worth noting that the fundamentalists have not made change altogether impossible in any era. Their mission has been not so much to oppose all change as to keep change and adaptation within the bounds of what could be seen as authentically Islamic. As the challenges changed, the fundamentalists' responses also changed, but their essential role remained constant: to preserve the visible Islamic authenticity of the life and faith of the community.

MODERN FUNDAMENTALISM

Islamic fundamentalism similarly takes different forms in the modern era. Some groups are in a line of direct continuity to premodern movements, whereas others appear to be responses to specifically modern conditions. In both cases, however, the foundations for modern fundamentalist structures were laid in the eighteenth century.

Eighteenth-Century Foundations

During that century, Muslim societies from Morocco to Southeast Asia were experiencing significant changes. Some of this was the result of the beginnings of European expansion, but there were important internal aspects as well. For the preceding four or five centuries, the Islamic world was a dynamically expanding one. By 1600, it had doubled in size from the days of Umayyad and Abbasid glory. This second wave of expansion consisted of more than military conquest; it included the gradual conversion of whole societies through the efforts of traveling teachers and of merchants. During this period, Islamic society "was not just one society among several non-Western civilizations. It was the one society that had come the closest to playing the world-dominating role which (as it turned out) the West was actually to play" (Hodgson 1974, 3:3).

Great empires had dominated the Mediterranean area, central Asia, and India, with smaller expanding states and societies prevailing in Africa and Southeast Asia. However, by the eighteenth century, these states were almost all deteriorating. The Ottoman Empire had ceased to expand and was beginning to lose territories to the rising states of Europe. The great Safavid empire in Iran came to an end during this century, and Iran entered an era of disorganization. In India, the Mughal Empire, which had dominated the whole of south Asia for two centuries, was disintegrating as the result both of outside attack and of internal division.

The great successes of the era of Islamic glory had created large and, by the eighteenth century, relatively conservative establishments. In many areas, compromises with local customs or adaptations by leaders to changing conditions had created environments ripe for fundamentalist reaction.

This reaction took a number of forms that aimed at the renewal of Islamic life and the sociomoral reconstruction of the Muslim community. Two features of this development were the ascension in importance of the scholars of the traditions (*hadiths*) and the emergence of what has been called neo-Sufism (Rahman 1970).

Scholars of hadith have often played an important role in the development of Islamic fundamentalist thought. Ahmad ibn Hanbal was, for example, primarily a scholar of hadith rather than of jurisprudence. This helped give the Hanbali legal tradition a special character. Similarly, more rigorist scholars in the Shafi'i legal tradition also emphasized the study of hadith as an important dimension in implementing the Islamic vision.

During the eighteenth century, a small but influential community of hadith scholars was located in the central cities of Islam—Mecca and Medina in the western part of the Arabian Peninsula. Believers and scholars came from all over the Islamic world to participate in the pilgrimage to Mecca and they frequently stayed to study. Thus, the hadith scholars of the two holy cities had a substantial impact. They helped to inspire many teachers to return to their homelands dedicated to the sociomoral reconstruction of their societies, using the early Muslim community led by Muhammad and described by the hadith as their model.

Many of these scholars became involved in the development of a new style of organization for devotional life. The Sufi or mystic tradition in Islam was expressed through brotherhood structures, or *tariqahs*. By the eighteenth century, some of these brotherhoods began to more actively mobilize the general population in an effort to create a more authentically Islamic society. This new format for Sufism, or neo-Sufism, was frequently the organizational vehicle for the programs of the hadith scholars as they sought to renew the Islamic spirit of their societies.

The eighteenth century was also a time of brotherhoodlike organizations, inspired by a vision of the early community of Muhammad, working to renew authentic Islam in the face of the decline that seemed to be taking place. This effort was the foundation for a large number of fundamentalist movements that are clearly discernible by the end of the eighteenth and early nineteenth centuries. In West Africa the way was prepared for the launching of the great Islamic holy wars inspired by Uthman dan Fodio. In Southeast Asia, purification movements were led by scholars who had studied in Mecca and Medina and then returned home to lead neo-Sufi/fundamentalist efforts. The most important of these teachers were men like 'Abd al-Ra'uf al-Sinkili, 'Abd al-Samad al-Palimbani, and the leaders of what was called the Padris movement. A little later, Middle Eastern studies helped to inspire a new movement of Islamic activism in China led by Ma Ming-hsin. (Pipes 1983, 64–67).

From the perspective of the 1980s, two renewalist leaders stand out as setting in motion traditions of Islamic revival that have direct tries to the present. These are Muhammed ibn 'Abd al-Wahhab (1703–92) in the Arabian Peninsula and Shah Wali Allah (1702–62) in India. The Wahhabi movement became almost synonymous with activist fundamentalism. Since the eighteenth century, the term "Wahhabism is not restricted to the actual Wahhabi movement as history knows it, but it is a kind of umbrella term—the 'Wahhabi-Idea' covering analogous rather than identical phenomena in the Muslim world" (Rahman 1968, 245). In a similar way, especially for the large Muslim communities of south Asia, Shah Wali Allah "forms the bridge between medieval and modern Islam" (Aziz Ahmed 1964, 201).

The Wahhabi movement arose in the central part of the Arabian Peninsula. Muhammad ibn 'Abd al-Wahhab had been born in that area in the region of Nejd and had studied in the Islamic holy cities. Following some travels, he returned to his homeland and began his efforts to persuade people to adhere more strictly to the guidance of the Qur'an and the sunnah of the Prophet. He found an ally in an able tribal leader, Muhammad ibn Sa'ud, and the pair created a fundamentalist Islamic community-state. This Wahhabi community continued to expand following the death of the two leaders and gained control of Mecca and Medina by the first part of the nineteenth century. In reaction, forces from the Ottoman province of Egypt were sent to Arabia and the Saudi-Wahhabi state was defeated by 1818.

This first Wahhabi movement arose in the context of opposition to popular religious compromises, the adaptability of local ulama, and a sense of the ineffectiveness of the ruling structures within the Arabian Peninsula. There was little modern Western challenge in eighteenth-century Arabia. The mission of the Wahhabi movement, the purification of Islamic society, was clearly Islamic in its origins and inspirations, thus allowing it to serve as a model or an example for later fundamentalist efforts. In the context of twentieth-century fundamentalism, the heritage of this type of fundamentalism is of critical importance. Even those contemporary thinkers who disagree with the descendents of Muhammad ibn 'Abd al-Wahhab still support the affirmation of an indigenous and authentic heritage of Islamic fundamentalism.

The later experience of the historical Wahhabi movement is also an important part of the modern development of fundamentalist movements. In the nineteenth century, a political revival of the Saudi-Wahhabi state helped confirm the renewalist mission of the original movement. However, it too was defeated militarily, and by the end of the century the descendents of the original leaders were political refugees.

At the beginning of the twentieth century, the Saudi-Wahhabi movement gained new life under the leadership of 'Abd al-'Aziz Ibn Sa'ud (1880–1953). He mobilized tribal soldiers and religious teachers in a successful movement of conquest and state building that resulted in the creation of the Kingdom of Saudi Arabia. The new state became a visible expression of the fundamentalist goal of creating a society whose "constitution" was the Qur'an. Although there has been much practical adaptation as Saudi leaders have faced problems of rapid social change, the Wahhabi tradition begun in the eighteenth century still provides the basic definition of the mission of the government.

Shah Wali Allah did not create a special organization or movement. His importance, rather, was as a scholar and intellectual who provided a rearticulation of the basic ideals of Islam in a way that inspired others facing first the great changes in the eighteenth and nineteenth centuries and then the problems of coping with modernization.

The ideological heirs of Shah Wali Allah are numerous. They include a wide spectrum of southern Asian Islam. They range from militant leaders of holy wars to quiet scholars of the traditions of the Prophet. Shah Wali Allah was, like Muhammad ibn 'Abd al-Wahhab, motivated by the weaknesses he saw in Islamic society itself rather than by the challenge from the expanding West. Thus, in South Asia there is also a tradition of renewalism that has lines of continuity with the era before the challenge of the West loomed large in the military and intellectual horizons of Muslims.

The Nineteenth Century

During the nineteenth century, Islamic fundamentalism again took a number of different forms. Some individuals and groups still lived in contexts that were similar to those of the eighteenth century, that is, in areas where the Western challenge still was not evident. In these areas the premodern dynamics of the emergence of fundamentalist movements continued. Perhaps the best example is the emergence of the great holy wars in West Africa, where Muslim teachers set out to create authentically Islamic societies through the conversion or defeat of compromising rulers and ulama who were viewed as virtual unbelievers because of the extent of their compromises. Uthman dan Fodio (1754–1817) was the great leader of this movement, which with others provided the foundations for the political systems that were in place at the time of the European conquests in West Africa. They laid at least some of the groundwork for the political structures that emerged in the twentieth century, especially in Nigeria, where the state structures themselves had been preserved and the leaders in the old traditional positions assumed roles like prime minister of the northern province in independent Nigeria. Similarly, renewalist movements arose in China where eighteenth-century traditions of revolt were revived in Kansu Province by Ma Hua-lung in 1862.

Most activist fundamentalist movements in the nineteenth century, however, involved a more complex mixture of local Islamic social dynamics and reactions to European imperialism and economic and intellectual forces. The headlines of nineteenth-century newspapers were filled with the news of Islamic fundamentalist movements. The Western news media painted a negative and threatening picture, whereas the new journalism in the Islamic world often hoped that such movements might begin the liberation of the Islamic world from the threats of foreign conquest and internal corruption.

The best known of the militant Muslim movements of the nineteenth century were not within the major political systems of the Middle East. The central parts of the Ottoman Empire were more directly involved in a modernizing adaptationism, led by strong personalities. The Ottoman sultan, Mahmud II (d. 1839), and the Ottoman governor who ruled virtually independently in Egypt, Muhammad 'Ali (d. 1849), both set in motion significant programs of modernization that were not particularly Islamic, either in inspiration or in implementation. It was outside of such central and cosmopolitan areas that the militant fundamentalist movements were most successful.

In India, the political aspects of Shah Wali Allah's teachings were given concrete form in the movement of Ahmad Brelwi (1786–1831). This leader hoped to create a well-defined Islamic society, opposed compromises with local religious customs, and worked for Muslim political and military independence from Hindu, Sikh, and European threats. Ahmad Brelwi was killed in battle in 1831 but other militant movements continued in South Asia for some time. The period of major militant movements reached a climax with the Muslim participation in the Indian uprising against British rule in the Great Mutiny of 1857. Following its suppression, some smaller militant revolts occurred, but Islamic renewalism moved in different directions, emphasizing intellectual and ideological rather than military aspects.

In North Africa, direct European invasion aroused an active response in Algeria under the leadership of the Amir 'Abd al-Qadir (1808–1883). The amir modeled his community on the early community of the Prophet and organized military resistance to the French after they invaded Algeria in 1830. Following his defeat in 1847, other less well-organized and less-effective revolts took place, many of them with Islamic dimensions in their inspiration and ideology.

A number of brotherhoods in the neo-Sufi model emerged as effective Islamic movements in the nineteenth century. Some were involved in direct opposition to expanding European control, whereas others were primarily concerned with the reformation of the faith and customs of the general population. In North Africa, one such movement was the Tijaniyyah Tariqah; in Libya and the central Sahara region, a neo-Sufi order, the Sanusiyyah, became important. The Sanusiyyah was established around the middle of the century by Muhammad ibn 'Ali al-Sanusi (1787–1859), who organized educational and devotional centers in the territories of modern Libya and the surrounding areas. Originally largely academic and inspirational in orientation, the Sanusiyyah came into conflict with expanding European control in central and northern Africa, finally leading the resistance to the Italian conquest of Libya in the first half of the twentieth century.

Many movements in the Middle East during the nineteenth century combined a fundamentalist concern for Islamic renewal with an activist opposition to Western conquest or Western-oriented local control. Depending on the degree of European interest, these movements often succeeded, when not openly attacked, in establishing relatively clearly Islamic states, using the fundamentals of Islam as a guide for the emerging sociopolitical systems. In 1881, for example, in the Egyptian-controlled Sudan, Muhammad Ahmad (1848–85) proclaimed himself the long-awaited mahdi who had come to establish a state and society based on God's will. In mood and teachings, the Sudanese mahdi fits clearly into the long-term patterns of Islamic fundamentalism (Voll 1979). The state that he established survived his death until it was conquered by an Anglo-Egyptian force at the end of the nineteenth century.

The militant face of Islamic fundamentalism in the nineteenth century combined relatively traditional ideology with direct opposition to foreign conquest and control. These fundamentalists were not rigid fanatics demanding a return to the conditions and structures of the seventh century. Instead, they demanded that the revelation received during the seventh century and the community created by the Prophet at that time should be the model for effective and authentically Islamic communities in their own times. 'Abd al-Qadir and the Sudanese mahdi vigorously worked to use the community of the Prophet as a model for their own movements but neither of them hesitated to adopt the modern military technology that seemed to be necessary for their survival. The fundamentalist tradition, then, is neither merely reactionary nor conservative. It is, in many ways, a revolutionary tradition, even in those cases where it does not come into open military conflict with political or religious establishments.

During the nineteenth century, there was much intellectual activity directed at interpreting the Islamic message in the modern context. The thrust of this effort was not primarily fundamentalist in mood or orientation; it sought to provide a basis for reconciling Islamic and modern Western concepts and ideas. The feeling had not yet arisen that the process of adaptationism had gone too far. The major intellectual effort was to create an Islamic modernism. The great figures in this process in the Middle East were Jamal al-Din al-Afghani (1839–97) and Muhammad Abduh (1849–1905). Although Jamal al-Din encouraged political militancy, opposing the expansion of Western imperial control within the Islamic world, he did not stop, and may even have encouraged, the expansion of a synthesis of Western and Islamic ideas. It was not until well into the twentieth century that a clearly fundamentalist intellectual alternative emerged within the Islamic world.

Evolution of Fundamentalism in the Twentieth Century

During the twentieth century, there have been significant developments in the ways the fundamentalist mood of the Islamic experience is expressed. At the beginning of the century, the major forms of expression were eighteenth-century-style neo-Sufi organizations or similar movements. These groups maintained a classical definition of what was required to purify Islamic society: primarily a relatively literalist interpretation of the rules in the Qur'an and the sunnah, with some recognition of the validity of the broad outlines of Islamic law as defined by the great medieval scholars.

These movements provided the basis for two rather different political-intellectual orientations. The first was to become somewhat conservative and pragmatic. As movements like the revived Saudi-Wahhabi state led by 'Abd al-'Aziz Ibn Sa'ud succeeded in establishing political systems, some of the revolutionary aspects of fundamentalism came to be replaced by efforts to preserve the existing gains. Thus, Wahhabi fundamentalism became oriented toward the preservation of the existing Saudi-Wahhabi state and the more revolutionary perspectives were overshadowed. In this way, in the late 1920s when the more extremist military brotherhood created by 'Abd al-'Aziz revolted in opposition to the negotiation of treaties with nonbelievers, the brotherhood was defeated and a less ideologically committed military emerged in the Kingdom of Saudi Arabia. Similarly, when the twentieth-century leader of the Sanusiyyah, Idris al-Sanusi (1890–1983), became king of independent Libya, his policies and those of the Sanusiyyah leadership were characterized more by cautious conservatism than by active fundamentalism.

The second orientation was a form of nationalism. The earlier resistance against foreign control and the unquestionable Islamic identity of these movements gave them, from the perspective of the late twentieth century, the character of proto-nationalist movements. By their resistance, they helped define the identity of regions that later were to become independent states, although they were not themselves inspired by nationalist ideas as such. Thus, one of the sources of Somali nationalism in East Africa is the memory of the struggle against European forces led by Muhammad 'Abd Allah Hasan (1864–1921), called by his British opponents the "Mad Mullah." The Sudanese mahdi provided a precedent that later nationalists would cite as the first independent state of the Sudan. The Amir 'Abd al-Qadir would inspire twentieth-century nationalists in Algeria, becoming a hero who could comfortably be called an "Algerian." However, this line of development leads away from the basic fundamentalist mood into a different context. The later nationalist movements are not themselves fundamentalist; they simply draw on earlier fundamentalist experiences for legitimation and as a source of effective symbols.

Islamic fundamentalism went beyond this initial base in the twentieth century. The internal dynamics of the Islamic experience in the face of challenges and changing conditions created a situation within which new fundamentalist movements emerged. Often taking significantly new forms, one important line of development was the modernization of the fundamentalist intellectual positions. Many of the older movements that continued into the twentieth century maintained their traditional style in their organizational structures as well as in their symbolism and ideology. However, following World War I, efforts were made to express the fundamentalist vision explicitly in terms of the modern context and challenges.

This expression again took many different forms, depending on local conditions, but they can be broadly classified into two general types: the intellectual, scholarly presentation of fundamentalist Islam, and more popular organizations promoting a fundamentalist program.

In the intellectual form, thinkers drawn from the ranks of both Islamic professionals and intellectuals with nontraditional, usually modern-style educations participated in the articulation of twentieth-century fundamentalism. In the Arabic-speaking world, the modernist tradition of 'Abduh and al-Afghani was taken up and developed in a more fundamentalist direction by their student, Rashid Rida (1865–1935). Through al-Manar, the journal he edited, and his other writings, he affirmed vigorously the universal validity of the fundamentals of Islam. al-Manar was widely read in the Muslim world and had an impact from northwest Africa to Southeast Asia.

Throughout the Islamic world, people like Rashid Rida were restating the fundamentalist vision in relation to the modern challenge to local conditions. Fundamentalists did not lose their conviction that "superstitious" popular religious customs needed to be opposed or that lax Islamic teachers should be criticized, but Western non-Islamic morals, concepts, and ideals came to be their main focus.

Following World War I, the nationalists and the secular radicals were usually the most visible on the intellectual scene. However, a number of hardworking but not widely known thinkers were creating the foundations for a modern fundamentalism. In addition to Rashid Rida, there was Said Nursi (1867–1960) in Turkey. He began as a member of the modernizing Young Turk movement, but then established the "Followers of Nur" (Light), which advocated the reestablishment of an Islamic state in the days of the creation of the modern Turkish secularist republic under the leadership of Mustafa Kemal Atatürk. Nursi's commentaries on the Qur'an went beyond a formalist fundamentalism to one that utilizes a more philosophical and mystic style of interpretation. Although the Nur movement had relatively limited numbers of followers, it has in recent years developed a growing appeal among Muslims both in Turkey and in Western countries (Mardin 1982, 191–92).

A more noticeable development in twentieth-century Islamic fundamentalism was the emergence of mass-oriented organizations. Their prototype was the Muslim Brotherhood in Egypt. It was established in the late 1920s by a schoolteacher with a modern rather than a strictly traditional Islamic education, Hasan al-Banna (1906–49). The Brothers viewed themselves as an important part of the development of the renewal process in modern Islamic societies. They did not reject the intellectual efforts of al-Afghani, 'Abduh, and Rida, but they believed it was important to go beyond simple intellectual work and establish a movement that would work actively and, if necessary, militantly for the renewal of Islamic society (Mitchell 1969, 321 and passim). The Brotherhood was organized to provide social services and to create political power in order to implement the fundamentalist vision in the modern Islamic world. In the era between the two world wars, the Brotherhood, which presented one of the most socially concerned programs in Egypt, attracted a large following. The political implications of its programs soon drew it into conflict with the Egyptian government. Terrorist acts and demonstrations became part of the Brotherhood's program following World War II. To some people, this compromised the integrity of the movement, but to others it was a necessary consequence of the political dimensions of the true fundamentalist vision.

Despite popular support for its opposition to the monarchy, the Brotherhood played only a small role in the 1952 revolution, cooperating with the young military officers who overthrew the government and established a new political system. The Brotherhood soon clashed with the nationalist and then socialist orientations of the military group led by Jamal 'Abd al-Nasir (Nasser), and the fundamentalists were outlawed. In underground opposition, however, they remained the voice of a radically fundamentalist and authentically Islamic alternative to the developing Arab socialism of Nasser and established formal and informal ties with fundamentalist groups in other countries. These groups were usually not quite as successful as the Brotherhood in winning mass followings. In South Asia, Abu al-A'la al-Mawdudi (1903–79) became the articulate leader of a strict intellectual fundamentalism. He organized the Jama'at-i Islami, which was an effective vehicle for propagating fundamentalist ideals but did not become a major mass movement. Mawdudi's organization is still a significant political force in South Asia, especially in Pakistan, and his writings are read by a growing circle of intellectuals from north Africa to Southeast Asia.

In Iran following World War II, fundamentalist groups developed within the context of Shi'i Islam. Ayatollah Abu al-Qasim Kashani had a long career of opposition to secularizing and modernizing reforms, and had been arrested and exiled for his activities. Following World War II, he returned to Iran and organized an activist Islamic party that, although it was not "dogmatically fundamentalist," called for repeal of secularist laws, the implementation of Islamic law, and Muslim unity against the West (Abrahamian 1982, 258). A more dogmatic fundamentalist group called the Feda'iyan-i Islam was established at the same time by a young theology student, Sayyid Navvab Safavi. It was often associated politically with Kashani, but was more militant and rigid, and was responsible for the murder of some prominent Iranians. The political implications and the potential for militant activism in this style of organizational fundamentalism are clear in the cases of the Feda'iyan and the Egyptian Brotherhood. In Iran, in contrast to Egypt, the organizations were disrupted by governmental suppression and there was less underground continuity in the fundamentalist efforts to reconstruct society on clearly Islamic grounds.

By the end of the 1960s, many of these developments of fundamentalism were reaching a point of important transition. There were still old-style groups and structures that were by that time relatively conservative in their orientation, but new forms were emerging. In addition to the "standard" fundamentalism, in the intellectual arena, thinkers were exploring more fully the implications of a return to Islamic fundamentals in a modern context. Although dogmatic standard fundamentalism still was tied to the specific rules and literal interpretations of the past, these provided the ideological basis for new and politically significant mass-oriented organizations.

In the Muslim Brotherhood tradition, Hasan al-Banna's writings were followed by the works of a persuasive and cosmopolitan intellectual, Sayyid Qutb, whose writings were to become an important part of the Islamic resurgence of the 1970s. Sayyid Qutb goes beyond the concerns of standard fundamentalist thought in an effort to create a legitimately Islamic (fundamentalist in mood) modern society. Similarly, in Iran, the dogmatic approaches of Kashani and the Feda'iyan-i Islam have been succeeded by the more modern-oriented but still vigorously fundamentalist approaches of Ayatollah Mahmud Taliqani and Dr. 'Ali Shari'ati. Thus, at the beginning of the time that is said to have seen the "resurgence of Islam" in the 1970s, Islamic fundamentalism was at an important point in its modern development.

FUNDAMENTALISM AND THE RESURGENCE OF THE 1970s

During the 1970s Islam became a major force in Middle Eastern and world affairs. It provided the symbols and rationale for domestic and international policies in many countries. There was a greater public adherence to explicitly Islamic rules of behavior and increased participation in clearly Islamic organizations and institutions. Islamic revolutionary movements in a number of countries worked to establish authentically Islamic regimes, the revolution in Iran being the most successful. This tremendous variety of activities and developments has come to be described as the resurgence of Islam.

Fundamentalism occupies a special place in this resurgence. Most of the manifestations of this increased Islamic activity have been called fundamentalist in one or another analysis. Given its dynamic variety, the labeling of every overtly Islamic movement or activity as fundamentalist is an oversimplification that sometimes leads to misunderstandings of the social and political developments taking place in the Islamic world. Not every act of Islamic militancy is the product of a fundamentalist group nor is every fundamentalist act militant. Similarly, there are affirmations of the validity of the Islamic message that are not, in themselves, fundamentalist in nature.

There are, however, important connections between the Islamic resurgence and the continuing development of Muslim fundamentalism. The dominant tone and mood of much of the contemporary resurgence is fundamentalist and grows out of the long tradition of the fundamentalist style of Islam. The fundamentalist tone of the resurgence provides some insight into the underlying dynamics within the Islamic world in the past decade, but has significance that goes beyond the simple assumption that any resurgence of Islam, by definition, will be fundamentalist. It underscores the fact that other major efforts of reform and renewal in Islamic societies have largely failed. One analysis of the resurgence states, for example, that "the movement back to Islam appears to be a reaction to the failure of the elites of Islamic countries to establish legitimate public order within viable political communities" (Dekmejian 1980, 3).

In the view of the leaders and participants in the resurgence, the adaptationist reforming efforts have failed. From one perspective at least, it is possible to say that there has been an effort to create a resurgence of the Islamic world community for more than a century. By the early 1970s, it seemed clear to many Muslims that the reform attempts that were based simply on borrowing ideas and techniques from the West and adapting Muslim practice to them were, at *best*, weak, and had generally failed. A vigorous new conceptualization emerged in which much of the earlier reform effort was called the product of the culturally pathological disease of *gharbzadegi* or "weststruckness."

The Islamic modes of operation that aimed at creating syntheses or adaptations to changing conditions became, in the modern era, associated with copying from the West. That type of reformism had not succeeded in bringing power and prosperity to Muslim states and societies. Western-style parliaments had become instruments of local corruption and foreign interference. Free enterprise meant the domination of local economies by large corporations, usually controlled by foreigners or a small, very wealthy local elite. By the end of the 1960s, radical regimes dedicated to social justice appeared to have become large despotic bureaucracies.

"Arab socialism" and other special variants of radical ideologies appeared to have failed as much as had the other borrowed ideologies. Moreover, it became clear that many of these new regimes were actively suppressing authentically Islamic movements. The shah in Iran jailed or exiled major Islamic leaders like the Ayatollah Khomeini or the Ayatollah Taliqani. Some "radical" leaders gained popular support by their success in eliminating overt imperialist interference in their countries. However, by the mid-1960s, the reputations of men like Nasir in Egypt were tarnished in the eyes of active Muslims because of the suppression of the Muslim Brotherhood and other Islamic organizations. In 1965, Nasir executed Sayyid Qutb, a fundamentalist writer who was well known in international Muslim circles and who was respected for his integrity. In the minds of many, this only strengthened reservations about the validity of the Arab socialist program.

The experience in Egypt was not unique. The failure of modernization and reform programs, whether led by conservative monarchs or by popular nationalists, seemed to indicate the weakness of a compromising and adaptationist position. By the early 1970s, then, many Muslims were ready to "return" to Islam as the way of coping effectively with the challenges of the modern world.

The consequence was that Islamic modes of social action and political articulation assumed increasing importance. A major transition began in the mode of expressing the goals of social behavior and political action. For decades, the goals of "progress," of "modernization," and of "development" had dominated Islamic societies both in political programs and in personal and cultural life. Emerging generations worked actively to become "modern," and their clothing, leisure habits, and reading reflected the effort. Blue jeans, transistor radios, and movies set the tone for many of the aspirations of the new generations of Muslims.

Political programs reflected much of the same motivation. Leaders in Muslim countries adopted programs of reform that would rapidly Westernize and modernize their societies. One of the most admired Middle Eastern leaders was Mustafa Kemal Atatürk, who worked to create a Turkey that was secular, modern, and basically Western. Leaders who hesitated to go that far or who tended to stress traditional Islamic values were frequently criticized as being reactionary or obstacles to the "progress" of their peoples.

During the twentieth century, there has been a gradual evolution of the vocabulary in which basic political and social goals were articulated. By the end of World War I, the ideals and symbols of nationalism had become important in shaping the goals and vocabulary of Muslims. *National* independence became an important thing for which to strive. Even conservative Muslims as well as relatively radical ideologues spoke primarily in nationalist terms.

Following World War II, the emphasis shifted. As independence was achieved, simple nationalism was insufficient to mobilize support for policies and programs. In addition, the older leadership groups seemed increasingly unable to cope with the rapid changes taking place in Muslim societies. New leaders began to emerge with new programs and symbols, built on the concept of the need for radical transformations or "revolutions." Just as nationalism tended to dominate much of the way people thought, so revolutionism became the basis for the social and political vocabulary of the emerging leadership. Even relatively conservative leaders came to call their programs revolutionary, with the symbolic difference in the 1960s being whether the revolution was to be "white" or "red." Both outside observers and many Muslims themselves believed that the wave of the future lay in radical approaches to the transformation of society.

There was already in existence in the 1960s a fully articulated set of symbols and ideas expressing the ideal of the revolutionary transformation of society. The ideas of the Left and the New Left provided the basis for much of the expression of social and political ideals by the late 1960s. The Arab socialism of Nasir in Egypt and the Ba'th party in both Syria and Iraq were the major manifestations of this approach to the social and political scene.

By the end of the 1960s, however, there was considerable disenchantment with the programs and operations of radical socialism. This was true not only within the Islamic world but elsewhere, especially outside of the West and the Communist areas. The great radicals of the early 1960s had lost their influence by the later years of that decade. In Arab countries, Nasir and the Syrian Ba'th party both faced real problems as a result of their catastrophic defeat in the Arab-Israeli war of 1967. Some of the most prominent radical figures who had been removed from power by the end of the decade included Kwame Nkrumah of Ghana, Sukarno of Indonesia, and Ahmad Ben Bella of Algeria. Other major radical socialist figures outside the Islamic world also suffered a loss of prominence because their countries had not enjoyed the great success that had been promised earlier. Fidel Castro in Cuba became increasingly dependent upon the Soviet Union, and Sékou Touré in Guinea gradually moved away from his militant positions until by the late 1970s he was working to encourage the capitalist investment in his country that he had at first rejected as a manifestation of neoimperialism.

In this atmosphere of discouragment, there was a shift from borrowed symbols toward "authentic" goals and ideologies that could express the genuine nature of the society. In Muslim countries, the Islamic heritage was a natural source of inspiration. For the general population, Islam had always been an important part of their social and political context. The more mass-oriented the nationalist movements were, the stronger the Islamic component became. Though the leadership may have been speaking in the symbols and terminology of nationalism with its secular and Western overtones, nationalism for the masses was meaningful largely as it related to basic Islamic concepts. Similarly, the radical socialists in Islamic countries always had to give at least some recognition to the Islamic ideals of the population. Ideologies like Arab socialism were often described as "Islamic socialism" or as being supported by the teaching of Islam. The elites, however, tended to use Islam in the service of some other cause rather than to value it directly.

By the beginning of the 1970s, this process began to be reversed. Politics, ideology, reforms, and programs of social change were expressed more and more in Islamic terms.

In this context, it was important that a statement of Islamic ideals not be compromised by association with foreign ideologies or external influence. And too many Muslim adaptationist programs, both conservative and radical, seemed to carry the disease of "weststruckness." The one style of Islam that had recognizably not compromised its integrity was fundamentalism, which as a result, provided the symbols and vocabulary necessary for a clear statement of purposes and goals. Thus, just as conservatives of the 1960s had articulated programs in terms of "revolutionism" (calling them "white revolutions"), now even secularist radicals identified and described their programs in fundamentalist Islamic terms. This process was aided by the fact that fundamentalism provided a clear set of actions to identify a program as authentically Islamic: the prohibition of alcoholic beverages, the banning of interest in financial dealings, the imposition of specified punishments for certain criminal acts, and so on. In this way, even nonfundamentalist aspects of the Islamic resurgence tended to be expressed in fundamentalist terms.

CURRENT STATUS OF FUNDAMENTALISM

To examine manifestations of the fundamentalist style during the past decade, we will consider three major types: first, the popular organizational style established by groups like the Muslim Brotherhood in Egypt; second, what might be termed the "official" fundamentalism of governmental policymakers; and third, the continuing intellectual development of fundamentalist thought away from the standard formulations of the past.

Popular Fundamentalist Organizations

The past decade has been one of much activity on the part of fundamentalist organizations in several areas. These groups have emerged as important sources of opposition to existing governments. They charge that these governments are encouraging secularism, that they have not succeeded in promoting the welfare of their populations, and they are immoral and irreligious. The history of these organizations varies depending on local conditions and the attitudes of those in political power.

In Egypt the tradition of the Muslim Brotherhood is still vigorous. Following the death of Nasir in 1970, his successor, Anwar al-Sadat, relaxed the controls on the Brotherhood and other fundamentalists. This came at a time when Egyptian Muslims were already increasing their visible adherence to Islam. Growing numbers of young women, especially in the high schools and universities, began to wear Islamic rather than "fashionably" Western clothing. Popular inspirational writings by Muslim teachers like Mustafa Mahmud were widely read and Islamic programs on television and radio had great popularity. A number of preachers in mosques at the Friday noon prayers gained large followings. People like Shaykh Muhammad Jalal Kishk became important influences among the educated leadership as well as among the working classes.

In addition to this popular resurgence, more militant groups developed in Egypt during the 1970s. They worked to bring to power a government that would establish a clearly fundamentalist Islamic program. Some of these groups operated in the underground of suppressed political opposition. Such groups were responsible for the attack on the Technical Military Academy in Cairo during 1974, the murder of a former cabinet minister in 1977, and the assassination of Sadat himself in 1981. While these groups frequently adopt positions similar to those of the older Muslim Brotherhood and are often inspired by the same writings, they may not have direct organizational connections with the Brotherhood itself.

There are many influential and powerful Islamic currents in Egypt. The cosmopolitan intellectual traditions are strong, and they have not always been particularly fundamentalist in their orientation. These dimensions still remain, but even relatively radical intellectuals like the Egyptian philosopher Hasan Hanafi and the conservative establishment of the al-Azhar ulama now speak in tones that have a fundamentalist ring. The case of Hanafi represents a significant new direction, and the views of the shaykhs of al-Azhar appear to be catching up with public opinion; both show the current vigor of the fundamentalist style in appealing to a wide variety of people.

In other areas of the Middle East, fundamentalist groups are most active in articulating the Islamic opposition to existing regimes. The Syrian Muslim Brotherhood represents the best organized opposition to the government of Hafiz al-Assad. The threat posed by this opposition can be gauged by the vigor of the measures taken by the Syrian government to repress it. During 1982, in order to suppress a Brotherhood-associated revolt that began in the city of Hama, large portions of the city were destroyed; there were thousands of casualties.

Most Muslim countries have some form of fundamentalist opposition movement. During 1983, these groups showed themselves in a number of ways, and the events mentioned at the beginning of this analysis should be read in this context. North African governments are concerned about the development of such groups in their countries. Although they did not achieve much strength in the Maghrib during the 1970s, they appear now to be gaining. The Islamic Liberation party in Tunisia and the student demonstrations in Algeria are part of a broader picture. At the other end of the Islamic world, the Dar al-Islam and Islamic Commando movements are similar groups working to establish a fundamentalist-style state in Indonesia.

At the end of 1983, an underground movement arising from the Shiite community of Iraq received wider notice when it was associated with the attack on Western embassies and installations in Kuwait. Militant Shiite opposition movements in Iraq emerged with some strength during the 1970s. The largest is al-Da'wah al-Islamiyyah, but there are others, too. The program that most of these organizations advocate reflects ideals similar to those that led to the establishment of the Islamic republic in Iran, and some of the Shiite opposition groups in Iraq have close ties to the movement of Ayatollah Khomeini. The intellectual leader of the Shiite opposition in Iraq was Sayyid Muhammad Baqir al-Sadr, who was executed by the Iraqi government in 1980. In his teachings and in the programs of the underground Shiite groups, the "concrete objective of the social revolution is the realization of the Islamic polity which would . . . apply the values of Islam in every sphere of life" (Batatu 1981, 579).

"Government" Fundamentalism

In recent years, there have been two governmental contexts for the implementation of relatively fundamentalist policies. Some governments, by their own definition and history, are clearly Islamic in some fundamentalist way, whereas others have gradually adopted fundamentalist policies over a period of time.

Established fundamentalist regimes are a relatively new feature in the Middle Eastern political landscape. For many years, the only notable one was the Saudi-Wahhabi kingdom. This was the one state that officially declared the Qur'an its constitution; others simply had a clause in the constitution that, for example, announced that Islam was the religion of the state. By the 1970s, the fundamentalism of the Saudi monarchy was relatively conservative and pragmatic. Under the leadership of King Faysal (d. 1975), Saudi Arabia had begun a well-organized program of industrialization and modernization. In this there is still a dedication to the Wahhabi principles, but the implications of Saudi fundamentalism are not socially or politically revolutionary.

This is in sharp contrast to the other two explicitly Islamic regimes in the Middle East in the 1980s, Iran and Libya. In both of these countries there has been a conscious effort to create an Islamic regime that is socially revolutionary. In Iran, the Islamic republic replaced the monarchy with a structure in which Islamic teachers play a prominent role in defining policy and implementing laws. Libya, under the leadership of Muammar Qaddafi, has striven to implement a third universal ideology, in contrast to capitalism and communism, that is based on the fundamental principles of Islam. Both Iran and Libya have many similarities to past fundamentalist approaches, but at the same time they represent significant experiments in alternative modes of implementing the fundamental principles of Islam. In this sense, they are fundamentalists who have gone beyond the guidelines of the standard fundamentalism of the past and are creating new forms.

Many other governments have adopted a more fundamentalist tone in recent years. For some this appears to be a pragmatic recognition of the current political strength of Islamic symbols and groups, whereas in other cases it may reflect a more deeply grounded change of perspective on the part of the leadership. However, whether Islamic themes are being manipulated by exploitative leaders or are a part of a gradual conversion of attitudes, it is apparent that many governments in the Islamic world have adopted more clearly Islamic policies.

The model in these cases is usually the formulations provided by standard Islamic fundamentalism in contrast to the more revolutionary nature of Libyan or Iranian fundamentalism. The most long-standing Islamization effort of this type is the one instituted by President Zia ul-Haq in Pakistan. Each year, as was the case in 1983, some new measures are introduced that bring official government policy closer to the rules and prescriptions of Islam as interpreted in the perspective of standard fundamentalism. This style of government policy was also seen in 1983 in the Sudan, when President Numayri introduced a ban on alcoholic beverages and imposed amputation as a punishment for theft.

Thus, as Islamic themes and symbols become more visible in social and political life in the Middle East, governments apparently will continue to adopt overtly Islamic policies. Because standard fundamentalism presents the simplest and most clearly articulated agenda for Islamization, it tends to provide the content of much governmental fundamentalism. The more revolutionary lines of fundamentalism might create threats to regimes even if the regimes begin to implement them. Standard fundamentalism, therefore, is a safer alternative than the new forms.

The "New" Fundamentalism of the 1980s

An important dimension of the Islamic resurgence in the past decade is the emergence of new formulations of the fundamentalist tradition. In Egypt, for example, a new articulation has been called "neo-fundamentalism" by Nazih Ayubi. He notes that the Egyptian Islamic establishment and the "conventional" Muslim Brothers tended to be rightist in their orientation and strong in their opposition to Marxism. The neo-fundamentalists, however, take a more radical position; they "are more militant than the Brothers and may represent a less orthodox orientation similar to what the new left represents within socialist circles" (Ayubi 1980, 488–89).

Within the whole Arab world, Fouad Ajami distinguished between "conservative fundamentalism" and "radical fundamentalism" (Ajami 1981, 50–75). In this contrast, the conservative version tends to be supportive of existing state structures, whereas the radical creates effective opposition of a populist style. The aim is to reject foreign elements and return to the authentic Islamic tradition. In his analysis of the writings of Muhammad Jalal Kishk as a representative of radical fundamentalism, Ajami notes that this position "cannot be dismissed simply as reactionary, fundamentalist, or theocratic. Kishk's quest is not just the resurrection of a lost and ideal past. . . . The virtue of Kishk's analysis was to demonstrate that traditionalist thought can be penetrating and unapologetic and can be turned onto social and political problems without excessive piety" (Ajami 1981, 59–60). Radical fundamentalism offers a concrete vision of the future that appeals to the general Islamic population as an authentic vision within the framework of meaningful symbols and aspirations. That it is fundamentalist does not, however, mean that it is a conservative vision. Rather, it is a radical vision based on the Qur'an and the sunnah.

One of the most controversial of the new forms of fundamentalism to emerge in the 1970s was what Daniel Pipes calls the "neo-Sanusiya" of Qaddafi in Libya. "Although al-Qadhdhafi overthrew *Sanusi* rule, denounced the *Sanusis* as non-Muslims, banned the *Sanusi* order, and totally reoriented Libyan politics, he in fact espoused many of the original *Sanusi* ideals" (Pipes 1980, 24). Qaddafi works for a total transformation of society based upon a new analysis of the fundamentals of the faith. He is unwilling to accept the traditional formulation of medieval and conservative modern Islamic scholars and rejects even many of the positions of standard fundamentalism. Qaddafi's neo-Sanusism is in the radical fundamentalist style of the original Sanusi, but the content is new. A restructuring of the social and political order has been undertaken in the past decade in Libya. Some Muslims reject Qaddafi's positions as going beyond Islamic principles, but whatever the evaluation of the contents or the results, Qaddafi's Libya represents a significant movement within the fundamentalist tradition away from the standard and conservative forms and toward a very new articulation of the fundamentals of the faith.

One of the most dynamic developments in the fundamentalist style of Islam during the 1970s was the number of thinkers who rose to prominence, becoming significant new spokesmen of Islamic resurgence. Some of these thinkers had been writing for a long time but only recently received widespread attention; others are themselves the products of the intellectual climate of the 1960s and 1970s.

Abu al-A'la al-Mawdudi (1903–79) is of an earlier generation of fundamentalist writers whose works are growing in popularity today. Originally, Mawdudi's influence was largely confined to the Muslim communities in South Asia. Even there his thinking ran counter to the sentiments of the majority of activist Muslims. For example, Mawdudi opposed on fundamentalist grounds the creation of a separate Muslim nation-state in India, since he believed that nationalism was contrary to the universalism inherent in Islam. Later, when he moved to Pakistan after its creation in 1947, his criticisms of the governments led to his occasional arrest. The organization he established, the Jama'at-i al-Islami, gained little mass support in the early days of the history of Pakistan.

Mawdudi wrote prolifically and his ideas gradually became more widely known. He traveled extensively in the Islamic world and in this way began to influence younger generations of Muslims both inside and outside of south Asia. By the early 1970s, Mawdudi's writings represented a comprehensive and accessible statement of what an Islamic revival should be. His emphasis on the universality and comprehensiveness of the Islamic message fit the mood of the time. Mawdudi's prescriptions went beyond the simple implementation of specific rules, as advocated by standard fundamentalists. Although he advocated those rules, he also attempted to create a broader framework of authentically Islamic analysis. For example, in his widely read commentary on the Qur'an, he "attempted to explain the verses of the Qur'an in the context of its total message" (K. Ahmad & Ansari 1979, 364).

Mawdudi's works have been translated into many languages, and the neo-fundamentalist students in Egypt and North Africa have been influenced by his work. A summary of his contribution by scholars sympathetic to his cause notes that "under the influence of Mawdudi's ideas a considerable amount of activity is visible in different parts of the world. . . . Mawdudi's contribution lies in initiating a process of change markedly inspired by Islamic ideals in an age which appeared insensitive, let alone unresponsive to God" (K. Ahmad & Ansari 1979, 381).

Another widely known fundamentalist writer is Sayyid Qutb, who was executed by the Egyptian government in 1965. Although he had been active in the Muslim Brotherhood for some time, it was not until the 1960s that he achieved special prominence. By the time of his execution, his works were beginning to be seen as the basis for a revolutionary fundamentalism directed at the Islamic transformation of society. In his writings, the basic symbols and themes of neo-fundamentalism are clearly defined. In this sense, much of his work, along with that of Mawdudi, provided the conceptual foundations for the radical fundamentalism of the contemporary world.

These basic themes include a major focus on the concept of oneness or unity, as represented by the Islamic concept of *tawhid*. Both Qutb and Mawdudi argue that the oneness of God in the Islamic perspective means that there can be no sphere that is separate from the Islamic vision. The secularist separation of church and state or of religion and politics is, in this view, the modern form of polytheism. The Islamic vision must be accepted as comprehensive and normative for every aspect of life; economics and politics are to be as Islamic as theology or philosophy.

In the writings of someone like Sayyid Qutb, this did not mean a rejection of modern science nor did it mean a demand for a return to the conditions of the seventh century. For example, Qutb speaks of the "material fruits of the creative genius of Europe," but says that it is now time for the Islamic community to step forward to provide the high ideals and moral leadership that will make it possible for humanity to have the material benefits of modern science without falling into the trap of the immoral materialism that has emerged in Western civilization (Qutb n.d., 7–13).

A third example of the intellectual leadership for the emergence of the new fundamentalism is an Iranian, 'Ali Shari'ati (1933–77). Although he wrote within the historical context of Shiite Iran, his works are now widely read throughout the Islamic world. He is said by many to be the intellectual or ideological founder of the Islamic revolutionary movement in Iran. He is, at least, the best known articulator of radical fundamentalism in Iran, although the more conservative or standard forms of the ulama followers of the Ayatollah Khomeini are also an important part of Iranian revolutionary fundamentalism.

Shari'ati, whose works advocate the Islamic transformation of society, also emphasizes the importance of *tawhid* or oneness as the necessary basis for the renewal of Islam in the contemporary era. He supported a careful study of the fundamentals of the faith, disregarding the corruptions that later religious establishments imposed upon believers. In his vocabulary, it was necessary to reject Safavid Shi'ism, that is, the governmental and establishment Shi'ism that had been created by making Shi'ism the state religion in the Safavid Empire in the sixteenth century. He advocated a return to the Shi'ism of 'Ali, that is, a return to the original inspiration and fundamentals of the Islamic tradition as accepted by Shiites. His work represents, in the eyes of many Muslims today, an "ideological revolution in the Muslim world" (Yadegari 1983).

Mawdudi, Qutb, and Shari'ati are only the most visible of a large number of Muslim intellectuals who are now in the process of transforming both the content of Islamic fundamentalism and the vocabulary of Islamic expression and loyalty in general. No program, whether it is standard, governmental, or radical fundamentalist, now ignores the mode of expression represented by these men.

The contemporary period is witnessing a resurgence of Islam and a restatement of the fundamentals of the faith. In recent years, this resurgence has been seen as a primarily fundamentalist phenomenon. This observation is true but it needs to be placed in the perspective of the broader reaches of Islamic history and also in the context of dynamic diversity, even within the fundamentalist style of Islam.

A final point must be made. The fundamentalist nature of the *Islamic* resurgence is not a unique phenomenon. In all major civilizations there seems to be a significant transition. The ideologies of the modernized West appear to have failed everyone, not just the Muslims who attempted to adapt them to their own societies. In the final quarter of the twentieth century, many people have sought a return to the fundamentals of their faith and their religious traditions.

Harvey Cox, a prominent Christian theologian, says that the structure of modernity "is already decomposing, that its quiet assurance of competence and efficiency cannot deliver what it promises. We know that here before us the five pillars of modernity are being eaten from the inside" (Cox 1984, 56D). Cox and others note that this has resulted in a significant postmodern world view evident in the Catholicism of Poland and the activist church in Latin America as well as the resurgence of Islam. Cox concludes that "it no longer looks as though the postmodern world will be a postreligious one" (Cox 1984, 56G).

In the postmodern world, Islamic fundamentalism maintains its traditional mission, even though its form and content may be changing. As it has since the early days of the Islamic community, fundamentalism represents the affirmation of the authentic Islamic vision in the face of rapid sociohistoric change. It is the safeguard that adaptation to change will not go so far as to destroy the clearly Islamic identity of the community of believers. Islamic fundamentalism reflects, in this way, the profound elements of continuity and change visible in the contemporary Islamic world.

REFERENCES

Abrahamian, Ervand. 1982. *Iran between two revolutions*. Princeton Studies on the Near East. Princeton: Princeton University Press.

Ahmad, Aziz. 1964. *Studies in Islamic culture in the Indian environment.* Oxford: Clarendon.

Ahmad, Khurshid, and Zafar Ishaq Ansari. 1979. Mawlana Sayyid Abul A'la Mawdudi: An introduction to his vision of Islam and Islamic revival. In *Islamic perspectives,* edited by Khurshid Ahmad and Zafar Ishaq Ansari, 359–83. London: Islamic Foundation.

Ajami, Fouad. 1981. *The Arab predicament.* Cambridge: Cambridge University Press.

Arab money in India. 1983. *Middle East,* no. 108 (October): 13.

Ayubi, Nazih N.M. 1980. Political revival of Islam: The case of Egypt. *International Journal of Middle East Studies* 12, no. 4 (December): 481–99.

Batatu, Hanna. 1981. Iraq's underground Shi'a movement: Characteristics, causes and prospects. *Middle East Journal* 35, no. 4 (Autumn): 578–94.

Cox, Harvey. 1984. The Devil is a modernist. *Harvard Magazine* 86, no. 3 (January–February): 56A–56H.

Das, K. 1983. Malaysia: A battle royal. *Far Eastern Economic Review,* 13 October, pp. 17–18.

Dekmejian, R. Hrair. 1980. Anatomy of Islamic revival: Legitimacy crisis, ethnic conflict and the search for Islamic alternatives. *Middle East Journal* 34, no. 1 (Winter): 1–12.

Delegation trip to Libya reviewed (Thailand). 1983. Joint publications research service 83858. *Southeast Asia Report,* no. 1309 (11 July): 37–38.

Execution of Islamic leader announced. 1983. Joint publications research service 83858. *Southeast Asia Report,* no. 1309 (11 July): 11–13.

Formation of Muslim foundation noted (Thailand). 1983. Joint publications research service 83858. *Southeast Asia Report,* no. 1309 (11 July): 35–36.

Gigot, Paul A. 1983. Islam fundamentalism stirs up much discord in Pakistan, elsewhere. *Wall Street Journal,* 1 December.

Hodgson, Marshall G.S. 1974. *Venture of Islam.* 3 vols. Chicago: University of Chicago Press.

Laoust, Henri. 1965. *Les schismes dans l'Islam.* Paris: Payot.

Lapidus, Ira M. 1975. The separation of state and religion in the development of early Islamic history. *International Journal of Middle East Studies* 6, no. 4 (October): 363–85.

Mardin, Şerif. 1982. Turkey: Islam and Westernization. In *Religion and societies: Asia and the Middle East,* edited by Carlo Caldarola, 171–98. Berlin: Mouton.

Memon, Muhammad Umar. 1976. *Ibn Taimiya's struggle against popular religion.* The Hague: Mouton.

Mitchell, Richard P. 1969. *Society of the Muslim Brothers.* London: Oxford University Press.

Pipes, Daniel. 1980. "This world is political!": The Islamic revival of the seventies. *Orbis* 24, no. 1 (Spring): 9–41.

———. 1983. *In the path of God: Islam and political power*. New York: Basic Books.

Qutb, Sayyid. n.d. *Milestones*. Cedar Rapids, Iowa: Unity Publishing.

Rahman, Fazlur. 1968. *Islam*. Garden City, N.Y.: Doubleday.

———. 1970. Revival and reform in Islam. In *Cambridge history of Islam*, edited by P.M. Holt, Ann K.S. Lambton, and Bernard Lewis, 2:632–56. Cambridge: Cambridge University Press.

Subversion trial of Muslim dissident concluded. 1983. Joint publications research service 83858. *Southeast Asia Report*, no. 1309 (11 July): 14–15.

Tasker, Rodney. 1983. Pakistan: Cracking the whip. *Far Eastern Economic Review*, 16 June, pp. 25–26.

Voll, John. 1979. Sudanese Mahdi: Frontier fundamentalist. *International Journal of Middle East Studies* 10, no. 2 (May): 145–66.

Yadegari, Mohammad. 1983. *Ideological revolution in the Muslim world*. Brentwood, Md.: IGPS.

ADDITIONAL READINGS

The following readings are of two types. The first group comprises general analyses and interpretations of modern Islamic developments that provide a variety of perspectives on the modern fundamentalist experience. The second group lists readings that present contemporary Islamic fundamentalist ideas and are readily available to the English-speaking reader.

Analyses

Esposito, John L., ed. *Voices of Resurgent Islam*. New York: Oxford University Press, 1983.

Mortimer, Edward. *Faith and Power: The Politics of Islam*. New York: Random House, 1982.

Pipes, Daniel. *In the Path of God: Islam and Political Power*. New York: Basic Books, 1983.

Voll, John Obert. *Islam: Continuity and Change in the Modern World*. Boulder, Colo.: Westview Press, 1982.

Islamic Viewpoints

Ahmad, Khurshid, and Zafar Ishaq Ansari, eds. *Islamic Perspectives*. London: Islamic Foundation, 1979.

Akhtar, Karm B., and Ahmad H. Sakr. *Islamic Fundamentalism*. Cedar Rapids, Iowa: Igram Press, 1982.

Azzam, Salem, ed. *Islam and Contemporary Society*. London: Longman, 1982.

Donohue, John J., and John L. Esposito, eds. *Islam in Transition*. New York: Oxford University Press, 1982.

Gauhar, Altaf, ed. *The Challenge of Islam*. London: Islamic Council of Europe, 1978.

The PLO
since Beirut

Philip Mattar

The Israeli invasion of Lebanon in the summer of 1982 dislocated the military structure of the Palestine Liberation Organization (PLO) and destroyed the socioeconomic infrastructure of Palestinian society in Lebanon. The evacuation of Palestinian fighters from Beirut in August meant the loss of a strategic, semiautonomous base close to Israel and to the West Bank and Gaza. Yasir Arafat, the chairman of the PLO, failed to acknowledge the magnitude of the defeat and the need for reform. He proceeded with his political maneuvers—negotiating with Jordan's King Hussein on the basis of President Ronald Reagan's peace plan and promoting his policies at the 16th Palestine National Council (PNC)—as if nothing had changed except the PLO's address. The defeat, however, catalyzed a rebellion within Fatah, the largest PLO group, which threatened the organization's unity and diplomatic effectiveness in its quest for self-determination and independence in Palestine for 4.5 million Palestinians.

The international media prematurely predicted that the PLO's defeat and dispersion would result in its permanent enfeeblement. With the rebellion under way in the summer of 1983, the PLO seemed, even to its senior officials, to be headed for a worse fate—an internal disintegration. (Kaddoumi 1983a; al-Hut, 1983a). Some Western analysts and journalists, carried away by the PLO's predicament or by their own wishful thinking, declared the demise of the organization and of the political fortune of Yasir Arafat.

Yet, although its activities were interrupted, the organization and its leader survived both the defeat and the rebellion; now it finds itself at a crossroad between rejectionism and moderation. Despite the PLO's setbacks, inherent weaknesses, and environmental constraints, it is likely to continue to assert itself on the international scene for some time to come. Its resiliency is largely due to four factors: democratic institutional structure, mobilization of the Palestinian community, economic and social achievements, and growing international recognition.

BACKGROUND

The PLO is the institutional framework of the Palestinian national movement, composed of the representatives of major sectors of Palestinian society. Foremost among its officials are members of a coalition of eight guerrilla groups that are fighting for one common goal: the establishment of an independent state in Palestine, a territory the Palestinians inhabited since ancient times until they fled or were driven out in 1948 by the Israel Defense Forces (IDF). Otherwise, the groups differ considerably in ideology, in the extent and method of the desired liberation, and in their development.

The oldest group within the PLO is Fatah, having been founded in the late 1950s by a Cairo University engineering student, Yasir Arafat (code name, Abu Ammar). Despite the 1982 dispersion, it remains the largest group, with perhaps 80 percent of the PLO's resources and fighters, and commands an equal percentage of constituency among Palestinians. Its popularity is derived from the personality and politics of its charismatic leader Arafat. To the masses he is both a father figure, affectionately called "the old man," and a Za'im, a leader with political authority. He and the cofounders of Fatah—Khalil al-Wazir (Abu Jihad) and Salah Khalaf (Abu 'Iyad)—are pragmatic nationalists, who discourage ideology within the group but nevertheless tolerate ideologists from the far right to the radical left. Its broad appeal is due to its simple national goal: the liberation of Palestine by Palestinians. Arab support is sought, but not at the cost of Palestinian independent decision making. Fatah has tried not to get involved in the internal politics of Arab states, though Jordan and Lebanon are costly, if inevitable, exceptions (Said 1979, 159–60).

There are other factors that make Fatah appealing to the majority. Its ethos is that of a modern Sunni Islamic culture, reflecting both the predominant religious values and the passion for modernity, animated by the necessity of living as minorities in hostile environments. Also, Fatah has been known as the group most willing to take action to fight for liberation. Its military branch, al-'Asifah, launched its first military raid in Israel in 1965. Its popularity and credibility increased enormously after the battle of Karamah on 21 March 1968. Karamah is a Jordanian town, which was attacked by large units from the IDF in retaliation for a Palestinian raid. Fatah put up a stiff resistance, ending in hand-to-hand combat, which resulted in the deaths of about thirty Israelis (not hundreds, as Fatah claimed) and one hundred Palestinians, together with forty Jordanians who had come to Fatah's assistance. Karamah (which means "dignity") became a symbol of resistance against the Israelis, who were considered invincible after their humiliating defeat of the Arabs in the 1967 war. The boost in Fatah's prestige brought it hundreds of new recruits, Arab recognition, and financial support. Most important, it provided Fatah an opportunity to take over the leadership of the PLO. (Said 1979, 160; Quandt, Jabber, and Lesch 1973, 57; Miller 1983, 25).

The PLO had been established in Jerusalem on 28 May 1964, with the blessings and under the shadow of the Arab states, who were responding to Palestinian demands for an organization to represent their national interests. Although the organization, under the leadership of a lawyer from Acre, Ahmad Shuqayri, articulated slogans that appealed to the masses—national unity, mobilization, and liberation—it accommodated organizational and external constraints unpalatable to the new generation of Palestinian political elite. Shuqayri's style of leadership was autocratic, like that of the first Palestinian leader, the mufti of Jerusalem, or of an Arab dictator. Rejecting elections, the Arab-selected Shuqayri chose delegates to the Palestine National Council (PNC), the PLO parliament (Hussain 1975, 16).

The charter passed by the council revealed the extent of Arab influence on the PLO and Shuqayri. In deference to Egypt and Jordan, article 24 of the PNC excluded the West Bank and Gaza from Palestinian claims to sovereignty over Palestine. Even though a Palestine Liberation Army (PLA) was established, it gave no priority to revolutionary action because it was controlled by Egypt. Indeed, the liberation of Palestine was dependent on the military performance of the Arab armies. Consequently, when the Arabs and the PLA were defeated by Israel in 1967, the PLO was discredited and Shuqayri was forced out in December and replaced by another lawyer, Yahya Hammuda, who served briefly (Hamid 1975, 98).

The 1967 Arab defeat and the 1968 Palestinian "victory" at Karamah enhanced Fatah's prestige and strength, and propelled it into the leadership position of the PLO. Fatah amended the 1964 charter at the 1968 PNC and elected its own spokesman, Yasir Arafat, as chairman of the PLO Executive Committee at the 1969 PNC. But the 1967 war had also spawned at least twenty other groups, of which only a few have survived in opposition to Fatah within the coalition.

Fatah's chief rival in the PLO is the Popular Front for the Liberation of Palestine. Headed by George Habash, a Christian Palestinian physician, the Popular Front is composed of men who adopted Marxism-Leninism to fight Zionism, Arab reaction, and world imperialism. They consider revolutions in Arab countries, which would create "Arab Hanois," necessary in the struggle to liberate Palestine (Fiche du monde arabe 1979, I-P27 PFLP).

The Popular Front leaders are more aware of the limitations within the Arab world that constrain the Palestinian movement than are the overly optimistic Fatah elite. They were, for example, more realistic about the extent and nature of Arab support before and during the 1982 war. Yet they idealistically insist on the use of military means to defeat Israel and on the rejection of any political settlement with the Jewish state, especially through the mediation of the "imperialist" American government or the "reactionary" Arab regimes. Their contempt for the government of Jordan led them to challenge Jordanian sovereignty, which helped trigger the 1970–71 war that resulted in a PLO defeat and relocation to Lebanon.

The Popular Front does not attract a mass appeal for two fundamental reasons: its Marxist-Leninist ideology is beyond the comprehension of most Palestinians and is alien to their religious and cultural ethos. Its influence, however, has been disproportionate to its numbers (about four thousand, mostly well educated), because it is considered a radical and necessary alternative to the centrist Fatah.

Another Marxist alternative to Fatah is the Democratic Front for the Liberation of Palestine. Led by Naif Hawatmeh, the Democratic Front split from the Popular Front in 1969 and has been far more imaginative and flexible in its ideological development. It initially subscribed to the establishment of a popular democratic state in Palestine in which Jews would enjoy full national rights rather than to a secular, democratic Palestine Arab state, which the other groups advocate. This objective was revised in 1973 when Hawatmeh proposed a state on the West Bank and Gaza as an "intermediary phase" (Fiche du monde arabe 1979, I-P20 DFLP).

Other rivals to Fatah include five groups, each of which is supported by a single Arab country that influences or dictates its policies. They are, therefore, less

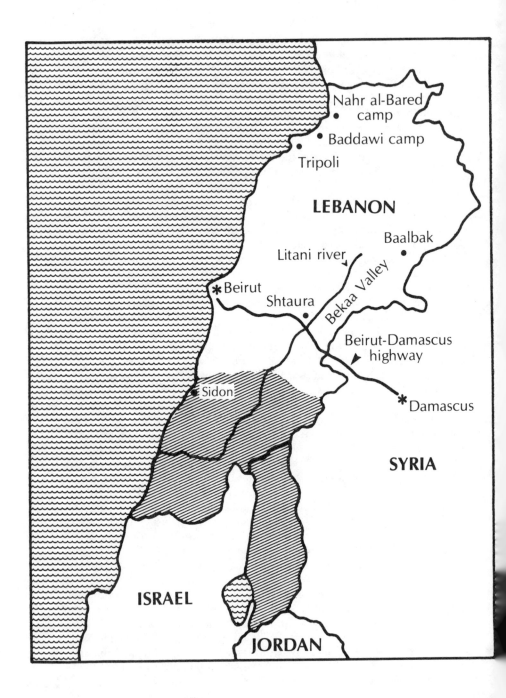

Nahr al-Bared camp

Baddawi camp

Tripoli

LEBANON

Litani river

Baalbak

Beirut

Shtaura

Bekaa Valley

Beirut-Damascus highway

Damascus

Sidon

SYRIA

ISRAEL

JORDAN

legitimate, less popular, and limited in political power to their resources and size of membership. The Popular Front for the Liberation of Palestine—General Command, which also split from the Popular Front, is led by Ahmad Jibril, whose pro-Syrian sentiments led him to join the rebels and the Syrians against Fatah in May 1983; al-Sa'iqa is Syrian-controlled and directed; the Palestine Liberation Front is pro-Iraqi; and the Arab Liberation Front is Iraqi controlled. Together these smaller groups have served as a counterweight to Fatah's otherwise total domination of the national movement and its institutions.

They also have served as gadflies, stimulating debates about Fatah's ideology, strategy, and organization. They have often charged that Fatah's nonideology produced an absence of vision of politics and society in the diaspora and in a future Palestine state; that the Fatah-led PLO promiscuously flirted with any nation—Saudi Arabia, Syria, Russia, the United States—leaving the organization without a clear policy of its own; that it had neither a military nor a political strategy but drifted from crisis to crisis (Said 1979, 162–63); that some of its revolutionaries had become self-perpetuating bureaucrats, more interested in improving their standard of living than in liberating Palestine; and that it had no strategy to induce more political or military resistance against the repressive Israeli occupation of the West Bank and Gaza, nor even to punish, with few exceptions, Palestinian quislings and land sellers.

The most vociferous denunciations have concerned Fatah's perceived moderation, the highlights of which were the Fatah-supported 1974 and 1977 PNC resolutions and Arafat's diplomacy, which was inexorably leading to the recognition of Israel. These criticisms generated heated and acrimonious debates, which could have degenerated into violence and disunity had it not been for the preponderance of Fatah and for the adherence to a set of democratic principles practiced within the PLO institutions.

Foremost of these institutions is the Palestine National Council, the parliament of the PLO. Most of the ideological political tendencies are represented by its members (numbering 355 in 1983) from eight commando groups and their political branches, ten unions, Palestinian communities, and some with a special status, such as leaders expelled from the occupied territories, intellectuals, and scientists. The PNC studies and debates, and then votes by a simple majority—though consensus is sought—on political and financial policies and programs (Rubenberg 1983, 54).

Arafat has been the central force in this political system since 1969 because of his Fatah power base, charisma, and political skills. These enabled him to survive within the volatile organization and region, and empowered him to maintain the unity of the coalition. The price for consensus has been high. He has had to appease or reflect diverse currents by articulating vague, incoherent, and at times, contradictory positions, which damaged his credibility abroad and created diplomatic immobility. Yet his politics of consensus and unity allowed the development of a sociopolitical infrastructure in Lebanon.

Palestinian presence in Lebanon began in 1948, when about 100,000 Palestinians, mostly from northern historic Palestine, migrated as a result of war conditions or were evicted from their homes by the IDF to make room for Jewish immigrants, on orders of Israel's first premier and minister of defense, David Ben-Gurion, according to Yitzhak Rabin (*New York Times*, 23 Oct. 1979). The Palestinians lived in refugee camps and were generally denied Lebanese citizenship, partly out of fear that, since most are Sunni Muslims, they would upset the delicate confessional balance of the state. But as a result of the 1969 Cairo agreement between Lebanon and the PLO and the transfer of the PLO headquarters from Amman to Beirut, the Palestinian community established a semiautonomous status (TEAM 1983, 20–22). This was at the expense of Lebanese sovereignty.

Over a period of a dozen years, the PLO developed an impressive infrastructure for the 360,000 Palestinians in Lebanon. Its annual budget was about $1 billion, larger than that of some developing countries. The size of its armed forces was about 25,000 fighters (including national guard and paramilitary units, but excluding the trained neighborhood *shabab*, or youth). These forces were armed with light and medium weapons and long-range artillery. Most of the PLO tanks were old medium-weight, short-range types such as the T-34, sufficient for the local theater of war but not for invading or shelling Israel. The PLO had a twenty-five plane "air force" for training and transport, but it was Arab-based; the planes rarely landed on the PLO airstrip near Ansar, partly because the Palestinians had no air defense system (PLO source, 19 March 1984).

The PLO's economic and social institutions served almost half a million Palestinian and Lebanese civilians. The Palestine Martyrs' Works Society (SAMED) operated businesses and light industries that grossed $40 million annually. The Palestine Red Crescent Society supervised clinics and hospitals for Palestinians and Lebanese. The Institute of Social Affairs and Welfare provided financial aid for the blind, for day centers for children, for the wounded, and for families of the "martyrs."

These political and economic institutions enhanced the PLO's prestige and legitimacy in the Arab world and among Palestinians everywhere. The Arab League recognized the PLO as the sole legitimate representative of the Palestinian people and accorded it government status at the Rabat Conference in 1974. Shortly thereafter the UN accorded observer status to the PLO, and over one hundred organizations recognized it. Palestinians on the West Bank and Gaza, in the 1976 municipal elections, voted out traditional pro-Jordanian mayors and replaced them with supporters of the PLO.

INVASION

The primary purpose of the Israeli invasion was to destroy the PLO. Defense Minister Ariel Sharon, the architect of the invasion, persuaded the Begin government, made up of hard-liners, that the elimination of the PLO would allow West Bank and Gaza Palestinians to seek an accommodation with Israel, presumably on Begin's terms of limited autonomy (Ha'aretz 1982). There was also a genuine alarm among hard-liners over growing American public support for the Palestinians which, if the PLO were to recognize Israel and the United States were to start talking with the PLO, could lead to American pressure on Israel to return the West Bank. This in turn could lead to a rift jeopardizing American aid and arms. In addition, the PLO's success in articulating Palestinian demands, its attainment of recognition as the only legitimate representative of the Palestinians, and its implicit acceptance of a West Bank–Gaza state were isolating the Begin government around the world and keeping U.S. and international attention on the occupied territories. An invasion not only would destroy the PLO but would relieve pressure on Israel and divert attention to Lebanon where, at the same time, Sharon would install a

Phalange government that would sign a peace treaty with Israel. All this could be done, Sharon promised, in a swift "surgical" operation with minimum loss of Israeli life (*New York Times*, 28 July 1982).

The timing of the invasion could not have been better. The Arab world was in disarray, and there was too much oil on the world market for it to be valued as a weapon. The strongest Arab power, Egypt, was isolated and neutralized by the Camp David peace treaty. Not since the Johnson administration had there been stronger support for Israel in Washington than during the Reagan administration. This was largely why, two weeks before the invasion, Secretary of State Alexander Haig gave Sharon the green light, according to former President Jimmy Carter and an editor of *Ha'aretz* (Schiff 1983, 80).

The stated reason for the operation, called "Peace for Galilee," was to remove PLO forces and missiles from southern Lebanon. Critics of the Israel invasion have underestimated the threat such weapons posed to inhabitants in northern Israel. Rocket attacks in July 1981 caused a number of casualties and sent Israeli inhabitants to shelters, paralyzing many towns and settlements in Galilee. Supporters of the invasion have argued that although it is true that the PLO did not represent an immediate threat to the state of Israel (which is reportedly the fourth strongest world power and the strongest in the region), nevertheless the threat was an unacceptable political weapon (Schueftan 1983, 6).

There was, however, no immediate threat from the north. The borders had been virtually quiet since July 1981, when U.S. emissary Philip Habib negotiated a successful cease-fire. The incident that triggered the invasion—the wounding of the Israeli ambassador to Great Britain, Shlomo Argov, by what the Begin government said was a PLO terrorist—was considered a pretext, particularly after Britain's Margaret Thatcher announced that the attacker belonged to the anti-PLO Abu Nidal group and that PLO officials were also on the hit list.

Still, the invasion might have been accepted in the West as a preemptive, self-defensive operation if it had been confined to a "surgical" operation against PLO forces within a twenty-five mile belt south of the Litani River, as Sharon declared to the Israeli public, American officials, and world media. But the operation quickly grew into a war which caused massive destruction in refugee camps, towns, and the large cities of Tyre, Sidon, and Beirut. The Israeli artillery and air attacks and the indiscriminate use of American-made cluster bombs and phosphorous shells on civilians were described in detail by reporters and graphically shown on television. According to the Lebanese authorities, 17,850 people were killed of whom 84 percent were Lebanese and Palestinian civilians (Hudson 1983, 9).

The destruction and killing damaged Israel's image as a nation threatened with destruction by its hostile Arab neighbors. A further blow to Israel's reputation occurred when the Sabra and Shatila massacres of over eight hundred Palestinians took place in September 1982 by Israeli-backed militias. Sharon and Begin denied direct responsibility, even though the IDF trained and transported the militias to the camps in the Israeli-controlled area of west Beirut, provided them with food and flares while the massacres were going on, and ignored reports of a massacre (*Jerusalem Post*, Jan. 1983).

The war also caused human and social losses for Israel. By 10 October 1982, the Jewish state had lost 368 soldiers in the war; another 200 perished in the occupation that followed. About 3,200 soldiers were wounded. It spent nearly $3 billion on the war, some of which was offset by increased American aid of $1.7 billion. The war divided Israeli society, many questioning their government's moral behavior, and led dozens of soldiers to refuse to serve in Lebanon and the West Bank.

The war was also costly to the PLO and the Palestinian community in Lebanon. The PLO lost between 600 and 800 fighters, large amounts of weapons, and ammunition. Thousands of Palestinian civilians were killed by the IDF and the militias, tens of thousands were left homeless, and Palestinians in the south were left vulnerable to militia attacks. Also damaged were support systems—the economic, social, and cultural institutions. The PLO's mass media, radio stations, and publications were gone, and the Palestine Research Center, containing historical documents and books on Palestinian society, was taken to Israel. (After Israeli institutions, such as the Israel State Archives, refused on moral grounds to house the center's collection, Israel returned it to the PLO during the prisoner exchange of November 1983.)

The PLO's greatest political loss was its quasi-sovereign base in Lebanon, where it already had an embryonic sociopolitical infrastructure for a future Palestinian state (Hudson 1983, 9). About 14,420 fighters and officials evacuated Beirut and were relocated to eight Arab countries—Tunisia, Jordan, Iraq, Syria, South Yemen, North Yemen, Algeria, and Sudan. Yet, because the command structure and the institutional frameworks survived, the PLO regrouped and began rebuilding its institutions in Tunisia, Jordan, and Cyprus.

The Israeli invasion produced world indignation and sympathy for the Palestinians. In the United States, despite ignorance of and hostility toward Palestinian national rights in the Reagan administration, the war and the massacres resulted in increased public support for Palestinian self-determination. The elite press, official and private analysts, and former national leaders called for a resolution to the Palestinian problem. An opinion poll in October 1982 indicated that 76 percent felt that the Palestinians should have a right to establish a state (Americans' attitudes 1983).

The Palestinian question had been put on the back burner by Secretary of State Haig in favor of a "strategic consensus" against the U.S.S.R. in the Middle East. Haig's replacement with George C. Shultz signaled a change in U.S. policy. President Reagan announced on 1 September 1982 a peace plan for the resolution of the Arab-Israeli problem. It did not differ in substance from the Camp David accords. Reagan opposed Israel's creeping annexation of the West Bank, asked for a freeze on new settlements, and called on Jordan to begin negotiations with Israel. At the same time, the plan opposed the establishment of a Palestinian state and excluded PLO participation in negotiations. American officials expected the PLO to give its blessings to King Hussein to negotiate on behalf of the Palestinians. Begin immediately rejected the plan, stating that it was a threat to the Jewish state. Hussein supported the plan but said that he needed Palestinian and Arab approval to negotiate. Arafat found it inadequate but saw "positive elements" in it.

The Reagan plan was promptly followed by two additional proposals to resolve the Palestinian problem. The Arab League summit at Fez, Morocco, announced an eight-point plan which implicitly recognized Israel's right to exist in peace and security. It also called for the return of Arab territories occupied in 1967 and for the establishment of a Palestinian state, after a UN–supervised transitional period, on the West Bank and Gaza under PLO leadership (*Middle East Economic*

Digest 1982). Arafat supported the plan, despite its rejection by four member groups of the PLO (*Washington Post,* 25 Sept. 1982). The second plan was put forward by Brezhnev, who called for the recognition of Israel and the establishment of a Palestinian state. Arafat proceeded to Amman in late September to explore the Jordanian position, but after a few weeks realized that he needed the authorization of the upcoming PNC session.

Arafat's primary preoccupation at the PNC's sixteenth session in Algiers from 14 to 22 February 1983 was unity not diplomacy. In a closed session, he declared: "It's true that we are being offered nothing of value, but we can't afford to say no to everything. We can't say yes to everything either. So we have to learn to say 'yes, but,' and 'no, but'." The resolutions that followed reflected Arafat's propensity for ambiguity. The Reagan plan was not rejected, but considered inadequate. The Fez and Brezhnev plans were supported, but otherwise ignored. Contacts with progressive and democratic Jews were encouraged, yet contacts with Zionist Israelis were also possible. Egypt was expected to distance itself from Camp David, but dialogue with Mubarak was implicitly allowed. The PNC resolutions, sarcastically called *la'am* ("no-yes") by Palestinians, also gave Arafat permission to resume negotiations with Hussein concerning the creation of a Jordanian-Palestinian confederation under two conditions: the PLO had to be accepted as the sole legitimate representative of the Palestinians, and the Palestinians should have the right to self-determination, including an independent state (Rouleau 1983, 150).

The no-yes resolutions gave Arafat room to maneuver, which is what he did in Amman where he resumed negotiations soon after the conference. Apparently, however, he went well beyond the limits of the resolutions. The protocol agreement he reached with Hussein violated at least three PNC decisions: like the Reagan plan, it excluded the PLO from the projected negotiations with Israel; it did not recognize the Palestinian national right to a sovereign state before joining Jordan; and on the insistence of Hussein, it mentioned the Reagan plan among projects that might lead to a peace settlement. Arafat prudently refused to countersign or initial the agreement until he received the approval of the PLO's Executive Committee and Fatah's Central Committee. Both rejected the protocol, despite Arafat's pleadings and threats to resign. Hussein, feeling betrayed, angrily ended his pursuit of the Reagan peace process on 10 April 1983 (Rouleau 1983, 151).

REBELLION

The rebellion began at a PLO military camp in the Bekaa, Lebanon's eastern valley, in mid-May 1983, when five senior Palestinian officers headed by Col. Abu Musa (Sa'id Musa Mragha) refused to accept the orders of their commander-in-chief, Yasir Arafat. The ostensible cause of this insubordination was the promotion of two officers, Col. Haj Isma'il and Col. Abu Hajim, to command posts in the Bekaa and northern Lebanon, even though neither had much to recommend him except loyalty to Arafat. According to the rebels, Isma'il had abandoned his men in Sidon during the Israeli invasion in June 1982, and Abu Hajim was known more for his high living than for his military prowess (*New York Times,* 5 June 1983).

Arafat rushed back to Lebanon, via Damascus, to put down the rebellion and reassert his authority. He traveled from one pep rally to another in the Bekaa and the Tripoli region, calling on Palestinians to remain united and accusing Lib-

yan Muammar Qaddafi and certain Arab regimes (Syria, his aides said) of foment-
ing dissension. Arafat's past interventions had frequently brought disgruntled Palestinians into line with PLO policy under his direction. But that was in Beirut and
southern Lebanon, not in the Bekaa where political conditions were far less
hospitable.

In the Bekaa, the PLO loyalists faced formidable forces. The territory was
controlled by thirty thousand Syrian soldiers who, in late June, began to back up
the few hundred rebels with tanks and artillery. Syria let fighters of Abu Nidal
(Sabri al-Banna), of the Syrian controlled al-Sa'iqa, led by Issam al-Qadi, and of the
PFLP—GC, led by the pro-Syrian Ahmad Jibril, to set up bases in the region, financed by a reported sum of $6 million from Qaddafi. More crucial, Syria allowed
supply depots in Damascus to fall to the rebels, blocked large shipments of arms
and food to the loyalists, and eventually froze PLO bank accounts (Arafat, Y. 1983).
Finally, the loyalists were left leaderless when Damascus expelled Arafat on 24
June for accusing Assad of inciting the rebellion.

Alarmed and desperate, Arafat traveled throughout the Arab world and
Europe seeking support. He hoped Saudi Arabia could use its financial leverage to
alter Syrian policies, but King Fahd proved too weak for the shrewd Assad. Other
Arabs either were unable or unwilling to intervene. Neither were the Russians inclined to antagonize the Syrians, whose strategic role in the Middle East was far
more useful than that of the weakened PLO, which in addition had recently flirted
with the Reagan plan against Soviet advice. The Russians gave Arafat early verbal
support, but went no further.

The Syrians continued their aid to the rebels, whose ranks grew into
thousands by early September. Arafat made some concessions to the rebels (Kaddoumi 1983b), but the rift was too wide and moreover concerned fundamental issues, most of which had been debated for years.

Criticism of Fatah and Arafat had often generated heated and acrimonious debates in meetings and PNC sessions. However, it was made by loyal critics
in the context of Palestinian democracy. Indeed, democracy was considered an essential principle that, together with the goal of national self-determination and Arafat's adroit leadership, kept the PLO coalition of diverse ideological groups united
for fifteen years. It was precisely the abandonment of this principle by the Bekaa
rebels that threatened the unity of the organization. Splits were of course not new,
but what alarmed the PLO leadership was that the nature of this split contained
the seeds of self-destruction for a number of unprecedented reasons (al-Hut
1983b).

First, the chief target of the violent rebellion was Arafat, the very symbol
of the national movement. Arafat's popularity among the rank and file, often
underestimated by Western "experts," is that of a father figure who has fought for
national rights and for the independence and unity of the PLO (New York Times,
15 Nov. 1983). An attack on his integrity and leadership threatened to damage his
credibility among the masses, reduce his ability as a great unifier within the organization, and diminish his effectiveness as the sole leader of the Palestinians in
Arab and world politics.

Second, it was the most serious rebellion within Fatah, and because Fatah's preponderance in resources, arms, and fighters made it the backbone of the
PLO, the mutiny threatened the disintegration of the organization. The rebels won

over thousands of fighters in the Bekaa, tried to assassinate top Fatah leaders Abu Jihad and Abu 'Iyad, and sought to drive out the rest of the loyalists from Lebanon. In addition, the revolt's military leaders—Col. Sa'id Musa Mragha (Abu Musa), Col. Nimir Salih (Abu Salih), Col. Abu Khalid al-'Amilah, Col. Muhammad Tariq al-Khadra, Col. Muhammad Zahran, Capt. Muhammad Hamdan, and Maj. Yusif Ajuri—were reputable officers who represented a variety of ideological positions found within Fatah, from rightist to Marxist.

Abu Musa was typical of the rebels. He was fifty-six, born in Silwan near Jerusalem, trained in Sandhurst, served in the Jordanian army, and distinguished himself in the 1970 Palestinian-Jordanian conflict and the Lebanese civil war in 1975–76. His military abilities, physical courage, and discipline were tested during the Israeli siege of West Beirut, where he effectively directed the defense of the city against the larger and better equipped forces of the IDF. His performance earned him a promotion after the war to deputy chief of military operations, as well as the command of Fatah's elite Yarmuk Brigade, which was the first army unit to join the mutiny (Rouleau 1983, 142).

Third, the dissension appeared on the eve of the revolt to represent the dissatisfaction of perhaps a majority of Palestinians over the handling of the 1982 war.

Except for the 1948 "disaster," the 1982 war was the most traumatic and catastrophic event in Palestinian history, raising many questions that begged painful reassessments and urgent reform. Why did Arafat and Abu Jihad (Khalil al-Wazir), the chief military commander, transform an elusive guerrilla fighting force into a conventional, stationary army with tank and artillery units, thus becoming sitting ducks for the IDF, which destroyed them and reached Beirut in four days? Why did the leadership not have contingency plans for an invasion force entrapping the PLO in Beirut? Why did the PLO evacuate Beirut, its vital and only military base and political sanctuary, when it could have stopped, or bled, the IDF if it had tried to enter the city? Why did Arafat abandon Palestinian civilians, on the basis of Habib's promises, when few in the movement thought that Habib, like Haig, should be trusted?

What has disturbed many Palestinians is Arafat's attempt, like Jamal 'Abd al-Nasir in 1956, to turn a military defeat into a political victory by declaring that the battle of Beirut was a "major victory" because it generated sympathy for the plight of the Palestinians and increased demands for the resolution of the Palestine problem (New York Times, 3 June 1982). His brother, Fathi, even declared to a subdued audience in Montreal, two months after the massacre, that "we are now in the third stage of Palestinian history since 1948, and it is the stage of victory." A listener reacted by saying that the Palestinians could no longer afford such victories and victors (Arafat, F. 1982.)

Of course, while the PLO's military performance in Beirut was impressive, it was not the PLO but media coverage of the brutal war that generated sympathy for the Palestinians. For the Arafat brothers to mistake such transient sympathy for a political victory was interpreted as either groundless optimism or an attempt to escape responsibility for the "second disaster" and to avoid reforms.

Neither corruption nor Arafat's mishandling of the war and subsequent boasting, however, was the primary cause of the revolt. Corruption was never considered endemic and, with one or two exceptions, it did not reach the top leadership. Also, most Palestinians were sympathetic to the PLO's military plight in the face of greater Israeli forces and blamed Begin, Reagan, and the Arab leaders for the military defeat, evacuation, and massacres far more than they did Arafat.

Causes of the Revolt

The fundamental cause of the revolt, for which the war was the catalyst and Syria the midwife, was the ideological division within Fatah between the purist ideologues and the pragmatic nationalists.

Arafat and his followers had been suspected, since the days of Amman, of playing the politics of compromise, which became obvious after the PLO defeat in Amman in 1970 and Jarash in 1971. Until then, at the core of Palestinian ideology, as expressed in the 1968 PLO charter, were two objectives: liberating Palestine (*Tahrir Filastin*) and establishing a democratic state (*Dawlah Dimuqratiyyah*) through the method of armed struggle (*al-Kifah al-Musallah*). These three concepts dominated until the shock of the 1970–71 defeat in Jordan and the 1973 war resulted in the revision of the political programs. Within Fatah, two trends emerged, one led by Arafat and the other by Abu Khalid al-'Amilah, the ideological leader of the 1983 revolt (PLO source, 14 Jan. 1984).

For Arafat only one thing mattered—Palestinians' self-determination in Palestine. Politics and ideology must be subordinated to this goal. Any method that gets his people closer to this goal should be employed, including soliciting the help of the "reactionary" Saudis, the "atheist" Russians, and the "imperialist" Americans. Military action should be used, not to defeat Israel, but for its nuisance value, to keep the pot boiling, to threaten interests. There must be no peace for Israel until the people of Palestine, are returned and an independent state is established (PLO source, 14 Jan. 1984).

To al-'Amilah and his followers, such "deviationism" threatened the revolution's purity as set forth in the charter. Most of these dissidents were Marxists though nationalist and, above all, militant and confrontational. They believed in the destruction of the "reactionary" Arab regimes, such as Jordan and Saudi Arabia, and in the replacement—therefore the destruction—of Israel with a bi-national democratic state, all of which sounds like the ideology of the Popular Front. In fact, they were closer to Habash's program than to Arafat's. They are said to have maintained personal contacts with Abu Nidal and political dialogues with Habash and Hawatmeh (PLO source, 14 Jan. 1984).

The first setback to al-'Amilah group came on 2 June 1974 when the pragmatists within Fatah and the rest of the PLO were able to dilute the 1968 charter. The PNC passed a resolution accepting a Palestine state on "liberated" territory, which to the delegates implicitly meant the West Bank and Gaza and, therefore, a state alongside Israel. The second major setback came in 1977 when the PNC affirmed the idea of accepting a state on the West Bank and Gaza.

It was clear to al-'Amilah where Arafat was heading, and he was unable to stop him as long as Arafat was popular, had the votes in the PNC and in Fatah, and was militarily secure in West Beirut and south Lebanon.

Once the dissidents found themselves in friendlier territory and Arafat's support seemed vulnerable, they secretly began to plan, shortly after the evacuation, a challenge—not necessarilay an all-out revolt—to Arafat and fellow leaders of Fatah. This was in coordination with Assad and Qaddafi, whom a dissident leader met (Rouleau 1983). None of their activity until November was picked up by Fatah's intelligence services, especially army intelligence, because they had been disrupted by the war and evacuation (PLO source, 14 Jan. 1983).

When information was received in Tunis in early 1983, the leaders of Fatah ignored it. They were accustomed to secret formations within Fatah by disgruntled leftists or rightists. Besides, the leaders doubted that Abu Musa and his comrades would cooperate with Syria, whose policies were antithetical to the dissidents. Syria had accepted UN Resolutions 242 and 338 (both rejected by the PLO), was willing to attend the Geneva Conference, signed with Israel a disengagement agreement mediated by Henry Kissinger, and signed the Fez plan, which implicitly recognized Israel's right to exist (Rouleau 1983, 145). And was it not Abu Musa who fought a bloody battle with the Syrian army which invaded Lebanon to aid the Phalange in 1976 and participated in the massacre of Palestinians at Tal al-Za'tar, and who was bitter when Syria agreed to a cease-fire with Israel only six days after the 1982 invasion, leaving the PLO and the Lebanese National Movement trapped in Beirut by Israeli troops?

The Fatah leaders also ignored two clear warnings from the dissidents and the Syrians. The first came on 27 January 1983 at Fatah's Revolutionary Council held in Aden, where Abu Musa, speaking on behalf of the dissident group, delivered a stinging denunciation of Fatah policy and of Arafat's diplomacy, both of which, he pointed out, were leading to a compromise with Israel in violation of the charter's objective of liberating "all" of Palestine. Generally, he attacked the watering down of the charter by many resolutions, not just the 1974 and 1977 ones. To Abu Musa, as someone who knew him said, the charter, like sacred scripture, was not to be altered. He also criticized Arafat for accepting the Fez plan, for negotiating with King Hussein on the basis of the Reagan plan, and for his contacts with Egypt and with Israeli peaceniks (Rouleau 1983, 143; PLO source, 14 Jan. 1984).

Citing the charter, Abu Musa declared that the "only" method of liberation is "armed struggle." Operations were to be launched in Lebanon, on the Golan, and from Jordan after the Hashimites were overthrown. American interests were to be destroyed and her hegemony ended. Such revolutionary rhetoric was preached to the masses at rallies, not to the hard-headed council leaders who were trying to cope with the consequences of the "second disaster."

The Fatah leaders also ignored Syrian warnings concerning Arafat's diplomacy and moderation. The Syrians were angered by Arafat's peace initiatives during the 1982 war. He supported a peace proposal drawn by three prominent Jews—Nahum Goldmann, Pierre Mendes-France, and Philip Klutznick; accepted a draft resolution to the UN Security Council calling for mutual recognition as a prelude to peace; and committed himself in writing to U.S. Congressman Paul McCloskey to adhere to all the UN resolutions concerning Palestine.

The last commitment caused as much consternation in Damascus as in Jerusalem. An American Jewish leader, who was visiting the Israeli Foreign Ministry, found that almost everyone he met there was anxious about the implication of the statement, for if the PLO recognized Israel, the United States would agree to talk to the PLO and would apply pressure on Israel to negotiate the return of the West Bank and Gaza to Arab control. Months later, a senior PLO representative in the West sent a message, via an Israeli peace activist, stating that the PLO would not even insist on the 1947 UN partition Resolution 181(II), but would recognize Israel's territorial acquisitions in the 1948 war. Arafat also called for an international peace conference. Assad responded by cutting off aid to Fatah and confiscating its Soviet arms.

Arafat continued his peace initiatives after his evacuation from Beirut. He established a dialogue with the Egyptians, sent aides to American officials, and allowed contacts, not just with Israeli peace activists, but even with a leading American Zionist, who was Begin's chief supporter in the United States. The aim of much of this activity was either to ascertain U.S. and Israeli interest in a statement of mutual recognition between the PLO and the Begin government or to explore alternative solutions.

None of these activities was as threatening to the Syrians as Arafat's negotiations with Hussein over the Reagan plan. The plan, based on the Camp David accords, had little to offer to the Syrians. If the Palestinians and the Jordanians, supported by Egypt and Saudi Arabia, signed a separate peace with Israel, the Syrians would find themselves isolated and the only confrontation state facing Israel. Assad could not stop Sadat from signing a separate peace treaty, but he was capable of reining in Arafat.

Syrian warnings came in a series of words and deeds. Ahmad Iskander, the information minister, stated in mid-October after the first round of talks with Jordan, that Arafat did not represent the whole PLO. Then Abu Nidal and Ahmad Jibril were allowed to set up bases in Syria. Abu Salih, a rebel political leader, declared in December that the Palestinians had lost confidence in Arafat because he negotiated with Hussein. This was followed by Abu Musa's criticism of Arafat in Adan in February and by a Damascus meeting of three Syrian-controlled PLO organizations that met to consider leaving the PLO. Finally, 'Isam Sartawi was assassinated by the Syria-based Abu Nidal on 10 April, days before the revolt.

The political interests of the Syrians and the rebels converged on the eve of the rebellion. Syria wanted to make Arafat and the PLO, which had about five thousand soldiers in Syrian-controlled Lebanon and needed a territorial base close to Israel, more manageable if not totally under its control. By controlling PLO policies and actions, Syria could improve its position in any diplomatic initiative from which it hoped to retrieve the occupied territories and maintain its interests in Lebanon. Syria had shown its willingness for a negotiated settlement and the recognition of Israel by accepting UN Security Council Resolution 242 and the Fez plan. The dissidents, on the other hand, were seeking a return to the basic aims and methods of the revolution, which rejected the recognition of Israel. The rebels obviously decided to ignore Syria's diplomatic record and to challenge Arafat's diplomacy by refusing to accept his orders in mid-May 1983. It is possible that they meant to go no further, as they claimed, but that events and the Syrians made the rebellion inevitable.

Arafat had three choices in the summer of 1983. He could accept Syrian and rebel demands that his "autocratic" leadership be replaced by a collective leadership in which the rebels would have half the seats of a reorganized Fatah. Syria and the rebels would then dominate PLO military actions and policies, thus depriving the organization of its independent decision making and Arafat of his freedom to maneuver. Such a concession would set a precedent that the gun, not the vote, determines Palestinian political decisions. On the other hand, the PLO would retain a territorial base in Lebanon and obtain the Syrian-Palestinian strategic cooperation that Habash, Hawatmeh, and such Fatah leaders as the Abu 'Iyad had been seeking (Kaddoumi 1983b).

Another option was to accept a split within the movement, minimize its consequences, and try to reach a compromise with Assad and the rebels that, while constraining the PLO, would leave him with the ability to maneuver. This was the least palatable option to the Syrians and the rebels because they were familiar with Arafat's ability to outwit his opponents. As one of the rebels reportedly said when questioned about a compromise with Arafat: "What do you want? You want me to just sit down and meet him? He'll kiss me, fool me, run me around and we'll have a reconciliation, and that will be it" (Khalidi 1983, 9).

Arafat's Last Stand

Arafat rejected both alternatives. He refused to subordinate PLO independence to the Syrians, and he spurned any meaningful compromise with the rebels. Instead, he confronted the rebels politically and militarily, while offering them minor concessions and trying to put diplomatic pressure on the Syrians to contain the rebellion. This became clear as events unfolded.

When the mutiny began in mid-May, he traveled in the Bekaa, campaigning against the dissidents and calling for unity, but as was pointed out earlier, his personal involvement failed to check the spread of the mutiny. The rebels seized Fatah's arms depots on 26 May in Damascus and attacked his troops in the Bekaa in June, overrunning eight of his bases.

Arafat made some concessions to the rebels on 21 June, when the Fatah's Revolutionary Council agreed to form a special committee to examine charges of corruption and dereliction of duty. In an effort to pacify the rebels on the issue of Arafat's diplomacy, the council declared that the Fez plan should be "bypassed" in favor of a military option. Neither Assad nor Abu Musa, however, were deceived. The following day, Abu Musa demanded a collective leadership, and the day after, the Syrians blocked supplies to the loyal forces of the PLO.

Uncharacteristically, Arafat harshly criticized Assad on 23 June for orchestrating the entire rebellion in order to undermine his leadership and bring the PLO under Syrian control. "The problem," he said, "is not Abu Musa or Abu Saleh. . . . All of them are being used. The problem is clearly and obviously with Syria, just as it was in 1976." He mocked Assad's authoritarian leadership and propensity for winning elections by saying: "I didn't arrive at my position on a tank or through a vote of 99.9 percent. I am here through a democratic action of the Palestinian people" (New York Times, 24 June 1983). Arafat was expelled from Syria the next day.

It appears in retrospect that Syria's support to the rebel attacks on Arafat's bases was a tactical error. Support for Abu Musa made him seem like a Syrian puppet, eager to undermine the PLO while callously shedding Palestinian blood. Support for the rebels quickly eroded, especially on the West Bank where a poll in early July showed that 92 percent still favored Arafat. Even Abu Musa's mother admonished her son. Assad's expulsion of Arafat from Syria, in an attempt to discredit the Palestinian leader among his people, proved costly. Habash called the expulsion an "insult to the entire PLO" (New York Times, 26 June 1983). Many Palestinians agreed.

From late June to mid-September, Arafat lost on the ground and in diplomacy. During the "war of the bases," the loyalists lost one base after another. Arafat tried to galvanize a reaction to Syria, but neither the Arabs nor the Russians were willing or able to apply the necessary pressure. A number of overtures were made to the rebels but they failed to satisfy them (Kaddoumi 1983b).

Having failed to pressure the Syrians, cajole the rebels, or stop the military retreat of his forces, Arafat slipped back into Lebanon by boat on 17 September. It is likely that he intended to establish a territorial base in northern Lebanon, the only hospitable region in the Arab world where he could be independent and close to Israel. Tripoli's 600,000 Lebanese residents were predominantly Sunni Muslims sympathetic to the Palestinians, and the two Palestinian camps near the city, Baddawi and Nahr al-Bared, were under Arafat's control. Some of his supporters and opponents claim that it was a typical Arafat trap: he was challenging both his opponents to attack him so he could discredit them among Palestinians and the rest of the Arab world (al-Ba'th, 11 Jan. 1984). Whatever his motives, his return presented his opponents with an unpleasant choice: either compromise on his terms and allow him a military base outside Syrian control or attack him in order to evict, capture, or kill him.

The Syrians wasted no time. They ordered one thousand remaining Fatah loyalists to leave the Bekaa for northeastern Lebanon. The action virtually eradicated Arafat's military presence in the Bekaa and kept his retreating troops from linking with his forces in northwestern Lebanon. However, most of these fighters made their way to Tripoli before Syrian and rebel forces arrived at the outskirts of the Nahr al-Bared and Baddawi camps, where they began to tighten the noose around Arafat. He in turn responded by calling for a "resumption of the dialogue with Jordan at every level."

Before storming the two Palestinian camps, the rebels indiscriminately shelled them, causing hundreds of deaths among civilians. The violence reminded many Palestinians, including supporters of the rebels, of similar attacks on civilians by the Arab Legion in 1970 and by the IDF in the 1970s and 1982. What the Syrian-backed rebels gained on the battlefield, they lost on the PLO political front, based as it was on popular support within a democratic system.

Disapproval turned into disgust when Arafat was finally trapped in Tripoli. The city was surrounded by two Syrian divisions and thousands of rebels. Arafat had only a few thousand fighters as well as the support of Sa'id Chaban, a Sunni cleric leader of the Islamic Unity Movement, whose six hundred guerrillas were prepared to defend Arafat and his fighters.

Arafat's last stand in Tripoli also evoked in Palestinians the bitter memories of the summer of 1982, when Arafat was trapped in Beirut. It seemed to many that Assad and Abu Musa were finishing what Begin and Sharon had begun—the destruction of the PLO. By the time Israel was pounding Arafat's positions from the sea and Syrian and rebel artillery was shelling him from the ground, the rebels had squandered whatever support they once had. They ceased to be legitimate dissenters seeking reforms and were now perceived as Syrian puppets. They won all the battles, costing Arafat six thousand defected guerrillas, his arms depots, bank accounts in Damascus, and a potential base in Tripoli. But theirs was a Pyrrhic victory.

When, with the help of Arab mediation, Arafat and 4,000 loyalists left on a Greek ship on 20 December, he had emerged with the "state" apparatus under his control. All of Fatah's and the PLO's political institutions had lined up behind him, particularly Fatah's Central Committee and the PLO's Executive Committee.

Not one delegation defected to the rebels during the seven months. The socioeconomic institutions stayed with him.

In addition, Arafat left behind the ideologues who had been the most cantankerous in Fatah. Once discredited, the key rebel leaders were expelled from Fatah. With fewer hard-liners nipping at his heels and with considerable popular support, Arafat resumed his independent diplomacy by visiting Egyptian president Hosni Mubarak in Cairo. The visit defied the remaining hard-liners of Fatah and of the PLO. After a seven-month interruption, Arafat at the end of 1983 seemed ready to resume his diplomacy, despite the potential for new splits within the PLO and the dismal prospects for a Palestine settlement.

REFERENCES

Americans' attitudes toward the Middle East. 1983. *Journal of Palestine Studies* 20, no. 3 (Spring): 135–46.

Arafat, Fathi. 1982. Speech at Association of Arab-American University Graduates Conference, Montreal, 22 October.

Arafat, Yasir. 1983. *al-Ra'y*, 9 November.

al-Ba'th, 11 January 1984.

Fiche du monde arabe. 1979. [Published in Beirut and Cyprus].

Ha'aretz, 23 May 1982.

Hamid, Rashid. 1975. What is the PLO? *Journal of Palestine Studies*, no. 16 (Summer 1975): 90–109.

Hudson, Michael C. 1983. The Palestinians after Lebanon. *Current History* 82 (January): 5–9, 34.

Hussain, Mehmood. 1975. *The Palestine Liberation Organization*. Delhi: University Publishers.

al-Hut, Shafiq. 1983a. Speech to Palestinian-Americans, New York, 2 October.

———. 1983b. Speech at the Palestine Congress, New York, 3 December.

Jerusalem Post. Various issues.

Khalidi, Rashid. 1983. Behind the Fatah rebellion. *MERIP Reports*. 13, no. 9 (November-December): 6–17.

Middle East Economic Digest, 17 September 1982.

Miller, Aaron David. 1983. *The PLO and the politics of survival*. Washington Papers, 99. New York: Praeger.

New York Times. Various issues.

Kaddoumi, Farouk. 1983a. Speech to Palestinian-Americans, New York, 3 October.

——. 1983b. Speech at the Palestine Congress, New York, 3 December.

PLO source. 1984. Source requested anonymity.

Quandt, William B., Fuad Jabber, and Ann Mosely Lesch. 1973. *The politics of Palestinian nationalism*. Berkeley: University of California Press.

al-Watan, 9 November 1983.

Rouleau, Eric. 1983. The future of the PLO. *Foreign Affairs* 62, no. 1 (Fall): 138–56.

Rubenberg, Cheryl A. 1983. The PLO response to the Reagan initiative: The PNC at Algiers, February 1983. *American-Arab Affairs*, no. 4 (Spring): 54–69.

Said, Edward. 1979. *The question of Palestine*. New York: Vintage.

Schiff, Zeev. 1983. The green light. *Foreign Policy*, no. 50 (Spring): 73–85.

Schueftan, Dan. 1983. The PLO after Lebanon. *Jerusalem Quarterly*, no. 28 (Summer): 3–24.

TEAM. 1983. *Summary of the final report on the economic and social situation and potential of the Palestinian Arab people in the region of western Asia*. Presented to United Nations Economic Commission for Western Asia. February.

Washington Post. Various issues.

ADDITIONAL READINGS

Abu-Lughod, Ibrahim, and Egbal Ahmad. "The Invasion of Lebanon." *Race & Class* 24, no. 4 (Spring 1983): 327–500.

al-'Amad, Salwa. "al-'Aqid Abu Musa." *Shu'un Filastiniyyah*, no. 134 (January): 53–69.

al-Banna, Sami. "The Defense of Beirut." *Arab Studies Quarterly* 5, no. 2 (Spring 1983): 105–15.

Chomsky, Noam. *The Fateful Triangle: The United States, Israel and the Palestinians*. Boston: South End Press, 1983.

Cobban, Helena. 1984. *The Palestinian Liberation Organization: People, Power, and Politics*. New Rochelle, N.Y.: Cambridge University Press.

Frangi, Abdullah. *The PLO and Palestine*. London: Zed, 1983.

The Israeli Invasion of Lebanon. Press Profile: June/July 1982. New York: Claremont Research and Publications, 1982.

The Israeli Invasion of Lebanon: Part II. Press Profile: August 1982/May 1983. New York: Claremont Research and Publications, 1983.

Jenkins, Loren. "Palestine, Exiled: A Nation without Borders in a War without End." *Rolling Stone*, 9 June 1983, pp. 29–32, 37, 62–63.

Miller, Aaron David. "Palestinians in the 1980's." *Current History* 83, no. 489 (January 1984): 17–20.

Miller, Aaron David. "The PLO: What Next?" *Washington Quarterly* 6, no. 1 (Winter 1983): 116–25.

Moughrabi, Fouad. "The Palestinians after Lebanon." *Arab Studies Quarterly* 5, no. 3 (Summer 1983): 211–19.

Pipes, Daniel. "How Important Is the PLO?" *Commentary* 75, no. 4 (April 1983): 17–25.

Rubenberg, Cheryl. *The Palestine Liberation Organization: Its Institutional Infrastructure.* Belmont, Mass.: Institute of Arab Studies, 1983.

Said, Edward W. "Palestinians in the Aftermath of Beirut: A Preliminary Stocktaking." *Arab Studies Quarterly* 4, no. 4 (Fall 1982): 301–8.

Stein, Kenneth W. "The PLO after Beirut." *Middle East Review* 15, nos. 3–4 (Spring-Summer 1983): 11–17.

The Soviet Union, Syria, and the Crisis in Lebanon: A Preliminary Analysis

Robert O. Freedman

Analyzing a major international crisis that is still in process is a difficult task at best. Compounding the difficulty in the case of the Lebanese crisis is the fact that there are so many actors, both foreign and domestic, each with different objectives in that long-troubled Arab country. It is for these reasons that the following analysis is only a preliminary one, although it is hoped that it will serve to describe the main thrust of Soviet policy during the Lebanese crisis from the Israeli invasion of June 1982 until the second exodus of PLO leader Yasir Arafat from Lebanon in December 1983.

In order to adequately describe Soviet activity during this period and in particular the interplay of Soviet and Syrian policies, it is first necessary to describe the policies of the two countries in the region prior to the Israeli invasion of Lebanon. This will be done in two parts. First, a brief overview of the policy of each country in the period leading up to the Soviet-Syrian Treaty of October 1980 will be presented. Second, the period from the October 1980 treaty until the June 1982 invasion will be analyzed, since their often tense relationship during this period foreshadowed similar tensions in the subsequent period as Damascus sought to manipulate the U.S.S.R. into support of Syrian objectives in Lebanon and elsewhere in the Middle East, while the Soviet leadership under both Brezhnev and Andropov remained wary of the Syrian moves.

SOVIET POLICY IN THE MIDDLE EAST TO OCTOBER 1980

In order to understand Soviet policy during the Lebanese crisis, it is necessary to deal first with the problem of determining Moscow's goals in the Middle East. Observers of Soviet policy in this oil-rich and strategically located region are generally divided into two schools of thought as to Soviet goals there. Both agree that the Soviet Union wants to be considered a major factor in Middle Eastern affairs if only because of the U.S.S.R.'s propinquity to the region, but they differ on the ultimate Soviet goals in the Middle East. One school of thought sees Soviet Middle East policy as being primarily defensive in nature, that is, as directed toward preventing the region from being used as a base for military attack or political subversion against the U.S.S.R. The other school of thought sees Soviet policy as primarily offensive in nature, as aimed at limiting and ultimately excluding Western influence from the region and replacing it with Soviet influence. It is my opinion that Soviet goals in the Middle East, at least since the mid-1960s, have been primarily offensive in nature; and in the Arab segment of the Middle East, the Soviet Union appears to have been engaged in a zero-sum game competition for influence with the United States. A brief discussion of the tactics and overall strategy employed by Moscow in its quest for Middle Eastern influence will serve as a background for the subsequent analysis of Soviet policy during the Lebanese crisis.[1]

In its efforts to weaken and ultimately eliminate Western influence from the Middle East, particularly from the Arab world, while promoting Soviet influence, the Soviet leadership has employed a number of tactics. First and foremost has been the supply of military aid to its regional clients.[2] Next in importance comes economic aid; the Aswan Dam in Egypt and the Euphrates Dam in Syria are prominent examples of Soviet economic assistance, although each project has had serious problems. In recent years, Moscow has also sought to solidify its influence through the conclusion of long-term friendship and cooperation treaties, such as the ones concluded with Egypt (1971), Iraq (1972), Somalia (1974), Ethiopia (1978), Afghanistan (1978), the Peoples Democratic Republic of Yemen (1979), and Syria (1980), although repudiation of the treaties by Egypt (1976) and Somalia (1977) indicate that this has not been too successful a tactic. Moscow has also attempted to exploit both the lingering memories of Western colonialism and Western threats against Arab oil producers. Still another tactic has been the establishment of party-to-party relations between the Communist Party of the Soviet Union (CPSU) and the ruling parties in a number of one-party states in the Middle East; Moscow has also provided assistance in developing a security apparatus and other elements of political infrastructure to selected states in the region. In addition, the Russians have offered the Arabs diplomatic support at such international forums as the UN and the Geneva Conference on an Arab-Israeli peace settlement. Finally, Moscow has offered the Arabs aid of both a military and diplomatic nature against Israel. That aid has been limited in scope, however, because Moscow continues to support Israel's right to exist both for fear of unduly alienating the United States with whom the Russians desire additional SALT agreements and improved trade relations and because Israel serves as a convenient rallying point for potentially anti-Western forces in the Arab world.[3]

While the U.S.S.R. has used all these tactics to a greater or lesser degree of success over the last two decades, it has also run into serious problems in its quest for influence in the Middle East. The numerous inter-Arab and regional conflicts (Syria-Iraq, North Yemen–South Yemen, Ethiopia-Somalia, Algeria-Morocco, Iran-Iraq, etc.) have usually meant that when the U.S.S.R. has favored one party, it has alienated the other, often driving it over to the West. Second, the existence of Arab Communist parties has proven to be a handicap for the U.S.S.R., as Communist activities have, on occasion, caused a sharp deterioration in relations between Moscow and the country in which the Arab Comunist party has operated.[4] The Communist-supported coup d'état in the Sudan in 1971, Communist efforts to organize cells in the Iraqi army in the mid and late 1970s, and the activities of the Tudeh party in Iran against the Khomeini regime are recent examples of this problem. Third, the wealth that flowed to the Arab world (or at least to its major oil producers) since the quadrupling of oil prices late in 1973 has enabled the Arabs to buy quality technology from the West and Japan, and this has helped weaken the economic bond between the U.S.S.R. and a number of Arab states such as Iraq. Fourth, since 1967 and particularly since the 1973 Arab-Israeli war, Islam has been resurgent throughout the Arab world, and the U.S.S.R., identified in the Arab world with atheism, has been hampered as a result.[5] Finally, the United States, and to a lesser extent France and China, have actively opposed Soviet efforts to achieve predominant influence in the region; this has frequently enabled Middle Eastern states to play the extraregional powers off against one another, thereby preventing any one of them from securing predominant influence.

To overcome these difficulties, Moscow has evolved one overall strategy—the development of an "antiimperialist" bloc of states in the Arab world. In Moscow's view, these states should bury their internecine rivalries and join, along with such political organizations as the Arab Communist parties and the PLO, in a united front against what the U.S.S.R. has called the linchpin of Western imperialism in the Middle East—Israel. Under such circumstances, it is the Soviet hope that the Arab states would then use their collective pressure against Israel's supporters, especially the United States. The ideal scenario for Moscow, and one that Soviet commentators have frequently referred to, was the situation during the 1973 Arab-Israeli war when virtually all the Arab states supported the war effort against Israel, while also imposing an oil embargo against the United States. As is well known, not only did the oil embargo create domestic difficulties for the United States, it caused serious problems in the NATO alliance, a development that was warmly welcomed by Moscow. Unfortunately for the U.S.S.R., however, this antiimperialist Arab unity was created not by Soviet efforts but by the diplomacy of Egyptian President Anwar Sadat; when Sadat changed his policies and turned toward the United States, the antiimperialist Arab unity sought by the U.S.S.R. fell apart. Nonetheless, so long as Soviet leaders think in terms of such Leninist categories of thought as "united fronts" (antiimperialist Arab unity, in Soviet parlance, is merely another way of describing a united front of Arab governmental and nongovernmental forces) and so long as there is a deep underlying psychological drive for unity in the Arab world, Moscow can be expected to continue to pursue this overall strategy as a long-term goal. It is in this context that Soviet policy during the Lebanese crisis can best be understood.

SYRIA'S ROAD TO THE SOVIET-SYRIAN TREATY

While Moscow has sought to rally the Arab world into an antiimperialist front against the West, Syria has primarily viewed Moscow as a supplier of military equipment and diplomatic assistance both to enhance Syria's prestige in the Arab world and to aid Syria in its confrontation with its main regional enemy, Israel, with whom it engaged in war in 1948, 1967, 1973, and 1982 and which still occupies Syrian territory in the Golan Heights. Relations between the U.S.S.R. and Syria became close for the first time in 1966 when a left-wing, Alawi-dominated, Ba'thist government seized power in Damascus. Relations remained close until 1970, although there was a disagreement within the Syrian regime between strongman Salah Jedid and then Defense Minister Hafiz al-Assad on how close to draw to Moscow. When Assad, who favored a more limited relationship, overthrew Jedid in November 1970, a marked cooling of Soviet-Syrian relations took place. Soviet support to Syria during the 1973 war helped to warm relations again, but the

Syrian refusal to attend the Soviet-cosponsored Geneva Peace Conference in December 1973 and the successful shuttle diplomacy of Henry Kissinger, which led both to a separation of forces agreement on the Golan Heights between Israel and Syria and the reestablishment of Syrian-American diplomatic relations, again chilled Soviet-Syrian ties. Yet another change in relations occurred in 1975 when Syria again turned to the U.S.S.R. after the Sinai II agreement, only to clash violently with Moscow the following year when the U.S.S.R. criticized Syria's military intervention in Lebanon and delayed promised shipments of arms.[6]

Interestingly enough, it was to be the Syrian intervention in Lebanon, coupled with Sadat's decision to sign a peace agreement with Israel, that was once again to turn Syria back to Moscow. Assad's decision to intervene in Lebanon on the side of the Christians in the Lebanese civil war was not popular in Syria where the majority Sunni Muslims had long suspected the Alawites, a Shi'i Muslim minority compromising only 11 percent of the population, of "deviationism." In addition, as Islamic fundamentalism began to rise in the Middle East in the aftermath of the 1973 war, the secular, Alawite-dominated Ba'thist regime, already noted for its widespread corruption, came in for increasing criticism. The result was the development of a group that called itself the Muslim Brotherhood and sought to overthrow Assad. This group began terrorist attacks against Alawi officials in Syria.[7] Compounding this domestic problem for Syrian President Assad was a difficult foreign policy situation. On his eastern front was a hostile Iraq (Syria and Iraq had long charged each other with sabotage and attempts to overthrow each other's regimes). On the west, the Syrian army, although under the mandate of the Arab League, was badly bogged down in Lebanon and by the fall of 1978 had changed sides and was aiding the PLO and Muslim forces against the Christians. On the southwest lay an increasingly powerful Israel, now recovered militarily from the 1973 war and led by hard-liner Menachem Begin. Only to the south was there an ally, Jordan, to which Syria had offered a military alliance in 1975 and with whom cooperation had reached the point of joint staff exercises in 1976.

As past history has shown, for Syria to have any hope in a confrontation with Israel, Egyptian participation on the side of Syria was a necessity. Yet Sadat's willingness to sign the Camp David agreements of September 1978 with Israel appeared to take Egypt, the most militarily powerful Arab state, out of the Arab ranks. Consequently, Assad denounced the Camp David agreements, thereby taking a position coinciding with that of the U.S.S.R., which also greeted Camp David with hostility, fearing it to be a major blow against the antiimperialist Arab unity it had long sought.[8]

Moscow was pleased by the fact that not only Syria but most of the rest of the Arab world also opposed Camp David. Although President Carter dispatched a series of administration representatives to try to sell the agreement to such key Arab states as Saudi Arabia (a major financial supporter of Egypt), Jordan (which according to the Camp David agreements was to play a major role in working out the West Bank–Gaza autonomy plan), and Syria, they met with little success. Indeed, only three days after the announcement of the Camp David agreements, the so-called Front of Steadfastness and Confrontation, composed of Syria, Algeria, Libya, South Yemen, and the PLO, met in Damascus. Not only did it condemn Camp David, which it termed illegal, and reaffirm the role of the PLO as the sole representative of the Palestinian people, it also decided on the need to "develop and strengthen friendly relations with the Socialist community led by the

U.S.S.R."[9] Reinforcing Soviet satisfaction with this development, PLO Moscow representative Mohammed Shaer stated that the Front for Steadfastness and Confrontation was "the core of a future broad pan-Arab anti-imperialist front."[10]

Soon after the Steadfastness Front meeting, Assad flew to Moscow for talks with the Soviet leadership, announcing that he was representing not only Syria but the entire Steadfastness Front in its quest for "more military and political support" from the U.S.S.R.[11] While the U.S.S.R. and Syria continued to disagree on Israel's right to exist (this was a central point in the Soviet peace plan which Syria refused to publicly accept), the two sides jointly denounced the Camp David agreements, stating that the PLO had to participate in any future peace talks, and emphasized the importance of the Geneva Peace Conference. This was a Syrian concession since heretofore Damascus had opposed such a meeting. In return, Assad appeared to get the military support he wanted, as the joint communiqué pledged that the U.S.S.R. would "further aid Syria in strengthening its defense potential," and it was specifically stated that "appropriate decisions" on this topic had been adopted.[12]

In addition to gaining further support from Syria and the other members of the rejectionist front for its policies, Moscow could also draw satisfaction from a number of other events in the Arab world that were precipitated by Camp David. Thus Syria and Iraq, which had long been feuding, had a rapprochement, with Syrian President Assad flying to Baghdad to personally work out an improvement in relations. The Syrian-Iraqi conflict had long bedeviled Soviet attempts to create a unified antiimperialist bloc of Arab states, and when Assad announced that he had accepted an invitation to visit Iraq, Moscow may well have seen this as a major step toward the creation of such a bloc. Indeed, Moscow Radio called Assad's visit "an event of truly enormous importance which has considerably strengthened the position of those forces that decisively reject the capitulatory plans for a settlement drawn up at Camp David."[13]

The reconciliation between Syria and Iraq helped set the stage for the Baghdad Arab summit conference (minus Egypt) which convened less than one week after the Syrian president's visit to the Iraqi capital. Not only were the Camp David agreements condemned, with even Saudi Arabia participating in the condemnation (the Saudis may have been influenced, if not intimidated, by the Syrian-Iraqi rapprochement), but Egypt was threatened with loss of Arab economic aid and its status in the Arab League, and a joint PLO–Jordanian commission was established, an event that appeared to foreshadow further cooperation between these two erstwhile enemies.[14]

The Soviet leadership was clearly pleased with the result of the Baghdad summit, with one commentator deeming it "a final blow" to imperialist intentions aimed at dissolving Arab unity and pressuring other Arabs to join Camp David.[15] Indeed, as what the Soviet Union hoped would be an anti–Camp David bloc of Arab states formed, one not limited to just the radicals in the Front of Steadfastness and Confrontation, but also including such conservative Arab states as Saudi Arabia and Kuwait, the Soviet leaders saw their position in the Middle East rapidly improving. Reinforcing this trend was the upheaval in Iran that led to the fall of the pro–U.S. shah and his replacement by the neutralist Ayatollah Khomeini who quickly pulled Iran out of CENTO and ended Iran's military ties to the United States. Indeed, as the Khomeini regime announced its support for the PLO, broke off trade and diplomatic relations with Israel (and with Egypt after it signed the peace treaty with Israel), Moscow may even have entertained the hope that a Khomeini-led Iran might join the antiimperialist front that Moscow viewed as being formed in response to Camp David.[16]

Although Moscow was undoubtedly pleased at the strong Arab response against Camp David, which was repeated in April at a second Arab summit in Baghdad following the signing of the Egyptian-Israeli treaty, its relations with Syria became somewhat strained. The dispute apparently centered on Soviet unwillingness to provide large amounts of sufficiently sophisticated armaments to Damascus. Indeed, less than a month after the first Baghdad summit, the Syrian army chief of staff, General Hikmat Shihabi, reportedly cut short a visit to Moscow after being unsuccessful in receiving the arms he requested (MIG-27s and SAM-9 mobile surface-to-air missiles).[17] From the Soviet perspective, with a SALT agreement with the United States now on the horizon, Moscow had to be cautious lest a too powerfully armed Syria go to war against Israel. In addition, with Syria and Iraq now cooperating, the U.S.S.R. may have felt that the two Arab states could pool their resources against Israel. Finally, Moscow may have hoped to use Syria's post–Camp David dependency on the U.S.S.R. to extract the friendship and cooperation treaty from Assad for which it had long been pressing.

Despite entertaining Soviet foreign minister Gromyko in Damascus at the time of the signing of the Egyptian-Israeli treaty (the two nations denounced the agreement and vowed to "rebuff any attempts to subvert Soviet-Arab friendship"),[18] it appears clear that strains in the Soviet-Syrian relationship over the arms issue continued, and a visit by Assad to Moscow in June was postponed. Assad's quest for additional Soviet arms was made more acute by two developments in the period following the signing of the Egyptian-Israeli peace treaty. On the domestic front, the Muslim Brotherhood was stepping up its attacks against the regime, with the murder on 16 June of thirty-two Alawi cadets an indication of the seriousness of the threat to Assad's Alawi-based regime. At the same time, Syrian-Iraqi relations began to cool because of disagreements over the nature of the proposed unity agreement between the two nations. Then, when Saddam Hussein took full power in Iraq at the end of July 1979 (he replaced Hassan Bakr), the Syrian-Iraqi conflict erupted anew as the new Iraqi president accused Syria of being involved in a plot to overthrow him.[19]

With the Egyptian-Israeli treaty now signed, with Iraq again an enemy, and with the Muslim Brotherhood stepping up its attacks against his regime, Assad was now in a weaker position than ever before. Adding to Assad's sense of isolation was a cooling of Syria's relationship with Jordan, which, undoubtedly to the chagrin of the regime in Damascus, had become increasingly friendly with Iraq, which was granting it large amounts of economic aid. Perhaps in response to these developments which isolated Syria in the Arab world, Assad felt it necessary to demonstrate his willingness to defend the Arab cause by sending up Syrian aircraft to challenge the Israeli planes that were periodically attacking PLO bases in Lebanon. This, of course, may also have been a ploy to demonstrate to Moscow his need for more sophisticated aircraft, since invariably the Syrian jets were shot down by the Israelis. In any case, by the fall of 1979, Syrian dependence on Moscow had increased markedly, and Assad was clearly anxious to improve relations.

For its part, Moscow was also interested in improving ties to Syria. With the rebirth of the Syrian-Iraqi quarrel, Moscow's hopes for the creation of an antiimperialist Arab front had begun to dissipate. It also had to be concerned about

American efforts to expand the Camp David process, as the United States had made a number of gestures to the Palestinians during the summer, a process that culminated in the meeting of American UN ambassador Andrew Young with a PLO representative. At the same time, Iraq was further distancing itself from the U.S.S.R. (its February 1980 Arab charter was to call for the exclusion of both superpowers from the Persian Gulf), and the only close Soviet Arab allies were South Yemen and Libya, countries all the other Arab states distrusted. For these reasons, Moscow was interested in improving relations with Syria, a pivotal Arab state and one important to the Arab world as a whole and also to the Arab-Israeli conflict. As a result, Assad's October 1979 visit to Moscow appears to have been a productive one.

Assad's main quest during his Moscow visit was, of course, weaponry, and he apparently was not to be disappointed in his quest, as the final communiqué released after his visit noted that "appropriate decisions were adopted on strengthening Syria's defense potential." For its part, Moscow obtained Syria's support on the need to strengthen Arab solidarity on an antiimperialist basis and to "rebuff all attempts to undermine Soviet-Arab friendship."[20] On balance, Assad's visit was a successful one (Assad called the talks "among the most successful we have held in recent years"), and the pattern was set for increasingly warm relations between Damascus and Moscow. This process was to accelerate rapidly following Syria's decision to support the Soviet invasion of Afghanistan in January and was to lead to the signing of a friendship and cooperation treaty between the two countries in October 1980.

In the year between the 1979 Assad visit to Moscow and the signing of the Soviet-Syrian treaty, the Middle East positions of both the Soviet Union and Syria sharply deteriorated. The Soviet invasion of Afghanistan created serious problems for Moscow in its relations with the United States (President Carter imposed a partial grain embargo, withdrew the SALT II treaty from Senate consideration and canceled American participation in the Moscow Olympics) and in its relations with the Muslim world. The United States also seized upon the invasion to try to rally the Muslim states of the Middle East (many of whom were suspicious of the United States because of its role in Camp David) against the U.S.S.R. while at the same time stepping up its search for Middle Eastern bases and hastening the deployment of its military forces near the Persian Gulf which Carter pledged to protect.[21] The Soviet invasion also led to a series of condemnations of Moscow both by the Islamic conference and by key states in the Arab world which Moscow had been seeking to win over to its long hoped-for antiimperialist unity.

Indeed, as a result of the invasion, it appeared as if the Arab world had become split into three major groupings. First, there was what might be called the "peace" camp of Egypt, the Sudan, Oman, and Somalia, all of whom were pro-Western (to the point of providing facilities for the U.S. Rapid Deployment Force [RDF]) and also to a greater or lesser degree committed to peace with Israel. On the other extreme was the so-called Front of Steadfastness and Confrontation composed of Libya, the Peoples Democratic Republic of Yemen, Syria, Algeria, and the PLO, who were all, at least on paper, opposed to any kind of peace with Israel and were also following a pro-Soviet line on such issues as the Soviet invasion of Afghanistan. Located between the "peace" camp and the Front of Steadfastness and Confrontation was the rather amorphous group of Arab states that can be called, for want of a better term, the "centrists." These states had indicated a willingness to live in peace with Israel (albeit under very stringent terms) and ran the spectrum from being mildly pro-Western (such as Morocco, Saudi Arabia, and the United Arab Emirates) to being neutralist as in the cases of the Yemen Arab Republic (North Yemen) and Kuwait. Even Iraq, before 1978 among the most hostile Arab states to Israel, moderated its position to that country and could be considered part of the centrist bloc for this reason as well as because of its improved relationship with the United States.

Given this situation, Moscow's goal was to try to move the centrist Arab states back toward the Front of Steadfastness and Confrontation into an antiimperialist bloc, much as had existed immediately after Camp David. On the other hand, the Soviet leadership had to be concerned about a rapprochement between the Egyptian camp and the centrists, since this would leave the pro-Soviet Steadfastness Front in an isolated position in the Arab world with its individual components engaged in their own intra-Arab and regional confrontations (Algeria-Morocco, PDRY–Oman, Libya-Egypt, Syria-Iraq, Syria-Jordan, Syria-Israel, and PLO–Israel), a development that would also exacerbate some internal strains within the Steadfastness Front, especially the conflict between Syrian President Hafiz al-Assad and PLO leader Yasir Arafat.

Although the majority of the Arab world, including both the Egyptian camp and the centrists, condemned the Soviet invasion of Afghanistan, Syria decided to endorse it. Indeed at the end of January 1980, at a time when the Islamic conference was denouncing the Soviet invasion, Assad hosted a visit of Soviet Foreign Minister Andrei Gromyko. Much to Moscow's satisfaction, the Soviet-Syrian communiqué issued after the meeting denounced U.S. efforts to exploit the invasion to weaken the Soviet position in the Middle East:

> Under the cover of an artificially fomented uproar over the events in Iran and Afghanistan, imperialist circles and their accomplices are striving to divert the Arab people's attention away from the struggle to liquidate the consequences of Israeli aggression, and are attempting to create a split in the ranks of the Arab and Muslim countries, drive a wedge between them and their friends—the U.S.S.R.—and subvert the unity and principles of the non-aligned movement. [The U.S.S.R. and Syria] condemn the continuing campaign by imperialist forces, led by the United States, which are displaying a false concern for Islam while simultaneously supporting Israel's seizure of the Holy places in Jerusalem [and] taking an openly hostile position toward the revolution in Iran.
>
> The facts indicate that imperialism has been and continues to be an enemy of all the Muslim countries as a whole and an enemy of Islam.[22]

While Moscow was thereby to obtain some Muslim support for its policies in Afghanistan as well as an Arab ally in its efforts to divert attention from the invasion of Afghanistan to the Arab-Israeli conflict, Syria was also to benefit. Thus, the communiqué also mentioned further Soviet provision of military aid to Syria, and Syria, which had begun to get sophisticated T-72 tanks even before Gromyko's visit,[23] reportedly received sharply increased amounts of Soviet weaponry in the postinvasion period as Moscow sought to bolster its position there.[24]

Although Assad's endorsement of the Soviet invasion of Afghanistan helped to increase the flow of Soviet arms to Syria, his increasingly close tie to Moscow was not noticeably popular domestically where the Muslim Brotherhood, in addition to stepping up its attacks on Alawi officials, had also begun to attack Soviet advisers, two of whom were killed in the city of Hama in January 1980.[25] Nonetheless, Assad pressed ahead with his policy of improving relations with the U.S.S.R. In February 1980, a Ba'thist party conference called for the upgrading of relations with the Soviet Union, a theme that was echoed in the government-controlled Syrian press. In addition, most likely as a gesture to Moscow, Assad also included two members of the pro-Soviet faction of the Syrian Communist party in pro-forma positions in the new government that was formed in January 1980.[26]

In moving even further toward Moscow, Assad's goals seemed clear. Isolated in the Arab world and under fire at home, the Syrian president needed support, particularly because of his continuing confrontation with Israel in Lebanon, part of which Assad was now claiming lay within Syria's air defense umbrella.[27] From the Syrian perspective, the Lebanese situation had become more dangerous in July 1980 when the Christian Phalangists decisively defeated their fellow Christians, the National Liberals, and became the dominant Christian faction in Lebanon, thus depriving Syria of the ability of playing one faction off against the other.[28] Syrian foreign minister 'Abd al-Halim Khaddam made it clear that what Syria wanted was a military balance not just between the Arab world as a whole and Israel but between Syria itself and Israel.[29]

The result of this process was a formal treaty of friendship and cooperation between Moscow and Damascus, something the Soviet leadership had been pressing Assad to agree to for almost a decade. It should be noted, however, that a month before flying to Moscow to conclude the treaty, Assad signed a unity agreement with Libya. Given the mercurial nature of Libyan leader Muammar Qaddafi and the strained relations between him and the Syrian president in the past, Assad's decision to conclude the unity agreement would appear to be primarily an effort to demonstrate to Moscow that Syria was not as isolated as it appeared. In addition, Assad may have also hoped that Libya would be willing to pay for the Soviet arms that Syria needed.[30]

While the Syrian interest in a treaty with Moscow had become increasingly clear, the outbreak of the war between Iran and Iraq in September 1980 had made it imperative for Moscow to conclude the treaty as well. Seeking good relations with both Iran and Iraq, Moscow had no choice but to remain neutral during the war, thus earning the animosity of both sides.[31] Of even greater concern to Moscow was the weakening of its overall Middle Eastern position caused by the war—and a concomitant strengthening of the American position. In the first place, there was a further split in the anti-Sadat forces in the Arab world, as Libya and Syria came out for Iran and Jordan openly backed Iraq. In addition to Iraq breaking diplomatic relations with Syria and Libya, Saudi Arabia broke diplomatic relations with Libya.[32] The result of the war was a major disruption of the antiimperialist Arab unity Moscow had wanted for so long. As *New Times* commentator Alexander Usvatov lamented:

> Fought between two non-aligned countries pursuing anti-imperialist policies, the war is bound to weaken them in the face of intensified imperialist scheming, and sows divisions

and disarray in the world's anti-imperialist front, creating a
serious threat to peace and international security.[33]

In addition to the split in the anti-Sadat front, Moscow feared a major
American gain in the conflict. The emplacement of American AWAC aircraft and
ground radar personnel in Saudi Arabia seemed to demonstrate American willingness to help defend Saudi Arabia and other Arab states in time of need and helped
refute Moscow's charge that the U.S. military buildup in the Indian Ocean was a
threat to the Arab world. Indeed, the AWACS move appeared to reverse the decline
in Saudi-American relations and held out the possibility of a significant improvement in U.S. ties to the oil-rich kingdom.[34] Thus, when Assad journeyed to Moscow in early October 1980, three weeks after the outbreak of the war, both the Soviet Union and Syria were anxious to sign the treaty. Nonetheless, despite the
outward harmony of the visit, there were clearly continuing disagreements as the
final communiqué noted "a thorough and fruitful exchange of opinions" had taken
place in an "atmosphere of mutual understanding"—code words for disagreement.[35] Part of the problem may have lain in open Syrian support for Iran in the
war while, as mentioned above, the U.S.S.R. wanted to remain neutral, although
Moscow may have leaned a bit in the direction of Syria on this point by warmly
praising the Iranian revolution in the joint communiqué. For its part, Syria endorsed the Soviet position on Afghanistan, stressed the need for Soviet participation in all stages of a Middle Eastern settlement and proclaimed Syria's willingness
to "continue to repulse any attempts to undermine Soviet-Arab friendship." As far
as Soviet military assistance was concerned, the joint communiqué merely stated
that "questions of the U.S.S.R. providing further assistance to Syria in strengthening her defense capability were discussed during the talks and relevant decisions
adopted."

The treaty itself was a fairly standard Soviet friendship and cooperation
treaty, unique only in its denunciation of "Zionism as a form of racism" both in the
preamble and in article 3.[36] Moscow, perhaps to maintain Syria's independent image, stated that it would "respect the policy of non-alignment pursued by Syria"
(similar language had been used in the Soviet-Afghan treaty of friendship and cooperation of December 1978).[37] As in other treaties, both sides promised to consult
regularly and to consult immediately in the case of situations jeopardizing the
peace and security of one of the parties, although the Soviet-Syrian treaty went a
bit further by adding the phrase "with a view to coordinating their positions and
to cooperation in order to remove the threat that had arisen."[38] As far as military
cooperation was concerned, article 10 of the treaty merely stated that "the parties
shall continue to develop cooperation in the military field on the basis of appropriate agreements concluded between them in the interest of strengthening their
defense capacity." Essentially, the treaty codified the existing relationship between
the U.S.S.R. and Syria and, in the absence of any secret military clauses, served to
provide a formal foundation for the improved Syrian-Soviet relationship.[39] Thus,
Moscow was assured of a formal presence in the very heart of the Arab world (the
other Soviet friendship and cooperation treaties still in effect with Arab states were
with peripheral Iraq, which, as mentioned above, was moving toward a neutral
position between the superpowers, and South Yemen), while also demonstrating
Soviet support for Syria in the face of its conflicts with surrounding Arab states
and Israel.

Yet, for Moscow, the signing of the treaty with Assad and the provision of additional military aid posed a number of problems. In the first place, Moscow had to be concerned that Assad, beset by internal and external difficulties, might provoke an international crisis either with Israel or with one of his Arab enemies and then drag in the U.S.S.R. Secondly, Assad, who had demonstrated his independence of Moscow on a number of occasions in the past, might do so again, thus complicating Soviet Middle Eastern policy at a time when, because of the Iran-Iraq war, Soviet policy was already in a state of disarray. Indeed, in the crisis with Jordan in late November 1980 and in the Lebanese "missile crisis" with Israel that began in April 1981, Assad was to demonstrate just such an independent turn.

SOVIET-SYRIAN RELATIONS FROM THE TREATY TO THE ISRAELI INVASION OF LEBANON

Moscow's first problem with Syria was to come less than two months after the signing of the Soviet-Syrian treaty. At the end of November 1980, an Arab summit took place in Amman, Jordan. Fearing that the Arab states would condemn it for aiding non-Arab Iran in the war, Syria boycotted the conference and pressured Lebanon and the PLO to do so as well (this was the first summit the PLO had ever missed); Libya, Algeria, and South Yemen, the other members of the Steadfastness Front, also boycotted the meeting. The Syrian-led boycott of the Arab summit was a blow to Moscow's efforts to help rebuild antiimperialist unity in the Arab world. An even more serious problem for Moscow took place in the aftermath of the summit when Syrian forces mobilized on Jordan's border in an effort to pressure King Hussein. Syria claimed that it was mobilizing because King Hussein was providing a base for the Muslim Brotherhood for its attacks on his regime, but it seems more likely that Assad was trying to punish Hussein for hosting the Arab summit, which came out in support of Iraq in the Iran-Iraq war. In any case, Moscow got pulled into the situation because Assad chose the time of a visit by Soviet Politburo member Vasili Kuznetzov, who had come to Damascus to transmit the Soviet-Syrian treaty ratification papers, to stage the crisis. In doing this, Assad clearly tried to demonstrate that Moscow backed him in the crisis. For his part, perhaps to dispel this impression, Kuznetzov in his Damascus speech at the height of the crisis, stressed the Soviet-Syrian treaty's importance in "eliminating hotbeds of dangerous tension in the Near East" and called for the peaceful solution of problems between Arab countries.[40]

In any case, although Saudi Arabia was ultimately to mediate the crisis, the confrontation between Syria and Jordan helped to halt the slow rapprochement between Moscow and Amman (Hussein postponed a planned visit to Moscow) while once again reinforcing American-Jordanian ties that had been strained since Camp David. Indeed, Hussein turned to Washington with a request for arms to counter what he called a Soviet-backed threat to the security of his country.[41] Furthermore, as a result of the Syrian move, Moscow may well have felt that Jordan was more susceptible to American pressure to join the Camp David peace process.[42]

While the Jordanian-Syrian crisis continued to simmer during the winter, Moscow had other problems in the Middle East to be concerned with as well. In January, the American hostages had finally been released from Iran, thus opening the door for an improvement in U.S.–Iranian relations. In addition, a new president, Ronald Reagan, had taken office in Washington, and he had openly proclaimed his desire to build a regional alliance against the Soviet Union composed of Israel and the key states of the Arab world. Although Brezhnev sought to deflect this—and the growth of American power in the proximity of the Persian Gulf—by his call at the 26th Communist Party Congress in Moscow for U.S.–Soviet negotiations and an international conference on the Middle East,[43] his efforts were in vain and the new American secretary of state, Alexander Haig, made a visit to the Middle East in early April in an effort to rally support for the U.S. anti-Soviet plan. Fortunately for Moscow, it quickly became apparent that most of the Arab states were more concerned with what they perceived as the threat from Israel (Saudi Arabia said this explicitly) than the threat from the Soviet Union. In addition, fighting between Christian and Syrian forces had again broken out in Lebanon, and Haig took the opportunity to strongly condemn Syria for its "brutal" actions in that country,[44] a move not calculated to drive a wedge between Damascus and Moscow. Thus Haig's Middle East visit did not prove too productive, and the subsequent escalation of the fighting in Lebanon was to precipitate a crisis from which both the Soviet Union and Syria were to benefit diplomatically.

At the outbreak of the April fighting in Lebanon, in which Syria attacked Phalangist positions in Beirut and near Zahle (the Phalange was seeking to consolidate a communications link between Zahle, a Christian Lebanese city which lay astride a major Syrian communication route into Lebanon, and the Christian positions in northern Lebanon), Syria remained in a state of isolation in the Arab world. In addition, because Saudi Arabia and Kuwait had cut off funds for the Syrian force in Lebanon, Syria's economic position had weakened, a development exacerbated by the continuing domestic unrest in Syria. When Syrian attacks against the Christians near Zahle escalated, Israel responded by shooting down two Syrian helicopters involved in the operation. Syria responded by moving surface-to-air (SAM) missiles across the border into Lebanon opposite Zahle, thus breaking the tacit agreement with Israel made in 1976 whereby Israel would not interfere with the Syrian invasion of Lebanon so long as no SAM missiles were moved into Lebanon and no Syrian forces were sent to south Lebanon. Israeli prime minister Begin responded by saying that if the missiles were not moved back into Syria, Israel would destroy them. The crisis was on.

An examination of the 1981 crisis is instructive in that it demonstrates certain patterns of Soviet and Syrian behavior that were to recur in the far more serious crisis in Lebanon two years later. Thus Assad's decision to move the missiles seems to have caught the U.S.S.R. by surprise (as in the crisis with Jordan, Assad apparently took action without consulting Moscow—despite the Soviet-Syrian treaty), and it was not until more than a week after the crisis began that Moscow made any public comment about it. Indeed, Moscow did not make any public comments about the crisis until after it became clear that other Arab countries, particularly such conservative states as Saudi Arabia and Kuwait, were rallying to Syria's side.[45] Such a development benefited the U.S.S.R. by moving its client out of isolation in the Arab world and held out the possibility of rebuilding the antiimperialist Arab unity that Moscow continued to hope for. An additional benefit flowing to the Soviet Union from the missile crisis was that it served to further weaken the American effort to build an anti-Soviet bloc of Arab states. It also complicated relations between Saudi Arabia, which promised to aid Syria, and the United States, Israel's main supporter, at a time when relations had already become strained over congressional opposition to the AWACS sale to Saudi Arabia. Yet another benefit of the crisis for Soviet diplomacy, albeit a fleeting one, lay in the fact that in the initial stages of the conflict the United States sought Soviet assistance in defusing it,[46] thereby once again demonstrating the importance of the Soviet Union to Middle East peacemaking. Although the United States was not pleased by the subsequent lack of Soviet assistance during the crisis, Brezhnev was to exploit the continuing Syrian-Israeli conflict by calling for an international conference to solve the crisis.

Although once the crisis was underway Moscow sought to exploit it for its own benefit, the Soviet Union faced a number of dangers in the crisis as well. First and foremost was the possibility that a full-scale war between Syria and Israel might erupt, into which Moscow could be drawn. For Moscow, this was not an opportune time for such a war. With Reagan now willing to allow grain sales to the U.S.S.R. and considering the resumption of the stalled SALT talks (a key Soviet priority), any major Middle Eastern war in which Moscow got involved might well reinforce the basically anti-Soviet tendency of the Reagan administration, doom the SALT talks, and possibly reverse Reagan's decision on grain sales. Although Moscow, as well as Damascus, would profit from the extension of the radar-SAM network to Lebanon,[47] it would be far better for Moscow if this could be done without war. So long as war threatened, but did not break out, the Soviet leaders may have felt that the Arabs would rally around Syria, and attention would be focused on the Arab-Israeli conflict—and away from the continuing Soviet ococupation of Afghanistan. A second problem facing Moscow lay in the fact that President Reagan had sent an experienced troubleshooter, Philip Habib, to the Middle East in early May to try to prevent a war. While Moscow and Damascus utilized the respite granted by the Habib mission to strengthen the missile position in Lebanon (Israel was unlikely to strike a blow at the missiles with Habib in the Middle East lest U.S.–Israeli relations be severely damaged), the Soviet leadership showed concern that Habib, in his shuttle diplomacy, might succeed in drawing Damascus away from Moscow, much as Kissinger had done in 1974. For this reason, Moscow bitterly attacked the Habib mission, claiming it was a device to impose Israel's will on Syria and the other Arabs.[48]

In the face of these dangers, Moscow adopted the dual policy of discrediting U.S. mediation efforts while also playing down the possibility of war. This strategy became evident in mid-May as the Soviet ambassador to Lebanon, Alexander Soldatov, on 16 May stated that the developments in Lebanon "are unrelated to the Soviet-Syrian treaty."[49] Soldatov's comments may well have been a response to the article which appeared several days earlier in the Syrian journal al-Ba'th which stated that if Israel attacked the SAM batteries it would risk confronting not only Syria and its Arab supporters but also "the strategic world of Syrian-Soviet Friendship and Cooperation."[50] Then Pravda, in a commentary by Soviet Middle East specialist Pavel Demchenko on 17 May, praised Syria as the main bastion of Arab forces opposed to Camp David and denounced Israel's demand for the removal of the Syrian missiles, which were there for "defensive purposes," as a maneuver worked out by the United States and Israel. Brezhnev himself entered the Middle East commentary with a speech in Tbilisi on 22 May in which he warned of the dangerous situation in the region, blamed Israel and the United States, and called for international talks to solve the crisis in a peaceful manner.[51] This was the theme of his speech at a dinner honoring the visit of King Hussein of Jordan on 27

May in which he also noted that the U.S.S.R. wanted good relations with Israel.[52] Significantly, in neither speech did he mention the Soviet-Syrian treaty.

As the crisis continued, Syria obtained increasing support for its position from the other Arabs as an Arab foreign ministers' conference, called on the initiative of Algeria and the PLO in late May, pledged financial support to Syria (Saudi Arabia and Kuwait, which had cut off funds for the Syrian forces in Lebanon, resumed their contributions), and the Arab states pledged "total" military assistance to Syria in case of an Israeli attack on Syrian forces in Lebanon or Syria.[53] Much to Moscow's satisfaction, the Arab states also warned the United States that continuation of its "unconditional" support to Israel "would lead to a serious confrontation between the Arab nation and the U.S."[54] Soon after this meeting, however, both Jordan and Iraq qualified their support to Syria, while for its part Syria did not even send a delegation to the Baghdad meeting of Islamic foreign ministers called to deal with the Lebanese crisis at the start of June. In any case, Arab inactivity during the Israeli invasion of Lebanon a year later demonstrated that Arab support of Syria was, in the main, merely rhetorical.

The Lebanese crisis was overshadowed in early June as attention was diverted to the Israeli attack on the Iraqi nuclear reactor, an event that kept the Middle East in turmoil until the Israeli elections of 30 June. Following the reelection of Begin's Likud party, Moscow and Syria staged a joint naval landing maneuver in Syria,[55] possibly as a signal to Begin and the Arab world that Moscow continued to stand behind Syria even if it did not actively support its policies in Lebanon.

In reviewing the crisis, three major points stand out. In the first place, whatever the military/political goals of the Syrians in Lebanon, Syria was to manipulate the crisis to demonstrate its role as the leading Arab confrontation state against Israel, thereby gaining Arab support. Second, Syria was to assert that the Soviet-Syrian treaty covered Syria's activities in Lebanon, thereby endeavoring to mobilize Soviet support for its policies in that war-torn country. Finally, for its part, Moscow was to downplay the crisis as it clearly did not wish to get involved in any major conflict in Lebanon. This pattern was to repeat itself two years later as Syria was to try to galvanize both Arab and Soviet support first against Israel and then against the United States.

In the year between the Lebanese missile crisis and the Israeli invasion of Lebanon, there was evident strain in the Soviet-Syrian relationship. As Israel and the United States began to talk about "strategic cooperation," Syria redoubled its efforts to obtain increased military equipment from the U.S.S.R. so as to increase its capability vis-à-vis Israel.[56] For its part, however, the U.S.S.R., perhaps remembering Syria's previous efforts to embroil Moscow in its adventures, appeared reluctant to meet Syrian requests. Thus a military delegation led by Syrian defense minister Mustafa Tlas which visited Moscow in September reportedly did not get all it wanted.[57] Even after Israel annexed the Golan Heights on 13 December (an event that led the United States to suspend the security agreement concluded with Israel two weeks earlier), Moscow did not move to step up its assistance to Damascus although the U.S.S.R. strongly denounced the Israeli move. One of the factors complicating Soviet-Syrian relations during this period was a clash between Assad and the Syrian Communist party which attacked Assad's domestic policies in a front-page article in the party newspaper.[58] In any case, when Syrian foreign minister 'Abd al-Halim Khaddam journeyed to Moscow in January 1982 in an apparent effort to gain increased Soviet support following the Golan annexation, he did not have a great deal of success. In his luncheon speech welcoming Khaddam, Gromyko, while debunking the U.S. suspension of the strategic cooperation agreement, pointedly avoided any specific commitment to Syria, and he reiterated the Soviet commitment to its three-point peace plan which included Israel's right to exist.[59] While Khaddam in his reply stated that "we are convinced that the Soviet Union, the countries of the Socialist commonwealth, and all progressive forces" would support Syria in its struggle,[60] the joint communiqué released upon his departure noted only that "both sides reaffirmed their desire to continue to strengthen cooperation between the Soviet Union and Syria in all fields, including the military field."[61] The fact that the talks took place in what the communiqué described as "an atmosphere of friendship and mutual understanding" indicates that serious disagreements remained between the two countries.

In the aftermath of the Khaddam visit, both Moscow and Damascus were to encounter increasing problems in their Middle East policies. Moscow's hopes for Arab unity on an antiimperialist basis deteriorated further as the Morocco-Algerian confrontation over the Spanish Sahara intensified and Morocco signed a major military agreement with the United States in which it provided transit facilities for the U.S. RDF, in an apparent quid pro quo for increased shipments of military equipment.[62] In addition, Morocco boycotted meetings of the Organization of African Unity, a pan-African organization which Moscow also wanted to see unified on an antiimperialist basis, because some OAU members recognized the Algerian-backed Polisario rebels. In the case of Syria, there was an antiregime uprising by the Muslim Brotherhood in the city of Hama in February in which as many as twelve thousand people are reported to have been killed. Two months later, Syria blocked the Iraqi oil pipeline that ran through Syria, an event that while weakening Iraq exacerbated the Syrian-Iraqi conflict and made Moscow's hopes for an antiimperialist Arab unity dim further. Meanwhile the Lebanese-based PLO, already under heavy Syrian pressure, found itself fighting against Shiite forces in southern Lebanon who were protesting PLO activities in their section of the country. This conflict was of particular worry to Moscow both because the Shiites, as the poorest element in the Lebanese population, were a prime recruiting ground for the Lebanese Communist party and other leftist Lebanese elements who were allied with the PLO, and also because the Shiite militia, Amal, was now also fighting against leftist and Communist forces.[63]

Perhaps the greatest problem for Moscow, however, was the gradual rapprochement between Egypt and the centrist Arabs. Induced in part by the Israeli withdrawal from the last part of the Sinai on 25 April 1982, the rapprochement was accelerated by Iran's success in its war with Iraq as the Iranians took the offensive and threatened Iraqi territory in the late spring. The Iranian advance frightened the Gulf states who turned both to the United States and to Egypt for support. Soon after the outbreak of the Iran-Iraq war, Iraq had become a recipient of Egyptian military equipment and had moderated its position toward Egypt as a result,[64] and now other Gulf states moved in the same direction. In addition, the warm official greetings by Jordan and Morocco to Egypt after the final Israeli Sinai withdrawal also appeared to signal their interest in improved ties with Egypt.[65] In the case of Jordan, there was evidently hope of Egyptian support against Jordan's enemy Syria, while in the case of Morocco, there may have been hope for Egyptian support against Algeria. In any case, by the time of the Israeli invasion of Lebanon, there was movement toward a rapprochement between Egypt and the centrist Arabs. Indeed, a special meeting of the Steadfastness Front took place at the end of May 1982 to try to reverse this trend, as the front proclaimed its opposition to any normalization of relations with Egypt until it renounced Camp David.[66]

In sum, it was a badly disunited Arab world—whose pro-Soviet members were isolated and whose centrist states were gradually moving toward a reconciliation with Egypt—which faced Soviet policymakers on the eve of the Israeli invasion of Lebanon.

THE SOVIET-SYRIAN RELATIONSHIP FROM THE INVASION OF LEBANON UNTIL THE DEPARTURE OF ARAFAT FROM TRIPOLI

Soviet Policy under Brezhnev: June-November 1982

The invasion on 6 June 1982, which had been predicted both by Western and by Soviet commentators, clearly came as no surprise. Israel had long proclaimed its desire to rid itself of the PLO artillery that threatened its northern towns, while the SAM missiles that Syria had emplaced in the Bekaa Valley of Lebanon in April 1981 had also been cited by Israeli spokesmen as targets for destruction. This being the case, it is surprising that there was no contingency planning among Syria, the PLO, and Moscow for an invasion. Although the lack of coordination between Syria and the PLO can perhaps be explained by the conflict between Assad and Arafat, who feared the Syrian leader was trying to take over the PLO, and the lack of contingency planning between Syria and the U.S.S.R. may possibly be explained by Moscow's unwillingness to extend the provisions of the Soviet-Syrian treaty to cover Syrian forces in Lebanon, the lack of Soviet–PLO coordination is somewhat surprising. Perhaps Moscow felt that any Israeli invasion would, because of Western and Arab pressure, be at most a repeat of the limited 1978 Litani operation; perhaps Moscow hoped that the PLO, which had frequently proclaimed its readiness for an Israeli assault (Arafat reportedly made an inspection of PLO military positions on 2 June),[67] could indeed cause so many casualties among the casualty-sensitive Israelis that the invasion would halt after only a few days; or perhaps Moscow simply did not wish to run the risks of too close a military involvement with such a fragmented organization.[68] In any case, the lack of prior consultation became evident in the first three days of the invasion as Israeli forces in a three-pronged operation overran PLO positions in south Lebanon and pushed the PLO back to Beirut.

Indeed, it must have been clear by as early as the end of the first day of the invasion when Israeli forces pushed by Tyre and drove well past the Litani River or at least by the second day when the Israeli army had pushed past Sidon and headed toward Damour that this was not to be a repetition of the Litani operation of 1978 when Israel drove only to the Litani River and never captured Tyre.[69] The PLO forces were unable to withstand the Israeli attack and rapidly fell back toward Beirut. It is not surprising, therefore, that Arafat made appeals to Moscow for aid, via the Soviet ambassador to Lebanon, Alexander Soldatov, on each of the first four days of the Israeli invasion.[70] Although Soldatov was quoted on Beirut radio as saying on 6 June that Moscow "will take all measures inside and outside the Security Council and will also resort to all the means and courses available to it to denounce the aggressors,"[71] the U.S.S.R. was to be rather hesitant in its response to the early stages of the Israeli invasion—a hesitancy that was to be maintained throughout the war. Thus, while *Pravda* noted on 7 June that Syrian president Hafiz al-Assad had promised Arafat that Syria would not let anyone destroy the Palestinian revolution and that "the Syrian people and troops would fight side by side with the Palestinian warriors," Moscow made no mention of its own troops. Instead, the U.S.S.R. emphasized the role of the UN in stopping the invasion by trying to get the UN Security Council to force an Israeli withdrawal. By going to the UN, Moscow avoided the necessity of direct action, although it was to try to obtain propaganda value from the vetoes cast by the United States to protect Israel while also using the Security Council debates to split the United States from its NATO allies who were far more critical of Israel. In addition, the official Tass statement on 8 June, although denouncing the Israeli invasion and emphasizing what it termed American complicity in it, contained only general threats, merely warning that the "adventure" might cost Israel and its people dearly and that Israel's aggression could threaten world peace.[72] The U.S.S.R.'s unwillingness to take further action was reflected in the comments of the PLO representative in Moscow, Mohammed Shaer, who in a press conference on 8 June praised the Tass statement, also noted that the U.S.S.R. would not send troops.[73]

The war heated up further on 9 June as Syria, which despite Assad's pledge to Arafat, was only giving the PLO limited assistance, suddenly found itself involved in a full-scale war with Israel in the Bekaa Valley as Israeli planes destroyed the disputed SAM missile emplacements. A major Israeli-Syrian dogfight ensued with Syria losing scores of planes, and a series of tank battles also took place. The same day, Soviet foreign minister Andrei Gromyko, who was in New York, met with Farouk Kaddoumi, head of the political department of the PLO Executive Committee, and pledged that the U.S.S.R. would invariably support "the just struggle of the Palestinians."[74] At the same time, a delegation of Arab ambassadors from Jordan, Algeria, Kuwait, and Tunisia and the chargé d'affaires of Lebanon visited the Soviet foreign ministry where they met with deputy Foreign Minister Viktor Shukatev.[75] Given the increased intensity of the fighting, it is quite possible that the Arab diplomats, who came from both the Steadfastness and centrists blocs in the Arab world, were calling for more Soviet support against Israel. Indeed, a Kuwaiti broadcast on 10 June went so far as to report that "an extensive Soviet political move was expected within the next twenty-four hours."[76] It is possible that the Arab demand for increased Soviet activity and the escalation of the fighting in Lebanon induced Brezhnev to send a letter to Reagan on 10 June in which the Soviet leader reportedly expressed his concern "that a most serious situation had been created which contained the possibility of wider hostilities."[77] Reagan, however, reportedly responded to the letter by warning of the dangers if outside powers became involved in the war.[78]

The day after the Brezhnev letter, Syria called for a cease-fire. It had lost one-fifth of its air force, its SAM emplacements in Lebanon had been destroyed, and it had incurred heavy losses to its tank forces, including the highly sophisticated T-72. Moscow may have been pleased that the possibility of a wider war was thereby averted. While PLO–Syrian relations were further strained by the fact that Syria agreed to the cease-fire while the PLO was still fighting, one day later, on 12 June, with its forces virtually surrounded in Beirut, the PLO also called for a cease-fire.

With the worst of the fighting apparently now over, Moscow had to decide its next moves. Hitherto the U.S.S.R. had acted in a manner that Secretary of

State Alexander Haig had publicly called "encouragingly cautious."[79] In truth, Moscow's options did not look too promising. In the first place, from a purely military standpoint, there were serious obstacles to any commitment of Soviet troops to the conflict. While in the past decade, the U.S.S.R. had committed its troops and/or those of surrogates like Cuba to Third World conflicts no less than three times (Angola in 1976, Ethiopia in 1978, and Afghanistan in 1979), in each case the opponent was not a significant military power and Moscow had secure bases of operation for its troops. In the case of Lebanon, however, Moscow's opponent would be Israel, a formidable military power, with a first-rate air force, a highly trained army, and the latest in military technology, much of which was supplied by the United States. In addition, given President Ronald Reagan's statement that outside powers should not intervene in the conflict, the Soviet leadership could not be sure that the United States would not actively intervene if Soviet troops entered the fighting. Third, the destruction of Syria's SAM missiles and its most modern tank, the T-72, in battles with the Israelis, along with eighty-five Syrian planes, had to give Moscow pause since these were the same weapons on which the defense of the U.S.S.R. was based and because Soviet military equipment was a prime export commodity earning the U.S.S.R. billions of dollars a year in hard currency.[80] Finally, it should also not be overlooked that the destruction of the SAM system in the Bekaa Valley and, by implication, Israel's ability to similarly destroy the SAMs located in Syrian territory meant that Israel virtually had air supremacy in the region of the fighting—a significant deterrent to any major Soviet operation.

This having been said, there was still a number of things Moscow could have done that it did not do, especially the airlifting of elements of an airborne division to Syria and the dispatch of "volunteers" via Syria to aid the PLO in areas of Lebanon such as Tripoli to which the Israeli army had not yet penetrated. Both moves would have been seen as major deterrents to further Israeli activity and would have been a demonstration to the Arabs as a whole that Moscow was indeed aiding them—and a reinforcement of the position of Moscow's Steadfastness Front allies. Such moves, however, entailed serious risks of involvement in the fighting and the possible escalation into a superpower confrontation as indeed occurred during the 1973 war. In 1973, by actively supplying the Arabs during the fighting and openly threatening armed intervention in the later stage of the war when Israel had successfully gone on the offensive, Moscow had been willing to take such risks.[81] In 1982, even when its strategic power had increased markedly vis-à-vis the United States, Moscow was to prove unwilling to risk an escalation of the fighting. In seeking to explain Soviet behavior, one can point to one major difference between 1973 and 1982. In 1973, the Arabs were united behind Cairo and Damascus in their war effort against Israel and had placed an oil embargo against the United States, and Moscow may well have seen the possibility of a decisive blow being struck against U.S. influence in the region. In 1982, however, the Arabs were so disunited that they proved unable to even call a summit conference to take action against Israel during the war. It must have seemed to Moscow that the bulk of the Arab world, unhappy with Syria because of its backing of Iran in the Iran-Iraq war, were not going to rally behind the Syrian regime of Hafiz al-Assad or, for that matter, behind the PLO which many distrusted.[82] In addition, given the increasingly severe Iranian military threat against Iraq and the Arab Gulf states as a whole, Saudi Arabia and its Gulf Cooperation Council allies were not about to place an oil embargo on the United States to whom they might have to turn for protection against Iran, especially at a time when an oil glut was forcing down prices. Under these circumstances, Moscow evidently decided that if the Arabs were not going to help themselves, Moscow was not going to take any risks to help them.

Nonetheless, as a superpower eager to have a hand in developments throughout the world and especially in the Middle East, a region Soviet leaders frequently remind the world is in "close proximity to the southern borders of the U.S.S.R.," Moscow had to at least give the appearance that it was taking an active role as events developed, particularly since the United States was sending its Middle East troubleshooter Philip Habib to try to peacefully end the Beirut seige. Should Habib's efforts prove successful, this would further enhance U.S. diplomatic credibility in the region while reinforcing the view of the late Egyptian president Anwar Sadat that the United States held "99 percent of the cards in the Arab-Israeli dispute." Moscow, therefore, adopted a two-tiered diplomatic approach. On the one hand, it issued a series of warnings to Israel about the consequences of its actions in Lebanon and sought wherever possible to link the United States to the Israeli invasion so as to discredit American diplomatic efforts to end the Lebanese crisis. On the other hand, it began to appeal openly to the Arabs to unite so as to confront the Israelis. The official Tass statement issued on 14 June echoed both of these themes. Published after the bulk of the fighting had ended (the PLO–Israeli cease-fire came into being on 12 June) Moscow, as it had done in the 1956 Suez conflict, sought to obtain diplomatic credit for taking strong action when the most serious fighting had already died down. Thus, Moscow warned Israel that the Middle East was an area lying in close proximity to the southern borders of the U.S.S.R. and that "developments there cannot help but affect the interests of the U.S.S.R." In addition, using terminology the Soviet leaders may later have regretted, the statement said "the U.S.S.R. takes the Arab side not in words but in deeds." Moscow also blamed the United States for aiding in Israel's "genocide" in Lebanon through its "strategic cooperation" with Israel. Finally the statement publicly deplored Arab disunity and asserted that "in carrying out its plans, Israel is using the fact that a number of Arab countries are virtually observing indifferently the destruction of the Palestinians in Lebanon."[83]

Interestingly enough, however, despite its strong words, there were two major omissions in the Tass statements. Thus, there was no mention of the Soviet-Syrian treaty (Moscow may well have remembered past Syrian efforts to embroil the U.S.S.R. in Lebanon) or of the PLO. These omissions, coupled with the termination of the fighting, indicated that the Soviet statement was essentially just rhetoric.

Nonetheless, Moscow did not totally refrain from military action during this period as the first deputy commander in chief of Soviet air defense forces was sent to Damascus on 13 June in an obvious attempt by Moscow to see what had gone wrong with the Soviet-supplied air defense system. In addition, the Soviet ambassador to Lebanon announced on 15 June that Soviet warships, including a nuclear submarine, were being sent to the eastern Mediterranean and that Moscow was resupplying both the PLO and Syria.[84] Still, Moscow was clearly playing down the possibility of its becoming openly involved in the fighting as a Soviet official, speaking with the *Christian Science Monitor* on 16 June, stated that he thought a wider war between Israel and the Syrians could be avoided because "we, the U.S., Syria and Israel are against it."[85] Similarly, on 18 June, Moscow agreed to a two-month extension of the UN force in Lebanon, despite previous unhappiness with its "ineffectiveness" for allowing Israeli forces to move unimpeded through its territory.[86]

While downplaying the possibility of its military intervention, Moscow stepped up its rhetoric. Moscow Radio Peace and Progress, the most radical of the Soviet broadcast media, which had appealed to the Arabs for an oil embargo on 12 June, three days later denounced "feeble and apathetic Arab countries who do not even raise a finger to halt this ugly crime against Palestine."[87]

While calling for the Arabs to unite against Israel, Moscow was beginning to come in for some serious Arab criticism for its own failure to provide more substantive support for the Arab effort against Israel. Thus, PLO leaders Salah Khalaf (Abu 'Iyad), Naif Hawatmeh, and Farouk Kaddoumi publicly complained about the lack of Soviet aid[88] (Kaddoumi also demanded warnings to the United States),[89] and Libyan leader Muammar Qaddafi openly berated a group of Soviet ambassadors, complaining that Arab friendship with the socialist countries was almost "ready to go up in flames, the way Beirut is going up in flames."[90]

Interestingly enough, however, Syria held aloof from the cascade of Arab criticism against the Soviet Union. Instead, Syrian information minister Ahmad Iskander told a press conference in Damascus that the Soviet Union was a "sincere friend" of Syria which had "helped us defend our lands, wives and children," and he called for a strategic alliance with the Soviet Union.[91] While the Syrians appeared to be using their battle losses against Israel and the Iskander press conference in yet another effort to obtain the strategic alliance with the Soviet Union they had long wanted, Moscow utilized the press conference, which was given prominent coverage by the Soviet news agency, Tass, to demonstrate its continuing importance in Arab affairs and the major role in aiding in Arab defense efforts it had already played.

Nonetheless, Moscow also called upon the Arabs to take a more active role in their own behalf, as a Tass commentary on 1 July by Grigory Vasilyev reminded the Arabs that they had "huge potentialities" that could be used—if intra-Arab differences could be resolved. Vasilyev then openly called for the use of the oil weapon against the United States and also cited the "impressive military potential" possessed by the Arabs.[92] Moscow's continued unwillingness to intervene actively in Lebanon was also made clear to a three-man Arab delegation which visited Moscow on 5 July on behalf of the Arab League. While the delegation met with Gromyko, the *Pravda* report of the talks noted that the discussions had taken place in a "businesslike, friendly atmosphere"—the usual Soviet code words for very limited agreement.[93] This interpretation of the talks was confirmed by Arab diplomats in Moscow who told *Washington Post* correspondent Dusko Doder that Gromyko had ruled out Soviet military involvement in the Lebanese fighting.[94]

Nonetheless, one day after the visit, when word of the possible dispatch of American Marines to Lebanon was made public, Moscow felt compelled to take action. On 8 July, Brezhnev, after calling on Reagan "to do everything in the United States' power to end the bloodshed," openly warned Reagan against sending U.S. troops to Lebanon. As *Pravda* noted:

> In connection with statements to the effect that the U.S. is
> prepared in principle to send a contingent of American troops
> to Lebanon, L.I. Brezhnev warned the U.S. President that if this

actually takes place, the Soviet Union will construct its policy with due regard to this fact.[95]

Soviet propaganda agencies gave extensive coverage to Brezhnev's warning,[96] with an Arabic-language broadcast by Alexandr Timoshkin on 9 July noting that "this warning has aroused widespread comment in the world, especially in the U.S. with which the message is primarily concerned."[97] It is, of course, possible that Moscow had several purposes behind the 8 July warning. At the minimum, it would be both a response to Farouk Kaddoumi's call for the U.S.S.R. to escalate the degree of warning to the United States and a response to the Arab League delegation's visit of 5 July. Moscow may also have hoped that Reagan would respond as former U.S. President Jimmy Carter did when the last major warning on a Middle East trouble spot was issued by the U.S.S.R.—in November 1978. At that time, Brezhnev warned Carter not to get involved in the turmoil that was then gripping Iran. Indeed, in a Persian-language broadcast to Iran on 14 July 1982, Soviet commentator Vera Lebedeva made an explicit comparison between the two warnings.[98] Nonetheless, Reagan was not Carter, and the United States simply shrugged off the warning and continued its diplomatic efforts to solve the Beirut siege—efforts that included the emplacement of U.S. troops as part of a multinational force to ensure the safe departure of the PLO. Then on 13 July, Tunisian president Habib Bourguiba, in whose country a proposed Arab summit to deal with the Israeli invasion of Lebanon was supposed to have taken place, announced its cancelation because of insufficient Arab cooperation.[99] A Tass commentary expressed Moscow's disappointment with this development:

> It is therefore not surprising that the disorder and vacillation,
> the inability of the Arab states to display political will and even
> a minimum degree of unity in the present stage arouses
> profound regret and anxiety amidst the progressive Arab
> public.[100]

The situation took a further negative turn as far as Moscow was concerned with the announcement that the foreign minister of Syria, the leading Steadfastness Front state, and the foreign minister of Saudi Arabia, the leading Arab centrist state, were journeying to Washington for discussions with Reagan. Not only did this development underline the continued centrality of the United States in Middle East diplomacy, Moscow may also have worried that Syria, seeing the changing balance of military and political power in the region, was making a change in its diplomatic orientation. The fact that rumors about a collapse of the Steadfastness Front had already begun to circulate in Arab circles may have heightened Moscow's concern.[101] Nonetheless, the problem before Moscow remained as it had been in the past—how to react. To add to the pressure on the Soviet leadership, PDFLP leader Naif Hawatmeh was again complaining about insufficient Soviet assistance, calling it "incomprehensible" and asserting that "we believe that the Soviet Union should resort to direct pressure, including sending troops in accordance with the Soviet-Syrian pact."[102] Moscow, however, was to react the opposite way and, in addition to not sending troops, began to deescalate its rhetoric. In a series of answers to questions from *Pravda* on 21 July, Brezhnev, perhaps seeing that the United States would not back down from its plan to send troops to Beirut despite Soviet threats, suggested a compromise: the use of a UN force to help in the disengagement of forces in Beirut as a first step toward an Israeli withdrawal from Lebanon. While again stating the U.S.S.R.'s categorical opposition to the dispatch of American troops to Lebanon, the tone of his comments was far milder than his 8 July warning. Thus, Brezhnev noted that "more and more people in Israel itself" were beginning to realize that the invasion of Lebanon was turning into a major political and moral defeat for Israel and that the world was realizing that the best solution to the Palestinian problem was the creation of a Palestinian state. The Soviet leader also repeated "Moscow's call for Arab unity in the present "crucial situation" and again urged the convening of an international conference on the Middle East, with the participation of the PLO, to achieve a Middle East settlement.

Brezhnev's comments of 21 July proved no more efficacious however, than his warning of 8 July and, as the Israelis grew impatient with PLO stalling during the Beirut negotiations, fighting again escalated. By early August, Israel had begun to penetrate West Beirut. At this point, Brezhnev did nothing but issue yet another appeal to Reagan in which the Soviet leader called on the U.S. president to "most urgently use the possibilities at his disposal to prevent the continuing annihilation of the people in Beirut."[103] The Brezhnev appeal again underlined the centrality of the U.S. diplomatic role, and when the Soviet leader on 6 August would do nothing more than send a telegram[104] to Arafat praising the PLO leader's courage as the Israeli pressure increased, Arafat and his colleagues must have realized that neither the U.S.S.R. nor their fellow Arabs would save them. Rejecting a call from Qaddafi to become martyrs, the PLO leaders began to negotiate in earnest for their departure from Beirut. Indeed, two days before the Brezhnev telegram to Arafat, Moscow had hinted that the PLO position in Beirut could no longer be maintained. Thus a *Pravda* editorial on 4 August cited French president François Mitterrand's statement that "even if Israel succeeds in neutralizing the PLO as a military force, this will not change the people's right to have their own country." On 20 August, with the PLO about to leave Beirut, *Pravda* simply noted that the evacuation plan had been approved by the PLO and the Lebanese government and that an international force with units from the United States, Italy, and France would be in place to monitor the evacuation.

Thus, the event that Moscow had long feared and which it had committed some of its prestige to prevent—the emplacement of U.S. troops in Lebanon—had taken place. This diplomatic defeat for Moscow was followed by what it feared would be yet another blow to its waning Middle East position. With the United States now ever more clearly holding the diplomatic initiative in the Arab world following the PLO departure from Beirut, President Reagan on 1 September—the eve of the long-delayed Arab summit—announced his plan for a Middle East peace settlement. In a clear effort to gain centrist Arab support for his plan, Reagan called for a stop to Israeli settlement activity on the West Bank and announced U.S. refusal to accept any Israeli claim to sovereignty over the West Bank. To satisfy the Israelis, Reagan emphasized U.S. concern for Israel's security, asserted that Israel's final borders should not be the pre-1967 war boundaries, called for the unity of Jerusalem and direct Arab-Israeli negotiations, and reaffirmed U.S. opposition to a Palestinian state on the West Bank. In his most controversial statement and one also aimed at obtaining centrist Arab support, Reagan called for a fully autonomous Palestinian entity linked to Jordan. Moscow, while denouncing the Reagan plan—and denigrating Begin's rapid rejection of it—was concerned that the plan might prove attractive in the Arab world. Indeed, *Izvestia* correspondent Vladimir Kudravtzev noted that "judging from press reports 'moderate' and 'pro-Western' Arab regimes find positive elements in the American initiative."[105]

Given this situation, Moscow seemed pleased by the outcome of the Arab summit at Fez, Morocco, which not only indicated that the Arab world had regained a semblance of unity [106] but also that it brought forth a peace plan[107] that, except for its lack of explicit clarity as to Israel's right to exist, was quite close to the long-standing Soviet peace plan.[108] Moscow also was pleased that the Sudanese proposal to formally readmit Egypt to the Arab League was rejected.[109] Nonetheless, the Fez conference did not reject the Reagan plan, thereby leaving it, along with the Fez plan, as one of the solutions the Arabs would consider to resolve the post-Beirut diplomatic situation in the Middle East. With both the Reagan and Fez plans now being considered, Moscow evidently felt that it too had to enter the diplomatic competition, and in a speech on 15 September during the visit of PDRY leader 'Ali Nasser Mohammed, one of Moscow's few remaining Arab allies, Brezhnev announced the Soviet Union's own peace plan.[110] While a number of its points were repetitions of previous Soviet proposals, others seem to have been added to emphasize the similarity between the Fez and Soviet plans. The elements of the Soviet peace plan that repeated earlier Soviet proposals were Moscow's call for the withdrawal of Israeli forces from the Golan Heights, the West Bank, the Gaza Strip, and Lebanon to the lines that existed before the June 1967 war; the establishment of a Palestinian state on the West Bank and Gaza; the right of all states in the region to a secure and independent existence; and the termination of the state of war between Israel and the Arab states. While these points in many ways resembled the Fez plan, except for Moscow's more explicit call for Israel's right to exist and an end to the state of war between Israel and the Arab world, the new elements in the Brezhnev peace plan seemed to be virtually modeled on the Fez plan. Thus, Moscow called for the Palestinian refugees to be given the right to return to their homes or receive compensation for their abandoned property, for the return of East Jerusalem to the Arabs and its incorporation into the Palestinian state with freedom of access for believers to the sacred places of the three religions throughout Jerusalem, and for Security Council guarantees for the final settlement. Brezhnev also took the opportunity to repeat the long-standing Soviet call for an international conference on the Middle East with all interested parties participating, including the PLO, which the Soviet leader again characterized as "the sole legitimate representative of the Arab people of Palestine."

In modeling the Soviet peace plan on Fez, Brezhnev evidently sought to prevent the Arabs from moving to embrace the Reagan plan. Nonetheless, with the United States clearly possessing the diplomatic initiative in the Middle East after the PLO pullout from Beirut, and both Jordan's King Hussein and PLO leader Arafat, along with other Arab leaders, expressing interest in the Reagan plan, Moscow was on the diplomatic defensive. Given this situation, it is not surprising that Brezhnev seized upon the massacres in the Sabra and Shatila refugee camps to point out to Arafat that "if anyone had any illusions that Washington was going to support the Arabs . . . these illusions have now been drowned in streams of blood in the Palestinian camps."[111]

Nonetheless, despite the massacres, Arafat evidently felt that there was value in pursuing the Reagan plan, and he began to meet with his erstwhile enemy,

King Hussein of Jordan, to work out a joint approach to the United States. Such maneuvering infuriated Syria, which sought to use pro-Syrian elements within the PLO to pressure Arafat into abandoning his new policy, a development that further exacerbated relations between Assad and Arafat. In addition, evidently fearing the weakening of the Steadfastness Front and the possibility of the PLO (or at least, of Arafat's followers) defecting from it, Moscow continued to warn the Arabs about what it called U.S. efforts to split the PLO and to draw Jordan and Saudi Arabia into supporting the Reagan plan, which the U.S.S.R. termed a cover for Camp David.

It was at this point in mid-November that Brezhnev passed from the scene. His successor, Yuri Andropov, had the task of rebuilding the Soviet position in the Middle East which had suffered a major blow during the Israeli invasion of Lebanon.

Soviet Policy toward the Lebanese Crisis under Andropov

When Andropov took power in mid-November 1982, he had to face the fact that the Soviet Union's Middle East position had deteriorated in three major areas as a result of the Israeli invasion of Lebanon. In the first place, Soviet credibility had suffered a major blow because its frequent warnings to the United States and Israel during the course of the war had proven to be ineffectual. Second, the quality of Soviet military equipment and, to a lesser degree, the quality of Soviet training had been called into question by the overwhelming victory of U.S.–supplied Israeli weaponry over the military equipment supplied by Moscow to Syria. Finally, Andropov had to deal with a situation in which the United States had the diplomatic initiative in the Middle East. Not only was the Reagan plan—and not the Soviet peace plan—the central factor in Middle East diplomatic discussions, but Arafat and King Hussein had begun to meet regularly and the governments of Israel and Lebanon had begun talks on a Lebanese-Israeli peace accord.

Andropov was to experience the weakened Soviet diplomatic position himself in early December when an Arab delegation, headed by King Hussein, journeyed to Moscow to discuss the Fez plan with the new Soviet leader. Thus, while *Pravda* gave page-one coverage to the talks and to the significance of the Arab delegation's visit, its report that the discussions took place in a "business-like and friendly atmosphere" and that there was "an exchange of opinions" reflected the fact that the Soviet leader was unable to get the Arab leaders to either criticize the Reagan plan or agree to Moscow's proposal for an international conference.[112]

Andropov was to receive additional evidence of Moscow's diminution of influence in the Middle East and the rise of American influence when PLO leader Yasir Arafat journeyed to Moscow in mid-January 1983. Arafat, who had long been a close Soviet ally in the Arab world, now was openly praising some aspects of the Reagan plan and had stated that he was resigned to dealing with the United States as the dominant superpower in the Middle East.[113] As a result, his visit to Moscow revealed a number of major Soviet–PLO differences. Thus, while in the past Arafat had supported Soviet plans for an international conference to solve the Arab-Israeli conflict, now he conceded only that such a conference "might open a road to a settlement."[114] Even more discouraging for Moscow must have been the PLO leader's announced agreement to the establishment of a confederation between Jordan and "an independent Palestinian state after its creation." While Moscow was in favor of the creation of an independent Palestinian state, the fact of its linkage to

Jordan, a centrist state, not only seemed to associate the PLO at least partially with the Reagan plan but also appeared to mean its defection from the Steadfastness Front, which had already been badly weakened by the Israeli invasion. Consequently, the U.S.S.R. expressed only its "understanding" of the PLO position—a diplomatic way of demonstrating its opposition.[115]

Yet another negative development, as far as Moscow was concerned, was a resumption of the momentum for a reconciliation between Egypt and the centrist bloc, which had been temporarily interrupted by the Israeli invasion of Lebanon. Indeed, the visit of Iraqi and U.A.E. military delegations to Cairo in December[116] and the calls by both Arafat and Iraqi deputy prime minister Tariq 'Aziz for Egypt to reenter the Arab world without having to renounce Camp David[117] seemed to signal that the end of Egypt's isolation in the Arab world might soon be at hand. Under these circumstances, the new Soviet leader, although preoccupied with consolidating his power and trying to block the installation of U.S. Pershing II and cruise missiles in Western Europe, evidently felt that Moscow had to move before Soviet influence in the Middle East fell any further.

In an effort to rebuild the Soviet position in the Middle East, Moscow moved both militarily and diplomatically. On the military front, it dispatched several batteries of SAM-5 missiles to Syria—along with the Soviet soldiers to operate and guard them.[118] This Soviet move went far beyond the Soviet resupply effort of tanks and planes to Syria which had been going on since the end of the Israeli-Syrian fighting in 1982. Indeed, by sending Syria a weapons system that had never been deployed outside the U.S.S.R. itself—a system that had the capability of engaging Israel's EC-2 aircraft system which had proven so effective during the Israeli-Syrian air battles in the first week of the Israeli invasion of Lebanon in June—Moscow was demonstrating to the Arab world, and especially to Syria, that it was willing to stand by its allies.[119] Nonetheless, by manning the SAM-5 missiles with Soviet soldiers, Moscow was also signaling that it, not Syria, would determine when the missiles would be fired. Given the fact that both in November 1980 and in April 1981 Assad had tried to involve the U.S.S.R. in his military adventures, this was probably a sensible precaution—especially, as will be shown below, when Assad and other Syrian government officials began to issue bellicose statements several months later. Yet another cautionary element in the dispatch of the missiles was that Moscow never formally announced that its own troops were involved in guarding the missiles, thus enabling the U.S.S.R. to avoid a direct confrontation with Israel (and possibly the United States) should Israel decide to attack the missile sites.

While Moscow was moving to enhance its political position in the Arab world by sending the SAM-5 missiles to Syria, it was also benefiting from developments in the PLO that challenged Arafat's opening to Washington. Indeed, Moscow's interest in preventing a PLO turn to the United States was shared by both Syria and Libya, which actively moved to undermine Arafat's position.[120] The efforts of the anti-Arafat forces were to prove successful as the Palestine National Council, which after a number of postponements finally convened in mid-February in Algiers, formally stated its refusal to consider the Reagan plan "as a sound basis for a just and lasting solution to the Palestine problem and the Arab-Israeli conflict."[121] Needless to say, Moscow was pleased with this development, and *Pravda* correspondent Yuri Vladimirov praised the council's policy document as a reaffirmation of the organization's determination to continue the struggle against imperialism and Zionism.[122]

As sentiment within the PLO hardened against the Reagan plan, King Hussein of Jordan, who on 10 January had stated that he would make his decision about joinging peace talks with Israel by 1 March, began to back away. Indeed, on 19 March, after delaying any official statement, the king indicated during a visit to London that, unless the United States succeeded in getting all of the foreign troops out of Lebanon and got Israel to stop building settlements on the West Bank, the talks could not get started.[123] Under these circumstances, and having linked (perhaps unwisely) progress on a troop withdrawal agreement in Lebanon to the Reagan plan, the United States stepped up its efforts to keep the plan alive. Thus, President Reagan both tied the promised sale to Israel of seventy-five F-16 fighter-bombers to an Israeli agreement to withdraw from Lebanon and promised King Hussein that if Jordan joined the Middle East peace talks, the U.S. would try to bring about a halt to the building of Israeli settlements on the West Bank.[124]

Despite these U.S. actions, by the end of March, it appeared that the Reajgan plan was in deep trouble. On 30 March, speaking at a Palestinian rally in Damascus, Arafat himself rejected the Reagan plan.[125] The Arafat rejection cast a predictable pall on the final round of the Arafat-Hussein talks in Jordan, and it was not surprising that on 10 April King Hussein, claiming that Arafat had reneged on an earlier agreement, stated that Jordan would not enter into the peace negotiations.[126] Hussein's statement was greeted with great relief by Moscow, which had long feared that Jordan would be attracted to the Reagan plan, seen by the Soviet leadership as an extension of Camp David. As Pravda correspondent Pavel Demchenko noted on 13 April:

> The authors of the "Reagan Plan" have especially been counting on Jordan. The government of that country has announced, however, that it would make a final decision only after meetings with the leaders of the Palestine Liberation Organization and would act only in concert with it. And now, after those meetings have ended, Amman has published a statement saying that, as in the past, Jordan will not hold talks on behalf of the Palestinians and refuses to take separate action to establish peace, in the Middle East.
>
> As the New York Times writes, Jordan's answer "killed President Reagan's plan."[127]

Meanwhile, as the Reagan plan faltered, a development that weakened U.S. influence in the Middle East, Moscow was seeking to underscore its improved position in the region by issuing a public warning to Israel not to attack Syria. The Soviet warning, released on 30 March, came after a series of Syrian warnings, yet was limited in nature. Thus while Moscow warned that Israel was "playing with fire" by preparing to attack Syria, it made no mention of the Soviet-Syrian treaty. Indeed, in listing those on Syria's side in the confrontation with Israel, the Soviet statement merely noted "on the side of the Syrian people are Arab patriots, the Socialist countries, and all who cherish the cause of peace, justice and honor." The statement also emphasized the need to settle the Arab-Israeli conflict politically, not through war.[128]

This rather curious Soviet warning can perhaps be understood if one assumes that Moscow did not seriously expect an Israeli attack on Syria. With the more cautious Moshe Arens as Israel's new defense minister and with rising opposition to Israel's presence in Lebanon being felt on the country's domestic political scene, it appeared unlikely that Israel would attack Syria, even to take out the newly installed SAM-5 missiles. Indeed, even the hawkish Israeli chief of staff, Gen. Rafael Eytan, in an interview on Israeli armed forces radio, stated that Israel had no intention of starting a war.[129] If Moscow, therefore, basically assumed that Israel would not go to war, then why the warning? Given the fact that Moscow's credibility in the Arab world had dropped precipitously as a result of the warnings it had issued during the Israeli invasion of Lebanon in the June-July 1982 period—warnings that had been ignored by both Israel and the United States—Moscow possibly saw a chance now to increase its credibility in the region. Thus if Moscow, assuming Israel would not attack Syria, issued a warning to Israel not to attack Syria and Israel then did not attack Syria, Moscow could take credit for the nonattack and could demonstrate to the Arab world that Soviet diplomacy was effective vis-à-vis Israel, at least as a deterrent. If this, in fact, was Moscow's thinking, however, not all the Arabs were to be convinced. Indeed, the Saudi paper al-Riyad expressed a lack of trust in the Soviet warning, noting that the limited value of Soviet statements had been proven during the Israeli invasion of Lebanon, "which dealt a sharp and severe blow to the Kremlin when the Soviet missiles became no more than timber towers in the face of the sophisticated weapons the United States had unconditionally supplied to Israel."[130]

In any case, only three days after the Soviet warning to Israel, Soviet foreign minister Andrei Gromyko, who had recently been promoted to deputy prime minister, held a major press conference in Moscow.[131] While the main emphasis of Gromyko's press conference was on strategic arms issues, he also took the opportunity to make two major points about the Middle East situation. In the first place, in response to a question from a correspondent of the Syrian newspaper al-Ba'th, Gromyko stated that "the Soviet Union is in favor of the withdrawal of all foreign troops from the territory of Lebanon, all of them. Syria is in favor of this."[132] Second, Gromyko noted once again that the U.S.S.R. was in favor of Israel's existing as a state. "We do not share the point of view of extremist Arab circles that Israel should be eliminated. This is an unrealistic and unjust point of view."[133] The thrust of Gromyko's remarks was clear. The Soviet leader, by urging the withdrawal of all foreign troops from Lebanon, including Syrian troops, and reemphasizing the Soviet commitment to Israel's existence, seemed to be telling Syria that despite the provision of SAM-5 missiles, Moscow was not desirous of being dragged into a war in Lebanon on Syria's behalf. If this was indeed the message Gromyko was trying to get across, the rapid pace of Middle Eastern events was soon to pose additional problems for the Soviet strategy. Thus, one week after King Hussein had announced his refusal to enter into peace negotiations, the U.S. embassy in Beirut was blown up by a car-bomb with massive loss of life. Reacting to both events, President Reagan dispatched his secretary of state, George Shultz, to salvage the stalled Israeli-Lebanese talks and regain the momentum for the United States in Middle East diplomacy. As Shultz toured the region and shuttled back and forth between Beirut and Jerusalem, prospects for a Lebanese-Israeli agreement began to improve. Both Moscow and Damascus, for different reasons, wanted to see the Shultz mission fail. The U.S.S.R. did not want to see any more Arab states following in Egypt's footsteps and agreeing to a U.S. plan for Middle East peace. Syria, for its part, had long sought the dominant position in Lebanon and feared that any

Lebanese-Israeli agreement would strengthen the Israeli position in Lebanon at Syria's expense. In addition, Syria also did not wish to see any more Arab states moving to make peace with Israel, since this would leave Syria increasingly isolated among the Arab confrontation states facing Israel. The result was a rise in tension and yet another war scare in which Moscow was to play a role, albeit perhaps a somewhat unwilling one.

Less than a week after King Hussein refused to enter the peace talks, the Syrian government raised its price for a Lebanese troop withdrawal. While as late as March Syria had been willing to have a simultaneous withdrawal of Israeli, Syrian, and PLO forces, on 16 April the Syrian government, strengthened both by its new Soviet weapons and by the Soviet warning to Israel, stated that Syria would not even discuss the withdrawal of its troops from Lebanon until all Israeli troops had left the country.[134] While the United States sought to assuage Syrian opposition in a letter from Reagan to Assad in which the U.S. president indicated that the United States was still pressing for Israeli withdrawal from the Golan Heights,[135] the U.S. ploy was not successful. Indeed, Syria appeared to step up tension by allowing guerrillas to infiltrate Israeli lines to attack Israeli troops while simultaneously accusing the Israeli government of reinforcing its troops in Lebanon's Bekaa Valley and of staging "provocative" military exercises on the Golan Heights.[136] Meanwhile, although Israeli foreign minister Shamir called the Syrian-induced tension "artificial,"[137] Israeli defense minister Arens, concerned about Soviet and Syrian intentions, put Israeli troops on alert and indicated that Israel would not leave Lebanon until Syria did.[138] Syria then stepped up its pressure on 26 April when Syrian forces opened fire on an Israeli bulldozer near the cease-fire line.[139]

Meanwhile, despite the rise in Syrian-Israeli tension, U.S. secretary of state Shultz continued to work for an Israeli-Lebanese troop withdrawal agreement, and on 6 May his efforts were crowned with success as the Israeli government accepted in principle a troop withdrawal agreement that had already been agreed to by Lebanon.[140] The next U.S. goal was to try to gain Arab support for the agreement so as to pressure Syria into also withdrawing its forces from Lebanon. As might be expected, neither Moscow nor Syria was in favor of a rapid Syrian withdrawal. Moscow, although interested in Syria ultimately withdrawing its troops from Lebanon, did not want any precipitate withdrawal in the aftermath of the Israeli-Lebanese agreement lest the United States reap the diplomatic benefit. Syria complained that Israel had gotten too much from the treaty and Damascus Radio asserted that Lebanon had "capitulated to the Israeli aggressor."[141] It was unclear, however, whether Syria opposed the withdrawal of its own troops on principle or whether President Assad was posturing so as to improve his bargaining position vis-à-vis Lebanon (so he could get a better deal than Israel did); vis-à-vis the Arab world (Syria, long isolated because of its support of Iran in the Iran-Iraq war was now openly confronting Israel and should, thereby, merit Arab support); and vis-à-vis the United States (so as to induce the United States to press Israel for a withdrawal from the Golan Heights). Indeed, as the crisis was played out until the end of May with military maneuvers and threats of war (almost all from the Syrians), it appeared as if Assad was enjoying the opportunity to play a major role once again in Middle East events.

While Syria was exploiting the Lebanese situation for its own ends, Moscow was cautiously supporting its Arab ally. Thus on 9 May, three days after Israel had agreed in principle to the accord, the Soviet Union issued an official statement denouncing the agreement, and in a gesture of support for Syria, demanded that "first and foremost" Israeli troops be withdrawn from Lebanon. The statement added, however, that "American and other foreign troops staying in Lebanon also must be withdrawn from it," an oblique reference to Moscow's continuing desire to see Syrian troops leave the country.[142] At the same time, perhaps to enhance the atmosphere of crisis, Soviet dependents were withdrawn from Beirut, although the Soviet ambassador to Lebanon stated that the departure of the dependents had occurred because of the beginning of summer camp in the U.S.S.R.[143] In helping to enhance the atmosphere of crisis, Moscow may also have seen that the situation could be used as a means of once again playing a role in the Middle East peace process after having been kept on the diplomatic sidelines since Sadat's trip to Jerusalem in 1977. Indeed, on 10 May, Shultz openly urged Moscow to use its influence to get Syria to withdraw its troops and stated he might meet Soviet foreign minister Gromyko to discuss the Middle East along with other international issues.[144] Shultz, however, indicated that the United States was not yet ready for an international conference on the Middle East, still a goal of Soviet diplomacy.[145]

Nonetheless, even in giving Syria a limited degree of support, Moscow had to be concerned about the possibility of war erupting, especially as Syria began to issue increasingly bellicose threats—threats that involved Soviet support for Syria in case of war.[146] Thus on 9 May, Syrian foreign minister Khaddam, in an interview, noted that in case war between Israel and Syria broke out, "we believe that the U.S.S.R. will fulfill its commitments in accordance with the [Soviet-Syrian] treaty." The next day, Syrian radio warned that any Israeli attack against Syrian forces anywhere, even in Lebanon, would mean an "unlimited war."[147] The Syrian bellicosity, however, may have overstepped the bounds of propriety insofar as Moscow was concerned. Thus, in a broadcast over Beirut Radio, the Soviet ambassador to Lebanon, Alexander Soldatov, when asked about Khaddam's assertion that Moscow would fully support Syria if war with Israel broke out, replied that "the U.S.S.R. does not reply to such hypothetical questions."[148] Soldatov added that the U.S.S.R. continued to support the withdrawal of all foreign forces from Lebanon. These themes of caution were repeated during the visits of a Soviet delegation to Israel in mid-May to attend ceremonies marking the thirty-eighth anniversary of the defeat of Nazi Germany. One of the leaders of the delegation, the well-known Soviet journalist Igor Belayev took the opportunity to state upon arrival at Ben Gurion Airport that Syria's recent military moves in the Bekaa Valley were purely defensive and that Syria had no aggressive intent toward Israel.[149] Similarly, Karen Khachaturev, deputy director of the Novosti news agency, noted that the U.S.S.R. favored a peace treaty between Israel and Lebanon—but only after all Israeli soldiers departed—and Khachaturev reiterated Moscow's support of Israel's right to live in peace and security.[150]

While Moscow was trying to play down the possibility of war, U.S. secretary of defense Caspar Weinberger, in a speech to the American Jewish Committee in New York, was publicly warning Moscow and Syria about their behavior in Lebanon:

> I want to make it very clear to the Soviets and any proxies they might have in Syria that any aggression by them would be met

by a retaliatory force that would make the aggression totally unworthwhile, totally lacking in any hope of gain to the aggressor.[151]

Although the State Department sought to somewhat tone down Weinberger's remarks several days later, there was no question but that the U.S. commitment to Israel remained strong.[152] Indeed, following Israel's signing of the U.S.–mediated agreement with Lebanon, U.S.–Israeli relations improved markedly and the U.S. government decided to release the seventy-five F-16 fighter-bombers for sale to Israel.

As might be expected, Moscow seized on Weinberger's comments and the end of the F-16 embargo to highlight the Israeli–U.S. relationship and to underline the close relationship between Israel "as an occupier of Arab lands" and the United States.[153] This was part of Moscow's efforts to try to prevent an Arab consensus from building up behind the Israeli-Lebanese accord, and Moscow hailed the statement by Saudi defense minister Prince Sultan Ibn 'Abd al-'Aziz that his country refused to put pressure on Syria on behalf of the United States.[154]

Meanwhile, Syria continued to escalate the political and military pressure to undermine the Israeli-Lebanese agreement. On the political front, it formed an alignment with a group of Lebanese leaders opposed to the agreement, including former Lebanese premier Rashid Karami, former president Suleiman Franjieh, Druze leader Walid Jumblat, and Lebanese Communist party first secretary George Hawi.[155] Given the fact that Franjieh and Jumblat had militias behind them, Assad may have felt that he had sufficient military as well as political support to sabotage the implementation of the agreement, or at least to maintain Syrian influence in Lebanon, should Syrian troops one day be withdrawn.

While moving to strengthen his political position Assad also stepped up the political and military pressure in the Bekaa. After refusing to see U.S. envoy Philip Habib, Assad on 23 May predicted a new war with Israel in which Syria would lose twenty thousand men.[156] Two days later, Syrian planes fired air-to-air missiles against Israeli jets flying over the Bekaa Valley—the first such encounter since the war in 1982.[157] Assad followed this up by conducting military exercises in the Golan and Bekaa, and the danger of war appeared to heighten.[158] Nonetheless, despite a limited countermobilization, Israel kept very cool during the crisis, and for its part Moscow kept a very low profile (although it did send a new aircraft carrier into the Mediterranean), supporting Syria politically but issuing no threats against the United States or Israel and again appealing for a full withdrawal of all forces in Lebanon. In any case, by the end of May, the crisis had subsided and the dangers of a Syrian-Israeli war in Lebanon had been replaced in the headlines by the growing revolt in the PLO against Arafat's leadership.

Assad, who continued to fear a deal between Arafat and King Hussein despite the breakdown of their talks in April, decided by the end of May, when his political position in the Arab world was enhanced because of his confrontation with Israel, to mount a challenge to Arafat from within the Fatah organization. Ironically, Assad had met with Arafat on 3 May as his confrontation with Israel was heating up so that he could demonstrate a modicum of PLO–Syrian cooperation before he further escalated the crisis with Israel.[159]

For his part, a weakened Arafat, under pressure from hard-liners within the PLO and having for the time being broken off his talks with Jordan, had no choice but to meet with Assad. Following the meeting, Arafat's deputy, Khalil al-Wazir, stated that Syria and the PLO had agreed to coordinate their military resources to face "the Israeli buildup and the Israeli threats that have reached their peak" in the Bekaa.[160] Nonetheless, the coordination—if indeed there was any coordination—was short-lived, because two weeks later the revolt against Arafat erupted.

The revolt was led by Abu Musa, a hard-liner who vehemently opposed any settlement with Israel.[161] Abu Musa was also outspoken in his opposition to a Jordanian–PLO negotiating arrangement. Initially, Libya gave even stronger support for the anti-Arafat uprising that took place in the Syrian-controlled Bekaa Valley of Lebanon than did Syria, but it soon became clear that Assad was utilizing the revolt within Fatah to try to bring the PLO under Syrian control once and for all.

The revolt against Arafat underlined the PLO leader's weakened position in the aftermath of the Israeli invasion of Lebanon, which had eliminated his main base of operations. While he was supported by the bulk of Palestinians living outside Syria and Syrian-controlled regions in Lebanon and while both Iraq and Algeria gave him support in the Arab world's diplomatic arena, he had no real power to resist Syria's crackdown against him. Thus, as the summer wore on, the positions of Arafat's supporters in the Bekaa Valley were overrun, and Arafat himself was expelled from Syria. In early August, the Palestine Central Council, meeting in Tunis, called for an "immediate dialogue" to rebuild relations with Syria,[162] but this effort, along with others attempted during the summer, proved to no avail. In early September Arafat, who had once again begun to meet with Jordanian officials, admitted that all attempts at negotiations with Syria had failed.[163]

As the revolt within Fatah developed, Moscow was faced by another of its serious problems of choice. On the one hand, a victory for the Fatah hard-liners would make it even more difficult for Moscow to succeed in promoting its Middle East peace plan. In addition, the very split with Fatah and the fact that Iraq and Algeria, key Arab countries, were backing Arafat against the Syrian-supported opposition further underlined the disunity in the Arab world. This was one more obstacle in the way of the antiimperialist Arab unity Moscow had sought for so long. On the other hand Moscow could not have been too unhappy with the fact that Arafat was being punished for his flirtation with the Reagan plan. In any case, in a showdown between Assad and Arafat, realpolitik impelled Moscow to side with Assad, who in the aftermath of the Israeli invasion of Lebanon was the main Arab state opposing U.S. diplomacy in the Middle East and who had granted to Moscow the use of Syrian naval and air force facilities as well.[164]

Given this situation, about all Moscow could do was to plead for Palestinian unity and PLO cooperation with Syria. Nonetheless, a Radio Peace and Progress Arabic-language broadcast early in the revolt indicated Soviet frustration with the split in Fatah:

> The U.S. exploits the smallest possible chance to weaken the
> PLO or at least split it if its total destruction proves impossible.
> In this context, one cannot ignore the irresponsible statements
> made in some Arab political quarters which help to deepen
> some of the disputes within the PLO. . . . The hasty and
> shortsighted calls in which the ambitions of certain political

quarters in the Arab world are reflected have nothing to do with the real interests of the Palestinian resistance movement and they in fact benefit imperialism.[165]

A series of PLO officials including Salah Khalaf, Naif Hawatmeh, and Farouk Kaddoumi journeyed to Moscow in June and July in an apparent effort to get the U.S.S.R. to intervene, but to no avail. While PLO media frequently reported that the U.S.S.R. was backing Arafat,[166] no public statement of support from Moscow was forthcoming. The most Moscow would do was to denounce the split within the PLO as the Pravda description of Kaddoumi's talks in Moscow noted:

> The Soviet side expressed its firm opinion about the impermissibility of strife and internecine dissension among the Palestinians faced with the Israeli aggressor, for they weaken the forces of the Palestinians and decimate the ranks of the Arabs. Discord within the PLO can and should be overcome by political means, through a dialogue.[167]

The fact that the talks were described as having taken place in an atmosphere of "mutual understanding" once again indicates that the two sides remained far apart, and this may have been the reason that Arafat did not undertake a rumored visit to Moscow after Kaddoumi's trip.[168] About the only positive development Moscow may have seen from the conflict within the PLO was the decision by Naif Hawatmeh's Democratic Front for the Liberation of Palestine and George Habash's Popular Front for the Liberation of Palestine to establish a single military and political leadership, as this was a step, albeit a small one, toward Palestinian unity.[169]

One of the reasons Moscow was standing on the sidelines during the clash between Assad's forces and those of Arafat may have been because the Soviet leadership was concerned that the unpredictable Assad might yet strike a deal with the United States over Lebanon. While Syria indicated that long-time U.S. mediator Philip Habib was persona non grata in Damascus, it did receive U.S. secretary of state George Shultz in July and Habib's replacement, Robert McFarlane, in August for talks about a Syrian troop withdrawal from Lebanon. Assad continued to denounce the 17 May Israeli-Lebanese agreement and to assert that Syria would not pull its forces out of Lebanon unless all Israeli forces left "without any political gains," but he did agree to establish a working group with the United States to consider the restoration of Lebanon's unity and independence.[170] In addition, he helped secure the release of the kidnapped president of the American University of Beirut, David Dodge, who had been abducted in the summer of 1982.[171]

While maintaining contact with the United States, Assad was also strengthening Syria's position in Lebanon. In addition to bringing Arafat's forces in the Bekaa under his control, he was profiting from the growing war-weariness of Israel which was planning a unilateral withdrawal of its forces from the Shuf Mountains and seemed in no mood to go to war to throw the Syrians out of Lebanon. Indeed, on 1 June, Prime Minister Begin had stated that Israel was not preparing to attack Syria,[172] and a week later Israel's deputy foreign minister, Yehuda Ben-Meir, ruled out military action to remove Syrian forces from Lebanon.[173] One month later, Shultz stated that U.S. Marines would not fill any vacuum created by a unilateral withdrawal by Israel in Lebanon.[174] Under these circumstances, Assad was able to fill the vacuum with Syrian-backed forces in large part because of mistakes by the Lebanese government. By July, the Lebanese government of Amin Gemayel had alienated two of the major forces within Lebanon, the Druze and the Shiite. In part because he did not establish an equitable power-sharing system and in part because Phalangist policies in the Shuf Mountains and in Shiite areas of Beirut angered the Druze and Shiite, they entered into an alignment with Syria. Druze leader Walid Jumblat did this explicitly by leading a newly proclaimed National Salvation Front (which also had as members Rashid Karami, a Sunni Muslim, and Suleiman Franjieh, a Christian opponent of Gemayel), while Shiite leader Nabih Berri gave tacit support to the organization.[175]

The strengthening of the Syrian position in Lebanon was, on balance, a plus for Moscow since by the end of August U.S. diplomatic efforts to secure a troop withdrawal agreement from Lebanon had all but collapsed and Moscow was again raising the possibility of a joint U.S.–Soviet effort to bring about a Middle East peace settlement.[176] Yet the situation also had its dangers for Moscow. As Israel stepped up its planning to withdraw its troops from the Shuf Mountains, the possibility that new fighting would erupt became increasingly strong, particularly since no agreement had been reached between the Druze and Gemayel about deploying the Lebanese army in the Shuf to replace the departing Israelis. Exacerbating the situation was the Syrian government statement on 27 August that it would defend its allies against the Lebanese army.[177] The danger for Moscow was that since the United States was backing the Gemayel government, a direct U.S.–Syrian confrontation could occur and then Moscow would again be faced with the problem of how to react to a military conflict in which its principal Arab ally was involved. This time, however, the opponent would most likely not be Israel backed by the United States, but the United States itself. In short, Moscow faced the prospect of a superpower confrontation over Lebanon, but when the crisis did occur, the U.S.S.R. adopted a very cautious policy so as to avoid any direct involvement.

The crisis began at the end of August when warfare broke out between the Lebanese government and the Shiite of western and southern Beirut who resisted a Lebanese army push into their neighborhoods on 30 and 31 August. The scale of fighting escalated sharply, however, after the Israeli redeployment of 3 September with Syrian-supported Druze forces clashing both with the Maronite (Phalange) militia and the Lebanese army. While the Phalangist forces were all but driven from the Shuf Mountains, the Lebanese army proved a tougher opponent for the Druze and a major battle was fought for the strategic mountain town of Suq al-Gharb which overlooks Beirut. Israel held off from intervening both because of pressure from its Druze minority and because of assurances from Druze leader Walid Jumblat that he would not permit the PLO to occupy positions in Druze-controlled areas. The United States, however, decided to play an active role in the fighting in support of the Lebanese army, which it was training. U.S. involvement in the conflict had actually begun before the Israeli withdrawal, for U.S. helicopters had fired on sniper and mortar positions that had harassed the Marines. The U.S. role escalated during the fighting in the Shuf when guns from U.S. warships in Beirut harbor were fired both in support of Lebanese army troops fighting in Suq al-Gharb[178] and against artillery positions that were firing on or near U.S. positions.[179] After holding aloof from the fighting, France also got involved when its forces came under fire.[180] As the fighting escalated, Syria felt constrained to issue threats against the United States so as to back its clients in the Shuf Mountains,[181] particularly when the U.S. battleship *New Jersey*, whose sixteen-inch guns had the capability of seriously damaging Syrian positions, neared Beirut.

As the crisis developed, Moscow reacted very cautiously. A Tass statement published in *Pravda* on 1 September merely noted that the Soviet Union was "deeply concerned" over the U.S. armed intervention in Lebanon. It also called for the end to U.S. intervention, the unconditional withdrawal of Israeli forces from Lebanon, and the withdrawal of U.S. troops and "the foreign troops that arrived with them." Interestingly enough, there were no Soviet threats against the United States, although Moscow may have balanced its lack of activity with the implicit support of Syria's right to remain in Lebanon, because there was no mention of any Syrian withdrawal in the Tass statement—a clear change from earlier Soviet policy.

The rapid escalation of the crisis, however, posed both problems and opportunities for the U.S.S.R. On the one hand, Moscow seized on the U.S. involvement in the fighting to discredit American policy in the Middle East by asserting that the United States was now directly fighting the Arabs. Vladimir Kudravtzev, one of *Izvestia*'s more colorful commentators, emphasized this Soviet propaganda line with the statement, "By shedding the blood of Arab patriots, the United States has de facto declared war on the Arabs."[182] In addition, Soviet commentators also utilized the intervention to discredit the U.S. RDF, whose forces it claimed were fighting in Lebanon.[183] Moscow also sought to exploit the Lebanese fighting to divert attention from its shooting down of a Korean airliner in early September. Nonetheless, as American participation in the fighting grew, Moscow faced the dilemma of whether it should get directly involved, particularly as Syrian positions came under American fire. The Soviet press noted the escalation of the fighting and also noted Syria's warning to the United States that it would fire back if fired upon, perhaps to prepare the Soviet public for a heightened crisis.[184] Nonetheless, on 20 September, the day after *Pravda* published the Syrian warning, the same Soviet newspaper published a Tass statement that carefully avoided any hint of Soviet involvement in the fighting. While it accused the United States of trying to intimidate Syria, and of seeking to establish its own hegemony in the Middle East, it issued no warning to the United States other than to state that Washington could not "evade responsibility" for the consequences of the escalated fighting.[185] To be sure, Moscow did not deny reports in the Kuwaiti press that the U.S.S.R. had placed its forces in the southern part of the U.S.S.R. on alert and that a joint Soviet-Syrian operations room was monitoring the situation in Lebanon.[186] In addition, Moscow rejected a U.S. offer to cooperate in limiting Syrian participation in the conflict.[187] Nonetheless, Moscow refused to formally offer military support to Syria; nor did it react to statements by Syrian officials that Damascus might turn to the U.S.S.R. for help.[188] It also ignored the leftist Lebanese newspaper *al-Safir*'s report that Assad had made a secret trip to Moscow in mid-September.[189] Perhaps most important of all, during the crisis Moscow failed to publicly mention the Soviet-Syrian treaty. In sum, Soviet behavior during the crisis was very cautious indeed, and it is not surprising that Moscow, which feared a superpower confrontation over Lebanon—an area of only tertiary interest to the U.S.S.R.—warmly welcomed the cease-fire that ended the crisis.[190]

In looking at the September 1983 crisis, it is clear that it differed substantially from the one four months earlier. In May, Assad had been basically in control of the situation and he maneuvered accordingly. Since that crisis was essentially a *political* one, over the Israeli-Lebanese treaty, Syrian mobilizations and threats of war were essentially political acts, unlikely to get out of control. In September, the crisis was essentially a military one that escalated rapidly. Under these circumstances, it is not surprising that the U.S.S.R. refrained from giving Syria overt support during the crisis; nor did Syria complain publicly about a lack of Soviet aid (thus repeating the strategy it followed during the Israeli invasion of June 1982), although Damascus could not have been too happy with the lack of Soviet support. Syria expressed its anger more openly against its fellow Arabs, intimating that whatever the position of the Arab governments, the Arab masses supported Syria.[191] The lack of Soviet and Arab support, coupled with the U.S. Congress's agreement to extend the stay of U.S. Marines in Beirut for an additional eighteen months and the arrival near Beirut of the U.S. battleship *New Jersey* seem to have persuaded Assad that at least a temporary compromise was in order, and he agreed to a Saudi-mediated cease-fire plan that held out the possibility of a new distribution of power in Lebanon.[192] No sooner had the cease-fire been achieved, however, than Assad moved to strengthen Syria's position in Lebanon further by expelling the remaining troops loyal to Arafat from the Bekaa Valley and forcing them to go over the mountains to Tripoli where Arafat had suddenly appeared in mid-September.

In the aftermath of the cease-fire, the Soviet Union adopted what, on the surface, appeared to be a contradictory policy toward Syria. On the one hand, perhaps to assuage Syrian unhappiness at the lack of support during its confrontation with the United States in September, Moscow dispatched to Syria modern SS-21 ground-to-ground missiles with a range of seventy miles—long enough to strike deep into Israel and with greater accuracy than the previously supplied SCUD or Frog missiles.[193] On the other hand, perhaps out of concern that if the Lebanese cease-fire should break down, Syria might become involved in a major confrontation with the United States, Moscow downplayed its military relationship to Syria. With Andropov ill, a major Soviet campaign to prevent the deployment of U.S. Pershing II and cruise missiles underway in Western Europe, and Moscow still trying to overcome the negative effects of the Korean airliner incident, the time was not opportune for the U.S.S.R. to become involved in a Middle Eastern war. Thus, Soviet treatment of the third anniversary of the Soviet-Syrian treaty was kept in very low key as far as Soviet military aid was concerned. A *New Times* article commemorating the treaty, for example, emphasized that Soviet aid had enabled Syria to enhance its defense potential and that the Syrian leaders had themselves repeatedly stressed that they possessed the means to repulse an aggressor.[194] Similarly, a *Pravda* commentatory by Yuri Glukhov on 8 October cited the Syrian prime minister's statement that Syria relies on its own efforts first and only then on the assistance of its friends. Perhaps to reinforce the point that the first friends Syria should look to for help were its fellow Arabs, an Arabic-language broadcast commemorating the tenth anniversary of the 1973 Arab-Israeli war asserted that the effectiveness of aid from the socialist countries would be increased manyfold if the Arab states themselves united to fight the aggressor.[195]

Moscow's low-key approach to the simmering Lebanese conflict was jarred by the blowing up of the U.S. Marine headquarters in Beirut on 24 October and subsequent American accusations that Syria was at least indirectly responsible. While *Pravda* senior Middle East correspondent Pavel Demchenko attributed the explosion to the work of "Lebanese patriots" and asserted that it was the direct result of Reagan's "adventurist policy,"[196] the deputy director of the CPSU International Department, Vadim Zagladin, in a *Le monde* interview on 25 October tried to play down the possibility of a Syrian–U.S. confrontation, calling the Beirut attack a "tragedy" and emphasizing that Soviet aid to Syria was defensive and that Moscow had always told the Syrians that it was in favor of a peaceful solution to the Middle East conflict.[197] Zagladin, however, also utilized the interview to emphasize, in light of the explosion, that Soviet participation in a Middle East peace settlement would be useful.

Soviet commentary on U.S. policy in Lebanon became more shrill, however, after the United States invaded Grenada, with the Soviet media warning that such moderate Arab states as Saudi Arabia, Morocco, and even Oman might be next.[198] Meanwhile, as threats of retaliation for the destruction of the Marine headquarters were repeated and the United States began flying reconnaissance missions over Syrian lines in Lebanon, the possibility of a Syrian–U.S. clash grew stronger. At this point, as if to disassociate Moscow from the possibility of intervening, a major Arabic-language broadcast minimized the Soviet military presence in Syria, repeating the now-familiar Soviet practice of citing Syrian statements that "Syria has enough means at its disposal to defend itself." In addition, the broadcast asserted that "there is no Soviet military presence in Syria at all, only experts helping Syria bolster its defense capability" and that Syria has "repeatedly replied vehemently to the lie of the alleged Soviet military presence on its soil."[199]

Nonetheless, as tension rose in Lebanon, Moscow evidently felt constrained to issue another warning to the United States, if only to show its support of the "progressive" Lebanese forces that were backed by Syria. Thus on 4 November a Soviet government Tass statement, citing remarks by Reagan, Weinberger, and Shultz that the United States was planning a "massive strike against Lebanese national patriotic forces," warned the United States "with all seriousness" about taking such action.[200] As in the case of the warning of 30 March to Israel, the Soviet warning of 4 November was very limited. Not only was there no mention of Syria, let alone the Soviet-Syrian treaty, but there was not even the usual Soviet statement that the Middle East lay close to the southern borders of the U.S.S.R. While *Pravda* commentator Pavel Demchenko two days later mentioned specifically that the United States was preparing "an act of retribution against Syria," he omitted any Soviet warning to the United States and also failed to mention the Soviet-Syrian treaty.[201]

Whereas Moscow was seeking to limit its involvement in the period of rising tensions, Assad was exploiting the possibility of an escalated U.S.–Syrian confrontation to crack down on the last redoubt of Arafat's supporters, the refugee camps north of Tripoli. At the same time, it was announced that Syrian foreign minister 'Abd al-Khaddam would shortly visit the Soviet Union.[202] It is not known whether the Khaddam visit was at the initiative of Moscow, which was unhappy at Assad's crackdown on Arafat's forces, or of Damascus. Whoever initiated it, it was clearly Damascus that was to exploit the atmosphere surrounding the visit. Thus, despite American and Israeli statements that they were not going to attack Syria, Assad mobilized his army on 8 November.[203] Although Moscow noted the Syrian mobilization in an Arabic-language broadcast on 9 November and also stated that Syria was exerting its additional defense efforts with the help of the U.S.S.R. on the basis of their bilateral treaty, the broadcast also stated that "the substance of this treaty is very well known."[204] The purpose of this qualification to the treaty may well have been to remind the Arabs that the treaty did not cover

Syrian activities in Lebanon. Indeed, the latter part of the broadcast was devoted to a call for the Arabs to strengthen their unity and act collectively in the face of the U.S. threat. Interestingly enough, in a possible backhand slap at Syria, the broadcast also noted Soviet support "for the efforts of some Arab states aimed at healing the rift in the ranks of the Palestinian resistance movement and at consolidating the ranks of the Arabs."

While Moscow was urging the Arabs to unite on an antiimperialist basis, Assad appeared to be painting his Soviet allies into a corner in which they had no choice but to support him, regardless of what he did to Arafat's forces. Thus, on the eve of Khaddam's visit to the U.S.S.R. Syrian forces opened fire on four American reconnaissance planes.[205] At the same time, the Syrian ambassador to Britain was stating in a television interview that a conflict caused by U.S. "aggression" against Syria would not be confined to one area, but would be "large scale because of the help which we are supposed to get from our brothers and friends."[206]

Thus, Syrian foreign minister Khaddam flew on to Moscow in the midst of a crisis which, like the one in May, seemed to have been orchestrated by Assad who at this critical moment, however, suddenly became seriously ill. For its part, Moscow could not have been too pleased either with Syrian claims to Soviet aid in a widened conflict or to Syria's crackdown on Arafat's forces in the Tripoli area, since Moscow still appeared to wish to see Arafat and the PLO as independent actors in the Middle East who would need Soviet support rather than as a dependent element of the Syrian army. Gromyko's luncheon speech to Khaddam made this point very clear:

> We regard as highly important and urgent the need for
> overcoming strife and restoring unity within the ranks of the
> liberation movement of the Arab people of Palestine which
> must remain an active and effective factor of the anti-
> Imperialist struggle in the Middle East.[207]

Gromyko also pointedly called for increased Arab unity, stating "the fact is that the enemies of the Arabs seek, in no small measure, to rely on their aggressive policy precisely on their disunity." While Gromyko also condemned U.S. and Israeli threats against the Lebanese National Patriotic Forces and Syria, he refrained from mentioning the Soviet-Syrian treaty. Khaddam, in his return speech, totally ignored the Palestinian issue while mentioning, in a segment of his speech ignored by *Pravda* but reported by Damascus Radio, that Soviet support "helped Syria in its steadfastness" and "enabled it to confront aggression."[208] Khaddam did, however, state Syrian aims in Lebanon that seemed to coincide with those of the Soviet Union: the renunciation of the 17 May agreement, the full withdrawal of Israeli and multinational forces, and the achievement of national unity and the restoration of security in Lebanon. The joint communiqué issued at the conclusion of the talks reflected the clearly differing viewpoints of the two sides as it reported an exchange of opinions—the usual Soviet code words for disagreement—"regarding the U.S. and Israeli threats against Syria and the danger of aggression against Syria in this connection."[209]

Moscow did, however, give a general statement of support for Syria against "the intrigues of imperialism and Zionism," and "confirmed its adherence" to its commitments under the Soviet-Syrian treaty.

If Moscow felt that it had succeeded in getting Syria to moderate its pressure on Arafat as a result of the Khaddam visit to Moscow, this proved not to be the case. Indeed, soon after Khaddam's return to Damascus, Syrian-backed troops stepped up their attacks on Arafat's forces and drove them out of the two Palestinian refugee camps north of Tripoli into the city itself. It is possible that Assad felt able to withstand Soviet pressure because at the same time his forces were fighting Arafat's followers near Tripoli, U.S. National Security Adviser Robert McFarlane was warning Syria that the United States would retaliate if Syria continued to fire on U.S. reconnaissance planes (he specifically reminded Damascus of what the United States had done in Grenada).[210] Moreover, French and Israeli planes were attacking purported terrorist bases in parts of Lebanon under Syrian control.[211] Indeed, at the height of the fighting in Tripoli, Syrian defense minister Mustafa Tlas was threatening suicide attacks against U.S. warships and proclaiming that the U.S.S.R. would never allow Syria to be defeated.[212] At the same time, Assad, in a Syrian television broadcast of his interview with the American columnists Evans and Novak, was stressing the possibility of a Soviet-American confrontation if a new war broke out.[213]

As the twin Lebanese crises escalated, Moscow increased its rhetorical activity. An article by Demchenko in *Pravda* on 17 November, citing McFarlane's comments on Grenada, noted that the United States and Israel counted "on deriving the maximum advantage from the present situation in the region, which is complex enough as it is, with the senseless Iran-Iraq war continuing, inter-Arab discord exacerbated, and the PLO's internal differences having led to bloody clashes between rival groups." He then appealed for cooperation among all "antiimperialist" forces to counter the "dangerous development of events" and the U.S.–Israeli threats. Two days later, a *Pravda* editorial discussing the fighting in Tripoli made the point even more strongly:

> It is no accident that the inter-Palestinian discord is being
> exploited in the framework of the anti-Syrian campaign
> unleashed by imperialist circles. In these conditions, the
> senseless and perverse nature of the fratricidal clashes in
> northern Lebanon are particularly vivid.[214]

The editorial also repeated the section of Gromyko's luncheon address during Khaddam's visit in which the Soviet foreign minister had stressed that the PLO "had to continue to operate as an active and effective factor of the antiimperialist struggle in the Near East." The editorial went on to say that Moscow was taking "active political steps to end the conflict."

As the Tripoli fighting escalated further despite the Soviet pleas, Moscow stepped up the level of its public complaints with an appeal from the Soviet Afro-Asian People's Solidarity Organization (AAPSO). Reminiscent of similar pleas at the time of Syrian–PLO fighting during the Syrian intervention in Lebanon in 1976,[215] the AAPSO called for an end to the "senseless bloodshed" and the restoration of unity in the ranks of the Palestinians, as well as the consolidation of all Arab antiimperialist forces "in the face of the mounting military and political pressure on the part of the U.S.A., Israel and their allies."[216]

Perhaps as a gesture to Arafat, Gromyko received Farouk Kaddoumi, one of Arafat's closest allies in the PLO, on 23 November. The fact that *Pravda* described the talks as having taken place in a "friendly, businesslike atmosphere," however, indicated that little agreement was reached—a probable indication that Kaddoumi was told Moscow would not take action against Syria—although Gromyko promised to help "in any way possible" to achieve a settlement among the Palestinian factions.[217] Fortunately for Moscow, however, an uneasy cease-fire was achieved in Tripoli several days later, although to what degree Assad agreed to halt the fighting owing to Saudi inducement, Soviet pressure, or the realization that Arafat continued to have widespread support in the Arab world and among Palestinians is not yet clear. In any case, Moscow warmly praised the cease-fire in an Arabic-language "Window on the Arab World" broadcast on 26 November,[218] and three days later, a joint Soviet party–government statement on the "international day of solidarity with the Palestinian people" saluted Arafat as the chairman of the PLO Executive Committee.[219] At the same time, it called for unity within the organization and its "close collaboration" with "those countries that are in the forefront of resistance to the U.S. and Israel," that is, Syria, as Moscow continued to try to maintain good relations with both Arafat and Assad.

While Moscow was clearly relieved by the Tripoli cease-fire, however tentative it may have been, it had to be concerned with the rise in U.S.–Syrian tensions. U.S. defense secretary Weinberger had asserted on 22 November that the attack on the Marine headquarters had been undertaken by Iranians with the "sponsorship and knowledge and authority of the Syrian government."[220] Although Syria rejected the charge,[221] it also again asserted that its planes had driven off U.S. jets flying over Syrian-controlled areas.[222] At this point, with the cease-fire holding in Tripoli, Moscow moved again to champion Syria, as a *Novosti* article by Demchenko that was distributed to Western correspondents warned that Syria was an ally of Moscow with whom it had a treaty of friendship and cooperation and that aggression against Syria was an "extremely dangerous venture." He also noted that the potential of forces opposing U.S. and Israeli policy in Syria and Lebanon did not compare "in any way with what the Pentagon faced on Grenada."[223] This was the strongest warning given by Moscow to the United States thus far in the Lebanese crisis and was perhaps aimed at deterring the United States from any strike against Syria, although the fact that it took the form of a *Novosti* article, not a Tass statement, indicated it was still low level. Nonetheless, such a warning again raised questions of Soviet credibility should a Syrian-American confrontation take place, either in the form of an American retaliation for the Marine headquarters explosion or an attack on Syrian positions in Lebanon in retaliation for the firing on U.S. reconnaissance planes. Syrian government statements, such as the one broadcast on Syrian radio on 29 November that "Syria expresses its pride—before the Arab nation and the world—at the fact that it agitates a superpower," appeared to make some form of confrontation even more likely.[224]

The U.S. attack came on 4 December, following Syrian antiaircraft fire on U.S. reconnaissance planes the previous day. The fact that the United States lost two planes and that one of its pilots was killed and another captured did not detract from the fact that the United States had openly attacked Syria and that a major confrontation was underway. Under these circumstances, Moscow was again faced with the dilemma of either supporting its client's policies in Lebanon—policies that the U.S.S.R. did not thoroughly agree with—or else once again losing some of its diplomatic credibility, particularly since Reagan was threatening to strike Syrian positions again if U.S. forces continued to come under attack.[225] Once again

Moscow was to take a cautious stand, although its diplomatic credibility was to suffer. Thus, a Tass statement simply noted that the Soviet Union "declared its solidarity with the peoples of Lebanon, Syria, and other Arab countries in defending their independence" and that "the aggressive actions of the United States against Syria constitute a serious threat to peace not only in the Middle East region."[226] The Tass statement also sought propaganda advantage by tying the U.S. attack to the strategic cooperation agreement concluded between Reagan and Israeli prime minister Yitzhak Shamir a week earlier, claiming that by its attack the United States no longer qualified as an "honest broker" in the Middle East. The failure of the Tass statement, however, to mention the Soviet-Syrian treaty indicated that Syria could not expect more than Soviet moral support against the United States so long as the confrontation was limited to Lebanon.

Although Moscow was not willing to aid Syria militarily to confront the United States, it did seek to utilize the American attack against Syria to undermine the U.S. position in the Middle East. Thus, a *Pravda* editorial on 10 December repeated the themes of the Tass statement that the United States no longer qualified as a mediator in the Arab-Israeli conflict and that the U.S. attack was the outgrowth of U.S.–Israeli strategic cooperation. The editorial went on to assert that the United States was now being opposed even in conservative Arab countries, and Moscow once again appealed for Arab unity on an antiimperialist basis. An Arabic-language broadcast on 12 December carried this theme further by asserting that when the United States signed its "strategic alliance" with Israel, it challenged "all Arabs without exception, the progressives and the moderates alike."[227] Interestingly, however, the broadcast mentioned Soviet support for Syria only in passing and again called on the Arabs to unite and use their economic pressure against the United States. It seems clear that Moscow, unwilling to use force to aid Syria, had returned to the course of action it had pursued since the September crisis—an appeal to the Arabs to help Syria themselves. Unfortunately for the U.S.S.R., which hoped that the U.S. attack would force the centrist Arabs to again rally around Syria and what was left of the Steadfastness Front, this was not to happen. With Syria's ally Iran again threatening to close the Straits of Hormuz, the centrist Arabs, and particularly the members of the Gulf Cooperation Council, had no choice but to rely on the United States for help. Syria, to its apparent bitter disappointment, also realized this soon after the U.S. attack as the Syrian media bewailed the lack of Arab support. As *al-Ba'th* noted on 8 December:

> It is illogical to have Arab resources remain idle, waiting for the circle of aggression to reach them. It is also illogical to restrict the role of this or that Arab country to mere condemnation or denunciation of the aggressor.[228]

The result was that Syria, lacking Soviet or Arab support against the United States and only moderately successful in its efforts to topple Arafat as leader of the PLO (he still commanded widespread Palestinian support and left Tripoli under the UN flag), moved to deescalate the tension. Thus, the Syrians returned the body of the dead U.S. airman to the United States, agreed to talk to U.S. mediator Donald Rumsfeld—despite the fact that the battleship *New Jersey* was firing on Syrian positions after U.S. reconnaissance planes were again fired upon—and finally, in a gesture they said was aimed at "creating a circumstance conducive to the withdrawal of U.S. forces from Lebanon," released the captured U.S. airman.[229] This was a major Syrian concession, given the fact that Syrian leaders had earlier said he would not be released until after the "war" was over and U.S. forces had withdrawn from Lebanon.[230]

It is clearly possible that Assad, who had now recovered from his illness, was trying to exploit the rising tide of opposition in the United States to the Marine presence in Lebanon; nonetheless, to release the airman at a time when U.S. naval guns were still pounding Syrian positions indicated that the Syrian leader realized his confrontation with the United States was in danger of getting out of control at a time when he could not count on either Soviet or Arab support. Meanwhile, Assad's enemy, Yasir Arafat, appeared to at least temporarily take the initiative in intra-Arab politics away from the Syrian leader by his surprise meeting with Egyptian president Hosni Mubarak, a meeting that held out the possibility of a new alignment in Arab politics, particularly since Egypt and Jordan were normalizing their relations. In any case, the Arafat-Mubarak meeting provides a useful point of departure for examining the course of Soviet policy during the Lebanese crisis in the 1982–83 period.

CONCLUSIONS

In evaluating Soviet policy during the Lebanese crisis of 1982–83 and the Soviet-Syrian relationship during this period, one can draw three general conclusions. First, in the aftermath of the Israeli invasion of Lebanon when the Soviet role was essentially limited to issuing a series of ineffectual threats to Israel and the United States, Moscow sought to block U.S. policy in Lebanon and throughout the Middle East as well primarily by reinforcing Syrian opposition to Israeli and U.S. policy. Second, Moscow sought to exploit the continuing Lebanese crisis to demonstrate that without its participation, no settlement was possible for the Arab-Israeli conflict. Finally, although issuing periodic warnings to both Israel and the United States throughout the 1982–83 period, Moscow sought to avoid a military confrontation with them. Thus, Moscow carefully limited the scope of its 1980 treaty with Syria to Syrian territory (excluding Lebanon), while at the same time urging the other Arab states to rally to the defense of Syria by using their economic and military resources to aid Syria in its confrontations with Israel and the United States.

Moscow's problem during this period was that while it was reinforcing Syria's ability to thwart U.S. diplomacy, whether in the form of U.S. efforts to expand the Camp David peace process, gain Arab acceptance for the Reagan plan, or obtain approval for the 17 May 1983 Israeli-Lebanese accord, it faced the dilemma that Damascus was exploiting Soviet support to achieve its own goals, both in Lebanon and in the Arab world as a whole, goals that were not always compatible with those of the Soviet Union. Thus, Syria sought predominant, if not exclusive, influence in Lebanon, control over the PLO, and a leading role in the Arab world during this period. To be sure, Moscow was not averse to Syria, a member of the pro-Soviet Steadfastness Front in the Arab world, obtaining a position of Arab leadership. This would mean that Syria would move out of its position of isolation in the Arab world caused by its backing of Iran in the Iran-Iraq war, and Moscow may have hoped that Syria could thereby win over some of the more important centrist Arab states or at least keep them from a reconciliation with Egypt.

Nonetheless, Syrian attempts to militarily confront first Israel in May 1983 and then the United States in the September-December 1983 period—confrontations the Syrian leadership attempted to portray as Syrian "defense of the Arab nation against Zionism and imperialism"—did not appear to meet with full Soviet approval. This was the case not only because most Arab states continued to remain cool toward Syria but also because Syrian leaders threatened to drag in the Soviet Union to help Syria fight its Lebanese battles, especially by claiming that the Soviet-Syrian treaty covered Syrian actions in Lebanon. Similarly, Assad's exploitation of the split in Fatah and his subsequent crackdown on Arafat's supporters in the Bekaa Valley and in Tripoli appeared to be unpopular in Moscow. In the first place, it further splintered the already badly divided Arab world, with not only Iraq but also Steadfastness Front member Algeria supporting Arafat, thus making Moscow's long-sought antiimperialist Arab unity even more difficult to achieve. Second, despite its unhappiness with Arafat's flirtation with the Reagan plan, Moscow gave every appearance of wanting to keep the PLO as an independent actor in Arab politics—one open to Soviet influence—rather than having it become a mere appendage of Syrian policy. Finally, should the hard-liners in the anti-Arafat movement in Fatah win out, it would be far more difficult for Moscow to gain acceptance for its Middle East peace plan which called for the existence of a Palestinian state alongside of, not in place of, Israel.

In sum, the Soviet-Syrian relationship during the 1982–83 period was an uneasy one as each country sought to use the other to help further its goals. Nonetheless, if one were to ask which country profited more from the relationship, the answer would appear to be Syria. Moscow benefited from Syrian opposition to the U.S. diplomatic initiatives, but the U.S.S.R. also had to make important concessions to Damascus during this period. First, after initially demanding that all foreign forces, including Syrian, leave Lebanon, the U.S.S.R. by September 1983 no longer publicly called for a Syrian troop withdrawal, even though it realized that the continued presence of Syrian troops in Lebanon carried with it the danger of a confrontation with the United States.

Second, after resisting a number of Syrian demands for more advanced weaponry so that it could have a degree of military power equivalent to that of Israel, Moscow agreed to send to Damascus two major weapons systems, the SAM-5 antiaircraft system and the SS-21 surface-to-surface missile. Both systems had never before been deployed outside the Warsaw Pact area. Interestingly enough, both weapons systems were sent after Moscow failed to give Syria support in a major military confrontation, the SAM-5 after Syria had been defeated by Israel during the Israeli invasion of Lebanon and the SS-21 after the September 1983 Syrian-American confrontation. By sending the two sophisticated weapons systems, Moscow may have tried to assuage Syrian unhappiness at the lack of Soviet support. It is, of course, possible that the weapons systems were sent to Syria with the primary purpose of helping it deter an attack, thus making Soviet support in a crisis situation unnecessary. In addition, Moscow emphasized during the Syrian military buildup and the subsequent crises that Syrian goals were defensive, another ploy aimed at averting war. Nonetheless, the reason that Soviet troops manned the SAM-5s may have been that Moscow was concerned that otherwise Syria would exploit the new weaponry to go to war in pursuit of its Lebanese or Middle Eastern goals. Indeed, by sending Assad such weapons, as well as by replenishing his 1982 losses to Israel, the U.S.S.R. not only enhanced the Syrian leader's bargaining position vis-à-vis Israel, the United States, and the other Arab states but also gave him the means to more successfully wage war, should he so choose, as Syria approached its long-sought strategic equivalence with Israel.

In taking such action, Moscow clearly ran a risk. On the one hand, its own credibility and that of its weaponry had come under strong attack by the Arabs during the Israeli invasion of Lebanon of 1982. By providing such advanced weaponry to Syria and also issuing warnings to both Israel and the United States, Moscow under Andropov's leadership evidently hoped to regain some of its lost credibility. The dilemma for the Soviet leadership was that Assad tended to exploit both the new weaponry and the Soviet warnings—limited as they may have been—to further his ambitions in Lebanon and elsewhere in the Arab world. What made matters so dangerous for the Kremlin, particularly at a time when Andropov was ill, was that in both September 1983 and December 1983 Assad provoked the United States into a military confrontation, thus putting Moscow in the unenviable position of either backing its most important Arab ally, thereby risking a confrontation with the United States, or remaining silent and losing credibility as it had in 1982. Moscow was to choose the latter course, although it may have hoped either that the U.S.–Syrian confrontation would so undermine the American position in the Arab world that the lack of direct Soviet support to Syria would be overlooked or that the growing war-weariness in Israel and the United States would lead both to withdraw, leaving Syria in the dominant position in Lebanon with no need of direct Soviet support.

Thus, while American diplomatic initiatives in the Lebanese crisis had been virtually stymied as a result of Soviet-reinforced Syrian opposition, Moscow was to run a considerable risk in providing Syria with the military and diplomatic support that helped it actively pursue its Lebanese and regional goals. Andropov's successors may one day wonder whether, in the volatile Middle East, the benefits they gained from their support of Syria were worth the costs.

NOTES

1. For recent studies of Soviet policy in the Middle East, see Robert O. Freedman, *Soviet Policy toward the Middle East Since 1970*, 3d ed., (New York: Praeger, 1982); Jon D. Glassman, *Arms for the Arabs: The Soviet Union and War in the Middle East* (Baltimore: Johns Hopkins, 1975); Galia Golan, *Yom Kippur and After: The Soviet Union and the Middle East Crisis* (London: Cambridge University Press, 1977); Yaacov Ro'i, ed., *The Limits to Power: Soviet Policy in the Middle East* (London: Croom, Helm, 1979); and Adeed Dawisha and Karen Dawisha, eds., *The Soviet Union in the Middle East: Policies and Perspectives* (New York: Holmes & Meier, 1982). For an Arab viewpoint, see Mohamed Heikal, *The Sphinx and the Commissar* (New York: Harper & Row, 1978). For a recent Soviet view, see E. M. Primakov, *Anatomiia Blizhnevostochnogo Konflikta* (Moscow: Mysl', 1978).

2. For studies of Soviet military aid, see Glassman, *Arms for the Arabs;* George Lenczowski, *Soviet Advances in the Middle East* (Washington: American Enterprise Institute, 1972); and Amnon Sella, "Changes in Soviet Political-Military Policy in the Middle East after 1973," in Ro'i, *The Limits to Power*, pp. 32–64.

3. For a view of the role of Israel in Soviet Middle East strategy, see Freedman, *Soviet Policy toward the Middle East*, chapter 8.

4. For a study of Soviet policy toward the Communist parties of the Arab world, see Robert O. Freedman, "The Soviet Union and the Communist Parties of the Arab World: An Uncertain Relationship," in *Soviet Economic and Political Relations with the Developing World*, (New York: Praeger, 1975), pp. 100–134; and John K. Cooley, "The Shifting Sands of Arab Communism," *Problems of Communism* 24, no. 2 (1975): 22–42.

5. For an analysis of the Islamic revival, see Daniel Pipes, "This World Is Political!! The Islamic Revivial of the Seventies," *Orbis* 24, no. 1 (Spring 1980): 9–41.

6. For analyses of Soviet-Syrian relations up to Camp David, see Freedman, *Soviet Policy toward the Middle East*; and Galia Golan, "Syria and the Soviet Union Since the Yom Kippur War," *Orbis* 21, no. 4 (Winter 1978): 777–801. For an analysis sympathetic to the Syrian role in Lebanon, see Adeed I. Dawisha, *Syria and the Lebanese Crisis* (New York: St. Martin's Press, 1980). For other analyses of Syrian politics and foreign policy, see John Devlin's studies, "Syria Since Camp David," in *The Middle East Since Camp David*, ed. Robert O. Freedman (Boulder, Colo.: Westview Press, 1984) and *Syria: Modern State in an Ancient Land* (Boulder, Colo.: Westview Press, 1983). See also David Pryce-Jones, "Bloody Assad," *New Republic*, 30 January 1984, pp. 20–25.

7. For analyses of the domestic situation in Syria, see Nikolas Van Dam, *The Struggle for Power in Syria* (New York: St. Martin's Press, 1979); Stanley Reed III, "Dateline Syria: Fin De Regime?" *Foreign Policy*, no. 39 (Summer 1980): 176–90; and Chris Kutscheria, "Sticks and Carrots," *Middle East*, no. 80 (June 1981): 8–9.

8. *Pravda*, 23 September 1978.

9. Leonid Medvenko, "Middle East: Fictions and Realities," *New Times* (Moscow), no. 40 (1978): 6.

10. A. Stepanov, "Hour of Trial for the Palestinians," *New Times*, no. 41 (1978): 7.

11. For a discussion of the Arab reaction to Camp David, see Robert O. Freedman, "Epilogue," in *World Politics and the Arab-Israeli Conflicts*, ed. Robert O. Freedman (New York: Pergamon, 1979).

12. For the text of the joint communiqué, see *Pravda*, 7 October 1978.

13. Moscow Radio, Domestic Service, 28 October 1978, in *Foreign Broadcast Information Service Daily Report: Soviet Union* (hereafter cited as *FBIS:USSR*, 30 October 1978, p. F-5.

14. For a report on the results of the Baghdad conference, see Baghdad INA, 5 November 1978, in *Foreign Broadcast Information Service Daily Report: Middle East* (hereafter cited as *FBIS:ME*), 6 November 1978, pp. A-13–A-15. See also *Amman al-Ra'y*, in Arabic, 6 November 1978, in ibid., pp. A-10–A-20.

15. Radio Moscow (in Arabic to the Arab world), 6 November 1978, in *FBIS:USSR* 7 November 1978, p. F-2.

16. For a discussion of Soviet policy toward the Khomeini regime in the early part of 1979, see Robert O. Freedman, "Soviet Policy in the Middle East: From the Sinai Accord to the Egyptian-Israeli Peace Agreement," in *Soviet Policy toward the Third World*, ed. W. Raymond Duncan (New York: Pergamon, 1980), pp. 179–81.

17. Ned Temko, *Christian Science Monitor*, 30 November 1978.

18. *Pravda*, 27 March 1979.

19. For an analysis of the resumption of the Iraq-Syria quarrel, see Graham Benton, "After the Coup Attempt," *Middle East*, no. 59 (September 1979): 13–14.

20. *Pravda*, 19 October 1979.

21. For the Soviet reaction to Carter's moves, see *Pravda*, 7 January 1980.

22. *Pravda*, 30 January 1980; translated in *Current Digest of the Soviet Press* (hereafter cited as *CDSP*) 32, no. 4:19–20.

23. Reuters report, *New York Times*, 29 August 1979.

24. Drew Middleton, *New York Times*, 14 March 1980.

25. *Washington Post*, 20 January 1980.

26. Reed, "Dateline Syria: Fin De Regime?" p. 180.

27. Edward Cody, *Washington Post*, 27 October 1979.

28. For a description of the Lebanese events, see Tewfik Mishlawi, "Breaking the 'No Victor, No Vanquished' Deadlock," *Middle East*, August 1980, pp. 21–23. See also Adeed I. Dawisha, "Syria in Lebanon—Assad's Vietnam?" *Foreign Policy*, no. 33 (Winter 1978–79): 135–50.

29. See Reuters report, *Washington Post*, 4 July 1980, and the report by Helena Cobban, *Christian Science Monitor*, 27 June 1980.

30. According to a report by David Ottaway in the *Washington Post*, 22 October 1980, Syria leaked a report that Libya had agreed to pay Moscow $1 billion for arms sent to Syria.

31. For an analysis of the Soviet dilemma in the Iran-Iraq war, see Freedman, *Soviet Policy Toward the Middle East*, pp. 391–93.

32. Libya had criticized Saudi Arabia's decision to allow the stationing of U.S. AWACS aircraft on Saudi soil where they could be used against Iran.

33. Alexander Usvatov, "Put Out the Fire," *New Times*, no. 40 (1980): 12.

34. See *Izvestia*, 3 October 1980.

35. *Pravda*, 11 October 1980.

36. *Pravda*, 9 October 1980. For a detailed analysis of the treaty, see Amiram Nir, *The Soviet-Syrian Friendship and Cooperation Treaty: Unfulfilled Expectations* (Tel Aviv: Jaffa Center for Strategic Studies, 1983).

37. *Pravda*, 6 December 1978.

38. Nir, *Soviet-Syrian Friendship*, pp. 10–13.

39. There were numerous rumors of such secret clauses. See the report by Anan Safadi, *Jerusalem Post*, 10 October 1980.

40. *Pravda*, 3 December 1980.

41. Cited in report of an interview with King Hussein by Pranay B. Gupte, *New York Times*, 2 December 1980. Hussein also stated that he had put aside plans to explore arms purchases from Moscow.

42. See Moscow Radio Arabic Broadcast, 5 December 1980, in *FBIS:USSR*, 8 December 1980, p. H-1.

43. *Pravda*, 24 February 1981.

44. Douglas Watson, *Baltimore Sun*, 7 April 1981.

45. By the end of the first week in May, Arab army chiefs, meeting in Tunis, had pledged to aid Syria as had Kuwait and Saudi Arabia (see report by Pranay Gupte, *New York Times*, 8 May 1981, and AP report, *Baltimore Sun*, 3 May 1981). *Tass* on 8 May and *Pravda* and Moscow Radio (Arabic-language broadcast) on 9 May carried stories about the missiles, referring to them as a defensive measure. The stories coincided with the end of a visit to Damascus by Soviet first deputy foreign minister Georgii Kornienko.

46. See report by Don Oberdorfer, *Washington Post*, 30 April 1981.

47. Soviet radar on Lebanese mountain peaks would aid Moscow's air deployments in the eastern Mediterranean.

48. Alexandr Timoshkin, Moscow Radio (Arabic) 13 May 1981, in *FBIS:USSR*, 14 May 1981, p. H-1.

49. Robert Rand, "The USSR and the Crisis over Syrian Missiles in Lebanon: An Analysis and Chronological Survey," *Radio Liberty Report*, no. 227–81 (3 June 1981): 6. Note: Tass on 5 May denied that Soldatov had said the U.S.S.R. regarded the Bekaa Valley (where Zahle is located) as a sector of substantial importance to the security of Syria. Rand's study is an excellent analysis of the missile crisis from 28 April 1981 to 29 May 1981.

50. *New York Times*, 13 May 1981.

51. *Pravda*, 23 May 1981.

52. *Pravda*, 27 May 1981.

53. *Jerusalem Post*, 24 May 1981.

54. *Pravda*, 26 May 1981.

55. *Christian Science Monitor*, 6 July 1981.

56. For a Soviet view of U.S.–Israel strategic cooperation, see *Pravda*, 15 September 1981.

57. Nir, *Soviet-Syrian Friendship*, p. 19.

58. Ibid., p. 20; interview with Hanna Batatu, Washington, D.C., 19 December 1983.

59. *Pravda*, 16 January 1982.

60. Ibid.

61. *Pravda*, 17 January 1982.

62. For Moscow's highly negative reaction to this development, see the Moscow Radio Arab-language broadcast on 28 May 1982, in *FBIS:USSR*, 1 June 1982, p. H-3.

63. For a description of the increasingly severe problems facing the PLO in Lebanon on the eve of the war, see David Butler, "In the Same Trench," *Middle East*, June 1982, p. 6. See also his report, "Shiites in Beirut Clashes," *Middle East*, February 1982, p. 14.

64. See remarks by Taha Ramadan, first deputy prime minister of Iraq, Baghdad Radio, 1 June 1982, in *FBIS:ME*, 2 June 1981, p. E-2.

65. The Moroccan foreign minister, Mohammed Boucetta, paid a visit to Cairo on 7 June 1982, thus further ending Egypt's ostracism, as did Egyptian President Mubarak's attendance at the funeral of King Khalid of Saudi Arabia later that month.

66. *Pravda*, 26 May 1982.

67. Voice of Palestine, 2 June 1982, cited in *FBIS:ME*, 3 June 1982, p. E-1.

68. For a detailed analysis of the difficulties inherent in the Soviet–PLO relationship, see Galia Golan, *The Soviet Union and the Palestine Liberation Organization* (New York: Praeger, 1980).

69. For Israeli military analyses of the war, see *Israel Defense Forces Journal* 1, no. 2 (December 1982): 11–28; and Chaim Herzog, *The Arab-Israeli Wars* (New York: Random House, 1982), pp. 339–59. For a view from the Palestinian side, see the special issue of the *Journal of Palestine Studies*, no. 44–45 (Summer-Fall 1982) devoted to the war, especially the chronology, pp. 135–92.

70. Voice of Palestine, 7 June 1982, 8 June 1982, in *FBIS:ME*, 8 June 1982, p. A-2; 9 June *FBIS:ME*, p. ii, and 10 June in *FBIS:ME*, 10 June 1982, p. A-3.

71. Voice of Lebanon, 6 June 1982, in *FBIS:ME*, 7 June 1982, p. G-9.

72. *Pravda*, 8 June 1982.

73. Tass, 8 June 1982, in *FBIS:USSR*, 9 June 1982, p. H-2, and AP report in *New York Times*, 9 June 1982.

74. Tass, 9 June 1982, in *FBIS:USSR*, 9 June 1982, p. H-1.

75. Tass, 9 June 1982, in *FBIS:USSR*, 10 June 1982, p. H-2.

76. *KUNA*, Kuwait, 10 June 1982, in *FBIS:ME*, 11 June 1982, p. A-1.

77. See report by David Shipler, *New York Times*, 30 June 1982, citing Israeli prime minister Menachem Begin, who also said he had received two messages from Moscow asking Israel not to hit the Soviet embassy in Beirut.

78. Hedrick Smith, *New York Times*, 11 June 1982.

79. Haig interview on ABC program "This Week with David Brinkley," 13 June 1982, reprinted in *Journal of Palestine Studies*, nos. 44–45 (Summer-Fall 1982): 330.

80. For an analysis of the economic benefits to Moscow of arms sales, see Andrew J. Pierre, *The Global Politics of Arms Sales* (Princeton: Princeton University Press, 1982), pp. 78–80.

81. For the best analysis of Soviet strategy during the war, see Golan, *Yom Kippur and After.*

82. *Pravda*, 15 June 1982.

83. *Pravda*, 14 June 1982.

84. Moscow Domestic Service, 13 June 1982, in *FBIS:USSR*, 16 June 1982, p. H-1, and *FBIS:ME*, 15 June 1982, p. i.

85. Ned Temko, *Christian Science Monitor*, 18 June 1982.

86. Tass, 17 June 1982, in *FBIS:USSR*, 18 June 1982, p. H-2.

87. Moscow Radio Peace and Progress (Arabic), 15 June 1982, in *FBIS:USSR*, 16 June 1982, p. H-2.

88. Radio Monte Carlo (Arabic) 18 June 1982, in *FBIS:ME*, 21 June 1982, pp. A-3, A-4; *Le monde*, 23 June 1982, cited in *FBIS:ME*, 23 June 1982, p. A-1.

89. *al-Anba* (Kuwait), 30 June 1983, in *FBIS:ME*, 1 July 1982, p. A-3.

90. Tripoli, *JANA*, 26 June 1982, in *FBIS:ME*, 26 June 1982, pp. Q-2, Q-3.

91. Tass, 22 June 1982, in *FBIS:USSR*, 22 June 1982, p. H-3.

92. *FBIS:USSR*, 2 July 1982, pp. H-3, H-4.

93. *Pravda*, 6 July 1982.

94. Dusko Doder, *Washington Post*, 6 July 1982.

95. *Pravda*, 9 July 1982, in *CDSP*, 34, no. 27:3.

96. Moscow Radio in Arabic to the Arab world, 8 July 1982 (Rafael Artonov, commentary) and Moscow Radio Domestic Service, 9 July 1982 (Yuri Kornilov, commentary).

97. Moscow Radio (Arabic) 9 July 1982, in *FBIS:USSR*, 12 July 1982, p. H-6.

98. *FBIS:USSR*, 15 July 1982, pp. H-1, H-2.

99. Tunis Domestic Service, 13 July 1982, in *FBIS:ME*, 14 July 1982, p. Q-6.

100. Tass, 15 July 1982, in *FBIS:USSR*, 16 July 1982, pp. H-6, H-7.

101. See *al-Anba* (Kuwait), 1 July 1982, in *FBIS:ME*, 2 July 1982, p. A-8.

102. AFP (Paris), 15 July 1982, in *FBIS:ME*, 16 July 1982, p. A-3.

103. *Pravda*, 3 August 1982.

104. *Pravda*, 6 August 1982.

105. *Izvestia*, 10 September 1982.

106. Dmitry Volsky, "Fez and the Bekaa Valley," *New Times* no. 38 (1982): 7–8.

107. For a description of the Fez plan, see *Middle East Journal* 37, no. 1 (Winter 1983): 71.

108. For an analysis of the status of the Soviet Middle East peace plan on the eve of the Israeli invasion of Lebanon, see Robert O. Freedman, "Moscow, Washington and the Gulf," *American-Arab Affairs*, no. 1 (Summer 1982): 132–34.

109. *Pravda*, 11 September 1982. The summit did agree, however, that any Arab countries that wished to renew ties with Egypt on a bilateral basis could do so.

110. *Pravda*, 16 September 1982.

111. *Pravda*, 21 September 1982.

112. *Pravda*, 4 December 1982.

113. Loren Jenkins, *Washington Post*, 13 November 1982.

114. *Pravda*, 13 January 1983.

115. Ibid.

116. *Washington Post*, 5 December 1982.

117. David Ottaway, *Washington Post*, 30 December 1982; comments by Yasir Arafat in the *Washington Post*, 18 January 1983.

118. Edward Walsh, *Washington Post*, 5 January 1983; Thomas L. Friedman, *New York Times*, 21 March 1983.

119. It is also possible that the Soviet move, in part, was a response to the emplacement of U.S. troops in Beirut, as well as a means of hampering U.S. air operations in the eastern Mediterranean near Lebanon.

120. The rise in opposition to Arafat within the PLO is discussed by Tewfik Mishlawi, *Wall Street Journal*, 12 January 1983, and 19 January 1983.

121. Cited in report by Thomas L. Friedman, *New York Times*, 23 February 1983. The fact that PLO moderate 'Isam Sartawi, who publicly advocated a compromise between Israel and the PLO, was forbidden to speak at the meeting was a further indication of the erosion of Arafat's position. Sartawi was subsequently assassinated in April while attending the Socialist International Congress in Portugal. For general discussions of the PNC Council session, see Judith Perera, "Hammering Out a Compromise," *Middle East*, no. 101 (March 1983): 8–9, and Cheryl A. Rubenberg, "The PNC and the Reagan Initiative," *American-Arab Affairs* 4 (Spring 1983): 53–69. For an analysis of trends within the PLO, see Aaron David Miller, "Palestinians in the 1980s," *Current History*, January 1984, pp. 17–20, 34–36; and "The PLO Since Camp David," in *The Middle East Since Camp David*, ed. Freedman.

122. *Pravda*, 25 February 1980.

123. Peter Osnos, *Washington Post*, 20 March 1983.

124. Bernard Gwertzman, *New York Times*, 9 April 1983.

125. Reuters report, *Washington Post*, 31 March 1983.

126. Herbert H. Denton, *Washington Post*, 11 April 1983. For a provocative interpretation of Hussein's decision, see the articles by Karen Elliott House in the *Wall Street Journal*, 14 April and 15 April 1983. For an analysis of Jordan's position vis-à-vis the Palestinians, see Adam M. Garfinkle, "Jordanian Foreign Policy," *Current History*, January 1984, pp. 21–24, 38–39.

127. *Pravda*, 13 April 1983, translated in CDSP 35, no. 15:9.

128. *Pravda*, 31 March 1983.

129. *Christian Science Monitor*, 30 March 1983.

130. Riyadh SPA, 2 April 1983, in FBIS:ME, 4 April 1983, p. C-6.

131. The text of Gromyko's press conference may be found in FBIS:USSR, 4 April 1983, pp. AA-1–AA-17.

132. Ibid., p. AA-15.

133. Ibid., p. AA-16.

134. Reuters report, *New York Times*, 17 April 1983.

135. David Landau, *Jerusalem Post*, 20 April 1983.

136. Herbert Denton, *Washington Post*, 22 April 1983.

137. *Jerusalem Post*, 24 April 1983.

138. *Jerusalem Post*, 26 April 1983.

139. *Jerusalem Post*, 27 April 1983.

140. For an analysis of the dynamics of the process leading to the Israel-Lebanon agreement, see the report by Bernard Gwertzman, *New York Times*, 10 May 1983.

141. Herbert Denton, *Washington Post*, 7 May 1983.

142. Tass report, 9 May 1983, in *FBIS:USSR*, 10 May 1983, p. H-1.

143. Thomas Friedman, *New York Times*, 10 May 1983, and Nora Boustany, *Washington Post*, 10 May 1983.

144. Bernard Gwertzman, *New York Times*, 11 May 1983.

145. John Goshko, *Washington Post*, 11 May 1983.

146. Damascus, *SANA*, 9 May 1983, in *FBIS:ME*, 9 May 1983, p. H-2.

147. Reuters report, *New York Times*, 11 May 1983.

148. Beirut Domestic Service (Arabic), 10 May 1983, in *FBIS:ME*, 16 May 1983, p. H-8.

149. *Jerusalem Post*, 15 May 1983.

150. Ibid.

151. Sam Roberts, *New York Times*, 14 May 1983.

152. John Goshko, *Washington Post*, 17 May 1983.

153. Radio Moscow, Window on the Arab World, 19 May 1983, in *FBIS:USSR*, 23 May 1983, p. H-4.

154. Radio Moscow, Window on the Arab World, 12 May 1983, in *FBIS:USSR*, 16 May 1983, p. H-6.

155. Robin Wright, *Christian Science Monitor*, 17 May 1983.

156. *Jerusalem Post*, 24 May 1983.

157. William E. Farrell, *New York Times*, 26 May 1983.

158. Hirsch Goodman, *Jerusalem Post*, 27 May 1983.

159. For an analysis of Syrian–PLO relations at this time, see the article by Eric Rouleau, *Manchester Guardian Weekly*, 15 May 1983.

160. Herbert Denton, *Washington Post*, 4 May 1983.

161. Denton, *Washington Post*, 5 July 1983.

162. *FBIS:ME*, 5 August 1983, p. A-1.

163. *al-Watan al-Arabi*, cited by INA, in *FBIS:ME*, 2 September 1983, p. A-1.

164. For a description of Soviet military facilities in Syria, see *Near East Report* 27, no. 23 (10 June 1983): 2.

165. Radio Peace and Progress, 26 May 1983, in *FBIS:USSR* 1 June 1983, p. H-3. See also A. Stepanov, "To Safeguard Palestinian Unity," *New Times*, no. 28 (1983): 14–15.

166. WAFA, 4 June 1983, cited in *Jerusalem Post*, 5 June 1983.

167. *Pravda*, 14 July 1983.

168. See report by Loren Jenkins in the *Washington Post*, 3 August 1983, and reports in the *Baltimore Sun*, 10 July 1983, *New York Times*, 15 July 1983, and *Washington Post* (AFP report), 17 July 1983.

169. Stepanov, "To Safeguard Palestinian Unity," p. 14.

170. Don Oberdorfer, *Washington Post*, 7 July 1983. For a European view of the Shultz visit, see the *Economist*, July 9, 1983, p. 31.

171. *Washington Post*, 24 July 1983.

172. David Shipler, *New York Times*, 2 June 1983.

173. Reuters report, *Baltimore Sun*, 8 June 1983.

174. Don Oberdorfer, *Washington Post*, 8 July 1983.

175. Nora Bustany, *Washington Post*, 24 July 1983.

176. *Novosti* article by Pavel Demchenko, cited in AP report in the *Jerusalem Post*, 3 August 1983. *Novosti* reports are often used as a direct means of trying to influence Western nations.

177. *Tishrin* editorial, cited in Reuters report, *Washington Post*, 28 August 1983.

178. E. J. Dionne, Jr., *New York Times*, 20 September 1983.

179. David Ottaway, *Washington Post*, 18 September 1983.

180. Thomas L. Friedman, *New York Times*, 23 September 1983.

181. Trudy Rubin, *Christian Science Monitor*, 19 September 1983.

182. *Izvestia*, 4 September 1983, in *FBIS:USSR*, 7 September 1983, p. H-4.

183. Editorial, *New Times*, no. 38 (1983): 1.

184. *Pravda*, 19 September 1983.

185. *Pravda*, 20 September 1983.

186. *al-Qabas* (Kuwait), 20 September 1983, in *FBIS:USSR*, 22 September 1983, p. H-1.

187. Bernard Gwertzman, *New York Times*, 23 September 1983.

188. *Tishrin*, 12 September 1983, cited on Radio Monte Carlo, in *FBIS:ME*, 13 September 1983, p. H-1.

189. Radio Monte Carlo, 23 September 1983, *FBIS:ME*, 23 September 1983, p. H-1.

190. Andropov himself praised the cease-fire (*Pravda*, 30 September 1983), in a page-one report of his meeting with PDRY leader 'Ali Nasser Mohammed. A Tass statement published in Pravda on 29 September noted that the cease-fire had been "favorably received" in the Soviet Union, and again opposed both the Israeli and American troop presence in Lebanon and the 17 May Israeli-Lebanese agreement.

191. Damascus Domestic Service, 15 September 1983, in *FBIS:ME*, 15 September 1983, p. H-1, 18 September 1983, in *FBIS:ME*, 19 September 1983, p. H-3, and 14 September 1983, in *FBIS:ME*, 20 September 1983, pp. H-1, H-2.

192. For the text of the cease-fire agreement, see the AP report, *New York Times*, 27 September 1983.

193. Michael Getler, *Washington Post*, 7 October 1983. A report in the Arabic-language *al-Majallah* asserted that Moscow had told Damascus that the missiles could only be used in self-defense (*FBIS:ME*, 31 October 1983, p. ii).

194. A. Stepanov, "Consistent Support," *New Times*, no. 42 (1983): 13.

195. Moscow Radio (Arabic), commentary by Alexandr Timoshkin, 6 October 1983, in *FBIS:USSR*, 7 October 1983, pp. H-2, H-3.

196. *Pravda*, 25 October 1983.

197. Cited in *FBIS:USSR*, 28 October 1983, p. H-2.

198. Moscow Radio (Arabic), commentary by Aleksey Zlatorunsky, 2 November 1983, in *FBIS:USSR*, 3 November 1983, pp. H-1, H-2.

199. Moscow Radio (Arabic), commentary by Rafael Artonov, 3 November 1983, in *FBIS:USSR*, 4 November 1983, p. H-3.

200. *Pravda*, 5 November 1983.

201. *Pravda*, 6 November 1983.

202. Tass, 4 November 1983, in *FBIS:USSR*, 8 November 1983, p. H-2.

203. Bernard Gwertzman, *New York Times*, 8 November 1983.

204. *FBIS:USSR,* 10 November 1983, p. H-2.

205. Thomas Friedman, *New York Times,* 11 November 1983.

206. *FBIS:ME,* 9 November 1983, p. i.

207. *FBIS:USSR,* 15 November 1983, p. H-2.

208. *FBIS:ME,* 14 November 1983, p. H-2.

209. *Pravda,* 13 November 1983.

210. AP report, *New York Times,* 14 November 1983.

211. For Moscow's reaction, see *Pravda,* 18 and 19 November 1983.

212. Radio Free Lebanon, 19 November 1983, in *FBIS:ME,* 21 November 1983, p. H-1.

213. Damascus television 15 November 1983, in *FBIS:ME,* 16 November 1983, p. H-1.

214. *Pravda,* 19 November 1983, in *CSDP* 35, no. 46:8.

215. Freedman, *Soviet Policy Toward the Middle East,* pp. 255, 261.

216. Tass, 20 November 1983, in *FBIS:USSR,* 21 November 1983, p. H-2.

217. *Pravda,* 24 November 1983.

218. *FBIS:USSR,* 29 November 1983, p. H-8. There was some indication that Arafat was publicly angry with the lack of Soviet aid, but he moved quickly to deny the report published to that effect in the Egyptian newspaper *al-Akhbar. See* Kuwait *KUNA,* 29 November 1983, in *FBIS:USSR,* 29 November 1983, p. H-1.

219. *Pravda,* 29 November 1983.

220. Richard Halloran, *New York Times,* 23 November 1983.

221. UPI report, *Washington Post,* 24 November 1983.

222. David Ottaway, *Washington Post,* 27 November 1983.

223. AP report, *New York Times,* 27 November 1983.

224. Damascus Domestic Service, 29 November 1983, in *FBIS:ME,* 30 November 1983, p. H-2.

225. *New York Times,* 5 December 1983.

226. *FBIS:USSR,* 6 December 1983, p. H-1.

227. *FBIS:USSR,* 14 December 1983, p. H-1.

228. The article was read on Damascus Radio, 8 December 1983, in *FBIS:ME,* 8 December 1983, p. H-4.

229. Damascus Domestic Service, 3 January 1984, in *FBIS:ME*, 3 January 1984, p. H-2.

230. This point had been repeatedly emphasized by Defense Minister Mustafa Tlas, while Syrian foreign minister Khaddam only a few days earlier had linked the airman's release to the suspension of U.S. reconnaissance flights over Syrian positions (Radio Monte Carlo, 1 January 1984, in *FBIS:ME*, 3 January 1984, pp. H-1, H-2).

Chad: Escalation Leads to Impasse

Edouard Bustin

> The great Libyan desert
> never spawned so vile a host
> Of plagues, nor all the lands of Ethiope
> Nor that which lies along the Red Sea coast.
> —Dante (*Inferno*, xxiv)

After more than fifteen years of almost continuous anarchy, Chad briefly erupted into the headlines of the American press during the summer of 1983, only to be crowded out again and relegated to the back pages by a succession of other trouble spots clamoring for the readers' attention. This brief stay in the limelight barely gave U.S. newswriters and their disconcerted but conscientious public enough time to spot the country on their atlases or to familiarize themselves with yet another set of outlandish locales with names such as Koro Toro or Umm Chalouba, and with a cast of characters whose identities were all the more puzzling since they appeared under several different spellings.[1]

Locating Chad on the map was the easy part: it is, after all, the fifth largest state in Africa (after Sudan, Algeria, Zaire, and Libya), with an area (495,753 square miles) exceeding that of Texas, Oklahoma, and New Mexico combined. Although its population (4.7 million) is smaller than that of tiny Rwanda, it is nevertheless larger—by nearly 50 percent—than that of Libya, whose visibility is hardly to be denied and whose alleged attempts to absorb its southern neighbor account for the sudden attention devoted to Chad. It is now ritualistic to note that the boundaries—and indeed, the very existence—of many African states are "artificial" and "arbitrary." Much the same thing can, of course, be said of dozens of other states in Latin America, Asia, the Middle East, and Europe—not to mention the United States, whose borders generously exhibit that oft-quoted hallmark of artificiality: the straight lines drawn across a map around a conference table.

Even so, however, it must be admitted that the boundaries of Chad are exceptionally irrelevant. They were, of course, negotiated among the dominant imperial powers in the region through a tortuous, but rather unhurried process that began long after the Berlin Conference in the aftermath of the Fachoda crisis (1898)

159

and continued over a period of nearly forty years, ending with the signing of the Mussolini-Laval agreements of 7 January 1935, which among other provisions transferred to Italy's colony of Libya the 114,000 square-kilometer Aozou Strip (occupied by Libya since 1973). Ratification of the 1935 treaty was stalled in the French parliament, and the deterioration of Franco-Italian relations that followed Mussolini's aggression against Ethiopia a few months later, his intervention in the Spanish civil war, and the emergence of the Berlin-Rome Axis further dampened France's inclination to accommodate Italian claims. With Italy's defeat in the war and the indirect state succession process that led to Libya's independence in 1951 after the limbo of an ill-defined international administration, the claims to the Aozou Strip (which had themselves been based on the pretensions of the Ottomans from whom Italy had wrested Libya) might have seemed a bit shopworn, but they were evidently not forgotten by the new Libyan kingdom now headed by King Idriss, heir to the leadership of the Sanusiyyah. The fact that French troops continued to be stationed in the Fezzan provided an additional irritant, which the outbreak of the Algerian uprising did nothing to alleviate. In February 1955, a Libyan patrol, apparently intent on occupying Aozou, was repulsed by the French. Later that year, with a notable lack of enthusiasm on both parts, France and Libya reached a settlement of their border dispute that made no reference to the Mussolini-Laval treaty, and the issue remained dormant for a few years. By 1968, however (i.e., before the advent to power of Col. Qaddafi), the FROLINAT rebels of northern Chad (discreetly supported by the Kingdom of Libya) had wrested Aozou from the government of Chad, which never recovered control over the area thereafter, despite French military backing.[2]

While less uncertain, Chad's other borders have also varied substantially since the area first passed under French rule. The border with the Sudan was determined at a relatively early stage and remained surprisingly stable, despite the deep historical affinities between the two territories and the steady flow of pilgrims and laborers across their common boundary. In the Southwest, the left bank of the Logone was briefly ceded to Germany (along with other, more substantial portions of French Equatorial Africa) as part of the 1911 settlement of the second Moroccan crisis, but France promptly took advantage of the outbreak of World War I to reoccupy these areas. By far the most sweeping vagaries in the delineation of Chad's borders, however, came from the French themselves. Since Chad was part of a continuous block of French possessions (constituting, in fact, the only link between the West African and Equatorial African territories), there were strictly speaking no international boundaries, but only administrative lines of demarcation between the various segments of French Africa. As a result, these lines were drawn and redrawn with great abandon for reasons of logistical convenience. The boundaries between Chad and Niger and, even more strikingly, those between Chad and Ubangui-Chari (today's Central African Republic) thus fluctuated almost continuously. As recently as the late 1930s, for example, the territory of Ubangui-Chari still included most of what is commonly known today as le Tchad utile—those southernmost districts that contain nearly half of its population and the bulk of its agricultural resources.[3] The Tibesti area, for its part, was not transferred from Niger to Chad (and thus from AOF to AEF) until November 1929.

Such vagaries are more readily understandable if one remembers that significant French expansion in the area of modern Chad did not begin until the turn of the century and that its northern reaches were not "pacified" until 1920, at which date a civilian administration was set up for what had previously been known as the Territoire Militaire des Pays et Protectorats du Tchad. In fact, even after that date, the northern part of Chad known as the Borkou-Ennedi-Tibesti (and commonly referred to as B.E.T.), with 43.5 percent of the country's area but less than 3 percent of its population, was kept under direct military rule for another forty-five years. It was not until 1965 (five years after independence) that military administration—still run by the French—gave way to civilian rule, but with such disastrous results that, within months, the whole area was engulfed in a state of rebellion which persists to this day and has now gradually eroded the rest of the country.

That condition of ceaseless strife, reducing a country that always was among the world's poorest to new depths of misery, has been ascribed to many causes, of which the artificiality of its borders is not necessarily the most pertinent. In fact, the deeper wisdom of the OAU's much-maligned decision to accept as permanent the boundaries, however absurd, that Africa inherited from its colonial masters was based on a tacit recognition of the fact that attempts to redraw them along more "logical" lines would create as many problems as it might solve and open the way to endless litigation.[4]

In any case, the fact that Chad's borders crystallized in their current outline less than twenty-five years before its independence matters less than their utter permeability. To an even greater degree than other areas lying along the southern edge of the Sahara from the Nile Valley to Western Sahara, most of Chad lies astride age-old paths of migration, commerce, nomadism, warfare, and pilgrimage that link it to all its neighbors, but particularly to the Mashriq and to the Middle Nile. This is reflected in the extraordinary diversity of its population, but while it would be pointless to deny the importance of ethnic cleavages, several qualifications are nevertheless in order. The fact that nearly half of the population is nomadic or seminomadic, in addition to the problems it raises for the operation of a modern state apparatus, implies a high degree of contact and interaction between communities, which does not, however, rule out an intricately "territorial" regulation of grazing rights. Second, the precolonial sultanates of central Chad (with about one-half of the population of the modern state) were themselves ethnically and religiously heterogeneous, yet generated some degree of popular identification, which French colonial rule, in its on-again-off-again flirtation with the convenience of indirect rule, did not seriously erode.[5]

To the precolonial patterns of nomadism, trade, and migrancy, which were never eradicated, colonial rule also added the centrifugal effect of new lines of communication (through Ubangui-Chari and Cameroun) and of new economic magnets (the "cotton kingdom" of the far South), which, on top of the disruption of the sultanates, led to further population movements and to a growing imbrication of ethnic groups.[6] Finally, it should be kept in mind that, as in other parts of Africa, ethnic labels are, at best, highly relative and almost invariably deceptive. The fact that they may reflect a measure of social proximity or of linguistic and cultural affinities does not exclude, on the one hand, the existence of important local cleavages based on patterns of economic or political conflict (both old and new) nor, on the other hand, the development of cross-cutting affiliations derived from occupational, religious, or ideological variables, from personal interest and from sheer tactical opportunism. The Sara "cluster" (over 1 million in 1977), for example, consists of over a dozen groups, most of them in turn divided into several segments. Among the nomadic Toubou, clan rivalries (occasionally mitigated by the arbitrating role of senior lineage heads) have long been in evidence. Thus, while ethnic identity has at times been a useful predictor of political alignments, its relevance and its reliability for the interpretation of conflicts have never offered more than a crude and often misleading yardstick. After the dizzying succession of realignments and alliance reversals that punctuate the history of independent Chad, no single ethnic group can boast of undivided allegiances. In the current confrontation, both sides claim partisans across ethnic lines—beginning, of course, with the nominal leaders of the two factions, Hissen Habré and Goukouni Oued-dei, both of them Toubou from opposite ends of the B.E.T.

What is true of ethnicity is also true, mutatis mutandis, of religion. No longer would it be accurate, as it once was, to use the phrase coined by Roger Pascal to describe the early phase of the insurrection: "Not all Moslems were rebels, but all rebels were Moslems."[7] This is not meant to minimize the importance of Islam in Chad; in fact, to say that Islam claims the allegiance of the larger half of the population would be misleading, in the sense that it would imply that it is more or less balanced by a non-Muslim bloc of comparable size and influence. In point of fact, however, Islam expanded into the area of modern Chad over a thousand years ago, and while its roots may have remained shallow among the common people, it had been adopted as the state religion by all the major precolonial states in the region (Ouadai, Baguirmi, Kanem-Bornu). By contrast, the first Christian missionaries (Protestant) who reached Chad from the South did not arrive until 1920. The first Catholic missions arrived around 1929 and did not expand their activity to the capital city (then known as Fort-Lamy) until 1946. There is, of course, little doubt that, whether or not it was deliberately exploited by the missionaries, the manifest association between Christianity and European colonial rule made it expedient, if not altogether mandatory, for many non-Muslim southerners to accept at least nominal conversion.

By the time of independence, over one-fourth of the population was officially listed as Christian (with the balance of non-Muslims continuing to adhere to traditional religions), but no one—and least of all the missionaries themselves—regarded these statistics as reliable. The fragility of Chadian Christianity was dramatically demonstrated in the early 1970s when the late President Tombalbaye (himself technically a Protestant) initiated a "cultural revolution" inspired in part by Mobutu's campaign for Zairean authenticité.

In pursuit of what was inelegantly referred to as Tchaditude, the names of cities and streets were Africanized and government officials were enjoined to drop their Christian names in favor of African appellations (with the president opting to call himself Ngarta Tombalbaye instead of François). Beyond this rather harmless exercise, however, Tombalbaye now went on to decree that all Chadians (with Muslims being, however, tacitly exempted from this obligation) should undergo the Yondo animist initiation rite of his own Sara group or some suitable equivalent. Protests by Christian religious circles led to the expulsion of several expatriate missionaries and even to the death of some indigenous Christian clerics. Tombalbaye's nativistic and anti-Christian zeal alienated most of his remaining educated southern supporters and was undoubtedly a major contributing factor in his April 1975 overthrow and assassination.

There is no doubt that the non-Muslim population of southern Chad responded much more positively than the northerners to the availability (limited though it was) of Western-style education, but this was only partly due to mission-ary activities. Other factors, such as population density and the demand by French employers for clerical and semiskilled workers in the South, also account for the differential impact of Western education. In 1965–66, the school attendance rate in the five southwesternmost districts ranged from 40.5 to 61.4 percent versus 2.8 to 6.3 percent for the five northernmost districts in that same year. Christian mission-ary schools, however, accounted for only one-eighth of the 163,962 students en-rolled in Western-style schools, whereas in other parts of ex-French Africa enroll-ments were more or less evenly divided between missionary and government schools.[8] Small as it was, however, the contingent of Western-educated Chadians (overwhelmingly made up of non-Muslim southerners) inevitably supplied the bulk of the bureaucratic cadres during the late colonial and early independence periods—a factor that clearly weakened the legitimacy of the postcolonial state in the eyes of its Muslim population.

Yet, while the importance of Islam may have been underestimated, the magnitude and relevance of its contribution to the chronic instability that has plagued Chad since independence can also be overstated, especially by Western observers who, as they swing from one extreme to the other, sometimes tend to endow Chadian Islam with a monolithic quality it is far from possessing. Over the ten centuries since Islam first penetrated the area, Chad has been exposed to most of the currents that affected the Sunnite Ummah. Its northern reaches were an in-tegral part of the Sanusi stronghold which successfully resisted French and Italian penetration for some twenty years, but while this shared experience reflects the artificiality of the Chad-Libya border, its relevance to Libya's current involvement in the Chad crisis is at best tenuous, not only because the Sanusi are very much a minority sect and played no idiosyncratic role in the ongoing civil war, but also because the contribution of the Sanusiyyah to the ideology of Qaddafist Libya ap-pears to be far from decisive.[9] The Tijaniyyah is by far the most numerous and influential order in Chad, but Sudanese influences in various forms are also in evidence, and pre-Islamic practices survive in many communities—even those that, like the Toubou, have been exposed to Islam for centuries.

THE LONG FUSE OF DISINTEGRATION

Chad's experience of colonial rule was briefer than that of any other African terri-tory, and nowhere—except perhaps in Mauritania—was its institutional legacy more fragile. Yet, because of France's centralizing and formalistic penchant for dealing with her overseas territories (whenever possible) in a categorically whole-sale manner, Chad experienced the vagaries of postwar French African policy—from the Union Française to the Loi Cadre and from community to cooperation—at exactly the same pace as its AOF and AEF neighbors and played these intricate charades according to French expectations by dispatching its handful of deputies to sit in the French National Assembly, by producing its share of indigenous "po-litical parties" and local elections (with only a slightly larger dose of transparent manipulation by the French administration), and by dutifully opting for member-ship in the Franco-African Community in 1958 and for independence in 1960 as De Gaulle shifted his ground toward an increasingly sophisticated form of neocolonialism.

Because of the artificial parallelism in French Africa's experience with guided decolonization and institutional transfer, Chad's acquisition of the legal attributes of international sovereignty seemed no less implausible in 1960 than that of, say, Niger or the Central African Republic. Even the familiar slide to a single-party system in 1962–63 was somehow true to form, except perhaps for the fact that the ruling PPT (*Parti Progressiste Tchadien*) had even shallower roots than most of its counterparts. The fragility of the state was exposed when, in a reckless attempt to translate its nominal sovereignty in "nation-building" terms, the Tombalbaye government insisted on dismantling the system of military administration the French had consistently maintained over the B.E.T. ever since the area had been officially "pacified." At the same time (1963–65), the chiefs who had served as convenient mediators of colonial rule (especially in central Chad) were stripped of most of their administrative, fiscal, and judicial powers. Those powers, together with the prerogatives of the French military commandants of the B.E.T. who had continued to serve the Chadian state, were turned over to a hastily Africanized civil service staffed almost exclusively with southerners.

The blunders and excesses of these raw and high-handed administrators triggered a number of incidents in the B.E.T. (Bardai) and in central Chad (Mangalme) during the latter part of 1965. A few months later, Ibrahim Abatcha, a former trade unionist who had exiled himself from Chad in 1963 and had drifted to Egypt, the Sudan, and Ghana, organized the Chad National Liberation Front (FROLINAT) in Khartum from a motley assortment of left-leaning and fundamentalist Muslim dissidents. Dissension promptly surfaced among the original founders of the movement, but Abatcha chose to reenter Chad where he joined the insurgent groups who, even before the creation of FROLINAT, had already taken up arms in the Ouaddai region bordering upon the Sudan. Meanwhile, a second rebel zone had emerged in the far North when the brutality of government officials alienated Kichidemi Oueddei, the spiritual leader, or *Derde*, of the Toubou of Tibesti, who thereupon exiled himself to Libya with his sons Hanneur, Hadj Moulinaye, and Goukouni.

Fighting continued through 1967 and 1968, prompting Tombalbaye to request French military intervention. In the ensuing campaigns, Abatcha and one of the Derde's sons were killed, and leadership of the FROLINAT passed into the hands of Abba Siddick, a physician born (1924) in the Central African Republic of a Chadian father, who had served as secretary-general of the PPT until 1959, when he had been purged from the party by Tombalbaye. By the spring of 1969, far from having eradicated the rebellion, the French had to send in reinforcements, but in the first of many attempts to combine military and political approaches, they compelled Tombalbaye to commit his government to a program of administrative reforms in return for expanded military support. The piecemeal "reforms," which consisted in the main of restoring the pre-1964 system, failed to meet the political grievances of the FROLINAT leadership, whose opposition stemmed, at least in part, from the way Tombalbaye had (with French assistance) captured the PPT from its veteran cadres and suppressed all opposition, and they were, in any case, surreptitiously sabotaged by Tombalbaye and by his clique of expatriate advisers. Military operations thus continued in a political vacuum, but in the meantime, Qaddafi's accession to power soon provided the northern insurgents with a more sustained source of assistance than the occasional and often passive support they had received from prerevolutionary Libya.

Among the reforms urged by the French was the appointment of more northerners to senior positions. One of the first beneficiaries of this policy was Hissen Habré, born in 1942 among the Anakaza clan of the Toubou of southern Borkou, who, after serving as a civilian employee of the French army and then as a civil servant in the administration of independent Chad, had been sent to France in 1964 upon the recommendation of a former French military superior to undergo advance administrative training. After studying at the Institut International des Hautes Etudes Administratives (a branch of the Institut d'Etudes Politiques) and taking time to earn a law degree, Habré returned to Chad in 1971 (somewhat reluctantly, it seems) and was offered a senior position in the Foreign Affairs Department. On his first assignment, he was dispatched to Tripoli and to Algiers for the purpose of approaching Abba Siddick and other FROLINAT leaders.[10] The exact nature of this mission was and remains a secret, but its probable purpose was to probe for divisions within the rebel camp and to determine which, if any, of their leaders might be persuaded to rally to the government side. At this point, however, Habré indicated his willingness to cast his lot with the FROLINAT. Siddick, who understandably suspected the would-be defector of wanting to infiltrate the movement, prudently kept him at arm's length and apparently suggested that he might prove his usefulness to the rebel cause by serving as a liaison with the Tibesti insurgents whose affiliation with FROLINAT had always been rather tenuous. Habré then met with fellow Toubou Goukouni Oueddei, who, following the death of his two elder brothers, had taken over the military command of the Tibesti rebels (officially known as the FROLINAT's "second army"); on the basis of his educational qualifications, he was invited to serve as their head political commissar.[11]

Whatever the motivation of Habré's double defection, the immediate effect of his affiliation with Goukouni's group was to widen the rift between the "second army" and Siddick's FROLINAT. Qaddafi vainly tried to reconcile the two factions, but ultimately chose to back Goukouni (and Habré) in preference to Siddick who, wary of Libyan designs, preferred to keep his base of operations in Algeria. France's gradual disengagement and Libya's increasing support of the Tibesti rebels prompted Tombalbaye to seek an accommodation with Qaddafi. Diplomatic relations with Tripoli, which had been ruptured in August 1971 following the attempted coup against Tombalbaye, were quietly restored in April 1972. In subsequent conversations between the two heads of state, Tombalbaye apparently offered to tacitly relinquish control of the Aozou Strip to Libya, presumably in exchange for the termination of that country's backing of the Goukouni-Habré group. Libya's response was evasive, but rumors of the secret deal infuriated not only the northern rebels, who saw the area as part of their homeland, but also the Chadian military. A renewed rebel offensive in the North in late 1972 was followed in January 1973 by an attempted putsch by a group of Chadian officers. The ongoing malaise in the ranks of the army was compounded in June with the arrest of General Félix (N'gakoutou Bey'ndi) Malloum, son of a Sara father and a northern mother, who had served for over a decade in the French army before rising to the rank of commander in chief of the Chadian armed forces. Faced with the rapid erosion of his political base, Tombalbaye thereupon decided to disband the country's single party and to replace it with a movement committed to his newly inaugurated "cultural revolution," the MNCRS (Mouvement National pour la Révolution Culturelle et Sociale). Meanwhile, sensing perhaps that Tombalbaye's days in power might be numbered, Libya proceeded to occupy the Aozou Strip.

The decline of Tombalbaye's power did not encourage the rebels to heed government appeals to national reconciliation, but the FROLINAT was not, at that time, in a position to take full advantage of the weakness of its opponents. In east-central Chad (site of the FROLINAT's "first army"), serious dissensions led to the elimination of several major field commanders without achieving a restoration of Siddick's authority, which also continued to be challenged by the Tibesti rebels. At the same time, however, Libya's occupation of the Aozou Strip had injected an element of bitterness and suspicion in the relations between Qaddafi and the Goukouni-Habré group (which had now taken to calling itself the Forces Armées du Nord, or FAN, rather than be known as the FROLINAT's "second army"). Habré's seizure of three European hostages[12] in April 1974 was in itself of no military significance and had no direct effect on the stalemated conflict between rebel and government forces, but it was a major publicity coup for Habré and soon led to a souring of relations between Paris and Ndjamena. Unlike the West Germans, who promptly ransomed Dr. Staewen by negotiating directly with Habré, France was reluctant to bypass the legal government of Chad by dealing openly with the rebels, while the French press kept public attention focused on the plight of the two French hostages.[13] Unable to conceal their clumsy and half-hearted attempts to covertly pay the ransom demanded by Habré, the French succeeded only in antagonizing the Tombalbaye government. Meanwhile, in an attempt to capitalize upon his opponents' disarray, Habré skillfully publicized his political demands, which covered the release of all political prisoners, including General Malloum and other Chadian officers arrested in 1973. The Chadian government reacted with plans for a further purge of the increasingly unreliable officer corps, but these maneuvers were forestalled by a successful military uprising on 13 April 1975, in which Tombalbaye lost his life.

In the aftermath of the coup (which seems to have met with tacit French approval),[14] Malloum took the head of a military junta known as the Conseil Supérieur Militaire (CSM), but the northern rebels remained unreconciled (and the hostages unreleased). Though reacting separately, both Siddick and Habré denounced Malloum as a figurehead, underlining the continued presence at the head of the Chadian secret services of Major Camille Gourvenec, a French officer who had been Tombalbaye's éminence grise before allegedly masterminding his overthrow. The Malloum regime scored some limited successes in securing the rallying of a handful of rebels and the return of Derde Oueddei from exile, but the old Toubou leader had by that time lost much of his influence, and his own son, Goukouni, remained unmoved. Relations with Paris continued to deteriorate as France pursued its desultory attempts to negotiate the fate of the French hostages with Habré, and by the end of September, Chad asked for the evacuation of all French forces. Diplomatic feelers failed to convince Libya to surrender the Aozou Strip, and Malloum himself was the target of an assassination attempt on the first anniversary of the 1975 coup.

The only redeeming feature in this dismal record was provided by the rebels' inability to take advantage of the CSM's weakness. This was the result not only of the continuing dissension between Siddick and the Tibesti rebels but also of the more ominous rift that developed in 1976 between Habré and Goukouni. Differences over the best way to end Libya's occupation of the Aozou Strip (which both leaders opposed) as well as over Habré's handling of the French hostages came to a head in October when Goukouni's supporters evicted Habré from the

FAN. Through Qaddafi's intercession, Goukouni promptly arranged for the "unconditional" release of the Claustres (earlier ransom payments, in the form of arms and money having already been appropriated by Habré) and thus emerged as the most prominent leader of the rebellion. Habré, for his part, withdrew across the B.E.T. and into the Sudan with a handful of followers, retaining for his group the name of FAN.

Divisions within the rebel camp now offered Malloum an opportunity to court Goukouni's rivals. The start of a new rebel offensive in June 1977 provided an additional incentive for Siddick and Habré to respond to Malloum's overtures, since the last thing that Goukouni's rivals wanted was for him to single-handedly topple the Chadian regime, but Siddick set impossibly high terms for rallying the CSM. Habré, for his part, was more noncommittal and kept dealing with Malloum's emissaries at a leisurely pace throughout the latter part of 1977 and 1978. By that time, however, Goukouni's rebel forces, assisted by some Libyan logistical support, were advancing rapidly throughout the B.E.T. By 5 February, as the northern oases fell one by one, the beleaguered Malloum government announced that it had reached a "secret agreement" two weeks earlier with Habré's forces.[15] Still, the rebels continued to advance, capturing Fada on 15 February and Faya-Largeau on 18 February. A few days later, through the intercession of Niger and the Sudan, Malloum met with Qaddafi to attempt a negotiated cease-fire. Although it recognized Oueddei's authority over the B.E.T., the agreement signed at Benghazi on 27 March was never implemented and the rebel forces resumed their southward march, finally prompting the French to dispatch 1,200 men and ten Jaguar fighter planes to halt the FAN offensive, more or less along the same lines as those where Goukouni's forces were again stopped in August 1983.

With its immediate survival assured by French military intervention, the Malloum regime returned to the task of broadening its political base. This meant coming to terms with Habré, but the wily northerner was not to be bought off with a mere cabinet post nor was he ready to relinquish control of the small group of armed followers he had assembled. Habré thus decided to consolidate his base in east-central Chad by purging the area of rival rebel groups. He was assisted in this task (which indirectly benefited the Chadian government) by French military cadres and equipment. By the end of August, Habré was able to join the Chadian government on his own terms. These included the disbanding of the CSM and its replacement by a new civilian-military government in which Habré would hold the office of prime minister while Malloum retained an ill-defined presidency. In addition, Habré demanded (and obtained) a seat on the Defense and Security Council (a stronghold of the military), the expulsion of Gourvenec, and the transfer to minor posts of two senior southern officers, Colonel Wadal Abdelkader Kamougué and General N'gué Djogo, who had made no secret of their hostility to the ex-rebel.[16]

Although it had been in the offing for almost a year, Habré's ascent to power and the CSM's virtual capitulation to his demands nevertheless came as a shock, not only in France, where Habré's image as a "Maoist" kidnapper still lingered, but also among southerners who, for the first time in twenty years, had lost their exclusive grip on the Chadian national government. Sporadic disturbances erupted in the South, presumably at the instigation of disgruntled non-Muslim officers and politicians. Meanwhile, however, the northern rebellion had lost its momentum and appeared to be foundering in the midst of fresh dissensions and conflicting ambitions, fueled in part by the spectacular success of Habré's own tortuous rise from dissident to premier.[17] But rather than exploit these differences, Habré committed the mistake of attempting to complete his takeover of the government apparatus. Tension between Malloum and Habré soon escalated into open conflict, and in February 1979, Habré's armed followers drove Malloum and the demoralized Chadian national army from the capital city.

At this point, and with the last semblance of a Chadian government in shambles, Goukouni's forces rushed into the fray and suddenly appeared in Ndjamena, having met no resistance from the French who, by that time, were themselves thoroughly confused and divided by the speed of Chad's disintegration. The diversion created by Goukouni's arrival paradoxically saved Malloum's army from annihilation. Malloum himself, who had holed up at the airport under French protection, now retired to Nigeria, but Kamougué and Djogo rallied their troops in the southern districts where they joined the tens of thousands of southern refugees who had fled the capital city at the height of the fighting. In the traumatized but still relatively prosperous South, vicious reprisals were now carried out against local Muslim minorities, and there were ominous rumblings of secession.

After Habré had, by his reckless ambition, destroyed the last shred of governmental legality, it was manifest that all power in Chad would henceforth stem from the barrel of a gun. In this contest for supremacy, the factions headed by Habré, by Goukouni, and to a lesser extent perhaps by Kamougué were the leading, but by no means the only, contenders. Outside of the capital city, several lesser warlords emerged to make their bid for a chunk of Chad's decaying carcass. In addition to Habré's own forces (now largely tied up in Ndjamena), four or five splinter groups (each claiming some more or less tenuous descent from past FROLINAT leaders) controlled portions of eastern and central Chad. One of these factions, headed by Ahmat Acyl and consisting mainly of Chadian Arabs, had built up its strength through Libyan largesse as Qaddafi became disenchanted with the independent-minded Goukouni who continued to object to Libya's occupation of the Aozou Strip. In the West, a small band led by Aboubakar Abdelrahmane, a renegade member of Goukouni's army, roamed the northeastern reaches of Lake Chad, where oil had recently been discovered, and insisted on calling itself the "third army" or the Forces Armées de l'Ouest (FAO), in obvious imitation of the more prominent factions. Even the South showed signs of splintering, and, of course, Abba Siddick, though professing to be thoroughly disgusted with all factions, nevertheless kept his hand in as the self-proclaimed leader of the "original FROLINAT."

Open concern for the situation in Chad was now voiced by neighboring states. Less explicit but equally preoccupying was the tempting opportunity for interference which the Chadian vacuum offered to Qaddafi, whose proclivities for rash adventurism were being amply demonstrated at the time by his backing for two of Africa's most unsavory autocrats, Idi Amin and "Emperor" Bokassa. This sense of urgency explains the hasty decision by Nigerian president Obasanjo to convene a "national reconciliation" conference at Kano in early March 1979. Attended by most Chadian factions as well as by Chad's neighbors, the conference ended with suspicious ease on a formal note of agreement. Upon returning home, the Chadian faction leaders then proceeded to hammer out their own makeshift coalition, led by Goukouni, while Nigeria, in an attempt to enforce its self-appointed role as mediator, dispatched a peacekeeping force that soon ran afoul of almost every Chadian faction. Three weeks after the first Kano conference, Nigeria hosted another round of talks with those factions that, in its haste and with an understandable lack of familiarity with the dizzying proliferation of Chadian splinter groups, it had neglected to invite to the first parley. On that occasion, Nigeria, Libya, and the Sudan each pushed their own protégés, thereby complicating rather than easing the task of national reconciliation. While ostensibly rallying behind Nigeria's choice to head a national coalition government, Habré, Goukouni, and Djogo worked out their own power-sharing arrangements, which, under the guise of achieving a semblance of national reconciliation, would leave them free to work out their differences in a more direct fashion. Nigeria thereupon withdrew its 1,600-man contingent and stopped oil deliveries to Chad, while Libya (equally incensed by the exclusion of Acyl from the coalition) embarked on a military buildup in the North. Goukouni ordered his followers to resist Libyan infiltration but was unable to prevent the growth of Acyl's zone of control. Meanwhile, in an attempt to gain hold of the South, Habré sent his forces into the Mayo-Kebbi district where they were decisively defeated by Kamougué, whose stature and claim to represent the South were thereby enhanced (largely at Djogo's expense).

By the end of July, the stillborn coalition was no more than a transparent fiction, and Nigeria, having won the endorsement of the OAU heads of state at their Monrovia summit, hosted yet another conciliation meeting (this time in Lagos) which, for the first time, was attended by the leaders of all Chadian factions. The conferees agreed to form the Transitional Government of National Unity (GUNT) to be replaced after eighteen months by a democratically elected regime. The choice of Goukouni to head the interim government was a testimony to the conciliatory and unassuming personality of the Toubou leader as well as to the increased credibility he had earned by standing up to the Libyans, but it also reflected, to an almost equal degree, the widespread hostility and suspicion the conferees increasingly harbored toward Habré's arrogance and boundless ambition. This was further confirmed by the choices of Kamougué—the man who had blocked Habré's raid into the South—to serve as vice-president of the provisional government. Since no viable coalition could be built in his absence, however, Habré was awarded the key ministry of national defense. The laborious process of distributing cabinet posts among the eleven factions represented in the GUNT took another two months, and the transitional government was eventually installed in November 1979. From the start, however, it was evident that the cabinet was not an operating body and that most of the factions were not interested in working with one another, treating their respective ministries as so many fiefdoms. In any case, lack of funds and of qualified personnel made it almost impossible for the administration to function properly.

One of the most striking resolutions of the Lagos conference in August had been to request the withdrawal of French troops, characterized as "an obstacle to peace." This was coupled with the rather vague promise that an African peacekeeping force would promptly be dispatched to Chad. France immediately responded by evacuating a portion of its contingent but, at the request of both Goukouni and Habré, agreed to postpone the completion of its pullout. Six hundred Congolese troops arrived in Ndjamena from Brazzaville on 18 January 1980, but by that time, Habré had already broken the uneasy truce by attacking the units led by Ahmat Acyl and his associates. Habré renewed his attacks in March, and the Congolese units promptly withdrew without having once intervened. In short order,

Kamougué's forces joined the fray, Habré and his faction were expelled from the GUNT, and the hapless Goukouni reluctantly concluded that a military showndown had now become inevitable. In mid-May, as Habré and Acyl called in reinforcements from their respective sanctuaries in the Sudan and Libya, the French completed the pullout of their remaining forces. In June, not without some misgivings, Goukouni agreed to the stationing in Ndjamena of a small, two-hundred-man detachment of Libyan troops to shore up the beleaguered GUNT which was held together by the common hostility of all participating factions to Habré's deliberate aggression.[18]

Up to that time, and with the exception of their occupation of the Aozou Strip, Libyan forces had never actually entered Chad. Assistance from Tripoli (initiated, as we have seen, before Qaddafi's accession to power) had simply taken the form of channeling a growing supply of equipment to the rebels and of providing them with sanctuary. By 1979, several factions (notably those led by Acyl and Kamougué) benefited from Qaddafi's largesse, but all of them were, in various degrees, anxious to keep him at arm's length, as evidenced by Goukouni's swift reaction to the threat of Libyan infiltration. The mutual defense treaty signed in June 1980 between Libya and the GUNT was an act of desperation, and Goukouni's inclination to limit its effects was shown by the small size of the initial Libyan contingent. Over the following months, unfortunately, the civil war escalated, and as any serious prospect of an OAU–sponsored force evaporated, Libya's embrace and offers of service could no longer be resisted. By the end of November, under the terms of the mutual defense treaty, the GUNT called Libya to the rescue, and within less than two weeks, Habré's forces (which already were in the process of being dislodged from the B.E.T. and Ouaddai prior to the dispatch of Libyan troops) were driven from the capital city.

Although a number of African leaders were clearly disturbed by Qaddafi's intervention (even if covered by a treaty with Chad's interim government), the OAU, conscious of its own failure to offer any viable alternative, grudgingly resigned itself to the fait accompli, while France itself appeared reconciled with the idea of dealing with Goukouni. It was at that point that, with characteristic flatfootedness, Qaddafi announced (on 6 January 1981) that Chad and Libya had agreed to a "merger." The OAU subcommittee on Chad immediately condemned the move as an infringement on Chad's sovereignty, and France reacted with a strong condemnation of Qaddafi's interference. It took some time for Goukouni to clarify the matter and to convince his fellow African leaders that Chad held a rather different view of its ties with Libya. Qaddafi's record with earlier spurious and unilaterally announced "mergers" contributed to restore Goukouni's credibility, and despite reservations about the continued Libyan presence, the OAU summit held in Nairobi at the end of June reaffirmed its recognition of the GUNT. Coming to terms with France was complicated by that country's transition to a socialist adminsitration, but by mid-September, Goukouni met with Mitterrand who, by virtue of his past association with them,[19] was particularly attuned to the sensitivities of veteran African leaders such as Houphouët-Boigny. Mitterrand impressed upon the Chadian leader the fact that normalization of his government's relations with Paris and notably his acceptability at the forthcoming Franco-African summit would be conditioned by his readiness to disentangle his country from its ambiguous ties with Libya.

Whether because of his trust in the new French administration or because he himself felt uncomfortable with the Libyan presence, Goukouni promptly responded to French suggestions and, on the eve of the Franco-African summit, abruptly requested Qaddafi to recall his troops from Chad. Libya immediately complied,[20] while at the Franco-African summit, Mobutu volunteered with suspicious alacrity to provide Zairian troops as the first contingent of an inter-African peacekeeping force, the principle of which had yet to be endorsed by the OAU. Ten days after the Libyan pullout, the first Zairian contingent (later joined by Senegalese and Nigerian units) had arrived in Ndjamena. Within a few weeks, Habré's forces, which had in the meantime regrouped in the Sudan and been thoroughly reequipped by the United States and its regional allies, launched a fresh offensive against the GUNT. It soon became clear that the so-called inter-African force was either unwilling or unable to protect the government it was supposed to uphold and whose sovereignty legitimized its presence in Chad. Instead, on 11 February 1982, Goukouni was enjoined in no uncertain terms to agree to a cease-fire and to negotiate with Habré.[21] Angered by what he saw, not unreasonably, as a "stab in the back," Goukouni tried to turn to Libya, but Qaddafi, still bitter over his unceremonious eviction (and anxious not to jeopardize his bid for the OAU chairmanship), coldly turned him down. Partners in the coalition began to tug their separate ways. Kamougué and Acyl pulled back to their respective strongholds, leaving Goukouni to defend the capital city, which fell on 7 June.

Acyl was killed in a mysterious "accident" in July. By September, Kamougué himself was driven out of his southern stronghold by an internal upheaval and, like Goukouni before him, he escaped to Cameroun and sought asylum in Libya. The remnants of the GUNT assembled in Tripoli and, with Qaddafi's backing, challenged Habré's claim to represent Chad during the second attempt to hold an OAU summit meeting in the Libyan capital. Like the initial attempt in August, however, this reconvened session aborted for lack of a quorum. Earlier, however, Habré had been accepted without any serious objections at the Franco-African summit held in Kinshasa, where he formally met with Mitterrand.

Habré's record of successive betrayals and his disinclination to share power with anyone did not encourage other Chadian leaders to rally behind the new regime. With the exception of Abba Siddick, who had little to offer except for his tarnished name, most of the significant power brokers (notably Kamougué and the St. Cyr–trained Djogo, viewed by many as Chad's most capable professional soldier) reaffirmed their support for the ousted GUNT and proceeded to regroup in Libya. Qaddafi, whose earlier willingness to disengage had been so cynically repaid, now had less reason than ever to refrain from assisting Goukouni, just as the Sudan and the United States had reequipped Habré in 1981.

In June 1983, as the OAU summit in Addis Ababa acknowledged the Habré regime (in the absence of delegates from Libya or the GUNT), Goukouni's forces, numbering 2,500 to 3,000 and probably including a handful of foreign "advisers," launched a major offensive from their bases in Bardai and the Aozou Strip. Within days, they had captured Faya-Largeau and were plunging South to seize Umm Chalouba and Abéché, briefly cutting Habré's lifeline to the Sudan. France immediately sped up the delivery of military supplies, as did Egypt and the Sudan. President Reagan dispatched a $10 million military aid package under emergency powers not subject to congressional approval. This was in addition to the $10 mil-

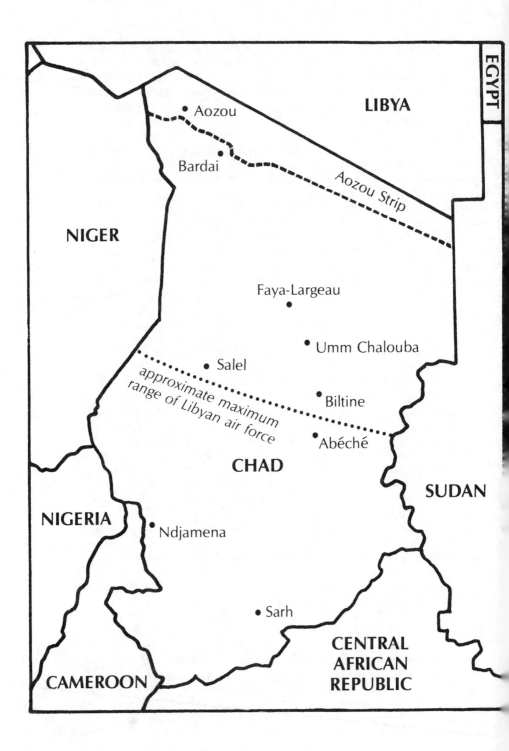

lion covertly provided to Habré through CIA channels in 1982 to help him over-throw the GUNT. Zaire's immediate contribution of a commando battalion was increased by the end of July to a force of 3,000 with air support, including three Mirage fighter jets. The Zairian contingent, bankrolled by the United States, did not take part in the fighting, but was deployed around Ndjamena, thereby freeing Habré's followers to mount a successful counteroffensive. By the end of July, Abéché, Umm Chalouba and Faya-Largeau had been recaptured by government forces. At that point, a Libyan contingent numbering some 2,000 and backed by jet bombers, heavy artillery, and armored vehicles came to the rescue and helped the GUNT forces regain control of Faya-Largeau and of most of the terrain they had lost to the Habré counteroffensive.

In his press conference of 11 August, President Reagan professed to see no circumstances that would call for a military intervention by the United States, but American concern for the region was attested by the fact that, even before Libya had intervened, the U.S. Rapid Deployment Force had been scheduled to hold ex-ercises in the Sudan during August. The chief effort of U.S. policymakers, how-ever, was directed at convincing France to commit itself to a full-scale military intervention. Through an orchestrated barrage of arm-twisting, cajoling, and veiled threats, the increasingly annoyed Mitterrand, who had already agreed to send some 500 French "instructors" to Ndjamena, finally approved the deployment of 2,500 French troops backed by armored vehicles, missile-firing helicopters, eight jet fighters, and four support and reconnaissance aircraft. Meanwhile, however, the plans to bring in a sizeable contingent of seasoned Moroccan troops to back up the Habré regime (as they had bolstered Mobutu in 1977 and 1978) evaporated when Qaddafi pledged to end his support for the Polisario insurgents of the Western Sa-hara in exchange for King Hassan's neutrality.

The deployment of the French expeditionary corps (known as Operation Manta) brought the Libyan-backed rebel advance to a halt, and without any major military confrontation, the fighting stabilized by early September along a line run-ning from east to west between the districts of Kanem and Biltine, that is, along the edge of the range the Libyan air force could cover from its bases. A small, but largely symbolic contingent of Chadian governmental troops clung on, under ha-rassment, to the outpost of Umm Chalouba, southernmost gateway to the B.E.T.; but despite Habré's bombastic pledges to march on to the North, the French re-fused to let their protégé dictate their choice of objectives. Indeed, even as French troops were still being deployed, President Mitterrand made it clear that any last-ing solution of the Chadian problem must be political rather than military and that foreign intervention was no substitute for a negotiated settlement (possibly in the form of a federal arrangement) among all Chadian factions.[22] Libya, for its part, wisely chose to parallel France's restraint, and by the end of the year, an uneasy stalemate and de facto partition had descended on Chad.

Despite discreet French nudgings, Habré refused to meet with Goukouni, while insisting (with no great risk of being taken up) that he was ready to negotiate with Qaddafi. By attempting to accredit the view that Goukouni and other GUNT leaders were merely Libyan puppets, Habré was, of course, trying to adhere to the simplistic version of events that represented his best (if not only) chance for polit-ical survival and allowed him to bask in the light of his improbable image as the pro-Western "good guy." In January 1984, Habré boycotted a reconciliation meet-ing to be held in Addis Ababa under OAU sponsorship. GUNT forces reacted with a limited attack, apparently intended to remind all parties concerned of the fragility of the truce, but the French immediately responded by moving their defense line some sixty-five miles northward, to the latitude of Umm Chalouba. By the spring, Goukouni appeared to be turning away from Qaddafi and leaning toward Algeria for alternative support. This opened the prospect of a direct negotiation (on neutral ground) between the GUNT and the Habré regime but prospects for an early settlement nevertheless remained tenuous.

INTERNATIONAL DIMENSIONS OF THE CHAD CRISIS

The Chadian situation reached an unprecedented degree of internationalization in 1983 with the explicit involvement of Libya, France, and the United States, not to mention a number of minor actors. Neither Libya's nor France's roles, however, are actually new, and the current stalemate appears in many ways like a replay of the situation that prevailed in mid-1978 (and, for that matter, at various earlier times). What is new, of course (although it remains far short of an all-out commitment), is the scale of Libya's intervention, but this is clearly due, in large part, to a prior escalation of the crisis by the United States—that move itself being only one of several actions directed by the United States against Libya within the context of its Middle East and African strategies. Whether or not they are fully rational (and Reagan's hyperbolic characterization of Qaddafi as "the world's most dangerous man" leaves some doubt on that score), the mutual hostility and suspicion between Libya and the United States are a matter of record. Nor are the reasons for this tension hard to identify. But, granting Qaddafi's proclivity to adventurism, it may be that the fundamental question to ask is not why (or how) Libya allegedly threatens the stability of every state from Morocco to the Gulf, from Ulster to the Congo, but rather what makes these regimes so vulnerable to this presumed subversion. The fragility and dubious legitimacy of most African states reflect the ambiguity of the decolonization process whereby they were ushered from a colonial to a neocolonial status. Many of these regimes were midwifed and nurtured by the barely concealed manipulations of the ex-colonial powers, with the United States occasionally stepping in when (as in Zaire) the former colonizers seemed unable to protect their spheres of influence.

The list of countries in which Qaddafi has truculently meddled or offered to meddle has been made even longer by the tendency on the part of a number of unstable regimes to attribute just about any form of domestic unrest to Libya's interference. Thus, Qaddafi's reputation has come to exceed his reach, and that reach, in turn, has consistently exceeded his grasp. The list of Qaddafi's "failures" is nearly as long as that of his interventions, real or alleged, even if one counts as "successes" the emergence in a given country of a government willing to entertain friendly ties with Tripoli in exchange for dollops of Libyan aid.[23]

Chad's case is different, however, not because it involves military action (though its occurrence is rare enough, with the only other notable case being Libya's limited involvement in the defense of Idi Amin), but because Chad is, quite simply, in Libya's own backyard. Whatever will-o'-the-wisp he might have been pursuing in Uganda or Liberia, whatever visions of an African Islamic empire he may have conjured, Qaddafi's interest in Chad is of a more conventional and indeed rational nature, as confirmed by the fact that pre-Qaddafi Libya also maintained an abiding interest in the Chadian situation. When Libya's ambassador to

Paris, Sa'id Hafiana, noted: "We consider that the stability and security of Chad are linked to our stability and our security. . . . This means that there must not be in Chad a political regime which is hostile to Libya and which might use Chad as a base for direct action,"[24] he was speaking a language that all international actors can recognize. Against the half-myth of a Protean Qaddafi sowing the seeds of subversion across the continents stands the more sober reality of an oil-rich but otherwise minor state surrounded on all sides by Western-backed neighbors—each with a substantially larger population than Libya's—while the U.S. Navy cruises along its Mediterranean frontage within sight of the "shores of Tripoli" (yes, that Tripoli, not the site of Arafat's last stand). Breaking this encirclement by preventing Chad from being turned into a base from which military operations can be conducted against Libya (as it was in World War II) is thus, from Tripoli's viewpoint, a rational objective. It is also a goal that, unlike some of Quaddafi's more grandiose dreams, has the advantage of feasibility, not only because Chad has been and is likely to remain the weakest link in the region, but also because of the very real historic and cultural ties between Libya and northern Chad.

These very same factors, however, can also work to Libya's detriment. Chad's chronic fragility and penetrability have left it permanently open to other external influences. After more than sixty years, France's presence in the area can almost be regarded as traditional, but the growing involvement of the Sudan and of the United States looms even more ominously. And when it comes to exploiting traditional linkages or irredenta, the Sudan (where Chadian migrants and refugees number some 500,000) holds a potential leverage that equals or exceeds that of Libya, as Habré discovered during his two periods of forced exile in Khartum.

The ironic dilemma of Libya's Chadian policy is that, in its attempt to contain or to roll back Western influence on its southern border, it has, in fact, contributed to the creation of a situation that invites a more overt form of involvement by the United States and its local clients. On the other hand, the crisis has allowed Libya to extend its southern glacis over the B.E.T., which now provides it with a convenient, if temporary, buffer zone and with some valuable chips for the inevitable negotiation. The cost of maintaining these tactical gains is one that Libya can easily afford, at least for the moment, and that would almost certainly be exceeded by the cost that France would incur by attempting to wrest them back at this stage. Over the longer run, however, Libya cannot overlook the fact that the prospect of a protracted Libyan occupation is the one issue on which all Chadian factions agree in common opposition. As is the case with many artificial states, Chad's uncertain sense of national identity is most easily affirmed through negatives. Thus, for lack of more solid criteria, being Chadian could best be defined as not being Libyan (or Sudanese or Centrafican). Practically as well as officially, Libya's territorial ambitions in Chad are probably limited to the Aozou Strip (and even those could conceivably be worked out amicably under the right circumstances), but Tripoli can almost certainly be expected to hang on to its goal of blocking any settlement that would run counter to its perceived security interests. In 1979, Libyan premier Jalloud bluntly stated that "any solution for Chad which does not meet with our approval is doomed to failure."[25] The subsequent five years have not eroded the credibility of that assertion, which still stands today as the most realistic expression of Libya's policy goals in Chad.

It would undoubtedly be much harder to come up with an equally clear-cut formulation of France's aims. This is not due in any particular degree to vacillation on the part of the Mitterrand administration, but rather to the number and complexity of variables that French policymakers have to reconcile by virtue of the scope and diversity of France's interests and alliance relationships. De Gaulle had retired from the political scene by the time it became apparent that it would take more than a routine police operation to control the Chadian insurgency (and, incidentally, before Qaddafi had taken control of Libya). Pompidou followed his own earthy common sense as well as the advice of those African leaders whose opinions he valued (notably his old classmate Senghor) by inclining toward a political settlement, and he accordingly did not discourage Tombalbaye from seeking an accommodation with Libya. The *affaire Claustre*, of course, fell into the lap of the Giscard administration as part of the Pompidou succession. And during the late 1970s, France, faced with an increasingly fragmented situation, was by and large reduced to waiting for the dust to settle while attempting to maintain a semblance of normalcy in its relations with whatever faction happened to have the upper hand.

France took the GUNT in stride, even though it had no direct part in its emergence, and appeared to proceed on the plausible assumption that, no matter what its ostensible ideological coloring, any Chadian regime would sooner or later have to reach a working understanding with Paris (as was indeed the case with Goukouni). Habré's defection and Libya's intervention at the request of the GUNT occurred while France was in the midst of a presidential election campaign and thus received only a modicum of immediate attention; but within a few months of his election, Mitterrand persuaded Goukouni to call for the withdrawal of Libyan troops. Throughout these years, however, the decisiveness of French policy was frequently blurred by the fluidity of the Chad situation which understandably made it difficult to transcend short-term perspectives, by the logic of neocolonialism which implies a preference for low-profile, behind-the-scenes intervention rather than for the series of inconclusive military operations in which France found itself repeatedly drawn, and by the very complexity of France's African policy apparatus with its many overlapping agencies, each pursuing its own tortuous path and often working in competition, if not at cross-purposes. Though the muddle was real enough, it did enable France to keep a finger in each of Chad's many pies: at no time were avenues of communication with any of the factions or warlords ever completely closed, and this probably remains France's greatest asset at the present juncture.

Over the past forty years, however, the premise of Chad's importance to France has been taken as a given and never seriously questioned. Much of this was based on the geopolitical value that France and the French military, in the idiosyncratic tradition of Continental powers, tended to attach to the control of large land masses. Chad was thus seen as a "necessary" linchpin between France's Equatorial holdings and her possessions in North and West Africa. In more mundane terms, of course, it also represented the residual increment of the French drive toward the Nile which the British had fended off at Fachoda. This rather irrelevant vestige of aborted expansionism acquired renewed significance during World War II when under the influence of its West Indian–born governor, Félix Eboué, Chad became the first African territory to rally to de Gaulle (soon to be followed by the rest of French Equatorial Africa) as well as the base from which the first Free French units, headed by the legendary General Leclerc and overwhelmingly made up of Chadian soldiers, reentered the war on the side of the Allies by mounting an unexpected attack from the South against the Italians. Chad thereby acquired a special place in the Gaullist legend, as well as in the annals of the French military, in whose postwar reorganization members of the Division Leclerc and other Free French forces played a central role. A whole generation of French officers preserved and transmitted their emotional commitment to the strategic value of Chad, which became an axiom of French military doctrine and was ostensibly reconfirmed by the rise of al-Nasir and by the traumatic effects of the Suez crisis and of the Algerian uprising. In the rather dubious logic that saw Egypt as the breeding ground of every form of anticolonial "subversion" and as a primary source of inspiration and supply for the Algerian freedom fighters, the belief in Chad's importance as the bulwark of the French presence in Africa was reinforced, and it even survived, in a more subliminal form, the end of the Algerian war and of direct French rule in sub-Saharan Africa. Thus, French military circles have probably carried more than their usual weight in the process of French policymaking toward that portion of the continent.

By contrast, French economic interests in Chad have, overall, played a more limited though not necessarily unimportant role. Even though its contribution to the economy of the franc zone is almost negligible, the cotton sector looms large in the Chadian context, and the French interests that control it have consistently reflected an emphasis on the "Tchad utile," whether in the form of favoring southern dominance of the central government or, more recently, by attempting to contain the extension of civil strife to the South and to preserve it as an enclave of relative prosperity, thereby fueling that region's autonomist tendencies.

Though receptive to the special views of business or military circles, successive French governments have nevertheless approached Chad from a broader perspective in the partly overlapping contexts of France's policies toward her former overseas territories, toward the rest of Africa, and toward the Arab world and the Middle East, or more recently and not without some reluctance, in the context of her relationship with the United States and thus, indirectly, of East-West confrontation.

Despite her extensive leverage, France's relationship to its African ex-colonies is not entirely a one-way street. French influence is a direct function of the extent of the French presence (in the broadest sense of the term) and of the degree of security that France can provide to the local regimes, whether in the form of economic and technical aid, in the cultivation of a sense of privileged and mutual relationships, or when the threat of destabilization arises, through the sharing of intelligence and the dispatch of troops. Failure to maintain this diversified supportive capacity thus theoretically weakens French influence, though not necessarily in a significant or permanent way. In fact, leverage can, in a very real sense, be enhanced by its discretionary nature, and France has indeed on several occasions withheld support (including in the form of military intervention) from regimes that were deemed objectionable or expendable. France's growing confidence in the strength of neocolonial ties also allowed her to countenance with equanimity the occasional advent in her former African empire of ostensibly radical regimes (such as those in Congo-Brazzaville, Benin, Madagascar, or lately, Upper Volta).[26]

France's capacity for adopting the long view and for taking African ideological stances with a solid grain of salt has, by and large, made her more skeptical than the United States toward African versions of the domino theory and has even allowed her to maintain working relationships with states that the United States tends to classify, somewhat hastily, as Soviet clients, such as Angola, Ethiopia, and of course, Libya.

Yet France cannot overlook the credibility of the protection she is expected to provide as part of the patron-client relationship, especially when it is being insidiously questioned (as happened last summer) by an "ally" that has been nibbling at the edges of her choice economic preserves. In addition, France is also mindful of the influence she has been patiently building up in areas that lie outside her former colonial domain, as reflected by the growing attendance at the annual Franco-African summit meetings, which in 1982, even outdrew the ill-fated Tripoli OAU summit. The choicest recruit into this "extended family" has been Zaire, where French influence increased markedly after the Foreign Legion was dispatched on a highly publicized, if somewhat futile, mission to the mining city of Kolwezi. While Mobutu's professed concern over Libya's intervention in Chad was visibly designed to curry favor with the Reagan administration, the pleas for a stepped-up French response by the Ivory Coast and Senegal (though also encouraged by U.S. diplomats) struck a more sensitive chord in Paris, if only because they came from France's two closest friends in Africa and could be addressed to Mitterrand in the name of ancient comradeship. It may also have been felt that, despite Mitterrand's personal friendship with several Francophone African leaders and his clear inclination to treat Franco-African relations, like his predecessors, as part of the "presidential domain," France's willingness to take direct and decisive action, which had been open to question since the 1981 advent to power of the Left, needed to be explicitly affirmed.

Even so, the decision to intervene in Chad was not embarked upon without some second thoughts. For one thing, it was bound to draw some negative reactions within the ranks of the ruling majority which had, after all, campaigned against the use of such practices by the previous administrations. France was also wary of jeopardizing her hard-won image as the only non-African power capable of maintaining friendly relations with almost every African state, from "progressives" to "moderates," through a reactivation of a style more reminiscent of her earlier and still remembered image as le gendarme de l'Occident (or worse yet, as "Uncle Sam's Cubans").

What made France's dilemma especially aggravating, of course, was the blatant badgering and deliberately visible way in which the Reagan administration prodded her to intervene in support of the Habré regime. From hints that France had become a paper tiger or that her African clients might "turn elsewhere" for protection to Reagan's flat-footed assertion (possibly intended as a form of flattery) that Chad was part of France's "sphere of influence," no effort was spared to broadcast the image of France as a muddled, yet ultimately dutiful satellite that had finally heeded the wisdom of her more perceptive Big Brother and realized the mortal danger that "mad dog" Qaddafi (instigated, of course, by the Evil Empire) represented for Africa and the rest of the free world. Though his own reading of the crisis, based on greater familiarity with the Chadian situation, inclined him toward an appropriate response, Mitterrand was understandably annoyed by the comic-book analysis pushed by the Reagan administration and especially by its arm-twisting style which deprived France of any credit she might have earned for her intervention and clashed with her usually more secretive modus operandi.

Although it ultimately involved a de facto confrontation with Libya, France's decision to intervene in Chad was apparently not affected to any substantial degree by her Middle East policies or by her overall relations with the Arab world, partly because Libya's maverick status in the region has left it with no unconditional friends and partly because of a tacit preference for avoiding an all-out conflict. Contrary to a widespread belief, France's reluctance to espouse the Reagan administration's unrestrained hostility toward Qaddafi is not primarily due to the magnitude of Franco-Libyan economic ties. France has indeed sold military equipment to Libya and bought some oil and natural gas from Tripoli, but her economic stake in Libya is puny in comparison to American business interests.[27]

In truth, Paris has determined, even before the latest crisis over Chad, that French national interests are not vitally threatened by Libya and would not in any case be served by an all-out military confrontation, even if (as is probable) France were able to defeat Libya in the course of an open war, if only because the chief beneficiary of such conflagration would be the United States and its regional clients rather than France herself. For somewhat comparable reasons (in that they too revolve about an assessment of national interest), Libya also has no wish to let itself be drawn into a military showdown with France and should accordingly be content to prolong the current stalemate, especially in view of the fact that a no-peace, no-war deadlock is more advantageous to Libya than to France because it is less costly and easier to perpetuate while leaving Tripoli in control of a useful buffer zone. In the final analysis, therefore, both France and Libya share an interest in limiting the scale of their present conflict and have a reasonably good chance of being able to contain their confrontation over Chad if they can control the bellicosity of their respective protégés and (in France's case) that of the United States.

After its theatrical insistence that Chad's problems really belong in France's lap, the Reagan administration is now to some extent the prisoner of its own rhetoric and cannot, without further straining Franco-American relations, claim to have had second thoughts and demand the leading part for itself. There is, in fact, no indication that the United States, no matter how "activist" its foreign policy has been in recent months, is particularly anxious (at least in an election year) to dispatch troops to yet another exotic hornet's nest. The situation might be somewhat different if the French, weary of bearing the costs of a thankless mission (which, unlike Mobutu, they cannot bill to the United States), decide to extricate themselves from Chad after patching together a face-saving political settlement— or worse yet, no settlement at all—thus leaving Chad pretty much as they found it. This unattractive, yet not implausible scenario argues strongly in favor of allowing France to proceed in her own way, at her own pace, and without any war whoops from Washington, toward a viable settlement involving all relevant parties (including Libya and the Sudan, whether officially or not).

At this point, however, the greatest obstacle to a successful defusing of the situation in Chad is not so much Qaddafi or, for that matter, the Soviets (even U.S. officials privately admit that "Libya does not coordinate its activities in Africa with Moscow")[28] but the rival Chadian leaders themselves, particularly Habré. Having apparently read Machiavelli even more closely than Mao, Habré seems to have come to the conclusion that his hold on power, and indeed his political survival, are best guaranteed if the situation is kept at the crisis pitch. Habré's belligerent posturing and theatrical pledges to march north, with or without French backing, have thus far amounted to little more than shadowboxing, and despite some provocative snide remarks by spokesmen for the Ndjamena regime France has apparently made it clear that she will not allow herself to be dragged recklessly into adventurist operations. Habré's rather flimsy excuses for dodging any meeting with Goukouni are obviously part of his overall strategy for preventing or at least delaying a settlement. Any time gained through such dilatory tactics also increases the chances that Habré's adversaries might be tempted to break the deadlock through renewed attacks, thus rekindling American alarm. The skirmishing reported in January 1984 around Zigey shows that this is not an implausible scenario.

France's decision to bring its forward lines up to the latitude of Umm Chalouba in response to this incident theoretically increased the chances of an open confrontation with Libya, but neither side seems to have been spoiling for a showdown. At the same time, however, the move enabled the French to keep a closer rein on Habré's forces. Prior to that decision, the forward posting of government troops in the northern salient of Umm Chalouba (beyond the line held by the French and within range of the Libyan air force) not only represented a baited trap—into which, however, the rebels avoided falling—but also a base from which armed provocations could be initiated without French clearance. As Habré's forces build up their strength through the delivery of Western military supplies, through the hiring of mercenaries, or through the injection of Egyptian and Sudanese advisers, the chances for a reopening of overt hostilities remain high. Should this happen, the French have the capability of rapidly reinforcing their contingent by bringing in additional troops and aircraft from their nearby bases in Gabon and the Central African Republic, but it is doubtful that this would be their preferred option, although it might be the only way for them to keep the situation from getting totally out of hand. The scope of Libya's involvement, in this hypothesis, would probably be the major determinant for the magnitude of France's response, but the most likely outcome of this resurgence of crisis would be a return to the current deadlock, unless other actors intervene more directly to alter the balance of forces.

Though many considerations should logically weigh against their direct entanglement in Chad, Egypt and the Sudan may be tempted—or prodded—into escalating their support of the Habré regime (possibly in the form of sending "volunteers"), especially if the United States is ready to provide financial and logistical backing. Qaddafi, on the other hand, despite the undue credit he has sometimes been given in the U.S. media for building up a network of clients, has few reliable friends and even fewer allies. The continuation of Soviet logistical support may be regarded as virtually certain (at least so long as Libya can pay for its arms purchases), but direct Soviet involvement is highly unlikely except, as a remote possibility, to prevent Libya's total collapse. Even this prospect, however, must be viewed as extremely doubtful, partly because there is no real precedent for it (as the Egyptians should know) and partly because, in his characteristically blunt and outspoken way, Qaddafi has never concealed his profound dislike of Marxist ideology and has taken pains to keep the Soviets at arm's length. In fact, any real chance that a regime more congenial to Moscow might emerge in Libya probably postulates the prior downfall of Qaddafi.

The use of common sense should therefore convince the Reagan administration to refrain from intervening in Chad any more directly than it has already done and to live by its professed belief that this is a problem that can and should be handled by France, even if Paris prefers to play by its own rules and views the problem in a somewhat different light. Yet, if common sense is, in Descartes's words, "the world's most evenly distributed commodity," it sometimes seems strangely absent in some policymaking circles. There is, however, another form of common sense that tends to emerge during election years and which, in the present instance, would argue against any major additional entanglement in an area where vital U.S. interests are not directly or immediately at stake and where, in any case, an alternative option already exists.

Given its heterogeneous nature, its inherent fragility, and its record of political instability, Chad may well remain a chronic trouble spot and a source of concern or conflict for its neighbors. Its value to anyone but the Chadians themselves is, at best, debatable, and the degree to which it could be controlled, in any lasting way, by an external actor is highly dubious. Although it has become a ritual for all those outsiders who have had a hand in attempting to solve them to say that Chad's problems can be settled only by the Chadians themselves, there is, in truth, no reason to believe that Chadians can achieve this goal easily or promptly, but there is, on the other hand, ample evidence that outside interference, in any form, has only served to make these problems more intractable.

NOTES

1. Such confusion is readily excusable, given the vacillations among "experts." The name of the ousted head of the Transitional National Unity Government (GUNT), Goukouni Oueddei, can be (and has been) spelled in at least a dozen different ways. Samuel Decalo, author of the generally reliable *Historical Dictionary of Chad*, lists him twice (with no cross-reference and differently phrased data) under "Ouaddaye, Goukouni" and "Wodei Goukouni" (pp. 214, 294). In the first of these two entries, he helpfully adds that "Ouaddaye" is "usually referred to by his first name," which is indeed the practice followed by many writers, including Virginia Thompson and Richard Adloff who, in their informative *Conflict in Chad*, index him under G rather than under O or W. As for *Africa Confidential*, it informed its readers in its issue of 7 September 1983 that it had decided to spell his name "Goukouni Oueddei," "rather than our traditional [*sic*] 'Waddeye.'" Meanwhile, Colin Legum, editor of *African Contemporary Record*, continues to adhere to his own preferred spelling of the GUNT leader's name as "Weddeye." From this sample, one can easily imagine the uncertainty that surrounds the exact names of less prominent actors.

2. For a detailed French account of the disputes, see Bernard Lanne, *Tchad-Libye: La querelle des frontières* (Paris: Editions Karthala, 1982). Lanne notes the many vagaries of current atlases on the precise delineation of the Chad-Libya border, which has, in any case, never been properly demarcated.

3. Specifically, the modern préfectures of Tandjile, Logone Occidental, Moyen-Chari, and Logone Oriental, including Sarh (formerly Fort-Archambault) and the Sara ethnic cluster, which represents roughly 25 percent of the total population of modern Chad.

4. The OAU's position of principle was never, in any case, meant to rule out bilateral renegotiations, and several minor adjustments have been or are currently in the process of being successfully negotiated.

5. After initially attempting to dismantle the sultanates which had been the chief bastion of resistance against colonial penetration, the French gradually chose to co-opt handpicked indigenous leaders without ever allowing them the degree of autonomy the British extended to the emirs of northern Nigeria. During the postwar period, chiefly influence was used as a bulwark against nationalist politicians. When, in 1969, the French forced Tombalbaye to accept an expatriate Administrative Reform Mission (MRA), one of the first "recommendations" of the French advisers was to restore to the chiefs much of the authority that had been stripped from them after independence. See Thompson and Adloff, *Conflict in Chad*, p. 72; also, Jacques Le Cornec, *Histoire politique du Tchad de 1900 à 1962*, (Paris: Librairie générale de droit et de jurisprudence, 1963).

6. Characteristically, transportation is, next to cotton, the most important sector of the modern economy and, given the fact that cotton growers represented a quasi-servile peasantry under the thumb of the French cotton monopolists, the only sector in which indigenous private entrepreneurs could really hope to flourish. An extraordinarily large number of political personalities of the "independence generation" were or had at some point been engaged in the trucking business.

7. Roger Pascal, *L'Islam au Tchad*, CHEAM, no. 4441 (1972), p. 9.

8. Decalo, *Historical Dictionary of Chad*, pp. 79, 116–18.

9. See Marius K. Deeb and Mary Jane Deeb, *Libya Since the Revolution* (New York: Praeger, 1982), pp. 93–105.

10. It is perhaps not coincidental that shortly before Habré was sent on his bizarre mission, France had begun to thin down its military presence in Chad, and Tombalbaye had survived an abortive coup. On this and subsequent occasions, French agents tied to different segments of the Chadian civilian and military establishments may well have been working at cross purposes. Habré himself has been accused of having been at the time an agent of Captain Pierre Galopin whom he captured and "executed" in 1975, and whose 1968 "secret" report on the abuses of Chadian government officials had been promptly leaked to Tombalbaye, making Galopin less than popular among the president's entourage.

11. On Habré's early career, see Thierry Desjardins, *Avec les otages du Tchad* (Paris: Presses de la Cité, 1975), pp. 29–31, 94–98; Jean Chapelle, *Le peuple Tchadien* (Paris: Editions L'Harmattan, 1980), pp. 277–79; Robert Bujitenhuijs, *Le Frolinat et les révoltes populaires du Tchad, 1965–1976* (The Hague: Mouton, 1978), pp. 243–46; and *Le monde*, 31 August 1978.

12. These were Dr. Staewen, a West German physician, Françoise Claustre, a French archaeologist, and Marc Combe, a French *coopérant*. Dr. Staewen's wife, who was the niece of the West German president, was accidentally killed in the kidnapping.

13. Combe managed to escape his captors in August 1975, but Françoise Claustre's husband Pierre, who had attempted to act as a self-appointed intercessor to secure his wife's release, was in turn held prisoner by Habré. Françoise Claustre was ultimately freed in January 1977, having spent a thousand days in captivity.

14. See, inter alia, Chapelle, *Le peuple Tchadien*, p. 270.

15. Ibid., p. 284.

16. Abba Siddick, who never lacked axes to grind, offered a bitter rejoinder when he characterized the new cabinet as one that was "headed by an executioner and a greedy seeker of ransoms" (*Afrique nouvelle*, 2 May 1978, quoted in Thompson and Adloff, *Conflict in Chad*, p. 82). Ironically, Siddick has now rallied to the Habré regime, in which he holds a minor cabinet post.

17. For a brief account, see Thompson and Adloff, *Conflict in Chad*, pp. 79–83.

18. President Eyadema of Togo, who can hardly be accused of pro-Libyan sympathies and who maintains close ties with the West and with Zaire's Mobutu, attempted at great personal risk to mediate between Habré and Goukouni and came to the conclusion that Habré was the greatest obstacle to peace in Chad. (See his interview in *Jeune Afrique*, 17 May 1980.)

19. After breaking its ties with the French Communist party in 1950, the supraterritorial RDA (Rassemblement Démocratique Africain), led by Houphouët, had become affiliated in the French National Assembly with Mitterrand's small left-of-center formation, the UDSR, and this had brought it back into the mainstream of Fourth Republic politics, with the result that Houphouët was named to a junior cabinet post, in which capacity he collaborated with Mitterrand on laying the foundations of what subsequently became the 1956 Loi Cadre.

20. Libya's uncharacteristic meekness was, in all likelihood, due to Qaddafi's desire to ensure his acceptability as the next chairman of the OAU and to improve his relations with the Mitterrand administration. Both expectations were disappointed.

21. Later in the year, as Habré's forces closed in on Ndjamena, the OAU belatedly disavowed the inter-African force, which it had halfheartedly endorsed earlier, and called for its immediate withdrawal, which was carried out when Goukouni's defeat was assured.

22. See Mitterrand's interview to *Le monde*, 26 August 1983.

23. For a tally of Qaddafi's reverses, see *Sunday Times* (London), 14 August 1983.

24. *Le monde*, 13 July 1983.

25. Interview in *Jeune Afrique*, 16 May 1979.

26. See Edouard Bustin, *The Limits of French Intervention in Africa: A Study in Applied Neo-Colonialism* (Boston: Boston University, African Studies Center, 1982), pp. 13–15.

27. See Eric Rouleau, "Guerre et intoxication au Tchad," *Le monde diplomatique*, September 1983.

28. *New York Times*, 9 August 1983.

ADDITIONAL READINGS

Buijtenhuijs, Robert. *Le Frolinat et les révoltes populaires du Tchad, 1965–1976*. The Hague: Mouton, 1978.

Bouquet, Christian. *Tchad: Genèse d'un conflit*. Paris: Eds. L'Harmattan, 1982.

Cabot, Jean, and Christian Bouquet. *Le Tchad*. 2d ed. Paris: Presses universitaires de France, 1978.

Decalo, Samuel. *Historical Dictionary of Chad*. Metuchen, N.J.: Scarecrow Press, 1977.

———. "Chad: Center-Periphery Cleavages and Civil Strife." *African Affairs*, July 1980.

Desjardins, Thierry. *Avec les otages du Tchad*. Paris: Presses de la cité, 1975.

Lanne, Bernard. *Tchad-Libye: La querelle des frontières*. Paris: Eds. Karthala, 1982.

Lebeuf, Annie. *Les populations du Tchad*. Paris: Berger-Levrault, 1959.

Le Cornec, Jacques. *Histoire politique du Tchad de 1900 à 1962*. Paris: Librairie générale de droit et de jurisprudence, 1963.

Le Rouvreur, Albert. *Sahariens et Sahéliens du Tchad*. Paris: Berger-Levrault, 1962.

Martin, B.G. "Kanem, Bornou and the Fezzan: Notes on the Political History of a Trade Route." *Journal of African History*, 10:1 (1969).

Ostheimer, John. "Playing the Arab Card: Niger and Chad's Ambivalent Relations with Libya." In *African Security Issues: Stability and Solidarity*. Ed. Bruce E. Arlinghaus. New York: Westview Press, 1983.

Pascal, Roger. "L'Islam au Tchad." *Cahiers du CHEAM*, no. 4441 (1972).

Thompson, Virginia, and Richard Adloff. *Conflict in Chad*. Berkeley: University of California, Institute of International Studies, 1981.

"Le Tchad déchiré." *Le monde: Dossiers et documents*, November 1983.

The Middle East in the U.S. Media

Edmund Ghareeb

The controversies surrounding television and print coverage of the Israeli invasion of Lebanon and of U.S. operations in Grenada have increased the charges that the media are elitist, negativistic, inaccurate, and superficial in dealing with complex issues. The lack of sympathy if not outright hostility shown by the public for the media in their dispute with the government over the handling of the Grenada coverage indicates that the problem has deeper roots than the immediate issue at stake.

Some critics have said that the media are overdue for serious examination and criticism for "cynicism and hostility towards American presidents and government institutions" (Janka 1983, 9), and for preoccupation with idol smashing and idle politicking (Shepley 1983, 10). Moreover, there has been a suspicion that journalists are showing increased disregard for accuracy and objectivity. Some people expressed delight when the *Washington Post*, the *New York Times*, and the *New York Daily News* were humiliated in 1981 and 1982 over the fact that they had printed stories their reporters had invented or embellished (Henry 1983). Robert MacNeil of PBS's "MacNeil-Lehrer News Hour" touched on the root of the problem when he stated, "More and more people have had the experience of being interviewed or being at an event that has been covered, and they know what they see on the screen is not the way it was" (Henry 1983, 79).

The increasing criticism leveled at the media may reflect unease over their power to channel and mold public opinion through their wide influence. Ben Bradlee, the editor of the *Washington Post*, has suggested that the national agenda—the topics the public takes to be the substantive issues of the day—is set by leaders of journalism, not leaders of government (Maddocks 1982). The print and broadcast organs are especially powerful in shaping public attitudes toward foreign affairs. Because most Americans are less interested in foreign than domestic issues, they are susceptible to interpretive reporting on foreign affairs. Often, such reporting affects U.S. policy on strategic issues without alternate points of view being aired or printed.

This situation has led one critic to state, "It is doubtful to put it bluntly whether anyone in this country, on the basis of reading the newspapers, listening

185

to the radio and viewing television, without the benefit of other sources, can be reasonably well-informed on world affairs. True, generalizations are always a little unfair. Some media devote more space or time to foreign affairs than others, and there are, of course, journalists and editorialists of the highest caliber. But when all allowances are made it is still true that foreign coverage and comment in the U.S. press is by and large quite bad. It is in fact on a lower level of competence and sophistication than it was in the 1930s" (Laqueur 1982, 100).

It has become obvious that in a technologically complex society, freedom of speech loses some of its value when it cannot be hooked up to the amplification system. Gay Talese, historiographer of the *New York Times,* has said that "news, if unreported, has no impact. It might well have not happened at all" (Karl 1983, 291). It may be that this view does not apply as much to international as to domestic events, for unreported international developments and the forces behind them will, sooner or later, come to world attention. Nevertheless, the media can distort perceptions of issues, actions, or foreign policy matters through the selective information it offers. Often such coverage critically affects and is affected by government policies.

One danger, as Patricia Karl points out, is that "everywhere the media have become part of the action," manipulating, manipulated, participating, building and destroying images, and acting as a bullhorn for what were once the whispers of diplomacy. Nowhere is this more obvious and more dangerous than in Middle East diplomacy (Karl 1983, 283).

There is little doubt that Washington reporters assist U.S. administrations and influence foreign policy in several ways. Reporters are "constantly used to transmit to foreign governments, through press, radio and television, those official views which the administration in Washington does not want to put in formal diplomatic communications. One reason for this is that the old diplomacy, with its polite but geometric language, has broken down and the new diplomacy—part secret, part public, part propaganda—has devised new techniques of communications between governments and peoples" (Reston 1967, 65).

It must be remembered, however, that journalists are not diplomats. They usually have, or ought to have, objectives different from those of the government officials upon whom they rely for much of their information. Nevertheless, these officials are playing an increasing role in deciding what is news, particularly in the coverage of foreign affairs, because of the way the media operate. The American media, especially television, focus on crisis coverage and depend on government officials who usually have the fastest access to sensitive information. Because of this dependence on government sources, they too often distort, exaggerate, and select and manipulate news happenings with little regard for the broader realities or the consequences. This can result in the creation of stereotyped or slanted and superficial images about the rest of the world. It makes it difficult for the public to understand conditions in foreign countries and to develop coherent policies that might reduce confrontations and violence. This situation bedevils the coverage of the Third World and particularly the Middle East (Ghareeb 1983; Hudson and Wolfe 1980).

SOURCES OF THE PROBLEM

What are the causes of the inadequate coverage of Middle Eastern affairs, and of foreign affairs in general, by the American media? One of the main limitations on foreign coverage derives from the fact that the approach of the media is one-dimensional; foreign news coverage begins and ends with issues of immediate concern to the United States (Trattner 1982, 103). This reflects to a large extent the society's belief concerning the centrality of the United States in world affairs. In order for any event in the Middle East to be covered, it must somehow have an American angle, and when it is reported, the perspective is likely to be slanted according to its compatibility or incompatibility with American values and interests.

William Adams, in a book on U.S. television coverage of the Middle East, revealed that the coverage was largely defined in terms of the threat to Israel and the Arab-Israeli conflict in which the United States was directly involved in supporting Israel (Adams and Heyl 1981, 12). Stories that were not related to the Arab-Israeli conflict, such as the Yemen war, the internal events in Iran, and the initial pro-Soviet coup in Afghanistan, were screened out as less newsworthy. Arab states bordering Israel received more coverage than the rest of the Arab world. The Gulf area, especially in these times of oil glut, or, even worse, the Arab states of the Maghreb—with the exception of Qaddafi's Libya—received much less coverage. "Only a few states broke the Israeli-Arab focus to a significant degree," said Adams. In addition to the Iran story, particularly the hostage crisis (which was the major exception to the pattern), other issues receiving attention were the Lebanese civil war and the Soviet occupation of Afghanistan, the October war, the Sadat trip to Jerusalem, and the Camp David summit. Even Iran received little coverage prior to 1978, and Iraq and Afghanistan were largely ignored prior to 1980 (70).

Following the defeat in Vietnam, the release of the American diplomats held hostage in Teheran, and more recently, the "redeployment" of American Marines from Lebanon, the coverage of developments in these countries was dramatically reduced. These facts reveal that U.S. strength and a sense of a U.S. global mission set the tone for the coverage of foreign affairs in the United States. There was little coverage of other societies regardless of their impact on and implications for U.S. policies. As one former spokesman for the State Department said, "Americans must recognize the superior and more practical logic of adapting one's analysis to the facts instead of the other way around" (Trattner 1982, 111).

Another factor that affects coverage of Middle East issues is the preoccupation with domestic problems and developments at the expense of foreign affairs. Since the early sixties, public interest in foreign developments has lost ground to the internal challenges and problems facing American society and institutions, such as civil rights, Watergate, the economy, and the environment. Some, in fact, credit the media for "displaying a socially responsible attitude about what the American public 'should' know about the world, even when that does not appear to be what they 'want' to know" (Bell 1980, 53).

Others, however, have disagreed with surveys that indicate that the public is not interested in foreign coverage. Former State Department spokesman Hodding Carter has stated:

> I happen to believe all those surveys are wrong, in that they
> only reflect the diet that people are given. A more intelligent
> and more consistent approach would change the perception of
> people's needs. (Ghareeb 1983, 248)

Nevertheless, the amount of coverage and analysis of foreign events remains small in much of the media. Few newspapers and networks maintain correspondents overseas. Only major newspapers, such as the *New York Times* and the *Washington Post,* the networks, and the wire services can afford to dispatch correspondents to foreign countries. As a result, a small number of reporters become the source for overall U.S. coverage of foreign news. The composition of a newspaper's readership also has a lot to do with its editorial policy. One newspaper chain editor justified his newspaper's practice of sending reporters only to the Israeli side on the ground that what constituted news for his paper was determined by the largely pro-Israel and ethnic Jewish population in cities served by his chain (Ghareeb 1983, 52).

Foreign correspondents have to cover many countries. Reporters stationed in Beirut or Cairo have had to cover not only those countries but the whole Middle East with the exception of Israel where correspondents and news bureaus are present. What is more, many of the correspondents have little knowledge of the cultures and languages of the region. At one time, correspondents covered local and regional economic and political developments and provided stories about the culture and customs of local peoples, but this has changed. Since the correspondent is responsible for such a wide area, there's no time for this kind of story. In addition, the reporter is likely to send stories that will get in the paper which too often means reports of conflict, confrontation, catastrophes, and other upheavals.

This leads to another factor affecting Middle East coverage by the U.S. media—that of crisis reporting. Too often, brewing tensions or ongoing conflicts that deserve attention before a flashpoint is reached are ignored. The situation prior to the 1973 war and to the Iranian revolution are good examples. When the crisis erupts, the news fills the front pages and the evening newscasts, at times to the exclusion of other foreign news. While several hundred correspondents are sent to Iran, Vietnam, or Lebanon to cover a crisis, not even a handful are sent when the crisis is still in the developing stage.

The relationship between the government and the media is still another important factor—the reliance of news reporters on official information and confirmation of information, or what correspondent Claudia Wright has described as the "Deep Throat" method of reporting (Wright 1983, 27–29). She speaks of the dependence on sources to support a story's validity and of the dubious logic that if a story has an official source it must be true. This method allows for a lot of coverage for a source who may be lying. On the other hand, there is little room for a truthful source if that source is not official. Relying on government leaks and sources is in many ways antithetical to real investigative journalism. Furthermore, sources who leak news usually do so because they have a point of view they want to advance or because they want to undermine certain policies.

According to Hodding Carter,

> Most leaks are in fact the calculated placing of information by major players trying to effect policy before it is enunciated, trying to change it after it is enunciated, trying to get it accepted or trying to send messages. (Ghareeb 1983, 249)

Another question to consider is how the leak came about. Was it the result of a reporter's initiative and knowledge of developments in a certain country or of the initiative of an insider who has an axe to grind? Jim Hoagland, the foreign editor of the *Washington Post,* has said that one of his great concerns is that we tend to be used much too much by people who leak us stories for specific and often unhealthy reasons. We have an obligation to examine the motivation of our sources and, taking that into consideration, make our decision about publishing. (Ghareeb 1983, 241)

Leaks usually are premeditated on the part of sources and are of a sensitive nature. They may be authorized or clandestine. And when it comes to Middle East coverage, the leak, as Hodding Carter puts it, "goes straight to the Israeli bait" (Ghareeb 1983, 249). Many examples can be cited of planted stories and deliberate distortions and misinformation that tend to have a wide-ranging impact. A leak published several years ago in the *Washington Post* concerned payments made by the CIA to Jordan's King Hussein. Appearing one day prior to the secretary of state's visit to Jordan, this story embarrassed both sides and undermined U.S.-Jordanian relations. A more recent example was the leak by Israeli radio of the story about the U.S. decision to help Jordan establish a regional defense force to be used in the Gulf. The Israelis also leaked President Reagan's statement on radio before the announcement was made in Washington and before the president had discussed it with members of Congress.

The press disclosures in Israel about U.S. decisions to send troops to Lebanon following the Israeli invasion forced President Reagan to announce that he had agreed to commit U.S. troops to the peacekeeping forces in Lebanon. Former secretary of state Alexander Haig stated that "with this ill-conceived announcement attention was diverted for several vital days from the peace effort and focused instead on the meaning of committing American troops" (*New York Times,* 1 April 1984). Although some may disagree with Secretary Haig's interpretation of the leaks, there is no doubt the leaks have had their effect on U.S. policy and developments in the region.

But the leaks have been used not only by the Israelis and their supporters. Opponents of the close Israeli-American relationship also leaked to the press secret information from a U.S. General Accounting Office report on the real extent of U.S. assistance to Israel. This information was leaked to the *Philadelphia Inquirer* in the fall of 1982, and the uncensored report was published by the American-Arab Anti-Discrimination Committee in July 1983.

The reporting system here is not as dependent on access to the truth as it is on access to official sources (Wright 1983, 27). Israel's supporters in the United States and the Israeli government know how to exploit the situation to their advantage by providing access to official sources and information suitable for media use. The Arabs to their detriment keep U.S. secrets, whereas the Israelis to their advantage leak them. Some argue that Arab leaders and lobbyists who think the key to changing U.S. policies in the Middle East lies in getting the media to print the facts fail to understand this process.

Yet another problem with coverage of the Middle East lies in the manipulation of op-ed pages, television editorials, and Sunday programs of the David Brinkley type (Wright 1983, 28).

Op-ed pages are intended to provide analysis and commentary on current events by experts and to offer alternative viewpoints, thus bringing continuity and some sense of balance and history to the coverage of major events. But op-ed pages and television commentaries have evolved in a different direction. Instead of writers expressing personal opinions or reporting news, too often slanted facts are contrived by reporters and their sources (Wright 1983, 28).

To demonstrate this, Claudia Wright cites a *New York Times* opinion piece by Benjamin Netanyahu, the deputy chief of the Israeli mission in the United States, claiming Syrian atrocities and bestiality. On the same day, the *Washington Post* published an opinion piece by syndicated columnist George Will in which he made similar allegations based on the same evidence. The official Israeli opinion was the source of the Will opinion. Both writers obtained the same information from the same sources. Both newspapers published the statements with no regular news report of the implicit facts. There was no investigation of the claims themselves—Syrian girls biting the heads of snakes, Syrian men drinking dogs' blood—no photographs, and no official statements discussing and interpreting the facts (Wright 1983, 28).

Although some balance is at times provided by outside contributors, this does not apply to regular columnists. This is even more of a problem for Arab officials. I was told by an Arab diplomat of his experience in trying to place an op-ed story in a leading U.S. daily. The diplomat approached the assistant foreign editor of the paper to complain of the coverage his country was receiving and was told to write an op-ed piece. When he did so, he was told by the foreign editor that the paper did not publish articles by foreign diplomats on the op-ed page but that it would publish it as a letter to the editor. A few weeks later, the same newspaper published an op-ed piece by an Israeli diplomat.

Embassies also retain professionals to write op-ed pieces, and they court journalists with expense paid trips, gifts, and dinners. "The result is that the op-ed system has become a watering hole for hidden interests, hybrid statements and intelligence disinformation" (Wright 1983, 28).

Finally, other limitations on Middle Eastern coverage include cultural and linguistic unfamiliarity, inexperienced reporters, a think-alike atmosphere among the media, the pro-Israeli lobby (when Arab-Israeli issues are covered), a tendency to fall prey to stereotyping when shorthand is used to discuss complex issues, and the failure of Middle Eastern officials and their representatives to present their case effectively.

Through their coverage of the Middle East in general and the Arab world in particular, the American media have projected certain preconceived images of Arabs, Jews, and Muslims to their viewers, readers, and listeners—images notable for being one-sided and stereotyped. The potential impact of slanted, superficial, and inaccurate coverage becomes apparent when one considers that in covering the region, the media are dealing with an extremely sensitive area of the world, one faced with regional conflicts that could under certain circumstances trigger a confrontation among the superpowers.

THE HISTORICAL BACKGROUND

The coverage of the Middle East and its peoples has been affected by the scarcity of historical writings about the area and its contributions to human civilization. And since the majority of the people of the Middle East are Muslims, the stereotypes of Middle Easterners in general and Arabs in particular have been influenced by the conflict between the European and Muslim worlds, which has existed since the spread of Islam. The mutual distrust grew out of a series of misunderstandings between Islam and the West.

The Crusades and the conflicts between Europeans and Moors manifested in the successes of Charles Martel and El-Cid against the Muslim conquerors of Spain contributed much to Western images of Muslims. The Crusades were organized in Europe in the midst of religious fervor to wrest the holy places from the "wicked race" (Nasir 1965, 3). Western travelers, such as Niebuhr, Burkhardt, Burton, and Lawrence of Arabia who for a long time lived among Arabs and wrote about their experiences and about Arab culture, language, and literature, helped shape the image of the Arab in the West. Stories of Aladdin and Sinbad from the *Arabian Nights* tales became equated with Muslims in general and were accepted as a reflection of real life in the Middle East. Early contacts between Americans and Middle Easterners also contributed to the image.

It was the negative rather than the positive experiences that were remembered, however. The fact that Morocco was among the first countries to recognize the independence of the United States was not remembered as well as the 1803–4 naval campaign against the Barbary pirates of Tripoli. There were the works of American archeologists and missionaries, the camel caravan (the United States imported camels and a guide from the Middle East before the Civil War), and the performance of Little Egypt in the Chicago International Fair in 1899 when belly dancing was introduced in the United States (Nasir 1965, 4). In these encounters, the Muslims, particularly urban dwellers, not bedouins, were portrayed as dirty and dishonest. Countering this image were writings by Western travelers about bedouins, which contributed to a more romantic stereotype exemplified by films like Rudolph Valentino's *The Sheik*. Here the Arab was portrayed as honest, hospitable, manly, and courageous. This image did not last long, however.

As U.S. interests in the Middle East grew and the struggles both for control of the region's resources and between nationalism and western colonialism developed, another image of Middle Easterners and Arabs began to emerge. The imposition of military force to serve Western interests (Teheran 1953, Suez, Algeria, Lebanon) has led both to stereotypical thinking and to subjecting the people of the region to an abusive exercise of armed aggression (Ghareeb 1983, 186–87). The relations between the West and Muslim countries have been further aggravated by the West's support for Israel, by Western inability to understand the forces of change in the area, by the misinterpretations of Arab intentions by U.S. administrations, and by the attempt to blame the West's economic ills on the Arabs because of the oil price hike (Heikal 1980, 226.) In July 1979, for example, the American press carried excerpts from a memo to President Carter written by his senior domestic affairs adviser Stuart Eisenstat in June, urging the president to lay the blame for the leadership crisis in the West at the door of OPEC, which was identified in the minds of many with the oil-rich Arabs (228–29).

THE ARAB-ISRAELI CONFLICT

The creation of the state of Israel and the ensuing Arab-Israeli conflict has also contributed to the deterioration of the Arab and Muslim image in the West. While anti-Semitism was directed against Jews during the thirties and forties, the same prejudice is today directed against the Arabs. A 1938 survey showed that the

American public believed that persecution of the Jews in Europe was entirely (10 percent) or partly (48 percent) their own fault, and as late as 1946, a majority (72 percent) of Americans disapproved of President Truman's plan to ask Congress to allow more Jews and other European refugees into the United States (Suleiman 1980, 14).

Today the American image of Jews and Israelis is quite positive, and the Arab image has deteriorated. A 1975 study showed that Arabs were perceived as backward (47 percent), barbaric (38 percent), arrogant (37 percent), underdeveloped (47 percent), greedy (41 percent), and poor (34 percent), whereas Israelis were perceived as peaceful (41 percent), honest (39 percent), intelligent (39 percent), similar to Americans (50 percent), and friendly (46 percent) (Suleiman 1979, 15).

In another poll taken in the spring of 1980, a plurality of the respondents (representative of mainstream America) had a low opinion of Arabs; a strong majority sided with Israel. A large percentage associated Arabs with the following qualities: barbaric, cruel (44 percent), treacherous, cunning (49 percent), warlike, bloodthirsty (50 percent), mistreaters of women, anti-Christian, and anti-Semitic (40 percent). The results of this poll can be partly explained by the fact that the media have consistently portrayed Arabs as threatening U.S. political and economic security. In spite of a perceived turnabout in 1974, during which there began a trend toward more balanced reporting, Arabs are still seen as the antagonists (Slade 1981, 143–62).

The press often speaks of the "Arab world" as though it were some kind of homogeneous mass. In truth, as any informed observer of the Middle East and Africa knows, there are vast differences among Arabs of different countries. In stories dealing with increases in oil prices or the squandering of oil wealth, for example, Persians are thrown in with Arabs, even though Persians are ethnically distinct from Arabs.

Israel has also been subjected to this sort of stereotyping, albeit of a different and certainly more positive kind. Owing to the media and in part to their own Judeo-Christian upbringing, Americans generally see Israel as little, brave, beleaguered, and heroic, as compared to backward, ignorant, and bloodthirsty Arabs. A *Time* magazine editorial (16 March 1970) characterized Israel as "a democratic, modern, stabilizing force in a chaotic and brutally backward corner of the world," adding that "the Israelis have created a nation and made the desert bloom, thereby more than earning the right to national existence. Israel needs U.S. support to survive, and if Israel were someday to fall, U.S. interests would suffer." Three years later, the same publication characterized the Arab nation as a "congeries of 24 republics, monarchies, sheikdoms and otherwise organized anomalies" (12 April 1973, 26). Such negative and derogatory portrayal of the Arabs was also manifested in an article by syndicated columnist R. Emmett Tyrell, Jr. (1980). "Arabs," he wrote, "are not like Philadelphians, nor are they like Frenchmen, nor even Israelis. . . . Arabs are religious fanatics devoted to a non-Western warrior religion. Their bequests to us include the words *assassin* and *jihad*. . . . On this earth only the Chinese and the Russians indulge in more wanton slaughter of one another. The Russians and the Chinese do it to make their societies more efficient and sequacious; the Arabs do it out of religious fervor. . . . Whatever the case, the Arab draws his blade with gusto, and when he is finished butchering, he is that much closer to Allah."

The unbalanced media coverage of Arab issues is manifested in the following ways:

1. A disproportionate amount of space is given to Israel and its news as against the space given to all twenty-one Arab countries.

2. The press generally looks upon the Israelis as the "good guys" and the Arabs as the "bad guys." Israel is viewed as an extension of Western civilization and culture against the chaotic and backward setting of the Arab world.

3. Israeli communiqués and propaganda tend to form the basis of news and, in fact, are usually interwoven *with* the news. The media adopt Israeli terminology when referring to Middle East events, which are in turn reported from the Israeli point of view.

4. A large number of verbs attributing information to Israeli speakers are neutral; they include such words as *ask, tell,* and *said.* Descriptive phrases such as "the grandmotherly leader" were used to refer to Golda Meir. In contrast, a large proportion of verbs and adverbs referring to the Arabs have unfavorable connotations. This category represents the most direct means of editorial image creation.

Edward Said has analyzed the ramifications of the "Islamic threat" as seen by many Americans:

> I do not think it is an exaggeration to say . . . that "Islam" can now have only two possible meanings, both of them unacceptable and impoverishing: on the one hand "Islam" represents the threat of a resurgent atavism, which suggests not only the menace of a return to the Middle Ages, but the destruction of what, according to Daniel Moynihan, is called the democratic order in the Western world. On the other hand, "Islam" is made to stand for a defensive counter-response to their first image of Islam as a threat. Anything said about "Islam" is more or less forced into the apologetic form of a plea for Islam's humanism, its contributions to civilization, development, and perhaps even to democratic niceness. (Said 1979, 91)

Indeed, it is interesting to note what the semantic field of the word *Arab* has come to be. The media have tended to subsume many meanings under the word, whether they are speaking of the United Arab Emirates where per capita income is over $15,000 or of Yemen where it is $177. *Arab* can refer to the 40 million people in Egypt or to the 170,000 in Qatar. Stories turn up in the newspapers about the "Arab" lobby or about "Arabs" who are buying up property in the United States. The result of all this is to reinforce an already negative image of Arabs.

CHANGES IN MEDIA COVERAGE OF THE MIDDLE EAST

American media coverage of the Middle East has by no means remained static through the years. It has undergone a gradual metamorphosis during the last few decades, as evidenced by the fact that although it was overwhelmingly pro-Israel during the 1967 war, a small number of pro-Arab and pro-Palestinian articles nevertheless appeared in the press. The trend was sustained during the 1973 war (Suleiman 1967, 138–54; Terry and Mendenhall 1974, 53–81).

Today one can justifiably say that the worst excesses associated with the portrayal of Arabs and Muslims are over. This is due to the fact that considerable changes have taken place in the Middle East.

The Camp David accords recast the shape of Egyptian-Israeli and Egyptian-Arab relations. The revolution in Iran transformed the social and political structures of that country. Iraq and Iran have fought a war of attrition for three years. Israel has invaded Lebanon and foreign troops occupy much of that country. Other factors influencing the change were the impact of the October War, the oil embargo, the increase in economic and cultural interaction between Americans and Middle Easterners, and the change in the image of Israel from little "David" to "Goliath."

Moreover, certain recent events have served not only to change the image of Arabs but also to divest Israel of its mantle of irreproachable virtue. Egyptian president Anwar Sadat's trip to Jerusalem, as well as his peace initiatives which led to the Camp David accords, are seen as key turning points, according to studies in Adams and Heyl's book, *Television Coverage of the Middle East.*

These developments have also focused the world's attention on the Middle East, with the result that we have been deluged with information about the area. This increase has made it possible for some journalists to take a more balanced approach toward Middle Eastern coverage. However, although crass or totally distasteful stereotypes are rather less common than before, Middle East coverage is still generally superficial and slanted.

This is partly due to the emergence of OPEC as a major economic power. Editorial cartoons, in particular, are responsible in no small way for popularizing the image of the greedy, grasping, crooked Arab bent on crippling the American economy (Damon 1983; Lendemann 1983). Also, one still sees many instances of hyperbole, euphemism, guilt by association, and extrapolation of the weakest evidence to heap opprobrium on Arabs. In his book, *Covering Islam,* Edward Said showed how even the Iranian revolution, a non-Arab event, was used to present the "rise of Islam" as a threat to American interests abroad. He points to the tendency to confuse Iranians and Arabs, and the unconscious but active propensity to malign Arabs and Muslims (Said 1981).

The attempted assassination of Pope John Paul II by a Turkish citizen, Muhammad Ali Ağca, revealed the degree to which Muslims and Arabs have been associated in the public mind with violence and terrorism. Syndicated columnist Joseph Kraft associated Islamic society with violence and instability in an article entitled "The Dark Side of Islam." He wrote, "At the root of the assassination attempt is a turbulent Islamic society . . . pregnant with nasty surprises" (Kraft 1981.) This attitude was reflected in media emphasis on the "Arab" and "Middle Eastern" appearance of the assassin. The use of such characterizations is all the more revealing since the incident occurred in Italy, a Mediterranean country, and there was no immediate reason during the early coverage to believe the accused assassin was a foreigner. Even after Ağca's nationality was determined, radio station announcers continued to describe him as an Arab from Turkey (Ghareeb 1983, 162). The theme of traditional Muslim confrontation contributed to this attitude. *Time* magazine said that oil brought the Arabs "a power they haven't known since the time of the Crusades" (*Time*, 2 April 1973).

On the positive side, however, one can point to increased awareness on the part of the media of the need for more accuracy (Ghareeb 1983). One example of this awareness was the way the media handled the Israeli air attacks on southern Lebanese villages on 9 November 1977. The chief of staff of Israel, Mordecai Gur, had declared the attacks to be "retaliation" against "purely terrorist bases" for the Palestinian guerrilla rocket attacks on Nahariyya. On-the-scene coverage revealed that there were no guerrilla bases and that the majority of the dead and wounded were noncombatants. The coverage also showed that the Israeli reprisal was out of proportion to the initial attack, in which 1 Israeli woman was killed and 2 children were wounded; the retaliation brought a death toll of 120 people and scores of wounded. The treatment by the *Washington Post* and the *New York Times* of the Israeli air attacks showed that the media had begun to grasp the true dimensions of the Middle East conflict.

During the last couple of years, there has also been an increase in in-depth reports about the Arabs and the Middle East problem, even in the major newspaper chains. A significant number of these articles was written by Jewish journalists, and although such stories remain small in number, they represent a step in the right direction. Nontraditional sources of information have increased, too. The Arab League, Arab embassies, PLO information offices, the American-Arab Affairs Council, the National Association of Arab Americans, the American-Arab Anti-Discrimination Committee, and other Arab-American groups have made great strides toward combating and eliminating Arab stereotypes. They have conducted lobbying and informational activities, and as a result more diverse Middle Eastern viewpoints have been represented in the media.

THE WAR IN LEBANON

If one could speak of a loss of innocence on the part of the American press, it would be traced to the 1982 Israeli blitzkrieg on Lebanon. The events surrounding the invasion—the cover-ups by the Israeli government, the massacres at Sabra and Shatila, the changing U.S. government attitude—combined to jolt the American press out of some of its comfortable assumptions about the Middle East.

The Israeli invasion of Lebanon generated as much media coverage as any other war in history (Collins 1982, 2). The media were taken to task for their coverage by supporters of both Israel and the Palestinians. Each side charged the media with bias and discrimination, inaccuracies, ineptitude, and failure to place events in context. The media were forced to analyze the coverage, the criticism, and its ramifications. But the complexity of the job led Thomas Collins, a writer for *Newsday* who spent two months assessing the coverage and the criticism, to declare: "In many ways, it is easier to review a book than it is the press. A book is contained; the media sprawl like a river in flood. Its two main branches, print and television, obey different rules and often go off in different directions. . . . The presumption that anyone can read the river accurately without running into contradictions and crosscurrents is immense" (Collins 1982, 6).

Roger Morris, writing for the *Columbia Journalism Review*, pointed to the fact that the coverage incensed both sides and that "increasingly supporters of Israel" attacked the coverage for "omission, distortion, or worse" (Morris 1982, 23). The media, he said, were bombarded by letters, protests, and angry delegations. He concluded that "when it was over there was a sense that nothing scarred by the conflict—journalism, public trust, the Middle East, Israel's moral and political standing with Americans—would ever be the same again." Another article by *Washington Post* correspondent Edward Cody and Pnina Ramati also delved into the issues raised by the coverage (Cody and Ramati 1982).

Protests from Israel's Supporters

Television and press coverage of the Israeli actions in Lebanon sparked a series of vociferous protests from supporters of Israel. During past decades, the Israelis had been the victors in every propaganda war, partly by default through Arab censorship. But in the summer of 1982, the Palestinians had learned their lesson, and this time they welcomed photographers and correspondents to report on their defeat and on Israeli bombings of Palestinian civilian areas.

For the first time, as several hundred reporters traced the developments from Beirut, the world was given the Arab view as well as the Israeli view. The result was devastating to the Israelis. Now the Israelis imposed censorship on the press with dire results. The *Jerusalem Post* noted in an editorial that

> for weeks now it has been apparent that there is something fundamentally wrong with Israel's information effort in the Lebanese war. . . . Little wonder, then, that the image of Israel that emerged from the war in Lebanon has not been that of plucky little David rising to defend himself against his enemies, but that of giant Goliath, immensely powerful but also crude and somewhat mindless. (Ottaway 1982)

The Anti-Defamation League of B'nai B'rith (ADL), in a report on network television coverage of the war, charged that it was marked by "lack of balance," factual errors, and exaggeration. The networks (particularly CBS News) denied these charges vigorously, saying that since both sides "tried to use the media," it was necessary to "sift out the truth from all the conflicting claims and right mistakes" as soon as they were discovered (Schwartz 1983; Anti-Defamation League of B'nai B'rith 1982).

Several other pro-Israel reports and articles were published in the media. The most notable were "Misreporting Lebanon" by Joshua Muravchik (1982), Norman Podhoretz's "J'accuse" (1982), Martin Peretz's "Lebanon Eyewitness" (1983), and Frank Gervasi's "Media Coverage: The War in Lebanon" (1982).

These and similar articles complained that the public relations ineptitude of Israel was compounded by what many Jewish sympathizers perceived as an obvious bias against Israel in the American media. The authors complained that the press reported the war as though it had no history or context of past atrocities by the PLO, thus making the Israeli government appear needlessly warmongering. They felt that it focused too much on the devastation in Beirut without examining its reasons, and that it humanized Yasir Arafat, making him look like a human being instead of a monster (Collins 1982, 2).

In his article, "Misreporting Lebanon," Muravchik singled out the *Washington Post* for attack for its part in publishing what he described as "phantom statistics"—dubious figures from mystery sources, such as Michael Berlin's estimate of "100,000 to 300,000" civilians affected by the war and a later *Post* estimate of "1.5 million" Lebanese in need of relief help. Both figures were never substantiated. Certain *Post* reporters (such as Cody) were accused of quoting Israeli estimates of the casualties and then refuting them in the same breath. The purported slant in the *Post*'s handling of the news was a result of the *Post*'s underlying sympathy for the PLO, which was reflected in the analysis that the issue of the fate of the Palestinians is "the root cause of the Arab-Israeli conflict" (Muravchik 1982, 25).

Muravchik also emphasized instances of misquoting, as when Bernard Nossiter changed Begin's remark about the right of self-defense being "the noblest concept of the human mind" into "wars of self-defense" to convey an image of Begin as bloodthirsty. Moreover, Muravchik complained that some columns in the *Post* (by John LeCarre, Granville Austin, William Claiborne, Milton Viorst) actually pushed an analogy of the Israelis and Nazis (20–21). Begin was compared to Khomeini by Jim Hoagland (21), and Jonathan C. Randal expressed the view that Israel was the source of terrorism and violence in the Middle East in his news reports (21).

Muravchik also attacked the magazines for perpetuating an anti-Israeli bias. According to him, *Newsweek* was careless in its war statisticss—the same phantom statistics syndrome that the major dailies suffered from (32). The magazine carried factual errors, as when it mistakenly attributed the damage in Damur to Israeli strikes instead of to the PLO. The casualties inflicted by Israeli fire were exaggerated, and in the case of the intense Israeli bombardment of West Beirut in August, the exaggeration turned into invention, as *Newsweek* described the "firestorm" brought on by Israeli attacks (34). *Newsweek* showed an underlying sympathy toward the PLO and a lack of sympathy toward the Israelis; this was manifested in the way it blurred the distinction between Palestinians and the PLO. *Newsweek* also played up dramatic descriptions of Palestinian "national feeling" (34–35).

According to Muravchik, *Newsweek* had an idée fixe of Arafat as a moderate, and it too hinted at a similarity between the Israelis and the Nazis. *Time*, on the other hand, which disapproved of Israel's action, said so in a rather straightforward manner. According to Muravchik, "*Time*'s unabashed editorializing often seemed fairer than *Newsweek*'s practice of insinuating its opinions into its news stories through inaccurate or tendentious reporting. The hitch was that *Time* also engaged in these practices" (38).

Israel's supporters raised the issue that television and photojournalism greatly distorted Israeli actions during the invasion. "The nature of television news demands that it shows whatever horror is available," wrote syndicated columnist Ben Wattenberg (Wattenberg 1982).

Muravchik pointed out that the problem with television is not so much one of bias (as it is with the press) as the nature of the medium itself. Television makes a case most strongly with the eye-catching horrors it shows. Unfortunately for Israel, most of these eye-catching horrors were caused by Israeli weapons (40–43).

Israel's friends' best example, however, was a UPI photo of a baby covered with bandages accompanied by a caption stating "Nurse feeds a seven-month-old baby who lost both arms and was severely burnt late yesterday when an Israeli jet accidentally bombed an area in East Beirut" (*Washington Post*, 2 August 1982). The picture triggered much reaction in Washington and led Secretary of State Schultz to remark that the symbol of this war was a baby with its arm shot off (Kohn 1983, 13). But the caption was in error because the baby had not lost his arms and his wounds may not have been caused by shelling from Israeli planes.

The ADL report emphasized what it saw as a media tendency to exaggerate and that "scenes of violence were inevitably and reflexively linked to Israel, however inadvertently and however understandably in a situation where the media competes for scoops and graphic depictions of a violent event."

Criticism by Israel's supporters was not confined to the press and television. A fifty-seven-minute movie written and produced by Peter Goldman, director of Americans for a Safe Israel, assembled extracts from NBC's televised news reports and comments during the war in Lebanon in the summer of 1982. The film targeted NBC in the "study in media representation" to exemplify "the abuse of privileges" by the use of "advocacy journalism," although Goldman and his organization emphasized that ABC and CBS were no better in their presentation of the war. Joseph Polakoff of *Jewish Week* described the film as tending to "convict" the network of sympathy toward the PLO and antagonism toward Israel (Polakoff 1983).

Gervasi and Muravchik also focused much of their criticism on the Lebanon press corps in order to discredit their work, accusing them of everything from anti-Semitism to being intimidated by the PLO. The Beirut correspondents, however, denied any intimidation and praised the PLO's conduct during the war. David Hurst of the *Guardian* affirmed that "the Palestinians have never given [me] any trouble" despite Hurst's occasional criticism (Romdhani 1983, 10).

Romdhani also criticized the efforts by pro-Israeli apologists who tried to excuse the war with charges about the number of dead. This was seen in the attitudes of Gervasi and Muravchik. In fact, as Romdhani pointed out, "moral reprobation and emotional abhorrence would have been the same whether the number of innocent casualties was one thousand or one hundred times more." Both men, Romdhani claimed, tried to cast a shadow of "relative legitimacy" over the war, by comparing the human losses incurred by Israel's invasion to "alleged massacres by Palestinians and Syrians" (9–10).

Protests from the Arabs' Supporters

Although the pro-Israeli groups were generally better organized than the Arabs in putting their viewpoint across in the media, Arab-Americans made their voices heard to a greater extent than ever before. They were able to launch their own public relations blitz (Collins 1982, 3), and the Arab League, Arab embassies, the PLO, the National Association of Arab Americans, and other groups and individuals were all active. An American-Arab Anti-Discrimination Committee (ADC) report on media coverage found a consistent pro-Israeli bias in the coverage of the war by the major daily newspapers.

The most important manner in which favor for Israel was shown was in the editorial decision-making processes: the choice of words for headlines and captions, the phrasing of editorials, and the selection of photographs, op-ed columns, and political cartoons. A second way was the wholesale adoption of the

Israeli point of view about the invasion. A third way was the use of terms or stereotypes that dehumanized the Palestinians and other Arabs (Hooglund 1983, 3). Hooglund's report pointed out that the pro-Israeli bias was also evident in the paucity of articles dealing with the human consequences of the war, in spite of the fact that civilian suffering was immense. A final manifestation of pro-Israeli bias was the implicit endorsement of the Israel invasion by editorials stating that the invasion "opened opportunities for peace." Such editorials expressed the hope that Israeli actions would lead to positive political gains not only for Israel but for the United States as well, and even expressed pride that the Israeli victory showed the superiority of U.S. technology (3).

Pro-Arab groups charged that the press sanitized the bombing by relegating it to the back pages and that it concentrated more on the evacuation of the PLO than on getting the Israelis out of Lebanon (Collins 1982, 2).

The Israeli argument, as reflected in their naming the campaign in Lebanon "Operation Peace for Galilee," tended to show that the war in Lebanon was not an act of aggression at all but a form of legitimate self-defense. The *New York Times*, for example, was accused not only of accepting this argument but also of questioning the validity of Lebanon as a country and dismissing its pleas for sovereignty and territorial integrity (Hooglund 1983, 5).

Another issue raised by the ADC report was that there is much inherent racism in the way the Israeli government refers to Palestinians and that this tendency has been adopted by the American media. The PLO, for example, is consistently described as a terrorist organization, in spite of the fact that the PLO formally renounced the use of terrorism as a political weapon in 1974 and dissociated itself from terrorist acts by Arabs and Palestinians in Europe. The PLO denounced the assassination attempt on the Israeli ambassador in London, but no newspaper discussed this. Even though the suspects rounded up by London police were not identified as Palestinians, the *Washington Post* blamed the PLO (Hooglund 1983, 6).

The ADC report pointed to the dehumanization of the Palestinians that occurred in almost all of the major dailies (with the notable example of the *Christian Science Monitor*) through their silence regarding Israeli treatment of Palestinian prisoners and civilians (Hooglund 1983, 9).

The critics of Israel also pointed to the use of visual imagery to convey messages. An example of this was the Associated Press's paired set of photos published in dozens of newspapers, including the *Los Angeles Times* of 25 July 1982. The left frame showed Israeli soldiers at prayer in Lebanon, and the right frame showed "PLO guerrillas firing a missile at Israeli jets." The unspoken implication here was that the PLO terrorists were attacking innocent Israelis. Yet, the press never described the Israeli bombings of Lebanese cities and towns as terrorist acts. Moreover, PLO shelling of Israel was never described as self-defense nor were PLO reprisals accepted as such (Hooglund 1983, 8).

It is important to note that both the U.S. government and the Israeli government also appear to have manipulated the U.S. press in the Lebanese crisis. Begin's assurances to Reagan in April were projecting a false image of Israeli intentions. Many reporters in Washington who cover Middle East affairs, for example, have said privately that had Alan Harry Goodman not attacked the Islamic Dome of the Rock and killed two people in mid-April (a media event in itself), thus diverting public attention, the Israelis would have invaded Lebanon then. In addition, the headlines in the press in April indicated, according to Patricia Karl, that the government wanted to create a climate inimical to an Israeli invasion because the return of Sinai (on 25 April 1982) would have been jeopardized and Egypt might have moved back to the Arab fold, thus undermining the Camp David framework (Karl 1983, 294).

In April 1982 Prime Minister Begin wrote a letter to President Reagan reassuring him that Israel would not attack positions in southern Lebanon unless it was provoked. The timing of this front-page story was interesting. It appeared a few weeks before the scheduled Israeli departure from Sinai on 25 April and only days after extensive media reports of violence and Israeli censorship of the Arab press on the West Bank (Karl 1983, 294).

The traditional pro-Israeli attitude within American popular culture was upset, and an image reversal took place in the American media. The subsequent Israeli invasion of Lebanon set in motion a tendency toward more balanced coverage. Several aspects differentiated this war from earlier ones. For the first time, Israel was conducting a war that was not perceived as one for solely defensive purposes and that was causing widespread suffering. This cast Israel in a different light. Moreover, both sides were equally accessible, as a result of which the humanity of Palestinians could be seen more clearly, according to Paul Varian of the UPI (Collins 1982, 2).

Although the Israeli invasion of Lebanon sparked an ongoing debate within the media, the coverage fell short in one crucial aspect. The invasion was not placed in historical context. Little or no attention was given to other factors surrounding the invasion, such as Lebanon's civil war and the significance of the invasion in relation to Israel's continued occupation of the West Bank.

The Trend toward More Balanced Coverage

The extensive coverage of Israel's invasion of Lebanon and the bombing and occupation of West Beirut in the summer of 1982, as we have noted, started the trend toward greater balance in the media's handling of Middle East issues, although against a backdrop of continued support for Israel's policy goals. The media shifted rapidly from their initial tone of pride in the swiftness and success of Israel's attack and in the superiority of the American weaponry as film footage and news dispatches bore graphic witness to the extent of the devastation wrought by these same weapons. This led many media critics, backed by the Israelis, to issue strong accusations against what the *Boston Globe*'s editorial-page editor Martin Nolan called "general angst about the media's coverage of Israel" (Morris 1982, 23). Yet detailed examination of reporting by the elite press and commercial television networks does not support the charges leveled against the media. On the contrary, it reveals many deliberate efforts to report events in Lebanon professionally and fairly.

Ironically, the evidence of the media's efforts at balance in reporting the war lies in the coverage most frequently cited by critics as anti-Israeli. The subjects that aroused the greatest controversy were the level of civilian casualties, the number of refugees, and the destruction of nonmilitary targets. Yet close analysis of the stories indicates that the media were, on the whole, very careful to note the uncertainty surrounding the statistics they published, as well as any discrepancy in their sources.

More often than not, television tried to assess general trends in casualty figures rather than reporting precise numbers. Peter Jennings, reporting for ABC on 8 June, spoke of "mounting casualties" suffered by both sides, noting that they were "particularly heavy among Palestinians and Lebanese" (Ghareeb 1983, 169). In the battle for the city of Tyre, NBC correspondent Vic Aiken provided "no figures" on the number of dead. On CBS, Bob Faw told viewers that "casualty lists climbed." When television reports did include figures, they were often vague, as in the case of NBC's story of a charge by Lebanon's president that the number of Lebanese killed or wounded "is in the thousands" (Ghareeb 1983, 170).

In contrast to television's lack of precision, the print media did attempt to provide its readership with exact numbers of the dead and wounded, although they too resorted to such caveats as "there was no independent confirmation of casualty totals," or phrases like Sidon's "uncounted dead" (*Washington Post,* 14 June 1982). Headlines such as "Disagreements Flare over Casualty Toll in Lebanon" (Ottaway, *Washington Post,* 25 June) bore witness to the press's conscientious effort to report the issue fully. Criticism of the media for offering "contradictory" and exaggerated casualty figures contributed to the overall charge of "lack of balance." But as Cable News Network correspondent Peter Arnett stated on an ABC News special program discussing television's war coverage, the statistics were "just a small part of what reporting war is all about. . . . Bombs explode without any political distinctions. . . . It seemed to me after coming home [from Beirut] and seeing the reaction to our reportage that it was less statistics than the fact of damage that the people in the United States reacted to" ("ABC Viewpoint," 15 October 1983).

Figures on the extent of the casualties proved only somewhat more explosive an issue than coverage of the siege and bombing of West Beirut. However, despite the mounting horror aroused by Israel's unrelenting attack, evidence suggests that the media made every effort to cover the story fairly and dispassionately. Films and descriptions of Israeli bombardments of civilian neighborhoods and living conditions after the Israelis cut off supplies of electricity, food, and water were consciously balanced by reminders that the Israeli "onslaught" was brought on by the "organized and continuing" resistance of the PLO (Ghareeb 1983, 170).

However, the *New York Times* showed reluctance to print the full story of Israel's terror bombing, as revealed in a telex sent over the Reuters wire by Beirut bureau chief Thomas L. Friedman. The *Times* recorded that the first week in August produced the "fiercest shelling" of the "Israeli onslaught," yet the editors clearly decided their correspondent had gone too far in a 5 August lead that described the previous day's bombardment of the city as "indiscriminate." In response to their deletion of that adjective, Friedman cabled the editors that he had always been careful "to note in previous stories that the Israelis were hitting Palestinian positions and if they were hitting residential areas to at least raise the possibility that the Palestinians had a gun there at one time or another." He defended his choice of the word *indiscriminate* to describe Israel's bombing of the previous day by saying that a hazardous tour of the city led him to conclude that "what happened yesterday was something fundamentally different from what has happened on the previous 63 days." His disillusionment over the paper's handling of the story was expressed in his "profound sadness" over the failure of the "newspaper of record" to tell "its readers and future historians" of Israel's actions (Ghareeb 1983, 171).

Reexamination of Israel's Policies

The war forced the media to reexamine their assumptions about the morality of Israel's policies and its exercise of power in the Middle East. Much of this critical examination took place in and through the media. Pulitzer Prize–winning journalist Richard Ben Cramer's stories in the *Philadelphia Inquirer* (30 June 1982) publicized in great detail the suffering caused by the war. *Washington Post* columnist Richard Cohen, a traditional supporter of Israel, wrote in his 27 June column that "the moral standing of Israel has been eroded not only by its actions but also by its words." Columnist Georgie Anne Geyer, in her *Washington Times* column of 14 June, described Menachem Begin as an "old terrorist" and Israeli defense minister Ariel Sharon as a "fanatic Israeli expansionist." Alexander Cockburn was one of the few journalists to point to the media's willingness to report the very real and tremendous tragedy of the war for the Lebanese people. According to Cockburn, "You do not have to be overly familiar with Lebanon to get a clearer idea of what is happening there than is available in most commentaries here. Southern Lebanon does not become 'a Palestinian stronghold' just on the say-so of Israeli spokesmen. The city of Sidon has, or had, a population of 300,000 and when Sidon or Tyre are 'pounded' by Israeli ships, aircraft and land artillery, a large number of Lebanese as well as Palestinians—refugees as well as fighters—are dying. Geo-politicians can say that Lebanon does not 'exist' as a nation. But there are still a lot of Lebanese around" (*Wall Street Journal*, 10 June 1982).

Well-known pro-Israel writers such as William Buckley began to question the impact of Israel's policies on U.S. interests in the Middle East and to support the right of the Palestinians to a homeland. Buckley advised Secretary of State George Shultz to suspend U.S. commitments to Israel's arsenal until it reaffirmed its willingness to cede the territories in the West Bank and Gaza to demilitarized Palestinian rule (*Washington Post*, 9 July 1982). Another well-known supporter of Israel, columnist Mary McGrory, who proclaimed in a column during the 1967 war that "we are all Israelis," devoted her 27 June column to Prime Minister Begin's visit to the United States. Entitled "Begin, Go Home," the column accused Begin of coming to Washington "with blood on [his] hands," and asked if Israeli security had to be achieved "by the slaughter of innocents." In an emotional broadcast from Beirut, on 2 August, NBC anchorman John Chancellor criticized the "savage" Israeli attack on Beirut, "one of the world's largest cities." He went on to point to the "stench of terror all across the city." He compared the bombing to the bombing of Madrid during the Spanish civil war and wondered "what in the world is going on," pointing out that Israel's security problem was "fifty miles to the south." He asked, "What's an Israeli army doing here in Beirut?" (Ghareeb 1983, 172).

The Israeli siege of Beirut and the enormous loss of life and devastation led to an ongoing debate among American Jews as well as Israelis. Some of the most sensitive articles in the American press dealing with the plight of Lebanese and Palestinian civilians and raising questions about Begin-Sharon policies were written by Jewish-American journalists, commentators, and intellectuals such as Nat Hentoff, Anthony Lewis, Noam Chomsky, Stanley Hoffman, I.F. Stone, Jonathan Randal, Richard Cohen, Milton Viorst, and Stanley Karnow.

The well-known critic and intellectual, Irving Howe, who traditionally has supported Israel's policies, wrote on 23 September in the *New York Times* that American Jews must not "waffle" or hesitate before going public with their criticism. "It is the bad policies and misconduct of Begin-Sharon that provide the most substantial help to enemies of Israel," he said. "Not those who express shame over the Israeli share of responsibility for Beirut, but those who would cover it up, give comfort to our enemies, so this is where some of us stand: warm friends of Israel, open critics of Begin-Sharon, we will probably make mistakes—but if there are mistakes of speech, there are also mistakes of silence. After Beirut, silence is impossible." And while some might question whether the "bad policies" and "misconduct" were the result of the policies of the Israel of Menachem Begin or whether they were the consequences of the policies adopted by Israeli leaders long before the invasion of Lebanon, it must be admitted that it took a great deal of moral courage and soul-searching for those Americans, Jews and Gentiles alike who have long had a special commitment to Israel, to publicly question Israeli policies.

During the early days of the invasion, many showed pride in Israel's victories and helped to justify its actions. Both television and the press virtually echoed each other in emphasizing the "retaliatory" nature of the Israeli bombing attacks on the Beirut stadium and the assault on PLO "strongholds" in southern Lebanon. Adopting the Israeli code name for the invasion, Peace for Galilee, the media noted that the invasion had been "triggered" by PLO attacks and that its "declared objective" (Claiborne, *Washington Post*, 8 June 1982) was to clear out the terrorists (NBC) and "eliminate" their bases (ABC).

The use of Israeli terms was prevalent during the early days of the war. Almost all the media used the term "twenty-five-mile buffer zone." The initial coverage of these events by the networks and the major papers, particularly until the latter part of June when Haig resigned, revealed that the United States continued to accept without much scrutiny the Israeli justification for the invasion. The attempted assassination of Israel's ambassador Schlomo Argov in London, the Israeli bombing of Beirut, and the rocket attack on northern Israel was the sequence of events that brought the media's attention to the unfolding tragedy in Lebanon. Up until then and despite the earlier predictions of an Israeli invasion, the crisis was overshadowed in the media by events in Poland and Afghanistan.

Other major themes during the first few weeks stressed the chaos into which Lebanon had fallen during the years prior to the invasion, the lawlessness of PLO occupation, and the welcome smiles and flowers with which Israeli troops were received. The stories that would have offset this picture of Israel as a liberating force received relatively little attention, however. The war was almost totally reported from the Israeli frame of reference, and the historical background to the invasion, which involved considerable advance preparation by Israel, was neglected. A more balanced coverage would have fleshed out the full story of Israel's interests in Lebanon, thereby giving the American audience a broader conception of the issues.

Reasons for the Change in Attitude

The initial U.S. government response to the invasion clearly supported Israel's goals of crushing the PLO and rebuilding Lebanese-Israeli relations on the basis of a political reorganization in Lebanon. The press faithfully represented this point of view in its early reports. But as the summer wore on and Secretary Haig was replaced by Secretary Shultz, who took a more balanced view of the regional situation, so, too, did the press. Although the military defeat of the PLO in Beirut was not bemoaned, the human suffering produced by the war and the new commitment by the U.S. administration to upholding the right of the Palestinians to a homeland received greater attention in the media.

The move toward greater objectivity and balance in the coverage of the Arab-Israeli conflict and particularly the Palestinian issue was first clearly manifested during the Israeli siege of Beirut. Undoubtedly this coverage contributed to the change in American public opinion toward Israel's leadership and policies, since Israel's actions in the words of syndicated columnist Nick Thimmesch "shocked Americans into a painful reassessment of the character and elevated moral standards of Israel" (Thimmesch 1982, 179).

Another factor contributing to the change was the increased sensitivity on the part of some Palestinians and Arab governments to the need to provide access and substantive information to journalists. The PLO's information offices and leaders appeared to have learned the benefits of cultivating the media. The Lebanese and the Palestinians were more than happy to allow Western correspondents to cover the story. Even Yasir Arafat, whose images was generally perceived in negative terms in the media and ultimately in public opinion, began to be viewed in positive terms as a wise and dedicated leader. According to Thimmesch, Arafat "became the media good guy" and Begin and Sharon the "bad guys during the siege of Beirut." Arafat's improved skills as a communicator were highlighted when he told an NBC interviewer on 11 January 1983 that even E.T. wanted to return home and kept repeating "home, home, home" (Ghareeb 1983, 181).

For their part, the Israelis also contributed to this trend. There is little doubt that Israel's actions in the occupied territories, the annexation of the Syrian Golan Heights, and more important, its invasion of Lebanon, particularly the siege of Beirut, changed American perceptions and attitudes toward the Arab-Israeli conflict. Correspondents were present and thus able to provide the American public with unusual insight into the suffering Israel could inflict with U.S. arms. The television cameras were able to show what Sharon wanted to conceal, that the Israelis were an invading army. Through personalizing the victims of war, the media coverage, despite its limitations, at least temporarily halted, if it did not begin to reverse, the process of stereotyping and dehumanizing the Arabs. Arab casualties and suffering were portrayed in the same way the media portrayed in the past, and continues to portray today, Israeli casualties. They were human beings, not statistics, with grieving families and friends (Ghareeb 1983, 182).

The behavior and words of Israeli leaders contributed to their negative images. The remoteness, stiffness, intransigence, and bellicosity of Begin, Sharon, and Shamir made an impact on public opinion, and more and more reporters began to refer to the "terrorist" background of these leaders. Begin's defiance of the reasonable and temperate requests of President Reagan, a well-known champion of Israeli causes, for Israeli moderation also had an impact on many, both in and out of the government. Still another contributing factor was the ever-changing proclamations about Israel's intentions in invading Lebanon. First, it was an operation to secure "Peace for Galilee" in a twenty-five-mile area aimed at preventing the PLO from infiltrating or shelling Israeli villages. Then a need was cited for an international force to guarantee that the PLO would not return to the buffer zone. Subsequent explanations included the need for the destruction of the PLO and its expulsion from Lebanon, the expulsion of the Syrians, and finally the establishment of a free independent Lebanon and normalized relations with the country (Salpeter 1982, 5–6).

The Israeli government's mishandling of the press, including heavy-handed attempts by its censors to influence coverage, contributed to the growing doubts about the wisdom or humaneness of Israel's actions. When the Israeli government's aggressive tactics in the Golan Heights and on the West Bank were questioned, the government responded by trying to place greater restrictions on reporters aimed at keeping them in the dark as long as possible. Begin is reported to have even threatened to cut the budget of Israeli television because of his disappointment with its coverage. Even before Lebanon, Israel began to act in a manner not dissimilar to Arab governments. Thimmesch has reported that Moshe Yegar, the Foreign Ministry's information chief, once proposed denying visas to foreign journalists "with hostile intentions." After the first week of the war, there were complaints from Western and even from some Israeli journalists about the lack of frankness and the infrequency of briefings by Israeli officials.

The underestimated, inaccurate, and contradictory Israeli figures on the number of civilian casualties in the south of Lebanon led some journalists to question Israeli government information, not only on casualties, but on other matters as well (Cody and Ramati 1982, 20). The Israeli attempts at censorship forced reporters to find other means to transmit information. They were able to send film through Cyprus and Damascus or to relay them by satellite from Beirut. CBS and NBC employed special graphics to indicate that their reports had been censored. On 24 June the CBS screen went dark and then these words appeared: 22 seconds deleted by the Israeli censors. The report then showed a weeping Lebanese woman begging the United States to act to end the fighting.

The increasingly strict Israeli censors were at times counterproductive despite their success at limiting photographic coverage. On 12 July 1982, *Time* magazine reported that Israeli censors reviewed shots of shattered residential areas and of wounded and dead civilians on the grounds that some scenes constituted "propaganda" (Ghareeb 1983, 185). The *New York Times* published an article on Israeli censorship on 29 June 1982 and described the way in which it was carried out. Other newspapers soon followed suit.

According to a 7 July 1982 *Baltimore Sun* editorial, Israeli officials, despite "astute planning, seemed to have overlooked the one key factor: the impact of a televised war in the American living room. . . . There is little doubt that the Israeli image in this country is suffering as never before."

Another contributing factor to the shift in coverage may have been the change in political stands on the part of the U.S. government. Secretary Haig and UN ambassador Jeane Kirkpatrick portrayed the invasion of Lebanon as a major victory for the United States and a humiliating defeat for the Soviets and their clients. Mrs. Kirkpatrick was reported by a former U.S. ambassador to have told a group of Japanese businessmen that their oil supplies had been secured by Israel's actions, which should have taken place long ago. The media coverage reflected the political stands adopted by high U.S. officials, who saw the invasion as a means of strengthening U.S. interests in the area. Statements made by Secretary Haig before his resignation undoubtedly had an impact on governmental and media policies. Secretary Haig described before television cameras the number of Israeli planes shot down in a dogfight with Syrian planes and said that "we" lost one F-16. As a former deputy undersecretary of state recently stated, "It was perhaps not just a Freudian slip when recently a senior U.S. official during the early days of the invasion referred to the Israeli forces as our side" (Newsom 1982, 62).

Although the full extent of the involvement of Haig and other high officials with the Israeli invasion may never be known, it is clear that after Haig's surprise resignation a noticeable change occurred in administration statements and actions. The new secretary of state George Shultz and others in the government criticized Israeli actions and spoke of Palestinian rights. This was paralleled by changes in the media's focus on Palestinian and Arab news and concerns. It is difficult to gauge the extent of this change, but it is obvious that the influence on the media of State Department and White House statements dealing with foreign affairs should not be underestimated.

CONCLUSION

In recent years, the Middle East has become big news. It has received more attention than many other regions in the world. The October war, the oil embargo, OPEC, the Sadat visit to Jerusalem and the Camp David agreement, the Iranian revolution and the hostage crisis, the Soviet invasion of Afghanistan, the Palestinian case and the invasion of Lebanon, and the Iraq-Iran war have all caught the media's attention.

These events have brought about some improvement both in the quantity and, to a lesser extent, in the quality of coverage and, therefore, some change in perceptions. The media also have achieved a more balanced approach to the area, less prone to distortion. But major problems remain. It is essential that some of the basic assumptions and preconceived notions about the Middle East be corrected and that the manner of coverage of the region—crisis journalism—change. Although it is natural that any foreign area coverage will start with the implications of stories for the United States and the American public, nevertheless the media must move beyond these considerations and cover in a more profound, sensitive, and balanced way all the issues at stake.

REFERENCES

Adams, William, and Philip Heyl. 1981. From Cairo to Kabul with the networks: 1972–1980. In *Television coverage of the Middle East*, edited by William C. Adams. Norwood, N.J.: Ablex Publishing Co.

Anti-Defamation League of B'nai B'rith. 1982. *Television network coverage of the war in Lebanon*. New York: Anti-Defamation League of B'nai B'rith.

Bell, Steve. 1980. American journalism: Practices, constraints, and Middle East reportage in the American media and the Arabs. In *The American media and the Arabs*, edited by Michael Hudson and Ronald Wolfe. Washington, D.C.: Georgetown University Press.

Cody, Edward, and Pnina Ramati. 1982. Covering the invasion of Lebanon. *Washington Journalism Review* 4, no. 7 (September): 18–21.

Collins, Thomas. 1982. Lebanon: The press caught in the crossfire. *Newsday*, 24–26 October.

Damon, George H., Jr. 1983. A survey of political cartoons dealing with the Middle East. In *Split vision: The portrayal of Arabs in the American media*, edited by Edmund Ghareeb. Washington, D.C.: American Arab Affairs Council.

Gervasi, Frank. 1982. *Media coverage: The war in Lebanon*. Washington, D.C.: Center for International Security.

Ghareeb, Edmund, ed. 1983. *Split vision: The portrayal of Arabs in the American media*, Washington, D.C.: American Arab Affairs Council.

Heikal, Mohammed H. 1980. The Arab image in Western mass media: What can be done to improve it? In *The Arab image in Western mass media*. Proceedings of the 1979 International Press Seminar. London: Outline Books.

Henry, William, III. 1983. Journalism under fire. *Time*, 12 December.

Hooglund, Eric. 1983. U.S. Press coverage of the Israeli invasion of Lebanon. American-Arab Anti-Discrimination Committee Issue No. 10. Washington, D.C.: American-Arab Anti-Discrimination Committee.

Hudson, Michael, and Ronald Wolfe, eds. 1980. *The American media and the Arabs*. Washington, D.C.: Georgetown University Press.

Janka, Les. 1983. Grenada: The media and national security. *Armed Forces Journal* 121, no. 5 (December).

Karl, Patricia. 1983. In the middle of the Middle East: The media and U.S. foreign policy. In *Split vision: The portrayal of Arabs in the American media*, edited by Edmund Ghareeb. Washington, D.C.: American Arab Affairs Council.

Kohn, Martin. 1983. An American Jewish view: Reporting on misreporting in Lebanon. *Arab Student Journal* 4, no. 2. (January-March).

Kraft, Joseph. 1981. The dark side of Islam. *Washington Post*, 19 May.

Laqueur, Walter. 1982. The devil and world coverage. *Washington Quarterly* 5, no. 3 (Summer).

Lendenmann, G. Neal. 1983. Arab stereotyping in contemporary American political cartoons. In *Split vision: The portrayal of Arabs in the American media*, edited by Edmund Ghareeb. Washington, D.C.: American Arab Affairs Council.

Maddocks, Melvin. 1982. Journalism's double agenda. *Christian Science Monitor*, 5 November.

Morris, Roger. 1982. Beirut and the press—under siege. *Columbia Journalism Review* 21 no. 4 (November-December).

Muravchik, Joshua. 1982. Misreporting Lebanon. *Policy Review*, no. 19 (Winter).

Nasir, Sari. 1965. The image of the Arab in American popular culture. *Arab Journal* 2 (Winter).

Newsom, David D. 1982. The Arabs and U.S. public opinion: Is there hope? *American-Arab Affairs*, no. 2 (Fall).

Ottaway, David. 1982. War coverage dismays Israel. *Washington Post*, 25 July.

Peretz, Martin. 1983. Lebanon Eyewitness. *New Republic*, 2 August.

Podhoretz, Norman. 1982. J'accuse. *Commentary*, September.

Polakoff, Joseph. 1983. Film released on bias in NBC coverage of Lebanon war. *Jewish Week*. 7–13 July.

Reston, James. 1967. *The artillery of the press.* New York: Harper & Row.

Romdhani, Oussama. 1983. The Lebanon war revisited: A not-so-easy whitewash. *Arab Student Journal* 4, no. 2 (January-March).

Said, Edward. 1979. The media revolution and the resurgence of Islam. In *The Arab image in Western mass media.* London: Outline Books.

———. 1981. *Covering Islam.* New York: Pantheon Books.

Salpeter, Eliahu. Views from Israel—Lebanon: The good, the bad, the misleading. *New Leader*, 28 July 1982.

Schwartz, Tony. 1983. ADL criticizes T.V. over coverage of Lebanon. *New York Times*, 21 October.

Shepley, James. 1983. Let's reconfigure the media for war. *Armed Forces Journal* 121, no. 13.

Slade, Shelley. 1981. The image of the Arab in America: Analysis of a poll on American attitudes. *Middle East Journal* 35, no. 2.

Suleiman, Michael. 1967. *American mass media and the confrontation of June 1967: An Arab perspective.* Evanston, Ill.: Northwestern University Press.

———. 1980. Summary of American public Support of Middle Eastern countries: 1939–1970. In *The American media and the Arabs*, edited by Michael Hudson and Ronald Wolfe. Washington, D.C.: Georgetown University Press.

Terry, Janice, and Gordon Mendenhall. 1974. 1983 press coverage on the Middle East. *Journal of Palestine Studies* 4, no. 1 (Autumn).

Thimmesch, Nick. 1982. The media and the Middle East. *American Arab Affairs*, no. 2 (Fall).

Trattner, John. 1982. Reporting foreign affairs. *Washington Quarterly*, 5, no. 3 (Summer).

Tyrell, R. Emmett, Jr. 1976. Chimera in the Middle East. *Harper's*, November.

Wattenberg, Ben. 1982. Column in *Philadelphia Inquirer*, 8 July.

Wright, Claudia. 1983. U.S. coverage of the Middle East. *Viewpoint* (Lahore) 9, no. 17 (December).

ADDITIONAL READINGS

Adams, William C. *Television Coverage of the Middle East.* Norwood, N.J.: Ablex Publishing Co., 1981.

The Arab Image in Western Mass Media. Proceedings of the 1979 International Press Seminar. London: Outline Books, 1980.

Bagnied, Magda, and Steven Schneider. "Sadat Goes to Jerusalem: Television Images, Themes and Agenda. In *Television Coverage of the Middle East,* edited by William C. Adams. Norwood, N.J.: Ablex Publishing Co., 1981.

Breger, Marshall J. "Who Ran the Show: Editors or Reporters?" *American Jewish Congress Monthly* 50, no. 2 (February-March).

Cooley, John. "The News from the Middle East: A Working Approach." *Middle East Journal* 35, no. 4 (Autumn 1981).

Isaacs, Stephen. "Jewish Bank, Newspaper Control Myth Continues." *Washington Post,* 21 November 1974.

Fulbright, J. William. "Fulbright on the Press." *Columbia Journalism Review* 14, no. 4 (November-December 1975).

Ghareeb, Edmund. "The American Media and the Palestine Problem." *Journal of Palestine Studies* 5, no. 1–2 (Autumn 1975-Winter 1976).

———. "Perceptions and the Media." *American-Arab Affairs,* no. 2 (Fall 1982).

———. *Split Vision: The Portrayal of Arabs in the American Media.* Washington, D.C.: American Arab Affairs Council, 1983.

Hershman, Robert, and Henry L. Griggs, Jr. "American Television News and the Middle East." *Middle East Journal* 35, no. 4 (Autumn 1981).

Lilienthal, Alfred M. *The Zionist Connection: What Price Peace?* New York: Dodd, Mead, 1978.

Mortimer, Edward. "Islam and the Western Journalist." *Middle East Journal* 35, no. 4 (Autumn 1981).

Raspberry, William. "Disagreeing or Distorting?" *Washington Post,* 7 May 1980.

Romdhani, Oussama. "The Arab Image in the U.S.: An Overview." *Arab Student Bulletin* 3, no. 3 (April-June 1982).

Shaheen, Jack. "The Arab Stereotype of Television." *Link* 13, no. 2 (April-May 1980).

————. "Do Television Programs Stereotype the Arabs?" *Wall Street Journal*, 12 October 1979.

————. "The Arab: T.V.'s Most Popular Villain." *Christian Century*, 13 December 1978.

Thimmesch, Nick. "War Coverage in a T.V. Age." *Public Opinion* 5, no. 5 (October-November 1982).

Weisman, John. "Why the Palestinians are Losing the Propaganda War: An On-the-Scene Report." *T.V. Guide*, 24–30 October and 31 October–6 November 1981. Part 2.

Bibliography: The Year's Publications in Middle Eastern Studies, 1983

Mark Tyler Day
David H. Partington

Monographs

The bibliography lists monographs in English, French, and German that appeared in 1983 on the modern Middle East, including major historical works that provide the background necessary to understand contemporary events. Certain 1982 imprints, which could not be included in volume 2 of the *Middle East Annual*, are also listed and identified by year of publication. So as not to overburden the bibliography with redundant titles, French and German translations of works that either originally appeared in English or are available in English-language versions have not been included, nor have reeditions and reprints of English-language works unless they are studies that have been revised extensively, have long been unavailable, or have particular relevance to contemporary events. On the other hand, an attempt has been made to include English, French, or German editions and translations of non-English-language publications, particularly those originally written in a Middle Eastern language.

Annotations in brackets are based on information derived from such secondary sources as publishers' catalogs, national bibliographies, and reviews; other annotations are based on examination of the books themselves. The alphabetical arrangement disregards the Arabic article *al* in its various permutations (*al, Al, el, El*, etc.); thus, El-Dareer will be found under D, Algosaibi under G, and so on.

Aba, Noureddine. *C'était hier Sabra et Chatila*. Ecritures arabes. Paris: L'Harmattan. 30 pp.
[This "song of trial," in recalling the massacres, challenges our consciences without hostility but with compassion.]

Abadi, Jacob. *Britain's Withdrawal from the Middle East, 1947–1971: The Economic and Strategic Imperatives*. Leaders, Politics and Social Change in the Islamic World, no. 2. Princeton, N.J.: Kingston Press. 283 pp. Bibl.; illus.; index.

Abdalla, Ibrahim S.E., Mahmoud Abdel-Fadil, and Ali Nassar. *Images of the Arab Future.* Translated by Maissa Talaat. New York: St. Martin's Press. 250 pp. Bibl.

Abd-Allah, Umar F. *The Islamic Struggle in Syria.* Forward and Postscript by Hamid Algar. Berkeley, Calif.: Mizan Press. 300 pp. Bibl.; index; maps.
"It is the purpose of this book to give an accurate portrayal of the Syrian Islamic Front" (p. 19). To achieve this aim, the author first surveys Syrian history since World War II and then argues in favor of an Islamic jihād against the regime of Hāfiz al-Assad. The argument relies heavily on eyewitness testimony from eight anonymous Syrians who support the front. An authorized English version of the front's "Proclamation and program of the Islamic revolution in Syria" (*Bayān al-thawrah al-Islāmīyah fī Sūrīyah wa-minhājuhā*) is appended.

Abdel-Malek, Anouar, ed. *Contemporary Arab Political Thought.* London: Zed Press. 288 pp.

Abdessalem, Ahmen. *Sadiki et les Sadikiens.* Tunis: Cérès Productions; Aix Provence: Edisud (distributor). 274 pp.
[A history of the Sadiki *lycée* in Tunis.]

Abitbol, Michel. *Les Juifs d'Afrique du Nord sous Vichy.* Judaïsme en terre d'Islam. Paris: Maisonneuve et Larose. 224 pp.
[A study on the margins of the universe of the Holocaust: an analysis of the anti-Semitic Vichy policy, of the consequences of the German presence in Tunisia, of the campaign to abolish the racial laws, and of the restoration of their rights to the Jews.]

————, ed. *Communautés juives des marges sahariennes du Maghreb.* Actes du colloque tenu en 1980 à Jérusalem. Jerusalem: Centre de Recherches sur les Juifs d'Afrique du Nord; Paris: Maisonneuve et Larose (distributor). 544 pp.

Abraham, Sameer Y., and Nabell Abraham, eds. *Arabs in the New World: Studies on Arab-American Communities.* Detroit: Wayne State University, Center for Urban Studies. 208 pp. Bibl.; illus.; index.
[This important volume is a result of a research project on the Arab ethnic heritage in America, particularly in Detroit. It is a unique and important study, emphasizing case studies, demographic data, and historical information. Partial contents include a historical overview of Arabs in America, emigration from Syria, Arab Muslims and Islamic institutions in America, and a selected bibliography on Arab-American immigration and settlement.]

Achenbach, Hermann. *Agrargeographie—Nordafrika (Tunesien, Algerien): Bodennutzung = Agricultural Geography—North Africa (Tunisia, Algeria) = Géographie agricole—Afrique du Nord (Tunisie, Algérie).* Afrika-Kartenwerk, Serie N, Nordafrika (Tunesien, Algerien): Beiheft, no. 11. Berlin and Stuttgart: Borntraeger. 83 pp. Bibl.; figures; graphs; illus.; table.
[Summary in English and French.]

Agarwal, Jamuna P., Hans H. Glismann, and Peter Nunnenkamp. *Ölpreisschocks und wirtschaftliche Entwicklung: Anpassungsprobleme in der Dritten Welt.* Kieler Studien, 176. Tübingen: Mohr. 261 pp. Bibl.

Ahmed, Akbar S., and David M. Hart, eds. *Islam in Tribal Societies: From the Atlas to the Indus.* London and Boston: Routledge & Kegan Paul. 320 pp. Index.

Ait-Ahmed, Hocine. *Mémoires d'un combattant: L'esprit d'indépendance 1942–1952.* Paris: S. Messinger. 240 pp.
[The revolt, the war, and the independence of Algeria recounted in the first person by one of its leaders. As the head of every rebellion and every organization, he was chief of an insurrection in Kabylie and founder of the bureau of the FLN in New York; he was arrested at the same time as Ben Bella.]

Āl-i Ahmad, Jalāl. *Occidentosis: A Plague from the West.* Translated by R. Campbell and edited by Hamid Algar. Contemporary Islamic Thought: Persian Series. Berkeley, Calif.: Mizan Press. Index.
[This is a translation of *Gharbzadeqi* written in 1962 by the influential author (1923–69). It is a critique of social conditions in Iran based upon the thesis that the Iranian monarchy was no more than a native brokerage for Western influence. A different translation by John Green and Ahmad Alizadeh was annotated in volume 2 of the *Middle East Annual.*]

Allan, J.A., ed. *The Sahara: Ecological Change and Early Economic History.* Boulder, Colo.: Westview Press. 146 pp.
[This book examines the complex interactions of man with a marginal environment, seeking to explain how human responses to extreme ecological circumstances provide insight into man's ability to adopt resource management practices in order to survive or prosper. Two main areas are covered: first, problems of ecological change are examined; second, a group of U.S., French, and British scholars analyze features of the early economic history of the Sahara. Together, these analyses provide a basis for understanding modern problems of drought and survival in the Sahara.]

Allen, Harry S., and Ivan Volgyes. *Israel, the Middle East, and U.S. Interests.* Introduction by Edmund S. Muskie. New York: Praeger. 190 pp. Bibl.; index.

American Friends Service Committee. *Lebanon: Toward Legal Order and Respect for Human Rights.* Philadelphia: American Friends Service Committee. 46 pp.

Anawati, Georges C., and Maurice Borrmans. *Tendances et courants de l'Islam arabe contemporain.* Vol. 1, *Egypte et Afrique du Nord.* Entwicklung and Frieden: Wissenschaftliche Reihe, vol. 26. Munich: Kaiser; Mayence: Grünewald; Paris: Maisonneuve, 1982. 276 pp. Bibl.; indexes. A collection of two works: "Les grands courants de la pensée religieuse musulmane dans l'Egypte contemporaine," by Anawati; and "L'Islam et ses courants actuels en Afrique du Nord," by Borrmans. Anawati discusses major thinkers and parties in four chapters: "Le réformisme"; "Le Coran et le Hadīth"; "La théologie et la mystique"; and "Présentation et défense de l'Islam." Borrmans relates Islam to law, education, science, politics, socialism, and humanism.

Arad, Ruth W., Seev Hirsch, and Alfred Tovias. *Economics of Peacemaking: Focus on the Egyptian-Israeli Situation.* New York: St. Martin's Press. 260 pp. Bibl.; index.

Arkoun, Mohammed. *Lectures du Coran*. Islam d'hier et d'aujourd'hui, no. 17. Paris: Maisonneuve et Larose. 210 pp.
[The author of these essays seeks to put in place the intellectual equipment and the cultural practice that would allow Muslims to radically rethink their relation to religion and history at a moment when their society needs to face up to modernity.]

Les Arméniens en cour d'assises: Terroristes ou résistants? Roquevaire: Editions Parenthèses; distributed by Presses universitaires de France. 216 pp.
[An unexpurgated account of the legal proceedings against Max Hrair Kilndjian, indicted for the attempted assassination of D. Turkmen, ambassador of Turkey in Berne (Aix-en-Provence, 22–23 January 1982). Preceded by *Les Arméniens, une lutte de libération contemporaine*, a text presenting the bases of the Armenian liberation struggle.]

Arnold. Anthony. *Afghanistan's Two-Party Communism: Parcham and Khalq*. Stanford, Calif.: Hoover Institution Press. 242 pp. Bibl.; index; map.

Aruri, Naseer Hasan, Fouad Moughrabi, and Joe Stork. *Reagan and the Middle East*. AAUG Monograph Series, no. 17. Belmont, Mass.: Association of Arab-American University Graduates. 95 pp. Bibl.; illus.; index.

Asad, Talal, and Roger Owen, eds. *The Middle East*. Sociology of "Developing Societies" Series. New York: Monthly Review Press, 1983. 240 pp. Bibl.; index.
[This reader, the second regional volume in the series, provides an overview of the sociology and politics of the contemporary Middle East. The texts have been arranged in three sections—the international context, the national context, and structures and processes. Each section is preceded by an introduction, and there is an extensive guide to further reading. The following topics are covered by the individual contributors: Iran, Egypt, Israel, labor migration, Lebanon, Turkey, Tunisia, nationalism, Algeria, Palestinian refugees, oil, the media, Iraq, and Syria.]

Aslan, Ibrahim, and Dietrich Klitzke, eds. *Kulturelle, Identität Kulturelle Praxis*. Photos by Horst Herkner and drawings by Selcuk Caydi. Berlin: Express Edition, 1982. 102 pp. Illus.
[Deals with Turkish immigrants to Europe.]

Azarya, Victor. *Urban Life behind Monastery Walls: Armenian Quarter of Jerusalem*. Berkeley: University of California Press. 224 pp. Bibl.

Aziz, Philippe. *Les sectes secrètes de l'Islam: De l'ordre des assassins aux frères musulmans*. Paris: Laffont. 360 pp.
[The convulsions of the Islamic world are illuminated by the history, the traditions, and the influence of the principal sects that already had arisen by the ninth century in Persia, Turkey, Lebanon, Egypt, Iraq, and Arabia.]

Bacque-Grammont, Jean-Louis, and Jean-Paul Roux. *Mustafa Kemal Atatürk et la Turquie nouvelle*. Paris: Maisonneuve et Larose. 62 pp. Illus.
[The life and work of the founder of the Turkish republic is the subject of this book.]

Bacque-Grammont, Jean-Louis, and Paul Dumont, eds. *Economie et sociétés dans*

l'empire ottoman: Fin du XVIIIe siècle, début du XXe siècle. Collque international du CNRS, no. 601, Strasbourg, 1er-5 juillet 1980. Paris: CNRS. 488 pp. Illus.; tables.
[A historical, social, economic, institutional, and political approach to the history of the countries of the Ottoman Empire. Fifteen communications in English, thirteen in French, and two in German.]

Badeau, John Stothoff. *The Middle East Remembered.* Washington, D.C.: Middle East Institute. 271 pp. Index.
[John Badeau describes a half-century of dramatic change and his personal involvement in the events that shaped the modern Middle East. As diplomat, scholar, educator, and missionary, John Badeau's memoirs bring a unique series of different perspectives to the Muslim world and to his role as ambassador to Nasir's Egypt. The book presents unvarnished views of Egyptian personalities.]

Bakalla, M.H. *Arabic Culture through Its Language and Literature.* London and Boston: Kegan Paul International. Bibl.

———. *Arabic Linguistics: An Introduction and Bibliography.* London: Mansell; distributed in North America by H.W. Wilson. 741 pp. Bibl.; index.
[More than 5,000 citations divided into Occidental and Oriental works with indexes by subject, author, translators, and so on. Prefatory matter is in English and Arabic. Essentially an update of the author's *Bibliography of Arabic Linguistics,* published in 1975 with 2,018 entries.]

Bakhtiar, Chapour. *Chapour Bakhtiar: Ma fidélité.* Paris: Albin Michel. 250 pp.

Bar-Siman-Tov, Yaacov. *Linkage Politics in the Middle East: Syria between Domestic and External Conflict, 1961–1970.* Boulder, Colo.: Westview Press. 176 pp. Bibl.; illus.; index.
[Traditional studies of linkage politics tend to assume that internal political instability leads the political leadership to divert attention from internal to external problems. Quantitative studies typically show little relationship between internal and external politics. In this case study of Syria's internal political instability and its involvement in the Arab-Israeli and inter-Arab conflicts, the author criticizes the exclusive use of quantitative methods and suggests employing traditional empirical methods to supply the basis for a well-substantiated quantitative analysis.]

Barthel, Günter, and Lothar Rathmann, eds. *The Arab World and Asia between Development and Change: Dedicated to the XXXIst International Congress of Human Sciences.* Studies of Asia, Africa, and Latin America, vol. 37. Berlin: Akademie-Verlag. 304 pp. Illus.

Bates, Daniel G., and Amal Rassam, eds. *Peoples and Cultures of the Middle East.* Englewood Cliffs, N.J.: Prentice-Hall. 289 pp. Illus.; index.

Bavly, Dan, and Eliahu Salpeter. *Fire in Beirut: Israel's War in Lebanon with the PLO.* New York: Stein and Day. Illus.; index.

Bayle, Pierre. *Les relations secrètes israélo-palestiniennes.* Paris: André Balland. 364 pp.
[The author lays out a balance sheet of all the negotiations claiming a place—

exhibiting all their complexity—and draws portraits of the negotiators he met while he was a correspondent for the A.F.P. in Beirut.]

Ben-Dor, Gabriel. *State and Conflict in the Middle East: The Emergence of the Post-Colonial State in Middle East Politics.* New York: Praeger. 288 pp. Index.

Benabdallal, Abdelkader. *La question du Chatt-el-Arab: Aspects géographique his-torique et juridique.* Montreal: Canada-Monde arabe. 170 pp. Bibl.; charts.
[The question of the Shatt-al-Arab River has been of great moment since the outbreak of the Iraqi-Iranian war, which has made of it an occasion for war. How does the situation present itself for litigation? How may this conflict, which still persists, be resolved? These are the questions the author addresses.]

Benchenane, Mustapha. *Pour un dialogue euro-arabe.* Mondes en devenir, série: Points chauds, no. 5. Paris: Berger-Levrault. 354 pp.
[The author does not content himself with merely retracing the efforts that have been made in this domain and striking a balance among them; he analyzes the complex nature of the Euro-Arab relationship in terms of its power relations and of relevant emotional and cultural factors. At the same time, he suggests ways to make the dialogue progress.]

Bendelac, Jacques. *Les fonds extérieurs d'Israël: La fin de l'Israël connection?* Pre-face by Pierre-Maurice Clair and commentary by Jacques Austruy. Per-spectives économiques et juridiques. Paris: Economica, 1982. 108 pp. Bibl.
[The author shows how the mechanism of mobilizing Jewish capital of the Diaspora has profoundly transformed the structure of funds received by Israel. He also discusses the nature of the financial contributions.]

Bennett, John Godolphin. *Der Sufi-Weg heute: Interviews und Informationen.* Translated by Angelika Nichols. Südergellersen: Martin. 181 pp. Figures; illus.

Bensalah, Anas. *La fiscalité face au développement économique et social du Maroc.* Bibliothèque de science financière, vol. 29. Paris: Librarie génér-ale de droit et de jurisprudence. 376 pp.

Bernard, Chantal. *La politique de l'emploi-formation au Maghreb (1970–1980).* Etudes de l'annuaire de l'Afrique de Nord, Centre de Recherches et d'Etudes sur les Sociétés Méditerranéennes. Paris: CNRS, 1982. 472 pp.
[After a study of the restructuring of the productive apparatus and of social mobility, the author analyzes the pertinence of the employment formation policy with regard to the logic of development. Extracted from *L'annuaire de l'Afrique de Nord.*]

Bernstein, Reiner, D. Hamdan, and Karlheinz Schneider, eds. *Der Palästinakon-flikt: Geschichte, Positionen, Perspektiven.* Bad Wörishofen: Sachon. 384 pp. Bibl.; illus.

Beyrouth, souvenirs . . . réalité. Preface by Ghassan Tuéni. Beirut: An Nahar Inter-national; Paris: Hachette. 96 pp. Illus.
[The 123 photographs of Beirut collected here represent a moment in life where the past and the present coexist as nowhere else in the world.]

Bleicher, Heinz M., ed. *Der Mann, der Friede heisst: Begegnungen, Texts, Bilder für Schalom Ben-Chorin; aus Anlass seines 70. Geburtstages im Juli 1983*. Gerlingen: Bleicher. 151, 32 pp. Illus.

Bogner, Heinz D. *Iran: Eine Revolution von ihr Selbstverständnis*. Puchheim: IDEA. 224 pp. Illus.

Bosworth, E., and Carole Hillenbrand. *Qajar Iran, 1800–1925: Political, Social, and Cultural Change*. Edinburgh: Edinburgh University Press. 300 pp.

Boulares, Habib. *L'Islam, la peur et l'espérance*. Paris: J.-C. Lattès. 246 pp.
[Ex-minister of culture and information, the author presents what is both a fact book and an essay. He makes us experience from the inside the actual situation of an Islam divided between retrograde conservatism and modernism.]

Bourgi, Albert, and Pierre Weiss. *Liban: La cinquième guerre du Proche-Orient*. Paris: Publisud. 314 pp. Maps.
[The authors attempt to interpret in as clear a manner as possible the Lebanese imbroglio and its regional and international implications.]

Bradsher, Henry S. *Afghanistan and the Soviet Union*. Durham, N.C.: Duke University Press. 324 pp. Bibl.; index; map.

Bräker, Hans. *The Implications of the Islam Question for Soviet Domestic and Foreign Policy*. Berichte des Bundesinstitut für Ostwissenschaftliche und Internationale Studien, 1983, no. 12. Cologne: Bundesinstitut. 34 pp. Bibl.
[Includes a summary in German.]

Breckle, Siegmar W., and Clas M. Naumann, eds. *Forschungen in und über Afghanistan: Situation der wissenschaftlichen Erforschung Afghanistans und Folgen der gegenwärtigen politischen Lage; in Bielefeld, 4.–6. Februar 1982*. Mitteilungen des Deutschen Orient-Instituts, no. 22. Hamburg: Deutschen Orient-Instituts. 230 pp. Bibl.; figures; illus.
[Lectures, part in German and part in English, from the Internationalen Arbeitstagung der Arbeitsgemeinschaft Afghanistan, 6.]

Brentjes, Burchard. *Libyens Weg durch die Jahrtausende*. Leipzig, Jena, and Berlin: Urania-Verlag. 128 pp. Illus.

Browne. Edward G. *The Press and Poetry of Modern Persia*. Los Angeles: Kalimat Press. 357 pp.
[A facsimile reprint, with new preface by professor Amin Banani, of Browne's classic study (Cambridge, England, 1914) of the journalism and poetry of the Iranian revolution of 1906–11. Half the study is an analysis and survey of the numerous newspapers that were published before and after the Constitutional Revolution. Section 2 consists of selections of Persian revolutionary poetry in the original and with translations by Professor Browne. An important historical sourcebook as well as background toward understanding contemporary Iranian affairs.]

Cahen, Claude. *Introduction à l'histoire du monde musulman médiéval, VIIe–XVe siècles*. Paris: Maisonneuve. 216 pp. Bibl.; index.
[A total recasting of *Introduction à l'histoire de l'orient musulman: Eléments*

de bibliographie, by Jean Sauvaget and Claude Cahen (Maisonneuve, 1961), which was translated into English as *Jean Sauvaget's Introduction to the History of the Muslim East: A Bibliographic Guide* (University of California Press, 1965), this reference book provides the basic information that will permit one to locate and consult the essential titles in the field of Near Eastern history and to understand the nature and limits of the sources available for particular periods and topics. Brings up to date a classic and necessary tool.]

Cantori, Louis J., and Iliya Harik, eds. *Local Politics and Development in the Middle East.* Boulder, Colo.: Westview Press. 250 pp.
[The authors of this book concentrate on how local politics influence development in the Middle East, with the intent of encouraging more appropriate—and thus more effective—assistance programs. They discuss general policy issues and the nature of center-periphery relations in Middle East countries and delve into specific problems encountered in Egypt, Jordan, Lebanon, Syria, Iraq, Turkey, Tunisia, and North Yemen. They show how information about local political schemes can help administrators of development programs provide assistance that is acceptable—and accepted— at the local level.]

Carré, Olivier, and Gérard Michaud. *Les frères musulmans: Egypte et Syrie (1928–1982).* Archives, no. 92. Paris: Gallimard. 238 pp. Illus.

Carroll, Raymond. *The Palestine Question.* New York: F. Watts. 90 pp. Bibl.; index.
[Discusses the complex problems of the land known historically as Palestine, including the question of to which, if any, people it belongs, and the possibilities of a peaceful settlement of the question.]

Chaliand, Gérard, and Yves Ternon. *The Armenians: From Genocide to Resistance.* Translanted by Tony Berrett. London: Zed Press. 125 pp. Bibl.; illus.; maps.
[Translation of *Le genocide des Armeniens, 1915–1917.*]

Chomsky, Noam. *The Fateful Triangle: The United States, Israel and the Palestinians.* Boston: South End Press. 481 pp. Index.

Clements, Frank A., and Robert L. Collision, eds. *United Arab Emirates.* World Bibliographical Series, vol. 43. Oxford and Santa Barbara, Calif.: ABC-Clio. 162 pp. Bibl.; index; map.

Clifton, Tony, and Catherine Leroy. *God Cried.* London and New York: Quartet. 141 pp. Illus.
[A history of the 1982 Beirut bombardment.]

Cohen, Amnon. *Political Parties in the West Bank under the Jordanian Regime, 1949–1967.* Ithaca, N.Y.: Cornell University Press. 278 pp. Index.

Cohen, Stuart A. *English Zionists and British Jews: The Communal Politics of Anglo-Jewry, 1895–1920.* Princeton, N.J.: Princeton University Press. 392 pp. Illus.
[This work analyzes the communal influences that alternately facilitated and retarded Anglo-Jewry's conversion to Zionism between 1895, when Theodore Herzl first visited London, and 1920, when Great Britain received the Mandate over Palestine. Cohen argues that the conflict between Zionists and anti-

Zionists evolved into a complex struggle for community control. To describe the struggle, the author draws on unpublished private papers and communal records, as well as secondary sources.]

Cohen, Warren I., ed. *Reflections on Orientalism: Edward Said, Roger Bresnahan, Surjit Dulai, Edward Graham, and Donald Lammers.* East Lansing: Asian Studies Center, Michigan State University. 62 pp.
[This volume, inspired by the notion of "orientalism" put forward by Edward Said in his two books *Orientalism* (Pantheon, 1978) and *Covering Islam* (Pantheon, 1981), is a collection of essays in which four Michigan State professors effectively balance Said's concentration on the Islamic "Orient" with studies of specific Western cultures in their relationship with other non-Western civilizations: Bresnahan on American views of the Pacific islands; Dulai on Orwell's *Burmese Days*; Graham and Lammers on China and Japan in Western literature.]

Communautés (Les) rurales = Rural Communities. Part 3, *Asie et Islam* = Asia and Islam. Recueils de la Société Jean-Bodin pour l'histoire comparative des institutions, no. 42. Paris: Dessain et Tolra. 412 pp.
[A study of rural communities from an institutional history point of view. Texts in French and English; preface by John Gilissen. Volumes 1–39 were published by the Librairie Pédagogique à Bruxelles.]

Cordesman, Anthony H. *Jordanian Arms and the Middle East Balance.* Washington, D.C.: Middle East Institute. 186 pp. Bibl.; illus.
[A detailed study of the arms balance in the Middle East by an acknowledged expert. Facts and figures to explain Israel's military superiority, why the Syrians lost the air war, the meaning of the SAM-5s around Damascus, the factors of terrain and supply as elements of weakness for Jordan, the comparative disadvantages of the weapons being supplied by the superpowers.]

Corm, Georges. *Le Proche-Orient éclaté: De Suez à l'invasion du Liban, 1956–1982.* Textes à l'appui, série: Histoire contemporaine. Paris: La Découverte/Maspero. 373 pp. Maps; index.
[More than a historical reflection, this work by a Lebanese economist and sociologist provides a key to comprehending the conflicts of the Near East and the parts played in them by France and the great powers.]

Covington, Sally, ed. *The Israeli Invasion of Lebanon: Part II—Press Profile, August 1982-March 1983.* Invasion of Lebanon Series. New York: Claremont. 300 pp.
[This work supplements an earlier one with the same title that covered the period of June-July 1982. The items in both works "are taken from newspapers and periodicals published in the U.S., Canada, Britain, Israel, and the West Bank."]

Crespi, Gabriele. *Die Araber in Europa.* Introduction by Francesco Gabrieli. Translated from the Italian by Konrad Norbert Braun. Stuttgart and Zurich: Belser. 334 pp. Bibl.; charts; illus.; maps.
[A German translation of *Gli Arabi in Europa* (Milan, 1982). The author displays the fundamental role played by Islam in the development of European civilization and points out its traces in France, Sicily, and Spain, after having retraced the particulars of Islamic civilization.]

————. *L'Europe musulmane*. Introduction by Francesco Gabrieli. Saint-Léger Vauban: Zodiaque; Paris: Weber-Diffusion. 336 pp. Bibl.; charts; illus.; maps.
[A French translation of *Gli Arabi in Europa* (Milan, 1982).]

Dahmani, Mohamed. *L'occidentalisation des pays du tiers monde: Mythes et réalités*. Algiers: Office des publications universitaires; Paris: Economica. 216 pp.
[This work relates attempts to modernize or Westernize non-Western societies, from Russia to the Islamic republic of Iran, passing Japan on the way. The author takes the opportunity in this context to denounce the perverse effects resulting from a superficial mimesis erected in lieu of economic and social development.]

Damis, John James. *Conflict in Northwest Africa: The Western Sahara Dispute*. Stanford, Calif.: Hoover Institution Press. 196 pp. Bibl.; illus.; index.
[Professor Damis has marshaled knowledge acquired in nearly two decades of close observation of events in Northwest Africa to produce a succinct account of the evolution of the Western Sahara problem and of its effect on the "concerned and interested parties." Following a thumbnail sketch of the Sahara and the Sahrawis, he describes the views and roles of the principal parties to the dispute—Morocco, Mauritania, Algeria, and the Polisario—and follows this with an account of the evolution of the conflict and a concluding chapter on the possibilities for achieving a solution.]

Danielsen, Albert L. *The Evolution of OPEC*. New York: Harcourt Brace Jovanovich, 1982. 305 pp. Bibl.; illus.; index; tables.

El-Dareer, Asma. *Woman, Why Do You Weep? Circumcision and Its Consequences*. London: Zed Press. 130 pp. Bibl.; illus.

Davis, Eric. *Challenging Colonialism: Bank Misr and Egyptian Industrialization, 1920–1941*. Princeton, N.J.: Princeton University Press. 232 pp. Bibl.; illus.; index.
[Describing the first solely Arab bank and its place in Egypt between the two world wars, this work discusses the Bank Misr's sponsorship of Egypt's first indigenously financed and directed industrialization movement, and develops a model to explain the bank's initial successes, its eventual failure to free Egypt from foreign economic control, and its crash in 1939. Eric Davis relates world market forces to Egypt's class structure, state regime, and nationalist movement to challenge classic theories of dependency and imperialism.]

Davis, Susan S. *Patience and Power: Women's Lives in a Moroccan Village*. Cambridge, Mass.: Schenkman. 198 pp. Bibl.; illus.; index.

Davis, Uri. *The Golan Heights under Israeli Occupation 1967–1981*. Centre for Middle Eastern and Islamic Studies: Occasional Papers Series, no. 18. Durham, England: University of Durham. 58 pp.

Delcorde, Raoul. *La sécurité et la stratégie dans le golfe arabo-persique*. Paris: Le sycomore. 124 pp.
[An inquiry into the different aspects of the strategic situation in this region and its influence on the worldwide equilibrium.]

Dempsey, Michael W., and Norman Barrett, comps. *Atlas of the Arab World*. New York: Facts on File. [125 pp.] Illus.; maps.
[This colorful atlas contains a wealth of information on the Arab world, which is defined as the twenty-one countries of the Arab League. Thirty-eight double-page maps are devoted to themes of physical, human, and economic geography; communication; government; the military; and, briefly, the historical dimension. Some questionable cartographic judgments and editorial lapses detract from the merit of the book: color gradations are inconsistent; transliteration is chaotic; some historical facts are incorrect; the notes are relegated to the end of the volume; and there is no index. A new edition should include revisions as well as updated data. A useful work, however.]

Dietl, Wilhelm. *Heiliger Krieg für Allah: Als Augenzeuge bei den geheimen Kommandos des Islam*. Munich: Kindler. 431 pp. Bibl.; illus.; index; map.

Diner, Dan. *Grenzprobleme im Palästinakonflikt*. Frankfurt am Main: Haag und Herchen. 172 pp. Map.

———. *Keine Zukunft auf den Gräbern der Palästinenser: Eine histori-politischen Bilanz der Palästinafrage*. Hamburg: VSA-Verlag, 1982. 167 pp.

Dodd, C.H. *The Crisis of Turkish Democracy*. Beverley, North Humberside, England: Eothen Press, distributed by Humanities Press.
[Events have moved rapidly in recent years in Turkey. The multiparty political system was suspended by the military when it intervened in September 1980 after a period of violence and terrorism. Since that date, the military has maintained law and order and has been taking steps to ensure that Turkey returns to a liberal and democratic system in the near future. This book deals with the breakdown of Turkish democracy, military rule, and the making of a new constitution.]

Dowty, Alan. *Middle East Crisis: U.S. Decision-Making in 1958, 1970 and 1973* Berkeley: University of California Press, Bibl.; index.
[Part of the International Crisis Behavior Project.]

Dumont, Paul. *Mustafa Kemal, 1919–1924*. Mémoire du siècle. Brussels: Complexe. 224 pp.
[As head of a troop of soldiers exhausted by four years of war, Mustafa Kemal, repudiated by the sultan, succeeded in effectively opposing the French and English, and then accomplished a revolution that has contributed greatly to fashioning the face of an important part of the world.]

Duri, Abd al-Aziz. *The Historical Formation of the Arab Nation*. CCAS Occasional Papers. Washington, D.C.: Center for Contemporary Arab Studies, Georgetown University, 17 pp.
[An examination of the historical influence of Islamic civilization on the evolution of Arab national consciousness and the Arab nation. Focusing on the causes that led to the formation of a unified Arab community, the author traces the social and economic changes encouraged by the spread of Islam.]

———. *The Rise of Historical Writing among the Arabs*. Edited and translated by Lawrence I. Conrad. Introduction by Fred. M. Donner. Princeton, N.J.: Princeton University Press. 192 pp.
[Translation of *Bahth fī nash'at 'ilm al-tārīkh 'inda al-'Arab*.]

Eban, Abba Soloman. *The New Diplomacy: International Affairs in the Modern Age*. London: Weidenfeld and Nicolson; New York: Random House. 427 pp. Index. Chapter 6 of this volume by Israel's distinguished statesman and foremost spokesman, Abba Eban, is entitled "The Unending Conflict: The Middle East."

Al-Ebraheem, Hassan Ali. *Kuwait and the Gulf: Small States and the International System*. Washington, D.C.: Center for Contemporary Arab Studies, Georgetown University; London: Croom Helm. 113 pp.
[An analysis of the foreign policy and economic factors governing the activity of small states, with a focus on Kuwait and other Gulf states. Kuwait is studied as an example of a small state that has succeeded in surviving amid the troubles of realpolitik in the international arena.]

Elwell-Sutton, L.P., ed. *Bibliographical Guide to Iran: The Middle East Library Committee Guide*. Sussex: Harvester Press; Totowa, N.Y.: Barnes and Noble. 462 pp. Bibl.; index.

Erol, Oguz. *Die naturräumliche Gliederung der Türkei*. Beihefte zum Tübinger Atlas des Vorderen Orients: Reihe A, Naturwissenschaftliche, no. 13. Wiesbaden: Reichert. 245 pp. Bibl.; figures; maps.

Esposito, John L. *Voices of Resurgent Islam*. New York: Oxford University Press.

Fahmy, Ismail. *Negotiating Peace in the Middle East*. Baltimore, Md.: Johns Hopkins University Press. 288 pp. Index.
[The author was Egypt's foreign minister throughout the four-year span from the October War in 1973 to Sadat's visit to Jerusalem in November 1977. He describes here the stormy years when prospects for a permanent peace in the Middle East seemed a real possibility.]

Farah, Tawfic E., ed. *Political Behavior in the Arab States*. Boulder, Colo.: Westview Press. 240 pp. Bibl.: figures; index; tables.
[This collection of research portrays political and social behavior in the Arab states. It offers new perspectives and illustrates the effectiveness of survey research as an analytical tool for investigating the problems of Arab societies— dealing with the political and social behavior of individuals in the Arab world in a comprehensive and interdisciplinary fashion. Malcolm H. Kerr, the recently assassinated president of the American University in Beirut, provides the Foreword.]

Fawaz, Leila Tarazi. *Merchants and Migrants in Nineteenth-Century Beirut*. Harvard Middle Eastern Studies, no. 18. Cambridge, Mass.: Harvard University Press. 240 pp. Bibl.; illus.; index.
[Fawaz examines the migration that lay behind the growth of Beirut—a small provincial town of 6,000 in the nineteenth century that grew into a political and cultural center of 120,000, making it the leading seaport of the eastern Mediterranean. She discusses why the migrants came, what economic changes resulted, and how social relations among the city's religious communities were transformed.]

Ferro, Marc. *Suez 1956: Naissance d'un tiers monde*. Mémoire du siècle, no. 24. Brussels: Editions complexe. 160 pp. Bibl.; index.

[By the author of *Comment on reconte l'histoire aux enfants: L'occident devant la révolution soviétique.*]

Fertl, Herbert L. *Abweichende Meinungen zu Israel: Die politischen Emanzipation den Juden durch eine Militärdemokratie mit imperialistischem Auftrag.* Munich: Resultate-Verlag, 1982. 128 pp. Illus.

Fesharaki, Fereidun, and David T. Isaak. *OPEC, the Gulf, and the World Petroleum Market: A Study in Government Policy and Downstream Operations.* Boulder, Colo.: Westview Press. 268 pp. Index; figures; tables.
[OPEC's dominant position as supplier of crude to the world oil market is well known. Recently, however, many of the OPEC nations, particularly those on the Gulf, have begun a large-scale move into hydrocarbon industries formerly controlled by the major oil companies. This book provides a detailed look at the OPEC nations' changing roles in the world oil market as they expand their participation in "downstream" activities.]

Feuillet, Claude. *Le système saoud.* Lausanne, Switzerland: P.M. Favre. 210 pp.
[The Arabia of the Saudis, a western economic and military base in the Gulf region: could it possibly crumble at any moment, as did the Iran of the Pahlavis? Do there exist opposition parties capable of overthrowing the dynasty founded on the despotic power of a single man, the present King Fahd?]

Fingerlin, Erika, and Michael Mildenberger, eds. *Ehen mit Muslimen: Am Beispiel deutschen-türkischen Ehen.* Beiträge Ausländerarbeit; 4. Frankfurt am Main: Lembeck. 58 pp. Illus.
[An appendix consists of a separate title: *Ehen in Ländern mit islamischem Recht.*]

Finkielkraut, Alain. *La réprobation d'Israël.* Bibliothèque médiations, vol. 237. Paris: Denoël/Gonthier. 181 pp. Bibl.
[The author of *Le Juif imaginaire* reacts to the accusations conveyed aginst Israel, not to proscribe the critique of the Jewish state, but to render possible a rational approach to Zionism and to Israel.]

Flores, Alexander, and Alexander Schölch, eds. *Palästinenser in Israel.* Frankfort am Main: Beliner Institut für Vergleichende Sozialforschung; New York: Campus-Verlag. 311 pp. Figures.

Follath, Erich. *Das Auge Davids: Die geheimen Kommando-Unternehmen den Israelis.* Munich: Goldmann. 279 pp.

Frangi, Abdallah. *The PLO and Palestine.* Translated by Paul Knight. London: Zed Press. 256 pp. Bibl.; illus.; maps.
A translation of *PLO und Palästina: Vergangenheit und Gegenwart* (Frankfurt, 1982), which was annotated in volume 2 of the *Middle East Annual.*

Frazee, Charles A. *Catholics and Sultans: The Church and the Ottoman Empire, 1453–1923.* New York: Cambridge University Press. 388 pp. Bibl.; index.
[This book provides a history of Catholicism inside the Ottoman Empire and traces the external relations of the papacy and Western Catholic countries with the Turkish government. The author focuses particularly on France's

diplomatic activities in pursuit of its role as protector of the Ottoman Catholics and on the founding of Eastern Catholic churches under French protection.]

Friedlander, Melvin A. *Sadat and Begin: The Domestic Politics of Peacemaking.* Boulder, Colo.: Westview Press. 338 pp. Bibl.; index.
[The architects of the Camp David process expected their efforts to become a broad, inclusive framework for peace in the Middle East. Friedlander demonstrates how domestic factors affecting policy decisions made in both Cairo and Jerusalem prevented Sadat and Begin from embracing a structure that would yield a more comprehensive arrangement. Both leaders, the author concludes, were able ultimately to guide their nations toward approval of the peace initiative primarily because of their mastery of techniques of domestic intraelite bargaining. This work was the author's American University dissertation.]

Front Polisario. *Dix ans de lutte contre le colonialisme et l'expansionnisme.* Ministère de la Culture et de l'Information de la République arabe sahraouie démocratique. Paris: Diffussion l'harmattan. 165 pp.

Gabriel, Richard A., ed. *Antagonists in the Middle East: A Combat Assessment.* Fighting Armies, vol. 2. Westport, Conn.: Greenwood Press. 176 pp. Bibl.; illus.; index.

Gallagher, Nancy Elizabeth. *Medicine and Power in Tunisia, 1780–1900.* New York: Cambridge University Press. 148 pp. Bibl.; illus.; index; maps; tables.
[In this study the author explores the ways in which medicine became a political tool that facilitated French domination of North Africa. Severe epidemics of plague, cholera, and typhus swept across Tunisia between 1780 and 1900. Muslim political leaders followed the practice of European ports in quickly imposing quarantines when news of disease arrived. The author shows how the transition to European-dominated quarantine boards, which had occurred by the 1830s, although stimulated by epidemics, was more fundamentally a part of the onset of European political domination.]

Garaudy, Roger. *L'affaire Israël: Le Sionisme politique.* Paris: S.P.A.G., Papyrus Editions. 201 pp.
[The author, familiar among other things as the founder of the LICRA and as a recent convert to Islam, approaches here the fundamental problem posed by the policy of the Israeli state. He analyzes the ideological and theological basis of that policy and extricates its internal logic.]

Garfinkle, Adam M. *Western Europe's Middle East Diplomacy and the United States.* Philadelphia Policy Papers. Philadelphia: Foreign Policy Research Institute. 118 pp.

Garthwaite, Gene R. *Khans and Shahs: A Documentary Analysis of the Bakhtiyārī in Iran.* New York: Cambridge University Press. 213 pp. Bibl.; illus.; index; 3 microfiche.
[An account of one of the most important nomadic societies of Iran, which constituted a quarter of the country's population in the nineteenth century. Professor Garthwaite's study outlines the society's interaction with the state and the effects the outside world had on its social and political structure. The volume enhances our understanding of how political power is created and

maintained in a tribal society. It is accompanied by microfiche of the documentation on which the study is based.]

Gaudio, Attilio. *Fès, joyau de la civilisation islamique.* Preface by Mohammed El Fasi. Paris: UNESCO, Nouvelles éditions latines, 1982. 312 pp. Bibl.; illus.
[The city of Fez is dilapidated, and UNESCO has launched an international campaign for safeguarding the Moroccan patrimony. This book retraces the history of the town and explains how to renovate the quarter. It describes the Fez of today through its artisans and its families.]

Gazit, Mordechai. *President Kennedy's Policy toward the Arab States and Israel: Analysis and Documents.* Tel Aviv: Shiloah Center for Middle Eastern Studies, Tel Aviv University; distributed by Syracuse University Press. 133 pp. Bibl.
[Under President Kennedy, U.S. Middle Eastern policy underwent important changes—some planned, some not. U.S. relations with Egypt and Israel are at the heart of this study, in particular, Kennedy's decision to authorize the Hawk missile deal with Israel—thereby breaking previous policy of no arms sales to Israel. Included are twenty-two documents dealing with U.S.–Israeli and U.S.–UAR relations and with the Palestine Arab refugee problem.]

Geiger, Andreas. *Herkunftsbedingungen der türkischen Arbeiter in der Bundesrepublik und ihr gewerkschaftliches Verhalten.* Berlin: Express-Edition, 1982. 229 pp.

Gershoni, Israel. *The Emergence of Pan-Arabism in Egypt.* Tel Aviv: Shiloah Center for Middle Eastern and African Studies, Tel-Aviv University, 1981. (Syracuse University Press) 142 pp. Bibl.; index.
[This book wrestles with the question of how and when pan-Arabism first appeared as a major ideological force in the consciousness of the cultural and political elite in Egypt. The author focuses on the years 1936–40 when pan-Arabism began to crystallize as a major factor affecting the national, political, and cultural consciousness of Egypt. He also examines the waning of pan-Arabism in the 1970s under Sadat.]

Ghareeb, Edmund, ed. *Split Vision: The Portrayal of Arabs in the American Media.* Washington, D.C.: American-Arab Affairs Council.
[To answer the question of how the media have influenced the public image of Arabs in the United States, the author conducted two series of interviews in 1975–77 and 1979–82. The results of the first set were published in 1977 by the Institute of Middle Eastern and North African Studies, Hyattsville, Md. This volume contains the second set as well. In the interviews, Ghareeb draws out well-known news media figures, such as Peter Jennings, Anthony Lewis, Georgie Anne Geyer, and John Cooley on the difficulties of achieving balanced news coverage on the Middle East and concludes that pro-Israeli attitudes dominate the U.S. media.]

Ghosh, Arabina. *OPEC, the Petroleum Industry, and United States Energy Policy.* Westport, Conn.: Greenwood Press, Quorum Books. 296 pp. Bibl.; charts; index; tables.

Gilmour, David. *Lebanon: The Fractured Country.* New York: St. Martin's Press. 232 pp. Bibl.; index.

Giniewski, Paul. *De Massada à Beyrouth: Une leçon d'histoire.* Paris: Presses universitaires de France. 272 pp. Index.
[A history of the Jewish people, from the resistance of Massada through the Roman epoch up to the Nazi genocide, the resurrection of the Jewish state, and the contemporary dominance of its military force as in Lebanon.]

Girgis, Maurice, ed. *Industrial Progress in Small Oil-Exporting Countries: The Prospect for Kuwait.* Boulder, Colo.: Westview Press. 195 pp. Index; tables.
[This book is an attempt to analyze some of the new and unique options for small oil-exporting countries not discussed in the traditional development literature. Recognizing Kuwait's three major areas of vulnerability—reliance on oil income, absence of food security, and need for immigrant workers—the contributors define a development strategy that would foster rapid growth without accentuating those vulnerabilities. They also examine other basic issues related to industrial expansion and diversification and suggest new methods to identify cost-advantageous industrial activities.]

Goldschmidt, Arthur, Jr. *A Concise History of the Middle East.* 2d rev. ed. Boulder, Colo.: Westview Press. 450 pp. Bibl.; chronology; figures; glossary; index; maps; tables.
[This second edition of the author's well-known text adds a chapter on the region since 1978 and an extensive chronology of events, and includes a revised and expanded chapter on the 1973–78 period, an updated glossary and bibliographic essay, and improved maps, as well as revisions throughout the book in response to comments from readers.]

Gordan, David C. *The Republic of Lebanon: Nation in Jeopardy.* Boulder, Colo.: Westview Press. 171 pp. Bibl.; illus.; index; tables.
[In this analytical survey of the present-day Republic of Lebanon, the author addresses such questions as why the republic—rooted in the distant past—has succumbed to disintegration. Lebanon's multiethnic character and the Palestinian presence are considered fully, and Lebanon is examined in the international context, necessarily with particular reference to the creation of Israel and its consequences.]

Algosaibi, Ghazi A., ed. and trans. *Lyrics of Arabia.* Washington, D.C.: Three Continents Press. 125 pp.
A collection of individual lines excerpted from the poems of forty-seven famous Arabic poets who composed the classics of Arabic poetry from 500 to 1100 A.D. This collection, compiled and translated by the Saudi minister of industry and electricity, reaffirms the continuing attraction of classical literary norms and of the individual poetic line for many contemporary Arabs. The text offers the reader an attractive bilingual English-Arabic format and includes short biographies of the poets.

Grandguillaume, Gilbert. *Arabisation et politique linguistique au Maghreb.* Islam d'hier et d'aujourd'hui, vol. 19. Paris: Maisonneuve et Larose. 216 pp.
[Discusses the Arab language as a means of unifying a country through the suppression of the foreign or regional influences carried by language. The policy of Arabization of education, of administration, and of the social environment raises questions and debates of which this book renders an account.]

Grose, Peter. *Israel in the Mind of America*. New York: Knopf. 361 pp. Bibl.; index.
A history of the relationship between the dreams and realities of the Christian and Jewish heritages as they have interacted in American thought and politics from North America's first encounter with Jews in 1654 when twenty-three emigrants landed on Manhattan Island until the present. The author focuses on how a variety of Jewish, Christian, and secular concepts of a restored Israel have been interpreted by Americans and how these interpretations have affected the intellectual and political history of the United States and its policy toward the actual Israeli state formed in 1948. Newly unsealed British, Israeli, and U.S. archives provide documentation for a very readable work.

Guecioueur, Adda, ed. *The Problems of Arab Economic Development and Integration: Proceedings of a Symposium Held at Yarmouk University, Jordan, November 4 and 5, 1981*. Boulder, Colo.: Westview Press. 275 pp. Figures; tables.
[In this book, scholars, journalists, researchers, and officials of Arab, pan-Arab, and non-Arab institutions afford insights into the problems of Arab economic integration. The contributors, who met on the occasion of what was called the Eleventh Arab Summit (also termed the First Arab Economic Summit), suggest that the best means by which individual Arab countries can achieve economic development is through Arab economic integration. The editor is with the Research and Statistics Department of the Arab Monetary Fund.]

La Guerre du Golfe. Proche-Orient et tiers monde, no. 8. Paris: Proche-Orient et tiers monde. 158 pp.
[In the course of history, Mesopotamia has always been a prize, a creator of conflict between Arabs and Persians, of which the war between Iran and Iraq is the present and painful illustration. This particular number of *Proche-Orient et tiers monde* is devoted to an analysis of the causes of the war and its consequences.]

Gysling, Erich. *Arabiens Uhren gehen anders: Eigendynamik und Welkpolitik in Nahost*. Texte und Thesen, vol. 149; Sachgebiet Politik. Zurich: Edition Interform; Osnabrück: Fromm, 1982. 115 pp. Bibl.

Haim, Yehoyada. *Abandonment of Illusions: Zionist Political Attitudes toward Palestinian Arab Nationalism, 1936–1939*. Boulder, Colo.: Westview Press. 170 pp. Bibl.
[According to the author, currently political counselor at the Israeli Embassy in London, the politics, attitudes, and assumptions prevailing in the pre–World War I Zionist movement are identical to those providing the dynamics of contemporary Israeli politics. Haim identifies the main factions of the Zionist movement, analyzing their basic assumptions and policies, their various interpretations of Palestinian Arab opposition to the Jewish state, and their different approaches to overcoming that obstacle. He deals with the Arab revolt of 1936–39 in detail, as it caused major Zionist reevaluations.]

Hammond, Thomas T. *Red Flag over Afghanistan: The Communist Coup, the Soviet Invasion, and Their Consequences*. Boulder, Colo.: Westview Press. 300 pp. Bibl.; figures; index.
[How did it happen that Afghanistan, a country populated almost entirely by devout Muslims, became Communist? Were the Soviets responsible for the Communist coup of April 1978, or was it a solely internal affair? Professor

Hammond, a leading authority on Communist coups, discusses these and related issues. He makes extensive use of previously classified documents that he obtained under the Freedom of Information Act. One important document, the Constitution of the People's Democratic (Communist) party, is included as an appendix. The book also benefits from the author's interviews with former U.S. officials who helped to formulate policy toward Afghanistan and the U.S.S.R.]

Hammoutene, Ali. *Reflexions sur la guerre d'Algérie*. Paris: Publisud, 1982. 153 pp.
[These reflections are those of an Algerian executed by a commando of the OAS in March 1962.]

Hanks, Robert J. *The U.S. Military Presence in the Middle East: Problems and Prospects*. Foreign Policy Reports. Cambridge, Mass.: Institute for Foreign Policy Analysis. 80 pp.

Hart, David. *Dadda 'Atta and His Forty Grandsons: The Socio-Political Organization of the Ait 'Atta of Southern Morocco*. Boulder, Colo.: Westview Press. 260 pp. Appendixes; figures; glossary; illus.; index; maps.
[The Ait 'Atta, the transhumant tribe living on the edge of the Sahara, resisted the imposition of French colonial rule longer than most tribes in Morocco, not submitting until 1934. This study of that tribe is an important addition to the anthropology of Morocco, taking forward earlier work by Ernest Gellner. It also is an important contribution to the understanding of rural structures in Morocco and tribal organization in the Muslim world.]

Heck, Gerhard, and Manfred Wöbcke. *Arabische Halbinsel: Saudi-Arabien und Golfstaaten; Reise-Handbuch*. Cologne: DuMont. 294 pp. Illus; maps.

Heikal, Mohamed. *Autumn of Fury: The Assassination of Sadat*. London: Andre Deutsch; New York: Random House. 290 pp. Illus.; index.
[*Autumn of Fury* is a controversial interpretation of Sadat's reign and the factors leading to his assassination, explaining why a man so admired in the West was so isolated in his own world. Mohamad Heikal, the well-known Egyptian journalist, political liberal, and former editor of *al-Ahrām*, was associated closely with Nasir and later Sadat until the 1973 October war. He was imprisoned during Sadat's mass arrests in September 1981.]

Heller, Mark A. *A Palestinian State: The Implications for Israel*. Cambridge, Mass.: Harvard University Press. 192 pp. Bibl.; index.
[At a time when a two-state solution to the Israeli-Palestinian conflict is popular in many circles, few who espouse such a position have studied its implications for the two peoples involved. Mark Heller has prepared such a study from the Israeli perspective for the Center for Strategic Studies of Tel Aviv University. The study is essentially a cost-benefit analysis of the various options facing Israel, written before the June 1982 invasion but still relevant. "The main conclusion . . . is that a settlement based on an independent Palestinian state . . . constitutes a recommended strategic choice for Israel."]

Heller, Mark A., Dov Tamari, and Zeev Eytan. *The Middle East Military Balance, 1983*. Boulder, Colo.: Westview Press. 338 pp. Glossary; maps; tables.
[A detailed data base and analysis of military forces in the Middle East, this volume also surveys strategic events in the area during the preceding year and

assesses military balances among potential Middle East adversaries. Distributed throughout the world by Westview Press for the Jaffee Center for Strategic Studies, Tel Aviv University.]

Heshmati, Manoochehr. *Die "Weisse Revolution" und deren Wirkung auf die sozio-ökonomische Entwicklung Persiens: Anatomie eines gescheiterten Modernisierungskonzeptes.* Introduction by Ulrich Albrecht. Frankfort am Main: Haag und Herschen, 1982. 493 pp. Bibl.
[A 1981 disseration from the Free University of Berlin.]

Hickman, William F. *Ravaged and Reborn: The Iranian Army, 1982.* Brookings Institute Staff Paper. Washington, D.C.: Brookings Institute, 1982. 33 pp.

Hodges, Tony. *Western Sahara: Polisario's War for Independence.* Westport, Conn.: Lawrence Hill. 448 pp. Bibl.; index.

Hofmann, Michael. *Entwicklungspotential und Entwicklungsstrategien der südarabischen Staaten: Jemitische Arabische Republik, Demokratische Volksrepublik Jemen Sultanat Oman.* Forschungsberichte des Bundesministeriums für Wirtschaftliche Zusammenarbeit, vol. 38. Munich, Cologne, and London: Weltform-Verlag, 1982. 146 pp. Bibl.; figures; maps.

Hollstein, Walter. *Vettern und Feinde: Der Palästina-Israel-Konflikt.* Politprint, vol. 11. Basel: Lenos-Verlag. 202 pp.

Hörth, Raimund, ed. *Das Arabien-Geschäft: Daten, Fakten, Perspektiven.* Frankfort am Main: Machinenbau-Verlag, 1982. 359 pp. Figures; maps.

Houchang, Nahavandi. *Iran, anatomie d'une révolution.* SEGEP, Revue universelle des faits et des idées. Paris: Duquesne (distributor). 216 pp.
[The objective of this work is to restore the truth about both the underlying and the immediate causes of the Iranian revolution, as well as about those who were its authors and acted in it.]

Hourani, Albert. *Arabic Thought in the Liberal Age, 1798–1939.* New York: Cambridge University Press. 416 pp. Bibl.
[This reissue (Oxford University Press, 1962) makes available again Hourani's comprehensive study of the roots of Arab nationalism in modern times. The author focuses on the movement of ideas in two countries, Egypt and Lebanon. He shows how a restatement of the social goals of Islam combined with a movement to separate religion from politics created the Egyptian and Arab nationalism of the present century. For this edition, the author has written a new preface that indicates new emphases in research and interpretation, and provides a new bibliography.]

Hovannisian, Richard G., and Speros Vryonis, Jr., eds. *Islam's Understanding of Itself.* Eighth Giorgio Levi Della Vida Biennial Conference, 1981, University of California, Los Angeles. Malibu, Calif.: Undena Publications. 149 pp. Bibl.; illus.; index.
[The occasion for the conference out of which this volume grew was the eighth presentation of the Giorgio Levi Della Vida Award in Islamic Studies to W. Montgomery Watt. The essays vary in the extent to which they are framed as specific responses to Watt's lifetime work on Islam. The range of presentations is broad and for the most part of high quality, although more often they are re-

presentations of researched materials than the results of new investigations, approaches, or theories.]

Hubel, Helmut. *Die USA im Nahost-Konflikt.* Arbeitspapiere zur internationalen Politik; 23. Bonn: Europa-Union-Verlag. 91 pp.

Hudson, Michael C., ed. *Alternative Approaches to the Arab-Israeli Conflict: A Comparative Analysis of the Principal Actors.* Washington, D.C.: Center for Contemporary Arab Studies, Georgetown University. 200 pp.
[This monograph comprises papers presented at a conference cosponsored by CCAS and the Al Ahram Center for Political and Strategic Studies in Cairo during March 1983. Contributors include Hisham Sharabi and Sami Mansour (Palestinian approach); Michael C. Hudson and Saad E. Ibrahim (Arab states' approach); Don Peretz and Ali H. Dessouki (Israeli); Philip Stoddard and Abdel M. Said (American); and Dimitri Simes and Mohammed Selim (Soviet approach).]

Hünseler, Peter. *Der Irak und sein Konflikt mit Iran: Entwicklung, innenpolitische Bestimmungsfaktoren und Perspektiven.* Arbeitspapiere zur internationalen Politik; 22. Bonn: Europa-Union-Verlag, 1982. 149 pp.

Hussain, Asaf. *Political Perspectives on the Muslim World.* New York: St. Martin's Press.

Ibrahim, Ibrahim, ed. *Arab Resources: The Transformation of a Society.* Washington, D.C.: Center for Contemporary Arab Studies, Georgetown University; London: Croom Helm. 304 pp.
[This paperback volume is a compilation of papers presented at Georgetown University's Sixth Annual Symposium at the Center for Contemporary Arab Studies (CCAS). Four themes are addressed in seventeen papers by authorities in their fields: "Sectoral Resources," "Institutional Mechanisms," "Political Economy of Development," and "Aspects of Arab Transformation." An excellent introduction and editorial summary provides a comprehensive overview.]

Institut Français de Polémologie. *Le crises du Liban.* Notes et études documentaires, nos. 4694–4695. Paris: La documentation française. 111 pp. Maps.
[After a general presentation of the country, this chronology describes the succession of Lebanese political and military crises from 1958 to 1980 and concludes with the continuing crises of 1981–82.]

Irfani, Suroosh. *Revolutionary Islam in Iran: Popular Liberation or Religious Dictatorship?* London: Zed Press. 320 pp.

L'Islamisme en effervescence. Peuples méditerranéens, no. 21. Paris: Anthropos. 218 pp.
[An analysis of the different currents of the revival of Islam with their spiritual and political principles.]

Israel. Commission of Inquiry into the Events at the Refugee Camps in Beirut. *The Beirut Massacre: The Complete Kahan Commission Report.* Princeton, N.J.: Karz-Cohl. 136 pp.
[Authorized translation of *Din ve-heshbon ha-Va'adah la-hakirat ha-eru'im be-mahanot ha-pelitim be-Beirut.* Introduction by Abba Eban, with

parliamentary speeches by Ariel Sharon and Shimon Peres. Based on the testimony of 163 witnesses and over 17,000 pages of documents, the report thoroughly examines the circumstances surrounding the Beirut massacre and exactly how much the highest ranking Israeli leaders knew, giving a rare view inside Israeli politics.]

Israeli, Raphael, ed. *The PLO in Lebanon: Selected Documents*. London: Weidenfeld and Nicolson. 330 pp. Index; illus.

Jackson, Elmore. *Middle East Mission: The Story of a Major Bid for Peace in the Time of Nasser and Ben-Gurion*. New York: Norton. 124 pp. Index.
"Sadat's dramatic trip to Jerusalem in Nov. 1977 was not the first Egyptian effort to bring peace between Israel and her Arab neighbors. In the spring of 1955, several months before Prime Minister Nasser . . . [turned] to Eastern Europe for massive arms supply, he initiated a major effort for a settlement with Israel. . . . American Quakers . . . were approached . . . to see if they would . . . explore the possibility of a peace settlement." This is the story of the ensuing negotiations told by the American Quaker asked to conduct them, the parties involved having recently consented to break their prior silence.

Jaidah, Ali M. *An Appraisal of OPEC Oil Policies*. Energy Resources and Policies of the Middle East and North Africa. London and New York: Longman. 150 pp. Illus.; index.

Jamālzādeh, Muhammad 'Ali. *Isfahan Is Half the World: Memories of a Persian Boyhood*. Translated by W.L. Heston. Princeton: Princeton University Press. 298 pp. Illus.
[Jamālzādeh, acclaimed as the father of the modern Persian short story, wrote this book to provide for his fellow Iranians a memoir in story form of traditional Islamic life in Iran before Westernization. This translation of his *Sarūtah-i yak karbās* begins with an account of the author's childhood in the city of Isfahan, in a family headed by an enlightened and outspoken Muslim clergyman. Jamālzādeh is a major figure in Persian literature, although little of his work is available in English. This translation was prepared with his cooperation and includes comments and notes from his correspondence and conversations with the translator.]

Jbara, Taysir. *Hajj Amin al-Husayni, Mufti of Jerusalem: The Palestine Years*. Leaders, Politics and Social Change in the Islamic World, no. 3. Princeton, N.J.: Kingston Press. 300 pp.

Jegou, Monique. *Les Emirats Arabes Unis*. Paris: Albin Michel. 198 pp. Maps.
[Three years of living in this young state on the Arabian Gulf put the author in a position to have done with the clichés that still cling to this region, ignored by the great powers up to the twentieth century.]

Johnson, Maxwell Orme. *The Military as an Instrument of U.S. Policy in Southwest Asia: The Rapid Deployment Joint Task Force, 1979–1982*. Boulder, Colo.: Westview Press. 134 pp. Bibl.
[This book traces the evolution of U.S. policy in the region and assesses the capability of the RDJTF for maintaining regional stability and security. Major Johnson, U.S. Marine Corps, examines the formation and execution of the Carter Doctrine and its reinterpretation under the Reagan administration and then analyzes the organization, training, and tactical doctrines of the RDJTF,

assessing its military capabilitay and its role as an instrument of U.S. foreign policy.]

Jones, Rodney W., ed. *Small Nuclear Forces and U.S. Security Policy: Threats and Potential Conflicts in the Middle East and South Asia.* Lexington, Mass.: Lexington Books. Bibl.; index.

Jurquet, Jacques. *Mouvement communiste de nationiste en Algérie: Chronologie commentée 1920–1962.* Paris: Presse d'aujourd'jui. 186 pp. Bibl.
[By the author of *La révolution nationale algérienne et le parti communiste français.*]

Kanafani, Aida Sami. *The Anthropology of Food and Personal Adornment among Arabian Women.* Beirut: American University of Beirut; distributed by Syracuse University Press. 134 pp. Bibl.; illus.
[This is a revision of the author's Ph.D. dissertation (University of Texas, 1979). It includes discussions of food and body rituals, the aesthetic significance of these rituals, and Islam and the rites of hospitality and aesthetics. Includes two appendixes on the aesthetics of the mask and food utensils.]

Kapeliouk, Amnon. *Sabra et Chatila: Enquête sur un massacre.* Paris: Seuil. 115 pp. Illus.

Kauppi, Mark V., and R. Craig Nation, eds. *The Soviet Union and the Middle East in the 1980's: Opportunities, Constraints, and Dilemmas.* Lexington, Mass.: Lexington Books. 292 pp. Index.
[These critical analyses by scholars and policymakers provide an update on Soviet–Middle East foreign relations. The topics are well coordinated and cover the major security and political concerns of the region, giving fair attention to such neglected aspects as the dilemmas facing the Soviet Union and the strictly regional sources of many of the tensions.]

Keddie, Nikki, ed. *Religion and Politics in Iran: Shi'ism from Quietism to Revolution.* New Haven, Conn.: Yale University Press. 258 pp. Bibl.; index; map; table.
[Based in part on papers prepared for a conference organized by the Berlin Institute for Comparative Social Research, summer 1980.]

———. *The Middle East and Beyond.* London: F. Cass; Totowa, N.J.: Biblio Distribution Center.

Kern, Montague. *Television and Middle East Diplomacy: President Carter's Fall 1977 Peace Initiative.* CCAS Occasional Papers. Washington, D.C.: Center for Contemporary Arab Studies, Georgetown University. 50 pp.
[In this study, the author provides a detailed analysis of television coverage involving Israel and the Arab "confrontation" states after the Carter administration's attempt to reconvene a conference on the Middle East in Geneva.]

Khalid, Detlev, and G. Hansen, eds. *Entwicklungspolitische Untersuchungen zur islamischen Herausforderung: Fallbeispiele Ägypten, Iran, Türkei.* Mitteilungen des Deutschen Orient-Instituts, no. 21. Hamburg: Deutsches Orient-Instituts. 315 pp.

Khalidi, Walid. *Conflict and Violence in Lebanon: Confrontation in the Middle East.* Harvard Studies in International Affairs, no. 38. Cambridge, Mass.: Harvard University Press. 216 pp.

Khatibi, Abdelkebir. *Maghreb pluriel.* Paris: SMER/Denoël. 256 pp.
[Grouping together studies spread out over ten years, this work consists of sociological discourses about the Maghreb; in passing, it also embarks on a polemic critique of orientalism, which continues to flourish there. Bilingualism, sexuality, and art all find their places in this discussion.]

Khomeini, Ruhollah. *Der islamische Staat: Ajatollah Chomeini.* Edited and translated from the Persian by Nader Hassen and Ilse Itscherenska. Islamkundliche Materialien, vol. 9. Berlin: K. Schwarz and Union-Verlag. 188 pp.
[A translation of *al-Hukūmah al-Islāmīyah.*]

Khoury, Adel-Theodor, comp. and trans. *Gottes ist der Orient—Gottes ist der Okzident: Lebensweisheit des Islam.* Frieburg im Breisgau, Basel, and Vienna: Herder. 124 pp.

———. *Tendances et courants de l'islam arabe contemporain.* vol. 2, *Un modèle d'état islamique: L'Arabie Saoudite.* Entwicklung and Frieden: Wissenschaftliche Reihe, vol. 30. Munich: Kaiser; Mayence: Grünewald; Paris: Maisonneuve.
[Summaries in English and German.]

Khoury, Philip. *Urban Notables and Arab Nationalism: The Politics of Damascus, 1860–1920.* New York: Cambridge University Press. Bibl.; index.

Khuri, Ra'if. *Modern Arab Thought: Channels of The French Revolution to the Arab East.* Translated by Ihsān 'Abbās. Revised and edited by Charles Issawi. Leaders, Politics, and Social Change in the Islamic World, no. 4. Princeton, N.J.: Kingston Press. 350 pp. Bibl.; index.
[Translation of *al-Fikr al-'Arabī al-hadīth.* This study by the late Ra'if Khuri is a work often quoted by specialists and is now available for the first time in English. The anthology includes selections from thirty-nine Arab writers of the nineteenth and twentieth centuries.]

Kimmerling, Baruch. *Zionism and Economy.* Cambridge, Mass.: Schenkman. 169 pp. Index.

———. *Zionism and Territory: The Socio-Territorial Dimensions of Zionist Politics.* Institute of International Studies, University of California at Berkeley, Research Series, no. 51. Berkeley, Calif.: Institute of International Studies. 289 pp. Bibl.; illus.; index; maps; tables.

Klein, Claude. *Le système politique d'Israel.* Thémis, section science politique. Paris: Presses universitaires de France. 232 pp.

Koszinowski, Thomas, ed. *Saudi-Arabien: Ölmacht und Entwicklungsland.* Beiträge zur Geschichte, Politik, Wirtschaft und Gesellschaft. Hamburg: Deutsches Orient Institut. 365 pp.

Kraemer, Joel L., and Ilai Alon, eds. *Religion and Government in the World of Is-*

lam. Israel Oriental Studies, no. 10. Tel Aviv: Faculty of Humanities, Tel Aviv University. 245 pp.
[Proceedings of a colloquium held at Tel-Aviv University 3–5 June 1979.]

Krahenbuhl, Margaret. *Lower Level Conflict on the Arabia Peninsula.* Santa Monica, Calif.: Rand corp.
["Prepared for the United States Air Force: R-2796-AF, September, 1982."]

Krautkrämer, Elmar. *Israel und Nahost: Der arab-israelischen Konflikt.* 2d ed. Frankfurt am Main, Berlin and Munich: Diesterweg. 135 pp.

Krupp, Michael. *Zionismus und Staat Israel: Ein geschichtlicher Abriss.* Gütersloh: Gütersloher Verlagshaus Mohn; Metzingen: Franz und Sternberg. 187 pp. Maps.

Kuderna, Michael. *Christliche Gruppen im Libanon: Kampf um Ideologie und Herrschaft in einer unfertigen Nation.* Wiesbaden: Steiner. 453 pp.
[A 1983 Munich University dissertation.]

Kunz, Hildegard. *Die amerikanische Palästina politik 1947, 48 im Spannungsfeld innen-und aussenpolitischer Interessen.* Beiträge zur internationalen Politik; 5. Munich: Hochschule der Bundeswehr. 130 pp. Bibl.

Lahlou, Abdelkader. *Le Maroc et le droit des pêches maritimes.* Bibliothèque de droit international, vol. 89. Paris: Libr. gén. de droit et de jurisprudence. 438 pp.
[A work of reference in the field of maritime fishing law that provides a general view of the subject. The author discusses the design of both domestic and international law from the economic and juridical points of view as well as from the administrative angle.]

Landau, Jacob M., ed. *Atatürk and the Modernization of Turkey.* Boulder, Colo.: Westview Press. 235 pp.
[In this attempt to evaluate Mustafa Kemal's overall contribution to the modernization of Turkey, an international group of scholars examines a broad range of subjects, including the Kemalist ideology in the context of Atatürk's quest for modernism, his impact on Turkey's political culture and civil bureaucracy, his experiments with state intervention in the economy, and his attempts to reform Turkish law, education, and language. The authors also consider both the legacy Atatürk inherited from the Ottoman past and the legacy he left his successors.]

Langher, Barbara. *Untersuchungen zur historischen Volkskunde Ägyptens nach mamlukischen Quellen.* Islamkundliche Untersuchungen, vol. 74. Berlin: Klaus Schwarz. 225 pp. Bibl.; index.
[A 1982 dissertation from Freiburg (Breisgan) University.]

Lapidus, Ira M. *Contemporary Islamic Movements in Historical Perspective.* Policy Papers in International Affairs, no. 18. Berkeley: Institute of International Studies, University of California. 66 pp.

Lasky, Melvin J., ed. *Nahost in Flammen: Araber, Juden und neue Hoffnungen für den Frieden.* Weinheim and Basel: Beltz, 1982. 192 pp. Illus.

Laurent, Anne, and Antoine Basbous. *Une proie pour deux fauves? Le Liban entre le lion de Juda et le lion de Syrie.* Paris: Dar al-Da'irah lil-Nashr. 216 pp.

Lawless, Dick, and Alan Findlay. *North Africa: Contemporary Politics and Economic Development.* London: Croom Helm; New York: St. Martin's Press. 240 pp. Index.

Lebrecht, Hans. *Die Palästinenser: Gesshichte und Gegenwart; die geschichtliche Entwicklung der Palästinafrage.* Frankfurt am Main: Verlag Marxistische Blätter, 1982. 272 pp. Illus.; maps.

Lemsine, Aicha. *Ordalie des vois.* Paris: Encre. 368 pp.
[A document on Arab society, consisting of a close inquiry into the life of the women of Syria, Iran, Iraq, Israel, and other Middle Eastern countries.]

Lessner-Abdin, Dietlinde. *Zur sozialen Lage der Frau in Entwicklungsländern: Eine Fallstudie, Algerien.* Rev. 2d ed. Munich: Tuduv-Verlagsgesellschaft, 1982. 201 pp.
[Originally a Munich University disseration.]

Levins, Hoag. *The Arab Reach: The Secret War against Israel.* Garden City, N.Y.: Doubleday. 324 pp. Bibl.; index.
[Jacket subtitle: The story of how billions of petro-dollars have been transformed into political power.]

Liebman, Charles S., and Eliezer Don-Yehiya. *Civil Religion in Israel: Traditional Judaism and Political Culture in the Jewish State.* Berkeley: University of California Press. 305 pp. Bibl.; index.
[The authors are concerned with the impact of Judaism on the political culture of the Jewish community in Israel from the 1920s to the present. Their focus is on civil religion—the ceremonials, myths, and creeds that legitimate the social order, unite the population, and mobilize the populace in pursuit of the dominant political goals; in short, that which is most holy and sacred in society. The authors are careful to set current developments in historical perspective throughout.]

Lings, Martin. *Muhammad: His Life Based on the Earliest Sources.* New York: Inner Traditions. 359 pp. Bibl.; index; map.
[A comprehensive yet extremely readable biography of the Prophet. The author weaves a narrative that brings to life the age of the Prophet. Martin Lings is an Islamic scholar and bibliographer as well as a British convert to Islam.]

Looney, Robert E. *Economic Origins of the Iranian Revolution.* Pergamon Policy Studies on International Development. New York: Pergamon Press, 1982. 303 pp. Bibl.; index.

Madkour, M. Monir, Aida Kudwah, and Zohair A. Sebal. *Saudi Medical Bibliography, 1889–1980.* Introduction by H.R.H. Prince Sultan Bin Abdul Aziz. Edinburgh and New York: Churchill Livingstone. 284 pp. Bibl.; illus.; indexes.

Manoukian, Pascal. *Le fruit de la patience: Mémoires nostalgiques d'un Arménien.* Paris: Centurion. 191 pp. Bibl.; illus.

[How might the 3 million Armenians of the Soviet Union and the other 3 million dispersed throughout the four corners of the world be able again to form a nation? This is the topic on which the author, an Armenian himself who remembers, expounds.]

Martin, Lenore G. *The Unstable Gulf: Threats from Within.* Lexington, Mass.: Lexington Books. Figures; index; tables.
[Martin offers a detailed analysis of disputes along the borders of countries in the Persian Gulf region and a thorough description of the religious, ethnic, and ideological tensions among the peoples. The pros and cons of various options for protecting American interests are outlined. The discussion covers Iran, Iraq, Kuwait, North and South Yemen, Oman, Saudi Arabia, Abu Dhabi, Bahrain, and Qatar.]

Massialas, Byron G., and Samir Ahmed Jarrar. *Education in the Arab World.* New York: Praeger. 394 pp. Index.

Massignon, Louis. *The Passion of Al-Hallaj: Mystic and Martyr of Islam.* 4 vols. Translated by Herbert Mason. Bollingen Series, no. XCVIII. Princeton, N.J.: Princeton University Press. Illus.
[This work explores the meaning of the life and teaching of the tenth-century Sufi, al-Hallāj. Massignon, scholar of religion and Islamicist, traveled throughout Southwest Asia to gather and verify al-Hallāj's surviving writing and biographical record. With profound spiritual insight and transcultural sympathy, he assembled the extant works by and about al-Hallāj (*La Passion d'al Hallāj*, 1922). A greatly expanded second edition was published posthumously in 1975, which Herbert Mason, the author's friend and pupil, has edited and translated from the French and Arabic.]

Mathis, Myrna E., and Lorena S. Yamine, eds. *Nursing Education in the Middle East: Community Health Needs and Curriculum Development.* Beirut: American University of Beirut; distributed by Syracuse University Press. 244 pp.
[Eleven essays and a symposia discuss such topics as health care delivery trends, the role of nongovernmental organizations in health care, the role of the nurse as a change agent, and recent trends in nursing education and practice.]

May, Fritz. *Israel zwischen Weltpolitik und Messiaserwartung: Die Nation Gottes, die religiöse Lage in Israel, der Nahostkonflikt, die Zukunft Israels in biblisch-prophetischer, theologischer und weltgeschichtlicher Sicht.* 7th ed. Moers: Brendow, 1982. 318 pp. Illus.; index; maps.

McCarthy, Justin. *Muslims and Minorities: The Populations of Ottoman Anatolia and the End of the Empire.* New York: New York University Press. 352 pp. Bibl.; index.

McLachlan, K.S., and W. Whittaker. *A Bibliography of Afghanistan.* Boulder, Colo.: Westview Press. 671 pp. Bibl.; index; map.
[Designed as a working bibliography for social scientists and historians, this book presents a wide range of materials on the history, geography, anthropology, and sociology of Afghanistan. Entries include items in English, French, and German.]

McTague, John J., Jr. *British Policy in Palestine, 1917–1922*. Lanham, Md.: University Press of America. 276 pp. Bibl.; index.

Mehrländer, Ursula. *Türkische Jugendliche: Keine beruflichen Chancen in Deutschland?* Forschungsinstitut der Friedrich-Ebert Stiftung: Reihe Arbeit, vol. 11. Bonn: Verlag Neue Gesellschaft. 228 pp. Bibl.

Meier-Braun, Karl-Heinz, and Yüksel Pazarkaya, eds. *Die Türken: Berichte und Informationen zum bessern Verstandis der Türken in Deutschland*. Frankfurt am Main, Berlin, and Vienna: Ullstein. 168 pp. Illus.

Mertz, Pamela M., and Robert A. Mertz. *Arab Aid to Sub-Saharan Africa*. Boulder, Colo.: Westview Press. 200 pp. Bibl.
[This study analyzes the political and economic dimensions of Arab aid to the countries of sub-Saharan Africa. The authors draw on extensive field research in the Middle East and Europe to focus on the bilateral aid programs of seven major Arab donor countries and on the aid programs of a variety of Arab-sponsored multilateral institutions. Assessing the foreign policy interests of the Arab donors, they also examine the role of Islam in the commitment of Arab aid and include an appraisal of Afro-Arab relations and a general survey of the growth of Arab aid in the 1973–80 period.]

Mikdadi, Lina. *Surviving the Siege of Beirut: A Personal Account*. London: Onyx. 152 pp.
Lina Mikdadi, writer, actress, mother of two girls, and author of *Survival in Beirut: A Diary of Civil War* (Onyx Press, 1979) follows up her previous personal account of the Lebanese tragedy with another eyewitness narrative. The author remained in West Beirut throughout the Israeli invasion of 1982 and gives a vivid and detailed report of how the war affected the daily life of its ordinary citizens. Seeing the situation from the viewpoint of this scrupulously honest reporter, we come to understand the malaise of the Lebanese people as they attempt to build ordinary lives in extraordinary circumstances—some bravely, many selfishly, but all hardened to the reality of daily death.

Miller, Aaron David. *The PLO and the Politics of Survival*. Foreword by William B. Quandt. The Washington Papers, vol. 11. Washington, D.C.: Center for Strategic and International Studies, Georgetown University; New York: Praeger.

Miller, James A. *IMLIL: A Moroccan Mountain Community in Change*. Boulder, Colo.: Westview Press. 230 pp. Bibl.
[Providing an important example of tribal adaptation to the modern world, this book shows how the High Atlas tribe of the village of Imlil remains a strong organizational force in the encounter between two economies: one set in the tradition of transhumant pastoralism and irrigated terraced agriculture, the other based on local tourism and religious shrine pilgrimage, migration to salaried jobs, and a series of shifts toward participation in the national and global economies.]

Miller, William G., and Philip H. Stoddard, eds. *Perspectives on the Middle East 1983*. Washington, D.C.: Middle East Institute. 150 pp.
[Proceedings of a conference held at the Cabot Intercultural Center of the

Fletcher School of Law and Diplomacy, Tufts University, 3 December 1982, 14 January 1983, and 4 February 1983. Papers by Charles McC. Mathias, Jr., Walid A. Khalidi, Haim Shaked, Shaul Bakhash, Hanna Batatu, Khodadad Farmanfarmaian, Harold H. Saunders, Oded Eran, and Herbert C. Kelman.]

Missen, François. *La nuit afghane*. Le Pré-aux-Clercs: Belfond; Paris: Hachette (distributor). 250 pp.
[This book contains the testimony of a true-life experience in a political prison suffered by a journalist and star reporter during two months in Afghanistan.]

Mojdehi, J.M. Moghtader. *Interpreting the Iranian Revolution*. London: Croom Helm. 224 pp.
[The author argues that the three common interpretations of the Iranian Revolution (overrapid modernization, political repression, and Shi'i Islam) are insufficient explanations of the first great social revolution in the Middle East.]

Molyneux, Maxine. *State Policies and the Position of Women Workers in the People's Democratic Republic of Yemen, 1967–1977*. Women, Work and Development, no. 3. Geneva: International Labour Office; New York: Unipub. 87 pp. Bibl.

Moosa, Matti. *The Origins of Modern Arabic Fiction*. Washington, D.C.: Three Continents. 250 pp. Bibl.; index.
This book is primarily a social and literary history that provides the background necessary for an understanding of the genesis and nature of modern Arabic literary forms—particularly the drama and the novel. The individual chapters do not tell a continuous, coherent story, but are more in the nature of individual essays, some of which have appeared previously in a different form as journal articles. Besides discussing the early rise of drama in Syria and Egypt, Moosa gives a detailed account of the translation of Western fiction, of the revival of the *maqama*, and of the development of modern fiction from al-Bustani to Jurgi Zaydan (1870–1914).

Mostyn, Trevor, ed. *Jordan: A MEED Practical Guide*. London: Middle East Economic Digest; distributed by Kegan Paul. 282 pp. Bibl.; illus.; index.

Moussa, Abdel Rafea. *Le consignataire du navire en droit français et égyptien*. Bibliothèque de droit maritime, fluvial, aérien et spatial, vol. 22. Paris: Librarie générale de droit et de jurisprudence. 494 pp.

Mussallam, Basim F. *Sex and Society in Islam: Birth Control before the Nineteenth Century*. New York: Cambridge University Press. 176 pp. Bibl.; index; tables.
[In this study the author demonstrates the wide range of evidence that contradicts many current assumptions. Medieval discussions about contraception and abortion in Islamic jurisprudence, medicine, materia medica, belles lettres, erotica, and population literature show that birth control was sanctioned by Islamic law and opinion and that contraceptive methods were available in premodern times to meet social, economic, personal, and medical needs. Mussallam also considers the impact of birth control as a factor in demographic change and therefore in social history.]

Nakhjavani, Mehran. *Arab Banks and the International Financial Markets*. Nicosia, Cyprus: Middle East Petroleum and Economic Publications. 98 pp. Illus.

Nakhleh, Khalil, and Clifford A. Wright. *After the Palestine-Israel War: Limits to U.S. and Israeli Policy.* Belmont, Mass.: Institute of Arab Studies. 150 pp.

Nashat, Guity, ed. *Women and Revolution in Iran.* Boulder, Colo.: Westview Press. 301 pp. Index.
[The role of women in the revolution, the reasons for their participation, and their subsequent fate are documented in this volume. The authors examine the status of women in prerevolutionary society, the ways in which their lives were affected by Islamic principles, and the changes that occurred throughout the twentieth century as increasing numbers of women entered the labor force and public life. They then turn to recent political events and describe the participation of working-class, rural, and educated women and of activists from both left and right. Finally, they consider the implications of recent government policies aimed at a return to more traditional roles.]

Nashif, Taysir. *Nuclear Warfare in the Middle East: Dimensions and Responsibilities.* Leaders, Politics and Social Change in the Islamic World, no. 5. Princeton, N.J.: Kingston Press. 150 pp.
[The author discusses "the direction nuclear warfare development and planning is taking in the Middle East in the absence of international controls."]

Neuman, Stephanie G., ed. *Defense Planning in Less-Industrialized States: The Middle East and South Asia.* Lexington, Mass.: Lexington Books.
[Despite growing material arsenals in less developed countries and persistent conflict in most areas of the world, little attention has been paid to the defense planning processes and the military strategies of less industrialized states. The contributors apply comparative foreign policy guidelines to analyze defense policy and behavior in Egypt, Israel, Iraq, India, Pakistan, Saudi Arabia, and Turkey. They investigate internal and external factors influencing the decision-making process, including weapons procurement, and they assess the implications for future U.S. security policies.]

Nienhaus, Volker. *Literature on Islamic Economics in English and German = Literature zur islamischen ökonomik.* Forschungsberichte islamische Wirtschaft; 2. Cologne: Al-Kitab-Verlag, 1982. 149 pp. Bibl.

Oesterdiekhoff, Peter, and Karl Wohlmuth, eds. *The Development Perspectives of the Democratic Republic of Sudan: The Limits of the Breadbasket Strategy.* Institut für Wirtschaftsforschung München, Abteilung Entwicklungsländer; Afrika-Studien, no. 109. Munich, Cologne, and London: Weltforum-Verlag. 339 pp.

Organization for Economic Cooperation and Development. *Aid from OPEC Countries: Efforts and Policies of the Members of OPEC and of the Aid Institutions Established by OPEC Countries.* Paris: OECD. 164 pp.
[For the period 1970–81, this work passes in review the aid furnished to countries on the road to development. It discusses the aid programs of both individual states and multilateral institutions—in terms of the volume and composition of the aid, its financial conditions and its geographic and sectoral distribution. The volume also is available in French under the title *L'Aide des pays de l'OPEP: Les efforts et les politiques de pays membres de l'OPEP et des organisms créés par eux.*]

Pahlavi, Princesse Ashraf. *Jamais résignée.* Paris: La table ronde. 233 pp. Illus.
[A testimony of the twin sister of the shah, who had fought for a modern Iran,

and who herself has become famous in the struggle for the emancipation of the Iranian woman.]

Peled, Mattityahu. *Religion, My Own: The Literary Works of Najīb Mahfūz.* Studies in Islamic Culture and History Series, Shiloah Center for Middle Eastern and African Studies, Tel-Aviv University. New Brunswick, N.J.: Transaction Books. 268 pp. Bibl.; index.
A revision of the author's Ph.D. dissertation (University of California at Los Angeles, 1971). The author concerns himself primarily with the themes and imagery of Mahfūz's novels, seen both as a reflection of Egyptian society and as the novelist's unique response to that society and its problems.

Penn-Paris-Dumbarton Oaks Colloquia (3d, 1980: La Napoule, France). *Prédiction et propagande au Moyen Age: Islam, Byzance, Occident.* Paris: Presses universitaires de France. 279 pp.
[The texts of twenty papers—in French with English summary or in English with French summary—presented at this third session organized by George Makdisi, Dominique Sourdel, and Janine Sourdel-Thomine. Added English title page: *Preaching and Propaganda in the Middle Ages: Islam, Byzantium, Latin West.*]

Peri, Yoram. *Between Battles and Ballots: Israeli Military in Politics.* 344 pp. Bibl.; figures; index; tables.
[A study of the relations of military institutions to civilian politics in Israel. The author demonstrates that state control over the military in Israel has been weak and that a pattern of civil-military partnership has emerged. This changing relationship involved the internal rivalries of Israel's Labour Party in particular. Peri, a former adviser to Prime Minister Rabin and a European representative of the Labour Party, traces the clashes and accommodations between politicians and military leaders through Israel's changing governments from Ben Gurion to Begin.]

Péroncel-Hugoz, Jean Pierre. *Le radeau de Mohomet.* Paris: Lieu commun. 243 pp. Index.
[The author, editor of the journal *Le monde,* denounces the threats that hover over the world of Islam caused by extremism.]

Perry, Glenn E. *The Middle East: Fourteen Islamic Centuries.* Englewood Cliffs, N.J.: Prentice-Hall. 336 pp. Illus.

Peterson, J.E., ed. *The Politics of Middle Eastern Oil.* Washington, D.C.: Middle East Institute. 530 pp. Bibl.; chronologies; glossary; maps.
[This is a collection of classic articles published in recent years, many updated for this volume, on various aspects of the petroleum question. The articles have been chosen for their current relevance and historical importance. Virtually every area and phase of the Middle Eastern oil industry is covered as it affects the societies, politics, and economies of the producers and the international community.]

Petran, Tabitha. *The Struggle over Lebanon.* New York: Monthly Review Press. 320 pp. Index.
[What was it that provoked the Israeli invasion of Lebanon in 1982? The author, a journalist who has lived in Beirut for many years, feels that this question can be answered only if we first understand the 1975–76 war in

Lebanon and the factors leading up to it—the developing national movement, the role of the Palestinians, and the consistent opposition of Arab states to any such movement—as well as recognizing Israel's long-term goals in Lebanon. Petran attempts to provide this understanding, as well as taking a hard look at Western policy, especially that of the United States. She concludes that the Lebanese national struggle goes beyond the Palestinian question.]

Pipes, Daniel. *In the Path of God: Islam and Political Power*. New York: Basic Books. 450 pp. Index.

Piscatori, James P., ed. *Islam in the Political Process*. Cambridge and New York: Cambridge University Press in association with the Royal Institute of International Affairs. 239 pp. Index.
[Papers presented at a conference sponsored by the Royal Institute of International Affairs, held at Chatham House, London. This collection of ten case studies analyzes the political role of Islam in different historical, cultural, social, and economic circumstances. Countries examined are: Saudi Arabia, Iran, Pakistan, Algeria, Egypt, Sudan, Turkey, Indonesia, Senegal, and Syria. In each case, the author explains how rulers use Islam to maintain power and opponents use Islam to oppose the regime. They also examine how religious authorities exercise power and how social change may affect Islam's potential for being used to facilitate or hinder development policies and ideologies.]

Poliakov, Léon. *De Moscou à Beyrouth: Essai sur la désinformation*. Paris: Calmann-Levy. 224 pp.
[The author of *La causalité diabolique* attempts to explain the reasons for the anti-Israeli explosion in the summer of 1982 by two remarkable facts of contemporary history: 1967 and the Six-Day war, which transformed the image of the persecuted Jew into that of the victorious Jew; and May 1968 and the enthusiasm of the youth for revolutionary movements, such as the PLO, and the manner in which the media have rendered an account of it.]

Politiques scientifiques et technologiques au Maghreb et Proche-Orient. Table-ronde du Centre de Recherches et d'Etudes sur les Sociétés Méditerranéenes, Aix-en-Provence, mai 1980. Paris: CNRS, 1982. 359 pp. Illus.
[Contains twenty communications.]

Preisler, Holger, and Martin Robbe, eds. *Islamic Studies in the German Democratic Republic*. Special issue (no. 10) of *Asia, Africa, Latin Amerika*. Berlin: Akademie-Verlag, 1982. 180 pp. Bibl.

Quataert, Donald. *Social Disintegration and Popular Resistance in the Ottoman Empire, 1881–1908: Reactions to European Economic Penetration*. New York: New York University Press. 205 pp. Bibl.; illus.; index; map.

Rachedi, Khorram. *Les femmes en Iran avant et après la révolution*. Paris: Nouvelles éditions rupture. 198 pp. Bibl.; illus.
[An Iranian journalist and Muslim living in France since 1971, K. Rachedi has been striving, during several years of inquiries and interviews, to unveil the ascendency of religion in Iran and to indicate to what extent the large demonstrations of women (notably against wearing the veil) have made the government of Khomeini retreat.]

Radjavi, Kazem. *La révolution iranienne et les Moudjahidin*. Preface by Maxime

Rodinson. Paris: Anthropos. 251 pp.
[The author carries out an inclusive analysis of Iranian society, displaying the importance of the Organization of the Mujāhidīn of the People in the development of Iran.]

Rahmy, Ali A. *The Egyptian Policy in the Arab World: Intervention in Yemen, 1962–1967: Case Study*. Washington, D.C.: University Press of America. 391 pp. Bibl.; illus.

Randal, Jonathan C. *Going All the Way: Christian Warlords, Israeli Adventurers and the PLO*. New York: Viking. 304 pp. Index; maps.

Rathmann, Lothar, ed. *Geschichte der Araber: Von den Anfängen bis zur Gegenwart*. Part 3, vols. 6 and 7, *Der Zussamenbruch des imperialistischen Kolonialsystems und der Kampf der Arabischen Befreiungsbewegung um sozialen Fortschritt: Der Kampf um dem Entwicklungsweg in der arabishen Welt*. 2 vols. Verfasst von einem Autorenkollektiv des Lehr- und Forschungsbereiches arabische Staaten der Sektion Afrika- und Nahostwissenschaften der Karl-Marx-Universität at Leipziq unter Leitung von Lothar Rathman. Berlin: Akademie-Verlag. 585 pp. Bibl.; illus.; maps.

Reid, James J. *Tribalism and Society in Islamic Iran, 1500–1629*. Studies in Near Eastern Culture and Society, vol. 4. Malibu Beach, Calif.: Undena. 214 pp.

Richards, Alan, and Philip L. Martin, eds. *Migration, Mechanization, and Agricultural Labor Markets in Egypt*. Boulder, Colo.: Westview Press. 288 pp. Index; figures; tables.
[After a long period of stability, Egypt's agricultural sector experienced sudden change because of the 1973 oil price increases and Sadat's open-door economic policies. Workers left rural Egypt for the cities and for high-wage jobs in the oil-exporting countries. The resulting "labor shortage" and rising real wages in agriculture coincided with a massive U.S. foreign assistance program that has been encouraging the rapid mechanization of Egyptian agriculture. This book treats the resulting changes in agricultural technology and labor markets and examines the social consequences and long-term mechanization prospects.]

Rizk, Charles. *Entre l'Islam et l'arabisme: Les Arabes jusqu'en 1945*. Paris: Albin Michel. 392 pp. Bibl.; index.
[For the author, a Lebanese telecaster, Arab nationalism has resulted in the disintegration and the subordination of his world. In need of being liberated from their anarchism, the Arabs no longer can emancipate themselves in this manner from the foreign dependence that holds them more than ever under its sway.]

Robbe, Martin. *Kein Freide in Nahost?: Die Araber, ihr Befreiungskampf und Israel*. 2d rev. ed. Berlin: Verlag Neues Leben, 1982. 205 pp. Illus.; indexes; maps.

Romey, Alain. *Les Sāid 'Atbā de N'Goussa: Histoire et étal de leur nomadisme*. Paris: L'Harmattan. 202 pp.
[This book examines the life of a tribe of nomads which persists despite the considerable sedentarization of the Algerian Sahara. The author, in charge of anthropological, prehistoric, and ethnographic research at the University of Algiers, examines some of the reasons for this persistence.]

Rosof, Patricia J., William Zeisel, and Jean B. Quandt, eds. *Middle East and North Africa: Medieval and Modern History.* Trends in History, vol. 2, no. 3. New York: Haworth Press. 134 pp. Bibl.; index.

Rubenberg, Cheryl. *The Palestine Liberation Organization: Its Institutional Infrastructure.* IAS Monograph Series: Palestine Studies, no. 1. Belmont, Mass.: Institute of Arab Studies. 66 pp.

Russel, Malcolm B. *The First Modern Arab State: Syria under Faysal, 1918–1920.* Studies in Middle Eastern History, vol. 7. Minneapolis, Minn.: Bibliotheca Islamica.

Sadaka, Linda, and Nawaf Salam, eds. *The Civil War in Lebanon, 1975–1976: A Bibliographical Guide.* Beirut: American University of Beirut; distributed by Syracuse University Press. 112 pp. Bibl.; indexes.
[Lists 572 Arabic and 338 English, French, German, Italian, Russian, and Japanese books and periodical articles (excluding newspaper material) on the civil war in Lebanon, 1975–76, for the period ending 1980. The bibliography includes theses, studies, memoirs, poems, plays, novels, drawings, and documents. There are alphabetical author and subject indexes.]

Saddy, Fehmy, ed. *Arab-Latin American Relations: Energy, Trade, and Investment.* New Brunswick, N.J.: Transaction Books. 175 pp. Index.

Said, Edward, Ibrahim Abu-Lughod, Janet L. Abu-Lughod, Muhammad Hallaj, and Elia Zureik, comps. *A Profile of the Palestinian People.* Chicago: Palestine Human Rights Campaign. 29 pp.
A narrative history of the Palestinian people with supporting data and references on their demographic, economic, and social condition. Written from an anti-Zionist perspective, the authors conclude that "the present situation of the Palestinian people then is fundamentally and seriously anomalous. The Palestinians have all the attributes of nationhood—a common history, language, and a set of traditions, a national culture, national institutions, a national representative, the Palestine Liberation Organization, . . . but they do not control Palestine" (p. 26).

Sallam, Kassim. *Le ba'th et la patrie arabe.* Paris: EMA; distributed by Hachette. 444 pp.
[A university study in which the author puts into relief what he believes to be the geographic, strategic, and political importance of the Arab nation.]

Sampson, Martin W., III. *International Policy Coordination: Issues in OPEC and EACM.* Monograph Series in World Affairs, vol. 19, bk. 4. Denver, Colo.: Graduate School of International Studies, University of Denver. 135 pp. Bibl.
[Revision of Indiana University Ph.D. dissertation.]

Sandler, Shmuel, and Hillel Frisch. *Israel, the Palestinians, and the West Bank: A Study in Intercommunal Conflict.* Federal Futures for Judea, Samaria and Gaza, Jerusalem Institute for Federal Studies. Lexington, Mass.: Lexington Books. 190 pp. Bibl.; index; map.
[The Arab-Israeli conflict has traditionally been viewed from an interstate perspective, yet it combines both interstate and intercommunal elements. Sandler and Frisch identify the three main powers in the West Bank—Israel,

Jordan and the PLO—and analyze the kinds of influence wielded by each. The authors contend that issue-area bargaining and shared-rule processes initiated at the local level could begin to break the political stalemate that has so far defied solution.]

Saudi-Arabien in den 80er Jahren: Expertengespräch in Bonn, 26. und 27. April 1982. Bonn: Friedrich-Ebert-Stiftung, Abteilung Entwicklungsländerforschung, 1982. 34 pp.

Sayigh, Yusif A. *Arab Oil Policies in the 1970s: Opportunity and Responsibility.* Baltimore: Johns Hopkins University Press. 271 pp. Index.

Sayyid-Marsot, Afaf Lutfi. *Egypt in the Reign of Muhammad Ali.* Cambridge Middle East Library. New York: Cambridge University Press. Bibl.; index.

Schenker, Hillel, ed. *After Lebanon, the Israeli-Palestinian Connection.* New York: Pilgrim Press. 522 pp. Illus.; maps.

Schneider, Steven A. *The Oil Price Revolution.* Baltimore: Johns Hopkins University Press. 630 pp. Index.

Scholl-Latour, Peter. *Allah ist mit den Standhaften: Begegnungen mit der islamischen Revolution.* 3d ed. Stuttgart: Deutsche Verlags-Anstalt. 766 pp. Maps.

Schreiber, Friedrich. *Die Palästinenser: Schicksal eines semitisches Volkes.* Munich: Molden Seewald. 320 pp. Illus.

Seale, Patrick, ed. *The Shaping of an Arab Statesman: Sharif Abd al-Hamid Sharaf and the Modern Arab World.* London and New York: Quartet Books. 237 pp. Illus.; tables.

Sebti-Lahrichi, Fadéla. *Répertoire de la législation marocaine.* Preface by M. Mustapha Belardi Alaoui. Paris: Librairie générale de droit et de jurisprudence. 400 pp.

See, Wolfgang. *Adieu Israel: Themen und Geschichten von Abraham bis Arafat.* Munich: Nymphenburger. 347 pp.

Selim, George D., comp. *American Doctoral Dissertations on the Arab World: Supplement, 1975–1981.* Washington, D.C.: Library of Congress; for sale by the Supt. of Docs., GPO. 200 pp. Bibl.; index.

———. *Arab Oil: A Bibliography of Materials in the Library of Congress.* Near East Series, no. 2. Washington, D.C.: Library of Congress; for sale by the Supt. of Documents, GPO. 203 pp. Bibl.; indexes.

Serageldin, Ismail. *Manpower and International Labor Migration in the Middle East and North Africa.* Oxford: Published for the World Bank by Oxford University Press. 252 pp. Charts; tables.

Seyppel, Joachim, and Tatjana Rilsky. *Hinten weit in der Türkei: Reisen und Leben.* Wiesbaden and Munich: Limes-Verlag. 309 pp.

Shaw, R. Paul. *Mobilizing Human Resources in the Arab World.* Arab World Studies. London and Boston: Kegan Paul International. 268 pp. Bibl.; charts; index; tables.
[A reference source for some twenty Arab countries, bringing together comprehensive empirical and bibliographic information on topics such as harnessing construction and labor migration, energizing traditional agriculture, manpower and educational shortages, and upgrading women's employment.]

Sherbiny, Naiem Ahmed, and Ismail Serageldin. *Labor Market of Saudi Arabia.* New York: Oxford University Press. 192 pp. Charts; tables.

Shinar, Pessah. *Essai de bibliographie sélective et annotée sur l'Islam maghrébin contemporain: Maroc, Algérie, Tunisie, Libye (1830–1978).* Paris: CNRS. 536 pp. Bibl.; indexes.
[First selective and annotated bibliography devoted exclusively to contemporary Islam in the Maghrib. Contains over 2,050 numbered references in French, English, Arabic, Spanish, Italian, and German; lists bibliographies, journals, and collections, general works and monographs, dissertations and unpublished masters' theses, as well as articles from over seventy journals. Arrangement is by country, subject, and author's name. Annotations are sometimes critical but primarily analytical. There are five indexes: authors, subjects, persons, places, Arabic and Berber terms.]

Sid-Ahmed, Abdelkader. *Développement sans croissance: L'expérience des économies pétrolières du tiers monde.* Paris: Editions publisud. 524 pp. Illus.
[Has the financial wealth derived from the exploitation of hydrocarbons been able to be converted into productive wealth? The author, an associate professor at the University of Paris, Dauphine, responds to this question and to others about OPEC and the problems of the petroleum industry in the Third World.]

Smith, Charles D. *Islam and the Search for Social Order in Modern Egypt: A Biography of Muhammad Husayn Haykal.* SUNY Series in Middle Eastern Studies. New York: State University of New York Press. 249 pp. Bibl.; indexes.
[This study fills an important gap in Egyptian intellectual and political history. Muhammad Husayn Haykal was one of the leading intellectuals of his generation and an important politician as well. By showing the difficulties and eventual defeat that Haykal faced both as a thinker and as a politician, the book furthers our understanding of why the old regime failed in Egypt in 1952.]

Spehl, Helmut, comp. *Hoffen auf den doppelten Holocaust: Texte zur Fortschaffung del Palästinenser aus Palästina.* Translated from the Hebrew by Ursula Spehl. Klartexte zum weltweiten Problem Palästina, Heft 5, 6. Freiburg: Holograph Edition, 1982. 36 pp. and 43 pp.

Starr, Joyce R., and Addeane S. Caelleigh, eds. *A Shared Destiny: Near East Regional Development and Cooperation.* New York: Praeger. 176 pp. Index.
[Published in cooperation with the Center for Strategic and International Studies, Georgetown University. Contains an introduction by Joyce Starr and "The European Contribution"; "The Marshall Plan Revisited"; "Establishing the Preconditions to Long-Run Development"; "After Sadat"; "Egypt and Israel"; "Middle East Development Funds and Banks"; "A Development Fund

for the Near East"; "Commentary—Rationale for a Near East Economic Consortium"; "Middle East Water"; and "Development Diplomacy."]

Stoddard, Philip H., ed. *The Middle East in the 1980's: Problems and Prospects*. Proceedings of a Conference Held at the National Defense University, Fort Lesley J. McNair, Washington, D.C., 8–9 June 1983. Washington, D.C.: Middle East Institute. 189 pp. Illus.
[Papers by Martha Caldwell Harris, Ragaei El Mallakh, Nazih N.M. Ayubi, Mangol Bayat, Richard H. Dekmejian, Michael Collins Dunn, Michael Lenker, Stephen Page, Dankwart A. Rustow, James A. Bill, Fred J. Khouri, J.E. Peterson, Ofira Seliktar, and Hermann Frederick Eilts.]

Sullivan, Antony Thrall. *Thomas-Robert Bugeaud, France and Algeria, 1784– 1849: Politics, Power, and the Good Society*. Hamden, Conn.: Shoestring Press, Archon Books. 216 pp. Bibl.; index.

Tabari, Azar, and Nahid Yeganeh, eds. *In the Shadow of Islam: The Women's Movement in Iran*. London: Zed Press; Westport, Conn.: U.S. distributor L. Hill, 1982. 239 pp.

Taleqani, Seyyed Mahmood. *Islam and Ownership*. Translated from the Persian by Ahmad Jabbari and Farhang Rajaee. Lexington, Ky.: Mazda Publishers. 380 pp.
[This volume is a meticulous analysis of economic activities and an examination of the system of ownership in Islam from a Shi'a perspective. The author (1911–79) was one of Iran's most respected religiopolitical figures, a leading authority on Islamic jurisprudence and a central actor in the Iranian revolution of 1978–79. This book provides a critical analysis of Western ideas of economics, particularly Marxism, regarding ownership of natural resources and property and presents a comprehensive view of ownership based on Islamic principles and precepts. A translation of *Islām va Mālikīyat*.]

Tapper, Richard, ed. *Conflict of Tribe and State in Iran and Afghanistan*. London: Croom Helm; New York; St. Martin's Press. 416 pp. Map.
[Presents new research on tribe-state relations from about 1800.]

Temmar, Hamid M. *Stratégie de développement indépendant: Le cas de l'Algérie, un bilan*. Paris: Publisud. 301 pp. Bibl.
[A university teacher, the author presently is principal technical counsel to the O.N.U.]

Ternon, Yves. *Le cause arménienne*. Paris: Editions du seuil. 311 pp. Bibl.; index; maps.
[The genocide of the Armenian people in 1915 caused a diaspora to follow. Ignored in their international entreaties, certain of their members have chosen the recourse of terrorism—a major point of contention concerning the Armenian question in the twentieth century.]

Terzian, Pierre. *L'étonnante histoire de l'OPEP. Le sens de l'histoire*. Paris: Jeune Afrique. 394 pp. Index.
[A history of the Organization of Petroleum Exporting Countries, which was born on 10 September 1960 in Baghdad amid general indifference but which has developed into the most powerful economic organization created by countries on the road to development.]

Thesiger, Wilfred. *Les Arabes des marais: Tigre et Euphrate*. Paris: Plon. 288 pp. Illus.; index; maps.
[In the Persian Gulf, the Shiite Arabs of South Iraq, an unknown people, face the Iranians. The author lived on intimate terms with them from the end of 1951 up to 1958. Since then, this society, one of the most unusual in Arabic history, has been moving toward its ruin—a development that the terrible Iran-Iraq war has precipitated.]

Thyssen, Xavier. *Des manières d'habiter dans le Sahel tunisien*. Les cahiers du Centre de Recherches et d'Etudes sur les Sociétés Méditerranéennes, no. 15. Paris: CNRS. 234 pp. Illus.
[A study of the Tunisian Sahel—a habitat reflecting at one and the same time a tradition and the imperatives and orientation of a modern socioeconomic and political regime.]

Touval, Saadia. *The Peace Brokers: Mediators in the Arab-Israeli Conflict, 1948–1979*. Princeton, N.J.: Princeton University Press, 1982. 377 pp. Index; maps.
[From Israel's establishment as a state to the Egyptian-Israeli peace treaty, the author analyzes the role of third-party mediators of the Arab-Israeli dispute and tests his conclusions against the existing theories of international relations. Including a discussion of both U.S. and UN attempts at mediation and providing a detailed picture of American-Israeli relations, he maintains that successful mediators do not have to be impartial. This book shows how various countries and institutions that have attempted to mediate the conflict have also acted out of self-interest.]

Tschirgi, Daniel. *The Politics of Indecision: Origins and Implications of American Involvement with the Palestine Problem*. New York: Praeger. 341 pp. Bibl.; index.
["Written under the auspices of the Center for International and Strategic Affairs, University of California, Los Angeles."]

U.S. Congress, House Committee on Foreign Affairs. *U.S. Policy toward the Conflict in the Western Sahara*. Report of a staff study mission to Morocco, Algeria, the Western Sahara, and France, 25 August-6 September 1982. 35 pp. Map.

U.S. Congress, House Committee on Foreign Affairs. *U.S. Policy toward the Persian Gulf*. Hearing, 10 May 1982, before the Subcommittee on Europe and the Middle East of the Committee on Foreign Affairs, House of Representatives, and the Joint Economic Committee. 97th Cong., 2d Sess. 110 pp. Illus.; tables.

U.S. Congress, House Committee on Foreign Affairs, Subcommittee on Europe and the Middle East. *The Unfinished Business of the Peace Process in the Middle East*. Report of a study mission to Israel, Egypt, Jordan, Saudi Arabia, Lebanon, Syria, France, and England, 6–20 November 1982. 97th Cong., 2d Sess. 74 pp. Maps; tables.

United Nations Environment Programme. *Basic Needs in the Arab Region: Environmental Aspects, Technologies and Policies*. UNEP Reports and Proceedings Series, no. 5. New York: Unipub. 216 pp. Bibl.; index.
[Report and background papers of an expert workshop sponsored by the Arab

League for Economic, Cultural and Scientific Organization, the Aspen Institute for Humanistic Studies, and the United Nations Environment Programme on "Technologies for Sustainable Satisfaction of Basic Human Needs with Special Reference to the Arab Region," Nairobi, 21 March to 3 April 1980.]

Université Catholique de Louvain, Départment de Démographie. *Normes famili-ales islamiques et fécondité en Jordanie, en Indonésie et au Pakistan*. Edited by A. Kouaouei. Louvain-Neuve Belgique: Cabay. 236 pp.

Valensi, Lucette, and Abraham L. Udovitch. *The Last Arab Jews: The Communities of Jerba, Tunisia*. Photographs by Jacques Perez. London and New York: Harwood Academic. Illus.

Vatikiotis, P.J. *Arab and Regional Politics in the Middle East*. London: Croom Helm. 256 pp.
[Examples are drawn from Egypt and the Fertile Crescent. The emphasis throughout is on the relation between tradition and politics, historical evolution and state policy, domestic factors and external constraints.]

————. *Islam and the Nation State*. London: Croom Helm. 192 pp.
[Examines the theoretical problems that arose when the modern European ideology of nationalism was adopted by Muslim societies organized into formally modern states. Also deals with the practical difficulties arising from the doctrinal incompatibility between Islam, itself a political ideology, and the non-Muslim concept of the territorial nation-state.]

Vatin, Jean-Claude. *L'Algérie politique: Histoire et société*. Rev. and enl. ed. Paris: Presses de la fondation nationale des sciences politiques. 396 pp.

Wagner, Ulrich. *Soziale Schichtzugehörigkeit, formales Bildungsniveau und eth-nische Vorurteile: Unterschiede in kognitiven Fähigkeiten und die sozi-alen Identität als Ursachen für Differenzen im Urteil über Türken; eine empirischen Untersuchung*. Berlin: Express-Edition. 229 pp.
[A 1982 Bochum University dissertation.]

Waterbury, John. *The Egypt of Nasser and Sadat: The Political Economy of Two Regimes*. Princeton Studies on the Near East. Princeton, N.J.: Princeton University Press. 475 pp. Bibl.; index.
[A balance sheet of thirty years of revolutionary experiment, this work is a comprehensive analysis of the failure of the socialist transformation of Egypt during the regimes of Nasir and Sadat. Testing recent theories on the nature of the developing states and their relation both to indigenous class forces and to external pressures from advanced industrial societies, the author describes the limited but complex choices available to Egyptian policymakers in their attempts to reconcile the goals of reform and capital accumulation.]

Wetzel, Dietrich, ed. *Die Verlängerung von Geschichte: Deutschen, Juden und der Palästinakonflikt*. Frankfurt am Main: Verlag Neuekritik. 134 pp. Maps.

Yadegari, Mohammad, and Hamid Quinlan, eds. *Ideological Revolution in the Muslim World*. Indianapolis, Ind.: American Trust Publications. 95 pp. Illus.

Yodfat, Aryeh Y. *The Soviet Union and the Arabian Peninsula: Soviet Policy to-*

wards the Persian Gulf and Arabia. London: Croom Helm; New York: St. Martin's Press. 191 pp. Bibl.; index.

[Yodfat presents in journalistic style a picture of Soviet policies as tactical and based on national and economic interests rather than strategic and based on specific doctrine. The work shows a scrupulous monitoring of the world press and an ability to discern trends in the Soviet's enigmatic and often erratic response to situations in all Arab states (not just in the Peninsula). The author divides the subject into four stages: 1917–75; the Egyptian open-door policy until the 1978 invasion of Afghanistan; the Iranian revolution; the September 1980 Iran-Iraq war until now.]

Young, Arthur N. *Saudi Arabia: The Making of a Financial Giant.* New York University Studies in Near Eastern Civilization, no. 8 New York: New York University Press. 176 pp. Index.

Zafrani, Haim. *Mille ans de vie juive au Maroc: Histoire et culture, religion et magie.* Judaisme en terre d'Islam, vol. 1. Paris: Maisonneuve and Larose. 315 pp. Bibl.; illus.

[Moroccan Judaism possesses the peculiarity of being at one and the same time implanted in the Jewish tradition and profoundly marked by the Maghrebi environment—as much in everyday life as in its foundations. The author describes the elaboration of this Judeo-Maghrebi personality.]

Zeppenfeld, Werner. *Medientraining für Entwicklungsländer: Projektevaluierung zu Praxis und Problematik journalisten Ausbildungsförderung in Agypten.* Studies in International Communication, vol. 4. Bochum: Studienverlag Brockmeyer. 366 pp. Illus.

[A 1982 Bochum University dissertation.]

Serials

Adam, André. "Les classes sociales urbaines dans la société musulmane du Maghrib." *L'Afrique et l'Asie modernes,* no. 137 (2ᵉ trim.): 23–40.

André Adam, a leading savant of French North Africa, starts with the fact that Morocco's population has doubled in the past twenty years, and there has been an exodus of rural population to the cities. After giving a clear and succinct enumeration of traditional North African social classes, the author describes in detail the urban classes: some have lost power, others have gained it. Adam believes that the absorption of the new "sous-proletariat" is the most difficult task facing the rulers of North Africa.

Arfi, Patrick. "La Syrie dans l'écheveau des rivalités ethniques et religieuses." *Le monde diplomatique,* no. 353 (August): 7.

Arfi stresses the sunni aspect of the PLO and what he sees to be irreconcilable differences with the Alawite regime of Hafiz al-Assad of Syria.

Arom, Eli. "Saudi Arabia's Oil Policy." *Jerusalem Quarterly,* no. 28 (Summer): 125–44.

The author argues that the oil policy of Saudi Arabia over several years has been one of "minimal risk" based essentially on a desire to preserve the Saudi family regime. He concludes that this policy, being at all times pragmatic, cannot be predicted.

Baram, A. "Qawmiyya and Wataniyya in Ba'thi Iraq: The Search for a New Balance." *Middle Eastern Studies* 19, no. 2 (April): 188–200.
Here is a scholarly examination of the Ba'th party's stress on the themes of patriotism and nationalism over the past twenty years.

Barsky, Neil. "The Media: Was the Messenger Blamed for the Message?" *Present Tense* 10, no. 2 (Winter): 20–22.
Barsky, editor of the Jewish Student Press Service, takes up media coverage of the 1982 Israeli invasion of Lebanon; this is a balanced presentation and a defense of the press against its many attackers, especially in the Israeli government.

Bayat, Mongol. "The Iranian Revolution of 1978–79: Fundamentalist or Modern?" *Middle East Journal* 37, no. 1 (Winter): 30–42.
Dr. Bayat points out how Khomeini's ideas differ from traditional Shiite thought. The author concentrates on politics and government, and stresses Khomeini's effort to politicize conservative Shiite doctrine, especially with his doctrine of the "government of the jurist." This is a complex subject and one of continuing importance for the ongoing revolution in Iran.

Brenner, Lenni. "Zionist-Revisionism: The Years of Fascism and Terror." *Journal of Palestine Studies* 13, no. 1 (Fall): 66–92.
The purpose of this article is to "explain" Menachim Begin as a disciple of Vladimir Jabotinsky, the founder and guiding force of the revisionist movement within Zionism during the 1920s and 1930s. Mussolini's fascism is seen to be the inspiration for certain aspects of Jabotinsky's career.

Caplan, Neil, and Ian Black. "Israel and Lebanon: Origins of a Relationship." *Jerusalem Quarterly*, no. 27 (Spring): 48–58.
Focuses on contacts in the 1930s and 1940s, with documentation, between Zionist settlers in Palestine and Maronite authorities in Lebanon who saw a community of interests in an era of growing pan-Arab sentiment. This article is especially interesting in light of the recent cooperation between Israel and Maronite forces.

Cobban, Helena. "Lebanon's Chinese Puzzle." *Foreign Affairs*, no. 53 (Winter): 34–48.
The author, a well-informed journalist with a scholarly background, displays a thorough familiarity with the internal political situation of Lebanon, giving a brief account of the four groups that determine events. She brings out the forces that act to keep Lebanon together, as well as those that divide the country, and is reasonably optimistic about a future accommodation so long as Lebanon is free of outside intervention.

———. "The PLO in the Mid-1980's: Between the Gun and the Olive Branch." *International Journal* 38, no. 4 (Autumn): 635–51.
Cobban carries the PLO story up to June 1983. She sees in the dominant PLO group, Arafat's al-Fatah, the important element for reestablishing and defining Palestinian identity; its role now is to support the nationalistic aspirations of Palestinians within Israel's borders.

Corm, Georges. "La Balkanisation du proche-orient, entre le mythe et la réalité." *Le monde diplomatique*, no. 346 (January): 2–3.
Reflections, both philosophical and practical, on the Middle Eastern mosaic

that perhaps is being "Balkanized" by design through the efforts of those whose interests are not advanced by regional stability.

―――. "La tragédie libanese au piège des schémas reducteurs." *Le monde diplomatique,* no. 356 (November): 6.
Corm, who always writes with a philosophical stance, here proposes that Lebanon is a viable entity and that the majority of its people desire a unitary state in which their communities can live in peace. He maintains that it is outside forces that have always threatened the natural symbiosis of Lebanon's communities.

Damis, John. "The Western Sahara Conflict: Myths and Realities." *Middle East Journal* 37, no. 2 (Spring): 169–79.
A survey, by one of the few American experts on the subject, of several generally accepted ideas about the Western Sahara conflict, which has been the leading North African regional problem since 1975. Damis, a professor at Portland State, narrows the conflict down to the rivalry between Morocco and Algeria by showing the irrelevance or falsity of other ideas that have been advanced to explain this international conflict.

Dawisha, Adeed. "Comprehensive Peace in the Middle East and the Comprehension of Arab Politics." *Middle East Journal* 37, no. 1 (Winter): 43–53.
Dawisha, a member of the Royal Institute of International Affairs in London, argues that any plan for peace must accommodate the two major value systems in the Arab world—Arabism and Islam. The Reagan peace initiative and Camp David failed because they did not provide for an accommodation with the tenets of either. Dawisha also points out that Arab leaders lack an institutionalized legitimacy and are therefore not secure in their power. Accordingly, any comprehensive peace plan must be presented in a manner that will not be contrary to a prevailing consensus in each concerned country. The United States is urged to pressure Israel to cease those actions and words that make an accommodation with Arab leaders impossible.

Dawisha, Karen. "The U.S.S.R. in the Middle East: Superpower in Eclipse?" *Foreign Affairs* 61, no. 2 (Winter 1982–1983); 438–52.
Although written before the rearming of Syria with up-to-date Soviet weapons, this article is recommended for its detailed exposition and many insights derived from a long study of the area.

Duclos, Louis-Jean. "Le discours politique jordanien: ideologies rivales." *L'Afrique et l'Asie modernes,* no. 136 (1ᵉʳ trim.): 3–26.
Duclos, a close student of the Arab world, reveals his confidence in the strengths of Jordan in political, economic, and social terms by means of an analysis of Hashimite ideology, Arabism, Arab nationalism, Jordanian patriotism, economic improvement, the Palestinian issue, and revolutionary socialism. Jordan seems fated to become a key factor in any future attempt to resolve the Palestinian problem.

Evron, Boas. "Une forteresse en perpétual état de guerre?" *Le monde diplomatique,* no. 348 (March): 10–11.
Dissects Zionism and concentrates on the massive influx of Oriental Jews into Israel. This peaceful invasion is certain to have far-reaching effects on the internal and external politics of present and future governments of Israel.

Fabian, Larry L. "The Red Light." *Foreign Policy*, no. 50 (Spring): 53–72.
Fabian reviews the West Bank–Palestine problem as a major issue dividing the United States and Israel. Both Likud's and Labor's approaches are laid out, and the dilemma confronting Washington is made clear. Fabian declares that Israel *must* deliver the West Bank; failure to do so will ultimately estrange the United States.

Forstner, Martin. "Die Kulturelle und nationale Identität Tunesiens angesichts der Reislamisierungsbestrebungen." *Orient* 24, no. 1 (March): 43–63.
Forstner, an Islamicist at the Institute for Arabic Language and Culture at Mainz, takes up the question of Tunisian national identity in a period of increasing signs of Islamic fundamentalism in the country. This issue may be the most pressing in the Arabo-Islamic world in this decade. Certainly, an understanding of the process by which this contest is worked out is essential to policymakers.

Freund, Wolfgang Slim. "Ägyptens nicht-arabische Presse: ein Überlick." *Orient* 24, no. 1 (March): 64–81.
A short treatment of some thirty-six titles, with most attention devoted to those published in Egypt.

Friedman, Robert. "Israeli Censorship of the Palestinian Press." *Journal of Palestine Studies* 13, no. 1 (Fall): 93–101.
Friedman, known for his reportage and analysis of Middle Eastern events, here details instances of censorship occurring since June 1982.

Garfinkle, Adam M. "Sources of the al-Fatah Mutiny." *Orbis* 27, no. 3 (Fall): 603–40.
This is an extraordinarily good essay. Although traces of sarcastic malice sometimes can be discerned, Garfinkle writes with assurance and often verve, presenting his detailed knowledge of events (even though he seems to lack Arabic) in a well-connected narrative. He stresses the importance of the Syrian-Jordanian rivalry and subjects U.S. policy to criticism. Garfinkle projects with brilliant insight that Yasir Arafat, now deprived of all military power, can be stronger than ever as a leader of the Palestinian movement by responding to the interests of the Palestinians (to whom he remains an important symbol) rather than to the interests of various Arab states or to the dictates of noncreative ideologies. Clearly, for Garfinkle, the path lies through Jordan.

Gunter, Michael M. "The Armenian Terrorist Campaign against Turkey." *Orbis* 27, no. 2 (Summer): 447–77.
Gunter first provides an historical review of the Armenian question. He then traces the current phase of Armenian terrorism to the Lebanese civil war of the 1970s, which acted as a catalyst, when leftist Armenians allied themselves with Palestinians against those right-wing Armenians who were close to the Phalangists. Attention is given to ties between the terrorists and certain countries. Gunter concludes that the terrorist activity of some 1,000 persons is not going to threaten the survival of Turkey.

Gutmann, Emanuel. "Begin's Israel: The End of an Era?" *International Journal* 38, no. 4 (Autumn): 690–99.
This is a rather cursory examination of the question, and no clear answer is given. Begin, of course, can be regarded as the last of the founding fathers of

Israel. Gutmann, a political scientist at Hebrew University, suggests that
Israel's future political leaders will be more technocratic than ideological.

Harrison, Selig S. "A Breakthrough in Afghanistan?" *Foreign Policy*, no. 51 (Summer): 3–26.
Harrison, a senior associate of the Carnegie Endowment, starts with the
premise that the U.S.S.R. is looking for a way out of Afghanistan via mediation
efforts at the UN. Two choices there face the United States: a UN–sponsored
withdrawal leaving a Soviet-controlled regime in Kabul or an escalation in aid
to the guerrillas. The author has interesting information on steps taken by the
Soviets to enhance their clients in Kabul, such as educational reforms,
economic development, the National Fatherland Front, and the decentralizing
of governmental authority. The focus of this essay, though, seems to be the
political/diplomatic position of Pakistan vis-à-vis a Russian pullout. One cause
of Zia ul-Haq's interest in a timely Russian departure is the present burden and
potential threat of the Afghan refugee population in Pakistan. Being almost
entirely composed of Pushtuns, those refugees might in time reach an accord
with the Pakistani Pushtuns and call for an independent Pushtunistan.
Harrison concludes that the United States should "encourage Pakistan to
pursue the U.N. negotiations to a successful conclusion" in accord with
Pakistan's interests. This is a thoughtful essay, rich with the potential
ramifications of an outwardly simple event.

Inbar, Efraim. "Israeli Strategic Thinking after 1973." *Journal of Strategic Studies*
6, no. 1 (March): 36–59.
The author of this study is a senior researcher at the Israel Research Institute of
Contemporary Society in Jerusalem. Two stages of strategic thinking are
analyzed, as are two political positions (Labor and Likud) and their influences.
In 1981, Israel switched from a defensive strategy to the doctrine of casus belli.
The process of adopting the new policy is detailed by the author.

Ishow, Habib. "L'Exode rural en Irak et ses consequences economiques et sociales."
L'Afrique et l'Asie modernes, no. 136 (1ᵉʳ trim.): 27–45.
This Iraqi scholar examines the massive movement of population from the
rural areas of Iraq, especially the central and southern regions, to the cities: in
1930, 75 percent of the population was rural, in 1977, 36 percent was rural.
After examining the causes of this movement, the author concentrates on the
social and economic effects in terms of public services, housing, labor, and
transport. The agricultural decline of the country—owing to insufficient
labor—is judged to be a most serious problem for Iraq.

Israeli, Raphael. "Policy Proposed: A Palestinian National Settlement." *Jerusalem
Quarterly*, no. 27 (Spring): 27–32.
The article urges a bold move by Israel to propose a comprehensive plan to
resolve all outstanding issues: (1) Palestinian people are a nation deserving
their own state, but the PLO must first revise its charter and recognize Israel;
(2) former Mandatory Palestine, the joint home of Jews and Arabs, must be
partitioned and population transfers made; (3) Jews and Arabs can opt for
citizenship in their state of residence if they do not want to move to their
national state, or they can remain nationals of the other state with permanent
residency in the host country; (4) borders between the two states will be open;
(5) Jerusalem will be one municipality; and (6) until Palestinian leaders accept
these principles, present conditions of military government and Israeli

settlements will continue. The author suggests that if maintaining the present situation becomes more costly to Israel's moral and economic resources, a radical solution must be sought. World public opinion will demand it, and Jews who wish to preserve the Jewish essence of Israel will advocate it.

Jabbra, Joseph G., and Nancy W. Jabbra. "Lebanon: Gateway to Peace in the Middle East?" *International Journal* 38, no. 4 (Autumn): 577–612.
Relates the high notes of the sad litany of Lebanese political history from 1975 to 1982, and describes the consequences of the Lebanon war.

James, Alan. "Painful Peacekeeping: The United Nations in Lebanon 1978–1982." *International Journal* 38, no. 4 (Autumn): 613–34.
A wordy essay struggling to show that UNIFIL has made a positive contribution. Little is known about the UN's efforts in Lebanon.

Kapeliouk, Amnon. "Les insuffisances de l'enquête israélienne sur les massacres de Sabra et Chatila." *Le monde diplomatique*, no. 351 (June): 1, 21.
Kapeliouk criticizes the Kahane report as follows: (1) the commission members could not visit the sites of the massacres; (2) of the 221 witnesses who testified, very few were non-Israelis; (3) inexplicable omissions occur, such as atrocities at the Akka hospital, south of Shatila; and (4) the IDF higher command should have been held more responsible for the massacres.

———. "Unité et moderation: la résistance palestinienne s'apprête à un jeu diplomatique serré." *Le monde diplomatique*, no. 348 (March): 9.
Sums up the PLO situation following the Algiers meeting in 14–22 February 1983 of the National Council.

Karaosmanoğlu, Ali L. "Turkey's Security and the Middle East." *Foreign Affairs* 62, no. 1 (Fall): 157–75.
Interesting for its concern with the Persian Gulf as an area of vital importance for Turkey—both for security reasons and for economic ones. In the area of security, Turkey is concerned about the global aspect (i.e., a Soviet threat) and about the regional concerns of the Gulf.

Kassir, Samir. "Entre phalangistes et Israéliens; convergences d'objectifs au Liban." *Le monde diplomatique*, no. 348 (March): 9.
On the commonality of interests between Israel and the right-wing Christian Phalange in destroying the PLO.

———. "Le Liban dans l'attente de l'après-guerre." *Le monde diplomatique*, no. 347 (February): 18–19.
An overview of the Lebanese situation, with most attention focused on the Phalangists.

———. "Perspectives et limites du dialogue israélo-palestinien." *Le monde diplomatique*, no. 351 (June): 20.
Recounts the history of PLO–Israel contacts, such as 'Isam Sartawi's, but sees little hope for their effectiveness.

———. "Le réadjustement de la diplomatie palestinienne: comment préserver les chances du futur état?" *Le monde diplomatique*, no. 346 (January): 4.
Explores the options for the PLO and Arafat, and, interestingly, hints of trouble to come from Abu Salih.

Katzir, Yael. "Yemenite Jewish Women in Israeli Rural Development: Female Power versus Male Authority." *Economic Development and Cultural Change* 32, no. 1 (October): 45–61.
An interesting study, based on fifteen months of fieldwork, of Jewish weavers from Yemen who moved to a Moshav in Israel in 1948. Male authority continued, but women greatly increased their economic and social power.

Kohlberg, Etan. "The Evolution of the Shīʻa." *Jerusalem Quarterly*, no. 27 (Spring): 109–26.
Kohlberg, a lecturer on Islam and Arabic literature at Hebrew University, sketches the features of the Imāmīyah branch of the Shiites. This is an excellent, concise account, not only of the theoretical bases of their theology, but also of the popular aspects of the faith. The author leads up to the Ayatollah Khomeini and the principle of *walāyat al-faqīh*.

Kuniholm, Bruce R. "Carrots or Stick? The Question of United States Influence over Israel." *International Journal* 38, no. 4 (Autumn): 700–712.
This is a review article covering three recent books that dwell upon the clashes of Israeli and American policies in the Middle East.

———. "Turkey and NATO: Past, Present, and Future." *Orbis* 27, no. 2 (Summer): 421–45.
Offers a good review of geopolitical factors and the important events in U.S.–Turkish relations. Due attention is given to Islam and Turkey's expanding economic activity in the Islamic world and to the difficulties caused by U.S. congressional politics for efforts to bolster Turkey's capacity for military effectiveness for NATO. As for the future, Kuniholm assures us that Turkey's lot is cast with the West.

Ludington, Nicholas S., and James W. Spain. "Dateline Turkey: The Case for Patience." *Foreign Policy*, no. 49 (Winter 1982–1983): 150–68.
In essence, this is a reasoned apologia for Turkey, explaining why some of the events in Turkey that Europe (and U.S. congressmen with Greek-Americans in their constituencies) finds distasteful deserve to be met with understanding and patience. The authors stress Turkey's importance to NATO and to U.S. strategic interests, and emphasize the Turkish desire for strong government. They end with the hope that Turkey will satisfy its critics by installing a government that is decent and democratic.

Lustick, Ian S. "Israeli Politics and American Foreign Policy." *Foreign Affairs* 61, no. 2 (Winter 1982–1983): 379–99.
This article proceeds from President Reagan's peace initiative of 1 September 1982 and attempts to indicate what actions by the United States are necessary in order to influence Israeli politics toward a more accommodating attitude. Lustick, a political scientist at Dartmouth, writes with a deep scholarly understanding of his subject.

Lutz, Eberhard. "Die 'Local Development Associations' in der Jemenitischen Arabischen Republik." *Orient* 24, no. 1 (March): 82–94.
Lutz, who has worked on the German–Yemen Haraz project, here develops in detail the institutionalizing of cooperatives in the mid 1970s, seeking to understand how they came to have an important sociopolitical influence.

Mabon, André. "Iran, un régime au bord du vide." *Le monde diplomatique*, no. 353 (July): 12–14.

A depiction of the reality of life in Iran. Concludes with a review of pertinent literature.

Mahdavi, Shireen. "Women and the Shii Ulema in Iran." *Middle Eastern Studies* 19, no. 1 (January): 17–27.
A competent essay, critical of the postrevolutionary position of women.

Malhuret, Claude. "Report from Afghanistan." *Foreign Affairs* 62, no. 2 (Winter): 426–35.
Malhuret, a director of the Medecins sans Frontières, relates the details of antiguerrilla warfare in Afghanistan. Despite seemingly good short-term results by the guerrillas, Malhuret is pessimistic over the long-term future of the insurgents.

Ma'oz, Moshe. "Israel and the Arabs after the Lebanese War." *Jerusalem Quarterly*, no. 28 (Summer): 25–34.
This article pursues the consequences, through imagined scenarios, of Ariel Sharon's policy vis-à-vis the Palestine problem. Sharon, according to Ma'oz, undercut PLO support among the Arab populace of Judea and Samaria, and destroyed the PLO military and civil infrastructure in Lebanon. Through the village leagues, Sharon instituted Israel's version of Palestine autonomy, and he intensified Jewish urban and rural settlement. The author urges Israel to seize the initiative at this historic juncture (May 1983) and pursue a Jordanian-Palestinian federation.

Morris, Benny. "After Begin, Who? Yitzhak Navon—a Profile." *Present Tense* 10, no. 2 (Winter): 24–27.
A panegyric on the former president of Israel, who may soon play an important role in Israeli politics.

Mossavar-Rahmani, Bijan. "The OPEC Multiplier." *Foreign Policy*, no. 52 (Fall): 136–48.
Although the American public seems to have gotten used to the higher cost of oil, Mossavar-Rahmani argues that the same factors that caused a crisis ten years ago can make for a repeat performance. The "OPEC multiplier" is the phenomenon, repeatedly observed, that a *small* increase in worldwide demand for oil results in a *large* increase for OPEC oil (and vice versa). The unhappy conclusion is that presently falling oil revenues will inevitably drive prices higher.

Nesvisky, Matthew. "David Levy—a Profile." *Present Tense* 10, no. 2 (Winter): 28–31.
A sprightly account of the rise of an immigrant from Morocco to a position of power in the Begin government. The wider significance of this example is the connection with the growing strength of Israel's Oriental Jewry who, as a group, have different expectations than the European Jews who have dominated Israel in past decades.

Neumann, Robert G. "Assad and the Future of the Middle East." *Foreign Affairs* 62, no. 2 (Winter): 237–56.
Most of this article recounts the recent past and present. The Israeli invasion of Lebanon in 1982 is recognized as the turning point, but predictions as to the future are vague. Certainly Syria is in an enhanced position. Neumann, a former ambassador and now the director of Middle East Studies at

Georgetown's Center for Strategic and International Studies, suggests that the United States should draw closer to Syria.

Oehring, Otmar. "Die Verfassung der Dritten Türkischen Republik: eine kritische Einführung." *Orient* 24, no. 2 (July): 301–57.
Oehring, a student of Near East civilization, gives here a brief account of what is new compared with earlier Turkish constitutions. His comments on religious freedom, freedom of thought, and the press are especially interesting.

Oren, Michael. "A Horseshoe in the Glove: Milson's Year on the West Bank." *Middle East Review* 16, no. 1 (Fall): 17–29.
This is an insider's account of the development of village leagues in the West Bank and of Menahem Milson's efforts to administer the occupied territories.

Orland, Nachum. "Die deutsch-israelischen Beziehungen aus der Beurteilung von Begin." *Orient* 24, no. 3 (September): 458–69.
Orland gives an interesting and valuable account of Begin's attitude toward Germany. Here is a quick review of the more or less strained relations between the two countries.

Pipes, Daniel. "The Real Problem." *Foreign Policy*, no. 51 (Summer): 139–59.
Pipes sees the "real problem" to lie in Lebanon's political and religious factions. He advocates that the United States do all it can to favor a new national pact. This excellent essay proves again the value of a good historical background to one who confronts the confusion of the contemporary Middle East.

———. "Understanding Islam in Politics." *Middle East Review* 16, no. 2 (Winter): 3–15.
All students (and many experts) of contemporary Middle Eastern politics should read this essay. Pipes approaches his subject with a good grounding in Islamic studies and with a knowledge of Arabic; his application of intelligence to the analysis of complex phenomena of the Islamic world is impressive; he is able to make meaningful comparisons with the West. As orientalists have long known, understanding the *shariʻa* is the key to understanding the Islamic world. Pipes reemphasizes this fact.

Razin, Assaf. "US Foreign Aid to Israel." *Jerusalem Quarterly*, no. 29 (Fall): 11–19.
A concise statement on the subject. The author, concerned about the 1980s when Israel is scheduled to begin repaying its loans from the United States, argues for a "permanent reduction in the import surplus."

"Rebondissement de la guerre civile au Liban: La mainmise phalangiste aggrave les antagonismes sur les rouages de l'état entre les communautés." *Le monde diplomatique*, no. 355 (October): 6–8.
A detailed account of the process of "Phalangization" that occurred in Lebanon from 1975 onward. This process antagonized all the other groups or communities in the country. Recommended reading, for most diplomatic historians are unaware of the local causes of regional conflicts.

de Riencourt, Amaury. "India and Pakistan in the Shadow of Afghanistan." *Foreign Affairs* 61, no. 2 (Winter 1982–1983): 416–37.
Long a student of South Asia, de Riencourt stresses that the Soviet occupation of Afghanistan is a threat to Western security. He urges the United States to

forge good relations between Pakistan and India, recognizing that India is the key to the future of South Asia.

Robert, Rüdiger. "Der Gulfkooperationsrat: Die arabischen Golfstaaten auf der Suche nach Sicherheit und Stabilität." *Orient* 24, no. 2 (June): 235–59.
This is a detailed and well-informed exposition of the origin, functions, and politics of the Gulf Cooperation Council. The author seems doubtful that the council can attain the cooperative goals for which it was created.

Rosenfeld, Stephen S. "The Politics of Foreign Aid." *Present Tense* 10, no. 2 (Winter): 6–7.
A brief, cogent article on American aid, now "a stunning and politically provocative $750 per Israeli." Rosenfeld, on the editorial staff of the *Washington Post*, "can discern no good reason why Israel should be regarded as the one nation in the world which can ignore with impunity . . . pleas for political cooperation"—meaning, pay heed to U.S. interests in the Middle East.

———. "Report from Washington II: Begin." *Present Tense* 11, no. 1 (Autumn): 15–16.
A sobering analysis of the U.S.–Israel relationship and the prospects for peace in the Middle East. The present problems all stem from the policies, strategies, and personality of former Prime Minister Begin.

Rouleau, Eric. "La force américaine dans le drame libanais." *Le monde diplomatique*, no. 355 (October): 1, 9.
Rouleau here reviews the use of U.S. military power in Lebanon. His thesis is that the United States prefers a destabilized Lebanon. During the civil war, we aided local factions in cooperation with Israel and the right-wing Phalangists. In 1983, we aided and supported the government, which in effect was but one faction among several in the country. Never able to pursue a policy contrary to Israel, the United States could not work toward a majority-rule government, for that would have placed a lay Muslim state on the north border of Israel.

———. "The Future of the PLO." *Foreign Affairs* 62, no. 1 (Fall): 138–56.
In this well-structured essay, Rouleau discusses the causes and the players in the drama of the May 1983 revolt of al-Fatah's dissident colonels. He stresses that accommodation with Syria is essential for Yasir Arafat and believes that Syria is not willing to make a complete break with the PLO.

———. "Guerre et intoxication au Tchad." *Le monde diplomatique*, no. 354 (September): 1, 8–9.
A useful article; it presents the policies, or intentions, of Colonel Qaddafi in Chad. American strategy toward events in that country seem to be explicable only in terms of President Reagan's global strategy against the U.S.S.R.: stabilize Chad with a strong man, while discomfiting Qaddafi whenever possible.

———. "La mutinerie contre M. Yasser Arafat." *Le monde diplomatique*, no. 353 (August): 1, 8.
An account, detailed, of events leading up to the revolt. This article contains the background material worked into Rouleau's *Foreign Affairs* article.

Safran, Nadov. "Middle East Update: The Continuing Tragedy of Lebanon." *Moment* 9, no. 1 (December): 55–57.

This is a conversational piece by a recognized authority on Middle Eastern politics. Blame is placed on President Reagan for the "poor timing of the Reagan initiative" that contributed to the present situation. Two choices confront the United States: (1) to try to rebuild Lebanese sovereignty or (2) to pull out entirely. Safran believes the United States should rebuild Lebanon after having reached a strategic understanding with Israel, i.e., the United States will support Israeli military efforts to force the Syrians out of Lebanon.

Sayigh, Yezid. "Israel's Military Performance in Lebanon, June 1982." *Journal of Palestine Studies* 13, no. 1 (Fall): 24–65.
This is a *detailed* account of Israeli tactics, strategy, and armament. The author concludes that the cost of maintaining the IDF's occupation of southern Lebanon will be high.

Schiff, Zeev. "The Green Light." *Foreign Policy*, no. 50 (Spring): 73–85.
Schiff pursues the thesis that the United States has encouraged the Israelis, both in the steps taken prior to the invasion of Lebanon and later. This encouragement was due to an identity of purpose and interest in some matters and to poor communication in others. Israel invaded Lebanon secure in the belief that Washington would welcome it.

Schlicht, Alfred. "Muslime und Kopten im heutigen Ägypten: zum Minoritäten problem im Zeitalter der Reislamisierung." *Orient* 24, no. 2 (June): 226–34.
This brief but interesting article reveals the rapid and recent development of fundamentalism in the Coptic community of Egypt and concentrates on the attitudes of the present-day Islamic resurgence toward the Christians of Egypt. These attitudes seem to say, "Have them revert to the Qur'anic, medieval status of *dhimmis*." Schlicht is an orientalist with a background in the philology of the Christian Orient, concerned with contemporary minority problems; this concern is well placed.

Schueftan, Dan. "The PLO after Lebanon." *Jerusalem Quarterly*, no. 28 (Summer): 3–24.
This careful analysis, by an Israeli professor of contemporary Arab history, looks at the political rather than the military effectiveness of the PLO presence in Lebanon, an effectiveness based upon an almost negligible military base in southern Lebanon. The 1982 war represents a turning point in the Palestinian national movement, with Arafat moving from a policy of coercion to one of playing on Western sympathies. Deprived of his traditional support, Arafat is losing out to Jordan in the ongoing process of finding solutions to the Palestine problem. This article is essential reading.

Shalev, Aryeh. "Security Dangers from the East (1)." *Jerusalem Quarterly*, no. 27 (Spring): 15–26.
The deputy director of the Center for Strategic Studies at Tel Aviv University takes up in theoretical fashion the West Bank as an element in Israel's security. Shalev assumes that a West Bank settlement will be reached through negotiations. Various scenarios are given, but Shalev concludes that Israel's security will require the stationing of the IDF in the West Bank.

Sigler, John. "United States Policy in the Aftermath of Lebanon: The Perils of Uni-lateralism." *International Journal* 38, no. 4 (Autumn): 556–76.
Starting with a discussion of a global approach versus a regional one to

international politics, the author focuses on the errors of U.S. policy and concludes that the United States and other great powers are unable to control and determine the outcomes of "wars of opportunity" such as Israel's invasion of Lebanon.

Sisco, Joseph J. "Middle East: Progress or Lost Opportunity?" *Foreign Affairs* 61, no. 3 (Spring): 611–40.
    Sisco, an experienced Middle East hand long at the State Department and now a consultant, here summarizes 1982 events in Afghanistan, the Gulf war, and Lebanon, with most of his wisdom applied to Arab-Israeli relations. Useful because of the broad perspective Sisco brings to the subject.

Sivan, Emmanuel. "The Two Faces of Islamic Fundamentalism." *Jerusalem Quarterly,* no. 27 (Spring): 127–44.
    The editor-in-chief of the *Jerusalem Quarterly* has been a member of the Institute of Advanced Studies in Princeton, N.J., and is professor of modern history at The Hebrew University. In this essay, Sivan commences by discussing the significance of the Egyptian journal *al-Liwā' al-Islāmī* in its preoccupation with the occult; he then moves into an informed presentation of "conservative fundamentalism" and "radical fundamentalism" in contemporary Egypt. This is a good contribution to the expanding field of fundamentalist studies.

Soffer, Arnon. "Geographical Aspects of Changes within the Arab Communities of Northern Israel." *Middle Eastern Studies* 19, no. 2 (April): 213–52.
    In this detailed and well-researched study of changes occurring since 1948, the emphasis is on land and the implication these changes have for Israeli politics.

Stein, Janice Gross. "The Alchemy of Peacemaking: The Prerequisites and Correquisites of Progress in the Arab-Israel Conflict." *International Journal* 38, no. 4 (Autumn): 531–55.
    Paints a not-very-hopeful picture of prospects for a solution to the Palestine problem.

Tibi, Bassam. "The Renewed Role of Islam in the Political and Social Development of the Middle East." *Middle East Journal* 37, no. 1 (Winter): 3–13.
    This is a theoretical exposition on the reasons for Islamic resurgence and the prospects of Islam for social development. Tibi's seemingly profound main points could be regarded as common sense clothed in excessive sociological garb.

Vandenbroucke, Lucien S. "Why Allah's Zealots? A Study of the Causes of Islamic Fundamentalism in Egypt and Saudi Arabia." *Middle East Review* 16, no. 1 (Fall): 30–41.
    The author presents an informed study of the relationship between modernization and the growth of Islamic fundamentalism.

Weinberger, Naomi Joy. "Peacekeeping Options in Lebanon." *Middle East Journal* 37, no. 3 (Summer): 341–69.
    This is a useful collection of information about UNIFIL (UN forces in southern Lebanon) and the MNF (multinational forces in Beirut).

Yovel, Yirmiyahu. "War and the Values of Society." *Jerusalem Quarterly,* no. 28 (Summer): 35–47.

Written by a professor of philosophy at The Hebrew University, this essay stressing the principle of humanism has a most interesting post scriptum on the Lebanese war which condemns (philosophically) the actions of the Israeli army in its pursuit of the PLO into Beirut.

Index

Contributors

Edouard Bustin is professor and past chairman in the Political Science Department at Boston University and is in charge of the political science division at that institution's African Studies Center. He was senior lecturer in public administration and comparative government at the State University of the Congo (1959–61), visiting professor at the National University of Zaire (1965–70), visiting lecturer at UCLA (1961–63), and a guest lecturer at several Central and West African universities. In 1983, he served as program director for the African Studies Association's annual meeting. His works in English and French have been published in the United States, Europe, and Africa.

Mark Tyler Day is an associate librarian in the Reference Department of the Indiana University Library. He has held a variety of library positions in a number of universities including the University of Riyadh, Saudi Arabia; Princeton University; and the University of New Brunswick, Canada. He recently earned an M.A. in Arabic language and literature from Indiana University and has completed course work for the Ph.D. He earned an M.A. in library science, an M.A.T. in social science, and a B.A. in political science from the University of Chicago. Current research activities include work on computer-assisted bibliographic reference service, the theory and practice of cross-cultural literary translation, and the development of modern literary cultures with their supporting social institutions—such as reading publics, libraries, and the book trade—in Middle Eastern countries. He is the author of "Contemporary Saudi Writers of Fiction: A Preliminary Bibliography of Published Books, Accompanied by Short Biographical Sketches," *Journal of the College of Arts, University of Riyadh* 7 (1980): 57–78.

Robert O. Freedman is dean of the Peggy Meyerhoff Pearlstone School of Graduate Studies and professor of political science at the Baltimore Hebrew College. He is the author of *Economic Warfare in the Communist Bloc* (New York: Praeger, 1970) and *Soviet Policy toward the Middle East Since 1970* (New York: Praeger, 1982), which is now in its third edition. He is also the editor of four volumes: *World Politics and the Arab-Israeli Conflict* (New York: Pergamon, 1979); *Israel in the Begin Era* (New York: Praeger, 1982); *Soviet Jewry in the*

Decisive Decade, 1971–1980 (Durham, N.C.: Duke University Press, 1984); and *The Middle East Since Camp David* (Boulder, Colo.: Westview Press, 1984). He also serves as a consultant to the Department of State and is a regular lecturer at the Foreign Service Institute of the Department of State. He received his B.A. in diplomatic history from the University of Pennsylvania and the M.A., Russian Institute Certificate, and Ph.D. from Columbia University.

Edmund Ghareeb is a specialist on Middle East affairs and media issues. He received a Ph.D. in history from Georgetown University. He is the author or editor of several books, including the revised and expanded edition of *Split Vision: The Portrayal of Arabs in the American Media* (Washington, D.C.: American Arab Affairs Council, 1983) and *The Kurdish Question in Iraq* (Syracuse, N.Y.: Syracuse University Press, 1981). He has contributed to other books and is the author of over 100 articles, book reviews, and interviews that have appeard in American, Arab, and European publications.

Philip Mattar is visiting scholar at the Middle East Institute, Columbia University, New York. He has taught at Yale University and the City College of the City University of New York. His interests have focused on Saudi Arabia and the Palestine problem about which he has written for such publications as *Middle Eastern Studies* and *Arab Studies Quarterly*; he is currently writing a postdoctoral work on the modern history of the Palestinians (1882–1982).

John O. Voll is professor of history at the University of New Hampshire. He is the author of *Islam: Continuity and Change in the Modern World* (Boulder, Colo.: Westview Press, 1982) and two books on the modern Sudan. He has published articles in the *International Journal of Middle East Studies*, *Der Islam*, *Muslim World*, and other journals as well as contributing chapters to a number of books.

David H. Partington was educated at Lehigh University, received an M.A. in European history from Rutgers University, and earned his doctorate in Oriental Studies at Princeton University in 1961. Successively employed by Princeton, Michigan, and Harvard universities, he has been since 1970 the Middle Eastern librarian in the Harvard College Library and an associate of the Harvard Middle East Center. The author of numerous reviews, articles, and studies related to bibliography and Middle Eastern librarianship, and articles on Arabic, Persian, and Turkish literatures in the *Reader's Adviser*, he has served on the board of directors of the Middle East Studies Association, been chairman of the Mid-East Committee of the Association of Research Libraries, and is now an editor of *Mundus Arabicus*, an annual devoted to modern Arabic literary topics. He brings to the editorship of the *Middle East Annual* a broad background in Arabic, Turkish, and Persian studies.

Previous Essays

DATE DUE

APR 3 0 '90			
MY8 '91			
GAYLORD			PRINTED IN U.S.A

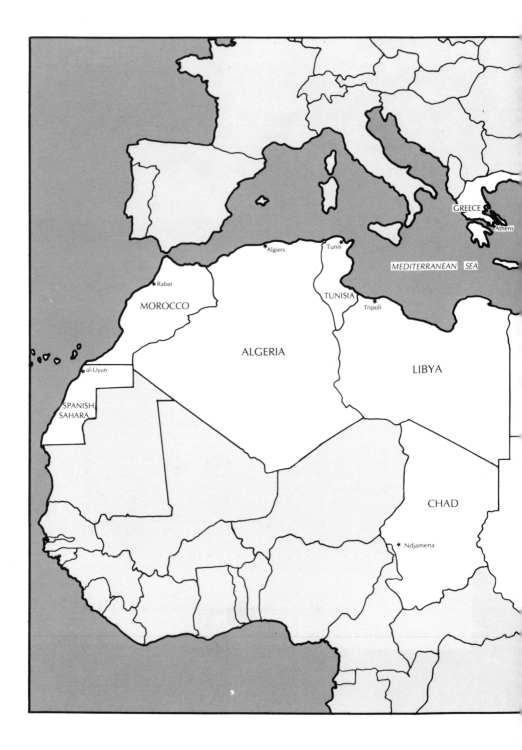

GREECE

Athens

MEDITERRANEAN SEA

Algiers

Tunis

Rabat

MOROCCO

TUNISIA

Tripoli

al-Uyun

ALGERIA

LIBYA

SPANISH
SAHARA

CHAD

Ndjamena